THE POLITICAL LIFE
OF CHILDREN

Books by ROBERT COLES

For Children

The
Political Life
of
Children

Robert Coles

HOUGHTON MIFFLIN COMPANY · BOSTON

For information about permission to reproduce selections
from this book, write to Atlantic Monthly Press,
19 Union Square West, 11th floor, New York, New York 10003.

Library of Congress Cataloging-in-Publication Data
Coles, Robert.
The political life of children/Robert Coles.
p.   cm.
Reprint. Originally published: Boston:
Atlantic Monthly Press, © 1986.
Includes bibliographical references and index.
ISBN 0-395-59922-9 (pbk.)
1. Children and politics—Cross-cultural studies.
2. Nationalism—Cross-cultural studies.   I. Title.
HQ784.P5C624   1987   87-16985
320'.088054—dc19   CIP

Printed in the United States of America

FFG 12 11 10 9 8 7 6 5 4 3

Houghton Mifflin Company paperback 1987

Published by arrangement with Atlantic Monthly Press

Parts of this book, often in different form, have appeared in the fol-
lowing publications: Chapter I in *The New York Review of Books*;
Chapter III in *The Atlantic* and *The New Republic*; Chapters VI and
VIII in the *Washington Post Magazine*; and Chapter VIII in *Harvard
Educational Review*.

To the memory of Dorothy Day

To Bob, Dan, Mike — their generation's future

CONTENTS

(Illustrations follow page 150)

THE POLITICAL LIFE
OF CHILDREN

INTRODUCTION

THE first patient assigned to me when I began a residency in child psychiatry at Children's Hospital in Boston[1] was a twelve-year-old boy who had a number of phobias. I remember his mother arriving with him — late, always late, because he was afraid to get on the subway, and also afraid to ride in cars, except in the country. He believed the chances of a city accident were substantial, and so he became nervous, jittery, reluctant to take his chances. Unfortunately the hospital was in a fairly crowded neighborhood and he could not avoid heavy traffic. By the time this boy and his mother entered our waiting room it was apparent that both had been through a lot.

I well recall my early conversations with him, because he did everything he could (so I decided at the time) to avoid discussing his worries and fears. Instead, he wanted to engage me in other discussions — mostly about his hobbies. He had a vast collection of trains, which he ran on the railroad tracks that covered his bedroom, as well as other parts of his home. He also read many adventure books and had amassed an impressive stamp collection. I tried to be patient with him, let him show me his accomplishments, yet also move toward the subject at hand, his increasing withdrawal from the world. But I had less and less success doing so, as the weeks followed one another, until, finally, three months into treatment, I decided upon a showdown — aided and abetted, I hasten to add, by my "supervisor," an austere, brilliant, elderly psychoanalyst who kept telling me to "remind" the child "why he was there." I now realize that the boy had, quite early, figured out why I lowered my voice and talked in such a cool, even-handed, deliberate manner. I was furious at him for obstructing "the course of treatment," meaning me and my plans to become an able, accomplished child psychiatrist.

One day we reached a comic impasse. The boy told me I was as scared as he was — scared I wasn't going to be able to "budge" him. I picked that up and asked him what he had in mind: "budge" him? He told me what he thought — that I wanted him to talk only about matters *I* believed important, and that he'd never get better if we kept that up. I was, he added, just like his father in that way. My eyes widened, of course, and I decided to relax a little and see where we'd go if I avoided "budging" him. I leaned back, and said to myself I'd try to be the model of the relaxed listener.

A few moments later the lad looked right at me, smiled, and told me he knew I was hiding something. My response was silence — though I still remember the thump in my chest, a feeling of being caught doing something wrong. I hesitated to ask him what he meant because I feared I'd sound as plaintive, uncertain, confused as I felt. At last he rescued me: "I saw you one day, when I came to see the other doctor [the boy had a chronic, eczematous skin condition], and you were wearing a Stevenson button, and now you're not."

More silence on my part. The child really had discovered something. I had indeed made a point of taking off the political button I wore most of the day during the time spent with my young patients. At that time we in psychiatry and psychoanalysis were much taken with the notion of a "value-free environment," and we all were making our gestures toward a "distance" from the dangerous swamps of familiarity, not to mention election-year partisanship. "Let the patients make of you what they want, with as little help from you as possible," my supervisor had cautioned me repeatedly, while I tried to figure out what kind of a person he was, only to notice how few cues his office supplied, to say nothing of his verbal responses.

When seeing the boy, I continued with my silence, though I had a hard time keeping my face from showing a faint smile, the significance of which he was quick to appraise: "A lot of Stevenson supporters are stuck-up! They're college professors!" Where in the world did those two sentences come from, I wondered. I waited vigilantly. The boy watched me with his own measure of circumspection, then boldly obliged: "Eisenhower beat the Nazis. He's strong, and he's been a great president. He doesn't talk fancy. He just leads."

I scribbled those statements down quickly and, while waiting for more, wondered where we were going. The boy was not at all hesitant to continue. He asked me what *I* thought of Eisenhower. I felt my answer on the tip of the tongue; but I shut up, and the boy promptly answered the question himself: "You don't think Eisenhower is smart."

I continued to look at my young patient, and I'm sure my face registered some amusement, because the boy had, indeed, said what I'd been thinking. He seemed quite unperturbed by my persisting refusal to engage in a direct exchange of opinion with him. He proceeded: "My father says the college people like Stevenson because he's a big talker. My mother says he's a nice man. My father says he may be nice but he's nowhere near the leader Eisenhower is. He's a general. He's a Commander-in-Chief."

I now plunged in and asked whether his mother and father usually agreed on politics, or disagreed. He replied that they disagreed on specific questions but usually came to an agreement before they went to vote. "Otherwise, they'd cancel each other out," he explained to me — clearly repeating what he'd heard at home. Did his mother or his father talk much with him about politics? No — and yes. He would be there at the kitchen table or in the dining room when they did talk about, say, the presidential elections, and though they didn't try hard to solicit his views, or to impress him with theirs, they most certainly welcomed his thoughts, and considered them carefully, so he earnestly believed.

I managed to get us deflected from further explicit political exchanges that day. I wrote up my notes and discussed them with my supervisor a week or so later.[2] He was interested in the words that were spoken in my office, but he also took pains to utter the kind of terse scrutiny one doesn't easily forget: "I think the boy feels he knows you better than you think he does."

Nothing more was forthcoming for the moment. I tried to get my supervisor talking about the patient by mentioning his various problems — to show that I knew what was happening inside his head, even if (up to then) not much actual "treatment" or "therapy" had taken place. As I got up to leave — having successfully pursued this line of presentation for the rest of the time allotted me — the elderly veteran of countless human entanglements said, "I'd let the political talk continue, if it comes up next time. See where you both end up."

I left the office perplexed, troubled. I'd never before even thought of politics as a likely or appropriate subject for psychotherapy with adults. I knew politics could provide a pretext for symbolic expression: A man or woman expresses his or her private attitudes by recourse to a news event, a public figure, a historical moment. I knew the next psychiatric step was to figure out what the patient was "really" saying — assuming for this fifty minutes that the ultimate reality was psychological.

The next time the boy was quite ready to continue where we'd left off — talk about his fear of roads crowded with cars, and subway trains that might, at any moment, go out of control. We pursued such a subject of inquiry for almost half our allotted time, my old notes tell me, but then found ourselves, once more, talking about politics. To be exact, the boy interrupted our discussion with an abrupt announcement: he'd brought me an Eisenhower button to wear! I smiled, thanked him. He was a smart boy, though — and quickly picked up my essentially noncommittal response. Would I wear the button? he wondered out loud. I hesitatingly told him I wouldn't. He didn't seem as upset as I worried he might be. He had known all along, he pointed out, that I would refuse: "We figured out you'd be for Stevenson, even before we saw you wearing the button."

Now I wasn't going to let that pronouncement go unchallenged. I wondered out loud who "we" was. He answered immediately: his parents. His father, I learned, had said several times that psychiatrists were "the kind of people" who voted for Stevenson. His mother had added that she thought most psychiatrists would like Stevenson's "intellect." The boy thought that his parents were right, though he was sorry that their analysis and prophecy had come true. He'd told them the night before that he was going to persuade me to change my vote. A question or two revealed that the boy had decided on his own, at the last minute, to bring me one of his father's Eisenhower buttons.

In the next few meetings we continued our political discussion, the boy and I — always at his initiation, but with my diminishing reluctance turning into outright, pleased willingness. I became more and more intrigued with this youth's political mind — his sharp asides on American social and cultural life. I did believe, then, that everything I was hearing was "really" about the patient's *parents, their* beliefs. (*That* word, "really," again! How often we use it, those of us in psychiatric training!) But I'd decided, at least, that what the mother and the father of this child had taught him was well worth knowing, even what they'd taught him about politics. I was no longer so eager to press him for *his* ideas, *his* feelings, *his* beliefs. Who hasn't learned such things from others, I began to ask myself, as I became less rigorously "patient-oriented" and more inclined to think of "families" and "neighborhoods" and even regions or sections of a country.

I have before me, as I write these words, a weathered old piece of hospital paper,[3] and on it a remark typed by a woman who spent her days listening to my ilk talk and talk and talk — so that she might "transcribe" what we said. "The patient says lots of people like Ike," the transcript reads, "and they're not going to change their minds 'just because other people look down their noses at us.' Asks do *you* know what he means? I say yes, I do." I had, upon reading the typescript, underlined the word "you," because I was sure it was a typing error.

My wife, going over all this with me later, had her own opinion of what the typist, to me forever nameless, faceless, had "really" meant to say: that some of us, in the name of our own political values, meant to be the spokespersons of others — the poorer folk who (we were sure) would be better served by a victory of Stevenson and the Democratic Party; but the typist, whose *lot* some of us, in the abstract, worried over long and hard, (but whose *everyday presence*, opinions, or preferences we had little time to notice) wanted me to stop and think. Do "you," after all, know what he means — what anyone means — when saying "I like Ike"? I noticed the next day (by chance, as we put it to ourselves afterward) that a number of "secretaries" in the hospital proudly wore "Ike" buttons.

I go into this long windup, with all its political, professional, sociological implications, because for me *The Political Life of Children* began right then — when an anxious child began to teach a young doctor that there most assuredly was a political life among children, and that its significance was well worth attending. Yet, the lesson was by no means learned quickly. As my wife and I have reviewed the tapes of our research during the early 1960s, when we studied school desegregation in Louisiana, Georgia, North Carolina, Alabama, and when we were very much involved in the civil rights movement, especially in Mississippi, we have found ourselves surprised by our chronic inability even to recognize the political implications of what we were hearing from both black and white children.[4] The tapes document not only the conversations themselves but also our continuing responses to what had been told us. We both kept notebooks as well. As we have finished twenty-five years of work, prepared to send all our records and papers to the University of North Carolina library in Chapel Hill,[5] we have tried to understand why it took us so long — several years, in fact — to regard our data (drawings, paintings, themes or compositions written in school or, for us, at home) as a sort of running political commentary by boys and girls who were, after all, involved in a dramatic moment of history.

Instead, we emphasized the racial aspects of thinking that came across in what the children said or pictured for us. Next we spotted the social and economic forces at work in their lives, though here, too, we needed time to extend the limits of our essentially psychoanalytic perspective to "factors" other than those of early childhood experience within the family. This time it was a mother who first jolted us. The year was 1964, when our first son was born, and I was heavily involved in the Mississippi Summer Project, an effort by college students from all over the country to register black voters in what was then the most segregationist of southern states — and by doing so, to challenge decisively its racial laws and customs.

In doing a long interview with a remarkable black woman, my wife heard her say: "I learned my politics when I was a little girl. My daddy would tell me that I'm one-hundred percent colored, and that means I'm one-hundred percent ineligible to vote, and *that* means I'm supposed to be an American citizen, but I'm not one. My little girl used to ask me, when she was in the first grade, what our country is — that's how she'd say it: 'Momma, what's our country?' I'd say, 'Clara, this is our country.' Then she'd come right back at me with another question: 'Okay, Momma, then is it Mississippi or is it Washington, D.C. where we belong?' I'd always tell her it's both, because you have these states, and then you have the government up there, that's the boss of all the states, but down here the states take care of themselves, all right, and let someone from up there try to change Mississippi, and he'll learn a few things before he's through, because the devil has his slippery shoes, is what I learned from *my* momma, and if that's not the first rule of politics, then what is? And when us folks, the colored people of hereabouts, win our freedom, and when we can vote and vote, and we have our own people in office — well, don't think there's no devil in us, because that wouldn't be right. We're *all* God's children, like we say in church, and that means there's the bad in us, no matter the shade of our skin, and in politics you have the bad, and you have the good, and they're fighting with each other, like it happens all the time."[6]

Such a moral and theological analysis of political life is worthy of Reinhold Niebuhr.[7] Yet it was spoken by a parent talking to another parent about her childhood, about her continuing attempts to teach her children something about the kind of political life they might well inherit. My wife and I, thinking about her and her outspoken declarations, slowly began to wonder (in the middle 1960s) whether our seeming indifference to matters explicitly political, while we had talked with children over the years, wasn't itself an expression of a kind of politics — or at least, the result of a specific kind of political education. I well remember Dr. Martin Luther King, Jr., telling my wife and me in 1963, in Atlanta, where we lived at the time, that he had noticed the various "luxuries" of white people, one of them being "their capacity to turn their backs on politics, while at the same time holding on to their power."[8] He was, maybe, telling us something about ourselves that we didn't know.

Only later, when we started our work among Pueblo and Hopi and Navajo Indians in New Mexico and Arizona, did we begin to think of the political side of children's life. Here we found children who were Americans but who, at the same time, belonged to another "nation." Here were children whose sense of commitment to a certain land was constantly being conveyed to us in terse and unforgettably powerful aphoristic comments, handed down from generation to generation. Here were children who were keenly aware of their double allegiances — and a startling inside-outside capacity to talk about the many Anglos with whom they constantly must deal. Not that my work, even out West, took on a predominantly political coloration. The other sides to Indian life — the religious myths, the naturalistic vein, the social and cultural values, very much entranced my wife and me. Moreover, Indian "nationalism" (at least among the Pueblos and Hopis, in contrast, say, to the Sioux or the Navajos, whom we knew much less well) is by no means a striking *contemporary* presence in the talk of children, or so it seemed to us Anglos. In the few years available we did our best to learn what a number of Indian children managed to tell us, noticing that a rather subtle and canny knowledge of political affairs is not necessarily beyond the ken of ordinary boys and girls.[9]

In spring 1974 we had just returned to New England when an invitation came from the University of Cape Town in South Africa — to give the annual T. B. Davie Memorial Lecture.[10] I had, up to that time, never stepped out of the territorial limits of the United States. The invitation from South Africa intimidated me — not so much because I had no experience as a traveler abroad but as a reminder that, in fact, I was utterly, provincially American, and so maybe the last person who should be making statements to people who live in a distant country, and who, naturally, expect of American visitors some "international perspective."

Thus it was that I first tried to talk about the political life of children. I had spent a good amount of time, before leaving for Johannesburg and Cape Town, poring over the notes my wife and I keep of our work, along with transcripts of interviews, childrens' crayon sketches and paintings — and was struck as much by my own lasting indifference as by the evident interest those I spoke to had maintained, sometimes (I began to realize) in spite of me. The college student who liked to read novels and study theology, but who scorned both political parties, and fussily called himself an "independent," had in my notes become a "field worker" who regarded most political references as "clichés," whether uttered by children or grown-ups. My long suspicion of political ideology had blinded me, it seemed, to the most ordinary, everyday expression, in the young and in their elders, of political perceptions.

We of this century know that sexuality is "repressed," that aggression has all sorts of underground manifestations — yet we often fail to ask ourselves what we do with some of the political passions that may occasionally come to the forefront of our minds, and so doing, scare us as mightily as a moment's sensuality or rage. In the words of a Pueblo mother I came to know fairly well in New Mexico during the early 1970s: "I have to tell my children what to say, and what not to say, when they talk with Anglos. I think you learn to keep some thoughts — well, keep them out of your mind completely. If you don't, you're headed for trouble. The Anglos own this country, and the Indians are guests, even if we were here first — that's what I remind my oldest son, especially. He tells me what he's read in school about 'all men being created equal,' and I tell him the words are great, but you should believe only what you see before your eyes if you want to survive in Albuquerque. When the government people don't like what you say or you do, the words from some history book won't help you much." This evocation of Freud's "reality principle" is, also, one woman's effort to comprehend a nation that has, at times, amazed her by the range of its political acts. Only when I was about to leave my native country was I able to begin to pay close attention to such a woman's remarks — to think of how her children viewed their political situation, their political landscape, their political possibilities, their political destiny. On a return to Albuquerque in early summer 1974, I sat and listened to children, yet again, and began to write the lecture I'd deliver later that year thousands of miles away, titled "Children and Political Authority."[11]

After several days in South Africa, before I delivered the lecture, I felt qualms about troubling a large, distinguished university audience with what was, essentially, a report on children based on work done in one country only, and it so far off. Moreover, so much near at hand required mention — in a lectureship that had been used for years by visiting speakers to denounce South Africa's racial laws. I felt it all too easy for me, a new visitor, to stand up and take rhetorical aim at the injustices so embedded in South Africa's legal codes and political structures. Better, it seemed, to state some general psychological principles on the capacity of children to figure out the nature of the political world around them, and begin to learn (in the seminars arranged by various University of Cape Town professors) how that political world works in South Africa.

During those seminars I heard much about South Africa, and

was invited to go see at first hand how various kinds of families live in that badly troubled country. I met some children in a school run for colored children; I heard them talk about their everyday troubles, their hopes for the future, their serious doubts, their prospects. As I asked them (out of obvious ignorance) about their country, I began to hear from them astounding political statements — the reasons, as they saw it, the Afrikaners behaved as they did, the reasons the British in Cape Town behaved as they did, the reasons South Africa had, so far, maintained a relatively stable and orderly society. I told these ten-, twelve-, fourteen-year-old boys and girls how impressively shrewd they seemed politically, how surprised I'd been as I noticed their strongly worded remarks. Thereupon, one girl raised her hand, and when I nodded to her in recognition, she asked: "Haven't you heard your American children tell you about America, their country?"

Of course. For years I'd heard all sorts of American children express their ideas about "America, their country." But I'd never heard them be as political as these boys and girls so outspokenly were — or so I thought at the time. I'd never heard, that is, such a shrewd and knowing appraisal of a nation by "mere children" living in it. Fortunately, I taped what I heard in South Africa so that my wife too could hear (she had not come to South Africa; my oldest son had accompanied me). When she did listen to those tapes she certainly was puzzled. She went to her study and pulled out transcripts of conversations she and I have had in the United States these past twenty-five years, and asked aloud whether the American children aren't also, in their own ways, emphatically political, when they choose to be. I still recall my immediate and quite brief reaction, word for word: "Yes, but indirectly." And her reaction to that generalization: "Maybe a South African visiting this country would think otherwise; and maybe the South Africans listening to their children talk don't think of them as uttering 'political' comments — just as saying more or less what they hear people say (what their parents say)."

My wife's contention was that I had been shifting many political observations by children in the United States to other rubrics, so to speak — to racial awareness, to regional loyalty, to social class, economic conflict, historical consciousness, cultural struggles, traditional sentiments of the neighborhood. I was not so persuaded; but we agreed I should return to South Africa and talk more systematically with that country's children — of all racial and cultural and social backgrounds — in order to study their political consciousness (if any). Moreover, she and I would go back to many of the American children we had been following, or (for those now virtually grown up) to their younger brothers and sisters, or to the sons and daughters of neighbors — in order to learn their thoughts about their country.

I can say now that we were, then, ten years ago, embarking upon a "cross-cultural" study of "political socialization," a study of the political consciousness of young citizens of various countries, a study of the political lives of children; but at the time we were trying to figure out how accurately we had been understanding the American children we knew in the Southwest, the South, the Northeast, and Alaska — work then being written up as Volumes IV and V of *Children of Crisis*.[12] But even before I left for my second South African trip (1975) I began asking American children some questions about South Africa. Where is it on the map? What kind of country is it? How to describe the people who live there? How to describe the country in general — as a desirable place to live, as thoroughly undesirable, and of course, why? I'd never before tried to get these children to talk about other countries at any length. True, sometimes children spontaneously declare a preference for one or another country, or a strong dislike for this part of the world, that part — and one pays heed, listens to the reasons, and makes an effort to comprehend them. But such encounters are deemed "idiosyncratic," or so I had thought. By the time I'd begun hearing American children of various class and racial backgrounds talk about South Africa, and (on our second visit there) South African children talk about their own country, and America (and England and the Soviet Union and Rhodesia and Japan), I had begun to see how inadequately I'd regarded children's political interests and ideas. Now I had begun to construct what

I hoped would be for me a new way of learning from children. The result, a decade later, is this book.

In the five volumes of *Children of Crisis* I have described in some detail how I do my work.[13] I carry my training as a child psychiatrist to the "field," where I have conversations with children in their homes, in schools, in neighborhood situations, such as a boy's club, a girl's club, in a church, say, or other neighborhood meeting place. I don't hand out tests or questionnaires; but I am much interested in children's drawings and paintings, and so I carry paper, crayons, paints with me — and a tape recorder, which I sometimes use during a first meeting with a child, but usually keep unused until I have gotten to know the person fairly well. I tell the children that I am trying to learn about their situation: their neighborhood, their country — from those who know best, the ones who live in it. I keep coming back, in weekly, sometimes twice-weekly visits, which can last an hour, sometimes two hours or more. Most of the interviews are done in the homes, enabled by willing, indeed wonderfully hospitable parents. In the United States and in other countries, too, I have been fortunate to obtain the considerable cooperation of school authorities, and so I have been enabled to sit with groups of children in school classrooms and hold continuing discussions with them, over a period, sometimes, of months. Their parents and teachers have of course given me clues about what I might want to talk about the next time, or the time after that, with boys or girls who may be reticent one moment, voluble the next.

Work for this book has been done in the United States, in South Africa, in Northern Ireland, in England, in Nicaragua, in Canada, in Poland, in Cambodia and Thailand, in Brazil. In footnotes to each of the chapters devoted to these countries I describe where I went, how many children (of what ages) I got to know and over what length of time. I also give information about my initial contacts and informants, as well as my long-term allies. A research effort is not always easy to accomplish in countries with governments such as those in South Africa, Poland, Cambodia, Nicaragua. Certain individuals whose assistance has been invaluable will have to go nameless, or be mentioned pseudonymously. It is one thing to meet families in Dublin or Belfast; it is quite another matter for a white man, an American, to keep visiting Soweto, outside Johannesburg; or for an American to go to today's Poland or Nicaragua and feel confident that no danger will befall the family in question as well as the American visitor.

Still, as American journalists well know, it is possible for many visitors to come and go with relative ease in countries whose governments are by no means on good terms with our own government. A young colleague of mine, Tom Davey, whose important assistance I shall acknowledge on several occasions in this book, was able to conduct interviews with children in East Germany (1982) without incident.[14] He also helped me by talking with families in Poland. In Nicaragua I found it possible to move freely, to talk with people as I wished, and on any subject I chose to mention, and I was welcomed in the schools, whether public or church-run. In Poland, Americans have friends everywhere, of course — and an American simply learns to be reasonably discreet. I wonder whether I could have done this work in the Soviet Union. As for South Africa, it is a political democracy — for whites who go along with the prevailing racial system, and for whites who come from abroad with a similarly obliging nature. It was against the apartheid laws for a small white group that eventually included me and my wife and three sons and Tom Davey to go in and out of Soweto and other black neighborhoods in Johannesburg and Cape Town. I fear I can't explain fully how we managed to do so, but we did — and in Chapter VI and its footnotes I try to tell how some of our work was done with the help of some Irish nuns, for instance. I can only thank black and colored colleagues in that beleaguered, tragedy-soaked country — its landscape so unnervingly beautiful, its people's lives so strikingly different in some respects from those of others anywhere.

This book appears at the same time as another titled *The Moral Life of Children*, and both are the result of twenty-five years of "fieldwork." I refer the reader to the *Children of Crisis* series for a description of the American places and the people met.[15] My wife and I have kept in touch with many of the families we've known in different parts of the United States, and so it was not difficult for us to renew contact with them, and with their neighbors or relatives, in the 1970s, when we decided to look at the moral anxieties, the political ideas, of some of our country's children. The hope is that a few dozen children, quite intensively visited, fairly well known (one hopes and prays) will shed some light on how children grow psychologically, and of course, morally and politically.[16]

I am not a survey social scientist. I claim no definitive conclusions about what any "group" feels or thinks. I don't even claim an exclusive say about what the limited number of children I've gotten to know "really" think. As clinicians know, patients possess within themselves many truths. Different doctors elicit different patterns of those truths — and often enough see different people in the same person. One can only insist on being as tentative as possible, claiming only impressions, observations, thoughts, reflections, surmises, speculations, and in the end, a "way of seeing." The limitations of this approach must be stressed again and again — no percentages, no statistics, no all-out conclusions. But there are a few rewards, too — those any doctor knows when he or she feels newly educated by another human being.

More space has been given to Northern Ireland and South Africa than to other national settings. I have been working steadily in Belfast and in parts of South Africa for more than a decade, and it is in those places that I think I've learned most about the way a "politics" gets worked into the texture of a child's life.

In this study I aim essentially to evoke, to suggest rather than to pursue a more cognitive approach or a psychopathological orientation. My chapter titles themselves, of course, offer a theory: the many "forces" that connect with the political life children experience. My notes offer further reading for anyone interested in learning about the "reality" these children are also trying to understand. The heart of my work is listening, years of it, and then describing what has been heard — selecting the most revealing excerpts, I hope, from the endless stories children have to tell.

Despite these disclaimers this work has a cognitive side, and elements of psychiatric pathology certainly do appear and require notice; but the telling is rendered through the narrative presentations of the children themselves.

Parts of this book have been previously published in a number of periodicals during the past decade: most of Chapter I in the *New York Review of Books*, parts of Chapter III in the *Atlantic* and the *New Republic*, part of Chapter VII in the *Harvard Educational Review*, and part of chapter VIII in the *Washington Post*.

I want to acknowledge the help of the Ford Foundation, the Rockefeller Foundation, the Hazen Foundation, and the Edna McConnell Clark Foundation in enabling the extremely costly travel required for this obviously international effort, done in five continents: North and South America, Africa, Europe, and Asia. I want to acknowledge, also, the very special help of the MacArthur Foundation for the five-year personal fellowship granted me — a gift that freed me to do this rather demanding travel and, very important, allowed me for the first time to hire others, in distant countries, to continue interviews I had begun with children, parents, teachers. I could never have finished this work in ten years — long as *that* span may seem to the reader! — had it not been for the MacArthur grant.

I want, further, to mention individuals who have helped me enormously in various and kindly ways — Shawn Maher, particularly, and Bonnie Harris, Larry Ronan, Phil Pulaski, Michael Jiminez, Adriana Monteverde Elia, Francis Wilson, Lindy Wilson — and a much-valued, fine colleague in these studies, Tom Davey. I also want to express my continuing gratitude to Peter Davison, who has been my editor for twenty-five years, from the very first days of my work with children in the American South. Those of us who have had the exceptional good luck to work with him know what he can mean to an inevitably faltering or self-preoccupied writer — his tact, his sound judgment, his decency, his patient willingness to extend himself on behalf of others. The names of others, where I can without potential jeopardy to them, will be included in the footnote descriptions of specific parts of the research. As for my wife Jane, and our sons, now grown, Bob and Dan and Mike, all of whom have put in their time in South Africa and Brazil, in Ulster and in Nicaragua, as we have moved across oceans and masses of land over and over again: God bless! And God bless the memory of Dorothy Day, whose "political life," whose everyday example, the use she made of her moral energy, has meant so much to me.

I

POLITICAL AUTHORITY
AND THE YOUNG

IN her long essay, "The Great Beast,"[1] written in 1939, Simone Weil tried to understand the "permanence and variability of national characteristics." She was intent on showing that though Hitlerism was indeed different from many other kinds of nationalist imperialism, it was by no means something new in the world's history. She insisted that Imperial Rome, long a *bête noire* of hers, had anticipated the Nazis, and in fact was far more successful as a conqueror: a larger number of people subdued absolutely for a much longer time. Yet, she was quick to point out, nations change, often unaccountably. She judged medieval Romans "completely unlike" the ancient Romans. The ancients had, in her eyes, perfected a ruthless military machine, harnessed to "a centralized state." Medieval Romans were "incapable of unity, order, or administration"; the various city-states to which they owed allegiance squabbled, but not in a vengeful, or even, it seems, murderous way. Machiavelli mentions that in one of Florence's campaigns not one soldier was killed. As for Mlle. Weil's native land, she scoffs at the expression "eternal France"; sometimes France has had more than a touch of Roman hauteur ("the state as sole fount of authority and object of devotion"), and sometimes it has been ruled quite differently. She considered Napoleon another of history's Roman consuls; whereas on occasion France has been among the more peaceful nations.

How does a nation maintain a notion of itself over a span of time — so that policies pursued by one government, with or without the consent of a particular citizenry, become policies believed in, accepted by succeeding generations of men and women? About Rome's lengthy tenure of military and political supremacy, Simone Weil observes, in partial explanation: "It is only from the conviction that she is chosen from all eternity for sovereign mastery over others that a nation can draw the force to behave in this way." Weil knows that a sustained "conviction" has to be passed down from parents to children. Myths are developed, and in one way or another they are transmitted; in the remote past by word of mouth, more recently by books and newspapers, and in our time over radio and television as well. The Nazis had their explicit propaganda, aimed at "public enlightenment"; for Mlle. Weil the renowned Virgil was not much more than a Goebbels who could write narrative poetry. She declares his "Thou, Roman, bethink thee to rule the people imperially" to be "the best formulation" of an empire's need for a myth of "universal dominion." The distinction she draws between the assaults of barbarians and those of Hitler deserves quotation:

There was always a limit to the harm done by the ravages of barbarians. Their destructiveness was like a natural disaster, which stimulated the spirit by its reminder of the uncertainty of human fate; their cruelty and perfidy, mixed with acts of loyalty and generosity and mitigated by inconstancy and caprice, represented no danger to any real values in those who survived their onslaught. It requires an extremely civilized State, but a basely civilized one, so to speak, such as Rome, to infect all those it threatens and all those it conquers with moral corruption, and thus not only to destroy in advance all hope of effective resistance but also to disrupt, brutally and finally, the continuity of spiritual life, which is then replaced by a bad imitation of undistinguished conquerors. For only a highly organized State is able to paralyze its adversaries' reactions by overpowering their imagination with its pitiless mechanism, a mechanism for seizing every advantage undeterred by human weakness or human virtue and equally able to pursue this aim by lies or the truth, by simulated respect for convention or open contempt for it. Our situation in Europe is not that of civilized men fighting a barbarian, but the much more difficult and dangerous one of independent countries threatened with colonization.

The "mechanism" is something more than a mixture of propaganda and sustained, ruthless military action. Rome's leading families, and those associated with them, had to believe strongly in their mission, and continue to do so not only in the midst of war, when patriotic passions are readily ignited, but in the years of apparent triumph. And though Rome ultimately did crumble, it took a long time to happen. Weil acknowledges the devilish genius of a kind of imperial rule: The slightest evidence of unrest was regarded as a life-and-death threat; indeed, turmoil was imagined, was conjured up — hence the arbitrary, agitated, senseless punitiveness of the *pax Romana*.

Not that Rome's well-to-do, influential people had Weil's image of themselves. Nor is the "conviction" Weil refers to a matter of mere rationalization and self-deception. In any empire there is always plenty of cynical exploitativeness — whether of the old territorial kind, or the more recent, thinly disguised version, in which a leading nation settles gladly for control of raw materials, leaving the day-to-day problems of the so-called underdeveloped nations to themselves, so long as they understand where the line of *ne plus ultra* is drawn. But, for staying power, political authority needs to become an object of belief, if not faith — especially among those who live closest to the center of things. In the outlying provinces or territories, in the remote corners of an empire, the *legatus* and his cohorts took care of any eruptions, threatened or actual. These days, a show of force with jets and warships accomplishes the same purpose. In the event of out-and-out war there is usually little need anywhere for elaborate persuasion of a population, only the waving of the flag. If, however, those who over the years live, so to speak, near the heart of an empire, and are nourished by it constantly and enormously, begin to have doubts or suspicions about its authority, its legitimacy, then all may well soon be lost. Simone Weil put her finger on the problem: "Since the sons of the great Roman families were trained for government by the spectacle of gladiatorial games and by commanding thousands or tens of thousand of slaves, it would have needed a miracle for the provinces to be governed with any humanity."

She refers to a process another writer would call "political socialization":

Only since the 1950s has a generic label — "political socialization" — become attached to the process of initiation into politics and have scholars started with some frequency to bemoan that "we know next to nothing about 'political socialization.' " The recency of systematic attention to political socialization can be traced to the slow process by which political science established itself as an academic discipline and liberated itself from its origins in departments of law, philosophy, and history, and to disciplinary compartmentalizations which assigned the study of children to psychologists and sociologists.

As the man who wrote those words, Fred Greenstein, acknowledges in his suggestive and thoughtful *Children and Politics*,[2] nothing is new about the notion that children ought to be systematically educated politically. Plato was what we would call a "psychologically oriented" political philosopher, well aware of the need each society has for the transmission of values and assumptions — and of political loyalty. Rousseau takes up the matter of political education at great length — as if he knew that at some moment a "social contract" lives or dies in the homes and schools where children learn what (and whom) to believe in. Napoleon observed that "as long as children are not taught whether they ought to be Republican or Monarchist, Catholic or irreligious, the State will not form a Nation."

Greenstein's work, carried out in New Haven during the last years of the Eisenhower administration with children between ages nine and thirteen of various backgrounds, indicates how well disposed elementary school boys and girls are (or more precisely, were then) toward the President, the flag, the government as a whole. They began in the third or fourth grade to learn which party their parents belonged to, well before they knew what the respective parties stood for. They tended to be more aware of national politics than state or local politics; the President was apt to be better known than the governor or mayor. If they came from upper-class homes, they were likely to be more critical, and at an earlier age, of the political status quo than if they came from poor or working-class families. The children studied, no matter what neighborhood they belonged to, by and large were less cynical politically than their parents. The child starts out with the inclination to idealize important national figures, and more broadly, the country as a whole, its history and its institutions. (Girls tended to be less interested in political matters and less opinionated than boys.) Studies conducted by Robert Hess, Judith Torney, David Easton, and Jack Dennis,[3] like Greenstein political scientists, tend to confirm, for the 1950s and early 1960s at least, a generally conservative quality to children's interest in our political life. True, those observers remarked that in adolescence cynicism sets in — not only directed against the President. But they offer little evidence that such cynicism ran deep — was part of an overall skepticism about our social and economic institutions. On the contrary, we are told that by the time youths are jobholders or parents themselves they have become, by and large, willing if not enthusiastic American citizens — as a result of relatively informal but persistent experiences at home, in the neighborhood, and at school, perhaps best described in summary form by Greenstein:

Socialization processes foster the status quo through the perpetuation of class and sex differences in political participation, continuity between the generations in party preferences, continuation (and perhaps even strengthening) of adult assessments of the relative importance of political institutions.

Back in 1965 the author took pains to indicate the need for "longitudinal study," as opposed to the usual cross-sectional research — it being one thing to tap a group of children with standardized questions and quite a different task to spend weeks, months, years with particular families. The more time one spends with a child the more complicated and ambiguous the "findings." All the inconsistencies and ambiguities of anyone's life, certainly including a child's, eventually become apparent to the long-term observer, whereas a series of questions, even open-ended ones, are likely to be felt by many (and *especially* children) as an occasion for quickly resolving those very mixed feelings which, soon after the interviewer is gone, reassert themselves in the mind. All of which is to say that so-called cross-sectional research (the basis of polling) and research based on long-term and close observation are complementary, rather than substitutes for each other.

Any research designed to study the relationship between individuals, however young, and the world around them requires detachment — the investigator's willingness to look at his or her own social and historical situation and ask "methodological" questions. Might the bias toward idealizing the prevailing political order reflect only a temporary or merely apparent kind of social and economic stability, with an attendant cultural conformity? Even more significantly, do many children consciously mouth pieties, all the while harboring a host of sly, mischievous, and maybe to some minds revolutionary ideas? In an important review of the literature of "political socialization,"[4] Richard Merelman worries that many of the studies done "committed the nascent field to a subtly biasing series of theoretical assumptions and methodological decisions based partly upon an atypical period of American politics." Unfortunately in his essay he fails to discuss the extraordinary work of the Australian social scientist (and literary essayist) Robert Connell, whose *Child's Construction of Politics*[5] contains wonderfully rich accounts of how the political world is regarded by children. He makes plain the difference between a child's remarks, spoken over a substantial length of time, and the so-called standardized responses of survey research, or even his own account of those remarks, which contains generalizations based on the theorist's need to formulate:

We have built up a collective portrait of the group of children and the developments to be seen among them. To do this it has been necessary to summarize and to use short extracts from here and there; but to do *that* is to violate the concrete whole of the interview, to tear statements from their contexts and to present them, in a way, as disembodied types or forms rather than real episodes. To overcome this drift into abstraction it is necessary to see the statement in the context of the full interview — itself a distorted projection of the life and thought of the child onto the plane of interrogation, but the nearest we can come, with these methods, to the actuality of which we wish to speak.

Among his observations, perhaps the most interesting and suggestive is the notion of "intuitive political thinking." Young and not-so-young children, from four or five to nine or ten, say, not only show evidence of "socialization," but of surprisingly outspoken, idiosyncratic, blunt, and imaginative political opinions. They can poke fun at the self-important, see through any number of phonies, and wryly take on subjects the rest of us have learned to skirt or get at only indirectly. But gradually something happens:

After the exuberant half-political fantasy of some of our children at the intuitive stage, the political outlooks become a rehash, sometimes an interesting rehash to be sure, of well-known themes from adult politics. Even the reassertion of personal control over political materials in adolescence is a flattened, rather chastened control, with little quality of political imagination.

Connell was interested in going a step beyond the documentation of "attitudes": the notion that the President is good beyond challenge (which many schoolchildren will say when questioned in a classroom) or that Australia, America, or some other country is the best country in the world (which those same children, among others, will also say). Presumably at some time a child begins to develop assumptions about his or her situation as an individual: The country beckons, or it doesn't; the political order is just or fearful and harmful or crooked to the core; the people who hold office, near and far, can be counted upon, or are, quite definitely, enemies, or indifferent, if not contemptuous. Race awareness, we know, takes root among preschool children; by three or four, they not only spot others who are black or white, or Indian or Chicano, but are quick to come up with pejorative or congratulatory remarks, tied to the person recognized as "other."[6] Professor Connell's studies show that some young Australian children are canny indeed about the motives and purposes of their own and other governments. Those same children, incidentally, are quick to distinguish themselves, racially, from the Vietnamese or the Japanese, whom they saw on television. Why do we so often assume that it takes ten or twenty years for children to begin to understand exactly what it is that works for or against them in the world?

In the South, for years, I heard black children speak of sheriffs and policemen as "devils," without picking up the hint they were giving me of attitudes long held.[7] In 1965, in McComb, Mississippi, I asked a six-year-old child who was President. She said she didn't know, "but they killed President Kennedy and they killed Medgar Evers." I asked who "they" were. She said, "the people who don't like us." There is a limit beyond which a guest begins to feel ever ruder and more arrogantly intrusive than he already may have good cause to feel. I may then have felt myself to have gone too far, because I shut up, and did not pursue the obvious chain of psychiatric interrogation: *Which* people don't like you, and *why* don't they, and so on. I realize now that I had made a psychological judgment, maybe a discovery: This child knows a great deal about what social scientists call the subject of "race relations," and I would be foolish, as well as insulting to her, if I persisted in making her spell out not only the obvious, but the exceedingly painful. And too, I probably felt (more than realized) that she would begin to wonder whether there was any point in talking about such matters with a white doctor. She was fully capable of a firm political assessment: The relatively well-off people don't *themselves* want to be reminded too pointedly how things work in their favor. It is a discomforting accusation.

Eventually, as some of the civil rights workers in rural Alabama and Mississippi turned their attention to the education of children, after dealing with issues like lunch-counter desegregation or voting rights, one began to hear astonishing exchanges between school-children and activists in the Student Nonviolent Coordinating Committee (SNCC) and the Congress of Racial Equality (CORE), or, up in the hollows of Kentucky and West Virginia, the Appalachian Volunteers. A young man or woman would enter a home to urge upon parents a course of action with respect to school desegregation, or a county official's attitude toward the school budget, and suddenly a child would speak up: "I don't like the teachers; they say bad things to us. They're always calling us names; they make you feel no good. We saw the man on the television, the governor, and he wasn't any good either." It is all too easy to take for granted such remarks, spoken by a ten-year-old boy whose father is a tenant farmer near Belzoni in the Mississippi Delta: Black children, badly treated by white *or* black schoolteachers (the latter can sometimes be especially mean to poor children of their own race) will inevitably pick up the rejection and scorn that others feel toward them. Yet, when a child of ten links the governor of his state with the schoolteachers who look down upon him in a rural, still all-black elementary school, he is making a significant judgment.

From that Belzoni boy, much more was to be heard, not then but at a later time. Many rural blacks in the South knew all along that those who came to fight on their behalf would soon enough leave; the apathy and lethargy they displayed to the political activists who asked for a signature, a declaration of support, a willingness to march, to picket were, in fact, also expressions of a political judgment. When asked whether he would one day want to vote, as blacks were then in small numbers beginning to do, the boy had this to say: "Maybe; I don't know. My daddy says what's the use, because even if every one of us voted, the whites would still run Mississippi and still own everything, the whole country. The teacher told us the President is a good man, and he's from the South, and he's trying to do good by the white, and by the colored. To tell the truth, I don't believe her. My sister, she laughed when I told her what the teacher said. My sister said that if I believe everything I hear teachers say, and the governor, and the President — then I'm still a baby, and have a lot of growing up to do. Well, I told her I try on something I hear, to see if it fits, but I know when it doesn't, and I throw it away real fast, because I'll tell you, if you're colored, you'd better learn the difference between a piece of real meat and streak o'lean. My mother cooks them their steaks, up at the boss man's house, and she knows the difference; and she's taught us. And I'll bet it's mostly streak o'lean that they hand out to you, a sheriff or a governor or a President. If they'd be handing out good meat, it would be better. But like my daddy says, there's nothing you can expect to get for the asking from the white people, so it's good the civil rights people are getting the governor mad and worrying the President, even if the teachers say we should obey the law and salute the flag and

America isn't second to any country. If you're not white, you're second, and a lot of whites, they're second, too; and my sister says that's the scene, and if you don't know what scene you're watching, you're dumb, dumb, dumb."

He was not especially precocious, for all his implicit sociological and political shrewdness. He never went to high school — and now, decades after he spoke like that, he works compliantly on a large Delta plantation. When I asked him, a grown man, the father of two children, what he thinks of the President, or the governor, or Watergate, or any of the important issues that have faced America and the world, he shrugged his shoulders and presented a blank look, or else smiled in a way that can only mystify: Does he, deep down, have some views, or is he utterly without them? After a drink or two he will speak his mind fully: "It's no good for the black man here, no matter who's up there in Washington as President or down in Jackson as governor. That's all I know. Watergate? They caught a few crooks and liars, I guess. Where are all the rest of them? Still in charge of us, still up to no good."

No one wiretaps his phone; he has none. But if he so much as speaks out of turn, the consequences are obvious. The black children I have known in our South, or in our northern ghettos sound — at six, eight, nine, or ten — like some articulate, politically conscious middle-class white college students. As these children grow older, they tend to become much less candid, though they do not change their opinions. While a number of American youths are becoming more critical politically (even disenchanted with the objects of childhood idealizations), many black youths in the South and mountain youths of Appalachia become less outspoken about what they have, it seems, known for a long time — that their situation in life, the conditions they must continue to face, day in, day out, are consequentially connected to the nation's political leadership. The black man whom I quoted as a child, and whom I have seen every year at least twice since I left Mississippi two decades ago, puts his feelings in perspective all too tersely: "I knew what's going on for us a long time, and I haven't seen a good reason yet to change my mind."

As a boy he watched not "the spectacle of gladiatorial games," but this kind of spectacle, no less persuasive: "You remember, when I was a kid I told you about the whippings they gave my daddy for saying he wanted to register to vote. Well, the sheriff did it; and that's the law for you. Now I can go vote, but the same sheriff is there, and even if the bigger politicians watch their language a little better these days, it's no different here. The other day my boy was called 'a little nigger' by the sheriff, just because he didn't say 'yes, sir' when told to stay on the sidewalk until the policeman said it's all right to cross the street. Later he asked me why the governor keeps talking about 'the good people' of the state and the 'bloc vote.' Actually, he's heard me say to my wife that the whites are 'the good people' and we're 'the bloc vote' — bloc instead of black is the way they do it these days!"

A cussing sheriff will do as well as a gladiator or two. The poor, or those who belong to the so-called working class, always live closer to the law, closer to the whims and fancies of political authority. A nine-year-old boy from Marion County, West Virginia, described the relationship between poor people, and those who get elected to office: "You make the wrong move, and they'll be on you, telling you off and ready to lock you up, if need be." What had he seen? What "trained" (Mlle. Weil's word) in him a specific attitude toward West Virginia's, America's government? The spectacle of a father's funeral; the man was one of seventy-eight miners killed in an "accident" whose causes, immediate and more distant, his children knew quite well. The boy sat in the church, with many other children; he heard various "principalities and powers" being exposed for their negligence, and worse. He saw on television the Secretary of Labor and the Secretary of the Interior and the governor and the mayor and a host of county officials and the president of the coal company utter their lamentations, apologies, and excuses: the litany of self-justifying explanations that miners' wives have a way of hearing as if a sounding brass or a tinkling cymbal. In the words of the child, again: "My mother says they can do what they want, the company people; and the sheriff, he listens to them, and that's it, they get their way. Last year there was going to be a strike, and daddy took us and we saw the company people and the sheriff and his people, and they were talking buddy-

buddy." Another "spectacle" that does not go unnoticed by children whose parents live or die, depending upon how sensitive they are to the implications of such a "spectacle."

Many upper-middle-class suburban children have quite a contrasting view of their nation and its leaders. A black child of eight, from southern Alabama, just above Mobile, told me in 1968 that she knew one thing for sure about who was going to be President: he'd be a white man; and as for his policies, "no matter what he said to be polite, he'd never really stand up for us." Already she knew herself to be a member of "us," as against "them." A few miles away, a white child of nine, the son of a lawyer and plantation owner, had a rather different perspective on the presidency: "The man who's elected will be a good man; even if he's not too good before he goes to Washington, he'll probably turn out good. This is the best nation there is, so the leader has to be the best, too." A child with keen ears who picks up exactly his father's mixture of patriotism and not easily acknowledged skepticism? Yes, but also a child who himself — by the tone of his voice and his earnestness — has come to believe in his nation's destiny, and in the office of the presidency. How about the governor? "He's better known than most governors," the boy boasts. Then he offers his source: "My daddy says that we have a better governor than they do in Louisiana or in Georgia." (The child has cousins in both states.) "And he says that our governor makes everyone stop and listen to him, so he's real good. He knows how to win; he won't let us be beaten by the Yankees."

More sectional bombast, absorbed rather too well by a boy who, now a teenager, hasn't had the slightest inclination to develop the "cynicism" a number of students of "political socialization" have repeatedly emphasized? Or the response of a child who knows what his parents really consider important, really believe in — and fear? "I took my boy over to my daddy's house," the child's father recalls, "and we watched Governor Wallace standing up to those people in Washington; he told the President of the United States that he was wrong." The boy was then four, and no doubt he would not at nine, never mind at fifteen, recall the specific event his father and grandfather both remember so clearly. But time and again he has heard members of his family stress how precarious they feel, in relation to Yankee (federal) power, and therefore how loyal they are to a governor who gives the illusion of successfully defending cherished social and political prerogatives.

Up North, in a suburb outside Boston, it is quite another story. At nine a girl speaks of America and its leaders like this: "I haven't been to Europe yet, but my parents came back last year and they were happy to be home." Then, after indicating how happy she was to have them home, she comments on the rest of the world, as opposed to her country: "It's better to be born here. Maybe you can live good in other places, but this is the best country. We have a good government. Everyone is good in it — if he's the President, he's ahead of everyone else, and if he's a governor, that means he's also one of the people who decide what the country is going to do. There might be a war, and somebody has to send the troops by plane across the ocean. If there is a lot of trouble someplace, then the government takes care of it. I'm going to Washington next year to see all the buildings. My brother went two years ago. He really liked the trip. He came back and said he wouldn't mind being in the government; it would be cool to go on that underground railroad the senators have. He said he visited someone's office, and he was given a pencil and a postcard, and he wrote a letter to say thank you, and he got a letter back. His whole class went, and they were taken all over. They went to see some battlefields, too."

She doesn't know which battlefields, however; nor does she know which war was fought on those fields. She is one of those whom southern children of her age have already learned to identify as "Yankees," even to fear or envy. There are no equivalents for her, however — no name she is wont to hurl at Southerners, or for that matter, anyone else. True, she learned long ago, at about four or five, that black children, whom she sees on television but has never gone to school with, are "funny" and the one Japanese child she had as a classmate in kindergarten was "strange, because of her eyes"; but such children never come up spontaneously in her remarks, and when they are brought up in conversation with a visitor, she is quick to change the subject or go firmly silent. Nor is there any great amount of prejudice in her, at least of a kind that she has directly on her mind. Her drawings reveal her to care about flowers, which she likes to help her mother arrange, about horses, which she loves to ride, and about stars, which she is proud to know rather a lot about.

The last interest prompts from her a bit of apologetic explanation: "My brother started being interested in the stars; my daddy gave him a telescope and a book. Then he lost interest. Then I started using the telescope, and my daddy said I shouldn't, because maybe my brother would mind, but he doesn't." And, in fact, her parents do have rather firm ideas about what boys ought to be interested in, what girls ought to find appealing. Men run for political office, she knows, and sometimes women do, but rarely; anyway, she won't be one of them. In 1971 she thought the President was "a very good man; he has to be — otherwise he wouldn't be President." The same held for the governor and the town officials who make sure that all goes well in her neighborhood. When the Watergate incident began to capture more and more of her parents' attention, she listened and wondered and tried to accommodate her lasting faith with her new knowledge: "The President made a mistake. It's too bad. You shouldn't do wrong; if you're President, it's bad for everyone when you go against the law. But the country is good. The President must feel real bad, for the mistake he made." After which she talks about *her* mistakes: she broke a valuable piece of china; she isn't doing as well in school as either her parents or her teachers feel she ought be doing; and not least, she forgets to make her bed a lot of the time, and her mother or the maid has to remind her of that responsibility. Then she briefly returns to the President, this time with a comment not unlike those "intuitive" ones made by Australian children (in New South Wales) to Professor Connell: "A friend of mine said she didn't believe a word the President says, because he himself doesn't believe what he says, so why should we." What did the girl herself believe? "Well, I believe my parents, but I believe my friend, too. Do you think the President's wife believes him? If he doesn't believe himself, what about her?" So much for the ambiguities of childhood, not to mention such legal and psychiatric matters as guilt, knowing deception, self-serving illusions, and political guile.

Unlike black children, or Appalachian children, or even the children of well-to-do southern white families, the girl I have just quoted has no vivid, politically tinged memories of her own, nor any conveyed by her parents — no governor's defiance; no sit-ins or demonstrations; no sheriff's car or sheriff's voice; no mass funeral after a mine disaster; no experience with a welfare worker; no strike, with the police there to "mediate"; no sudden layoff, followed by accusations and recriminations and drastically curbed family spending. Such unforgettable events in the lives of children very definitely help shape their attitudes toward their nation and its political authority. The black children I have come to know in different parts of this country, even those from relatively well-off homes, say critical things about America and its leaders at an earlier age than white children do — and connect their general observations to specific experiences. A black child of eight, in rural Mississippi or in a northern ghetto, an Indian or Chicano or Appalachian child, can sound like a disillusioned old radical.

The pledge of allegiance to the flag can be an occasion for boredom, at the very least, among some elementary schoolchildren; the phrase "with liberty and justice for all" simply rings hollow, or is perceived as an ironic boast. Here is what a *white* schoolteacher in Barbour County, Alabama, has observed over the years: "I'm no great fan of the colored; I don't have anything against them, either. I do my work, teaching the colored, and I like the children I teach, because they don't put on airs with you, the way some of our own children do — if their daddy is big and important. The uppity niggers — well, they leave this state. We won't put up with them. The good colored people, they're fine. I grew up with them. I know their children, and I try to teach them as best I can. I understand how they feel; I believe I do. I have a very bright boy, James; he told me that he didn't want to draw a picture of the American flag. I asked him why not. He said that he just wasn't interested. It's hard for them — they don't feel completely part of this country. I had a girl once, she was quite fresh; she told me that she didn't believe a word of that salute to the flag, and she didn't believe a word of what I read to them about our history. I sent her to the principal. I was ready to have her expelled, for good. The principal said she was going to be a civil rights type one day, but by then I'd simmered down. 'To tell the truth,' I said, 'I don't believe most of the colored children think any different than her.' The principal gave me a look and said 'Yes, I can see what you mean.' A lot of times I skip the salute to the flag; the children start laughing, and they forget the words, and they become restless. It's not a good way to start the day. I'd have to threaten them, if I wanted them to behave while saluting. So, we go right into our arithmetic lessons."

In contrast, among middle-class white children of our northern suburbs, who have no Confederate flag to divide their loyalties, the morning salute can be an occasion for real emotional expression. It is all too easy for some of us to be amused at, or to scorn, the roots of smug nationalism. But for thousands of such children, as for their parents, the flag has a great deal of meaning, and the political authority of the federal, state, and local governments is not to be impugned in any way. Among many working-class families policemen, firemen, clerks in the post office or city hall are likely to be friends, relatives, neighbors. Among upper-middle-class families, one can observe a strong sense of loyalty to a system that clearly, to them, has been friendly indeed. And the children learn to express what their parents feel and often enough say, loud and clear.

"My uncle is a sergeant in the army," the nine-year-old son of a Boston factory worker told me. He went on to remind me that another uncle belongs to the Boston Police Department. The child has watched parades, been taken to an army base, visited an old warship, climbed the steps of a historic shrine. He has seen the flag in school and in church. He has heard his country prayed for, extolled, defended against all sorts of critics. He said when he was eight, and in the third grade, that he would one day be a policeman. Other friends of his, without relatives on the force, echo the ambition. Now nearer to ten, he speaks of motorcycles and baseball and hockey; and when he goes to a game he sings the national anthem in a strong and sure voice. Our government? It is "the best you can have." Our President? He's "good."

One pushes a little: Is the President in any trouble now? (It is 1973, and the President is Nixon.) Yes, he is, and he might have made some mistakes. Beyond that the child will not easily go. His parents had for the first time voted Republican in 1972, and now they are disappointed with, disgusted by, the President's Watergate-related behavior. But they have been reluctant to be too critical of the President in front of their children: "I don't want to make the kids feel that there's anything wrong with the *country*," the father says. There's *plenty* wrong with the President, he admits, and with the way the country is being run — and, he adds, with big business, so greedy all the time, as well as with the universities and those who go to them or teach at them; but America, he believes, is the greatest nation that ever has been — something, one has to remember, every President's speech-writers, Democratic or Republican, liberal or conservative, manage to work into just about every televised address. Only indirectly, in drawings or comic exaggeration or metaphorical flights of fancy does the boy dare show what he has been making of Watergate, news of which has, of course, come to him primarily through television. Asked to draw a picture of the President, the boy laughs, says he doesn't know how (he had had no such trouble a year earlier), and finally manages to sketch an exceedingly small man, literally half the size of the earlier portrait. Then, as he prepares to hand over the completed project, he has second thoughts. He adds a blue sky. Then he blackens the sky. He puts earth under the man, but not, as is his usual custom, grass. Then he proceeds to make two big round black circles, with what seem to be pieces of string attached to them. What are they? He is not sure: "Well, either they could be bombs, and someone could light the fuse, and they could explode and he'd get hurt, and people would be sad; or they could be balls and chains — you know, if you're going to jail." (Figure 1.)

Way across the tracks, out in part of "rich suburbia," as I hear factory workers sometimes refer to certain towns well to the north and west of Boston, adults have a slightly different kind of love of country — less outspoken, perhaps, less defensive, but not casual and certainly appreciative. In those towns, too, children respond quite directly and sensitively to the various messages they have learned from their parents — and to a number of low-key "spectacles": flags out on July Fourth; the deference paid to civil employees; pictures of father in uniform during one or another war; and perhaps most of all, conversations heard at the table. "My father hears bad news on television, and he says 'thank God we're Americans,'" says a girl of eleven. She goes on to register her mother's gentle, thoughtful qualification: "It's lucky we live where we do." Her mother's sister, older and attracted to the cultural activity that only a city can offer, has to live a more nervous life: "My aunt has huge locks on her doors. My mother leaves the keys right in the car." Nevertheless, the United States of America, for the girl's aunt as well as her parents, is nowhere near collapse: "Everything is going to be all right with the country. This is the best place to live in the whole world. That's what my aunt says." The girl pauses. Now is the time to ask her what *she* has to say. But she needs no prodding; immediately she goes on: "No place is perfect. We're in trouble now. The President and his friends, they've been caught doing bad things. It's too bad. My older brother argues with daddy; he told daddy that it's wrong to let the President get away with all he's done, while everyone else has to go to jail; and he told daddy there's a lot of trouble in the country, and no one is doing anything to stop the trouble. The President, I think he's running as fast as he can from the police. I guess I would if I knew I'd done wrong. But I'd never be able to get to Egypt or Russia, so he's lucky, that President." (Nixon had just gone to both countries.)

It is simply not altogether true, as concluded in some studies of "political socialization," that she and other children like her *only* tend to "idealize" the President, or give a totally "romanticized" kind of loyalty to the country, on the basis of what they hear, or choose to hear, from their parents or teachers. Many parents do select carefully what they say in front of their children; and children are indeed encouraged by their teachers, and the books they read, to see presidents and governors and Supreme Court justices and senators as figures much larger than life. Yet, in no time — at least these days — children can lay such influences aside, much to the astonishment even of parents who *don't* try to shield their children from "bad news" or "the evils of this world," two ways of putting it that one hears again and again. Black children laugh at books given them to read in school, snicker while the teacher recites historical pieties that exclude mention of many things, and often challenge their own parents when they understandably try to temper the actuality of black people in America. White children, too, as James Agee noticed in the 1930s, pick up the hypocrisies and banalities about them and connect what they see or hear to a larger vision — a notion of those who have a lot and those who have very little at all.

"The President checks in with the people who own the coal company," a miner's shy son, aged eleven, remarked in Harlan, Kentucky, where the Duke Power Company was fighting hard to prevent the United Mine Workers from becoming a spokesman of the workers. The child may well be incorrect; but one suspects that a log of the calls made by the President would show him in contact with people very much like those who are on the board of the Duke Power Company, as opposed to people like the boy's parents. By the same token, when a child whose father happens to be on the board of a utility company, or a lawyer who represents such clients, appears to overlook whatever remarks his or her parents have made about the United States and instead emphasizes without exception the nation's virtues, including those of its leaders, by no means is psychological distortion necessarily at work. The child may well have taken the measure of what has been heard (and overheard) and come to a conclusion: this is what his parents really believe. The reason they believe it is to support a whole way of life — the one we are all living. And so, it is best for the child to keep certain thoughts (in older people, called "views") to himself.

Too complicated and subtle an analysis for a child under ten, or even under fifteen? We who in this century have learned to give children credit for the most astonishing refinements of perception or feeling about the nuances of family life or the ups and downs of neighborhood play, for some reason are less inclined to picture those same children as canny social observers or political analysts. No one teaches children sociology or psychology; yet, children are constantly noticing who gets along with whom, and why. If in school, or even when approached by a visitor with a questionnaire (or more casually, with an all-too-interested face and manner), those same children tighten up and say little or nothing, or come up with platitudinous remarks, they may well have applied another of their sophisticated psychological judgments — reserving the expression of any controversial political asides for another, a more private occasion.[8]

As for some of those children who are called "rebellious" or "aggressive," and sent off to guidance counselors or psychiatrists, they can occasionally help us know the thoughts of many other, more "normal" children. "My poor father is scared," says the son of a well-to-do businessman, the owner of large tracts of Florida's land, employing hundreds of migrant farm workers (who, believe me, are also scared). What frightens the boy's father? His twelve-year-old namesake, who is described by his teachers as fresh and surly, tries hard to provide an answer, almost as if whatever he comes up with will help him as much as his father: "I don't know, but there will be times he's sweating, and he's swearing, and he's saying he gave money to all those politicians, and they'd better do right by the growers, or they'll regret it. Then he says he's tired of living here, and maybe he should go back to Michigan where his granddaddy was born. The other day the sheriff came by and said he didn't know if he could keep those television people out indefinitely. So, Daddy got on the phone to our senator, and we're waiting. But it may cost us a lot, and we may lose. Daddy says we will either get machines to replace the migrants, or we'll go broke, what with the trouble they're beginning to cause. But I don't think he really means it. He's always threatening us with trouble ahead, my mother says, but you have to pour salt on what he says."

That same boy scoffs at what he hears his teachers say about American history; one day he blurted out in class that his father had "coolies" working for him. Another time he said we'd had to kill a lot of Indians, because they had the land, and we wanted it, and they wouldn't "bow to us, the way we wanted." His teacher felt that she had witnessed yet another neurotic outburst, but a number of his classmates did not. One of them, not especially a friend of his, remarked several days later, "He only said what everyone knows. I told my mother what he said, and she said it wasn't so bad, and why did they get so upset? But she told me that sometimes it's best to keep quiet, and not say a lot of things you think." It so happens that the child's mother, when spoken with, and in front of her three sons, and without any evidence of shame or embarrassment, willingly picks up where she left off a day earlier with one of her boys: "Yes, I feel we had to conquer the Indians, or there wouldn't be the America we all know and love today. I tell my children that you ought to keep your eye on the positive, accentuate it, you know, and push aside anything negative about this country. Or else we'll sink into more trouble; and it's been good to us, very good, America has." Her husband is also a grower. Her sons do indeed "idealize" America's political system — but when a classmate begins to stir things up a little with a few blunt comments, there is no great surprise, simply the nod of recognition and agreement. And, very important, a boy demonstrates evidence of moral development, a capacity for ethical reflection, even though both at home and at school he has been given scant encouragement to regard either migrants or Indians with compassion. Both Piaget[9] and Lawrence Kohlberg[10] suggest that cognitive and moral development in children have their own rhythm, tempo, and subtlety. Children ingeniously use every scrap of emotional life available to them in their "psychosexual development," and they do likewise as they try to figure out how (and for whom) the world works. A friend's remarks, a classmate's comments, a statement heard on television can give a child surprising moral perspective and distance on himself and his heritage — though, of course, he is not necessarily thereby "liberated" from the (often countervailing) day-to-day realities of, say, class and race.

* * *

What of the Indians? How do, say, Hopi or Pueblo boys or girls in Arizona and New Mexico regard the United States of America, its leaders, its political system, and its traditions as a democracy? Listening to those boys and girls it is, more often than not, hard to believe that the scene is the United States of America.[11] These children are enormously indifferent to the political authority that is vested in Washington or the various state capitals. The Indians in theory have their own nations — but for all practical purposes they live on reservations under the control of the federal government, which runs schools and supposedly provides medical care for, and looks after the "welfare" of, half a million rural people. (Perhaps another half million, it is hard to estimate precisely, live in our cities.) For those who have wanted to work with the Indians in their various economic and political struggles, the enemy has rather obviously been the federal government. It provides schools that have long taught children to think little of themselves; medical facilities that are thoroughly inadequate, often staffed with the rudest and most inconsiderate of doctors and nurses; and administrators who are all too willing to operate arbitrarily, with condescension, and sometimes (in connection with land and water rights) quite exploitatively on behalf of whatever white power happened to exert some influence.

For many Hopi children, however, the presence and power of that government bureau — its agents and teachers and bureaucrats — inspires much less animosity. At first the temptation is to call upon various psychological "traits" (culturally induced, of course) in explanation. The Hopis are "passive," or have trouble expressing their "aggressive" feelings, or are afraid to level with themselves, or with white people. In a much more sophisticated and subtle vein, the Hopi, who call themselves "the peaceful people," are said to have a "world view" thoroughly different from ours, hence an indifference to the white world and all that it holds precious — among other things the authority of the military-industrial nation-state.

"Do not ask of these children that they reconcile all their feelings," a Hopi mother-teacher once warned me — as if she knew in her bones that any number of us white child psychiatrists forget to observe (among our patients, among our own children) how various and contradictory a child's inclinations and perceptions turn out to be. The woman's own daughter, at twelve both extraordinarily childlike and on the brink of becoming a woman, had this way of saying a striking yes to Simone Weil's essay on Rome: "We are nothing to the white people; we are a few Hopis, but they are Americans, millions of them. My father told me that their leader, whoever he is, ends his speech by saying that God is on their side; and then he shakes his fist and says to all the other nations: You had better pay attention, because we are big, and we will shoot to kill, if you don't watch out. My mother says all the big countries are like that, but I only know this one. We belong to it, that is what the government of the United States says. They come here, the BIA [Bureau of Indian Affairs] people, and they give us their orders. This law says . . . another law says . . . and soon there will be a new law. In case we have any objections, they have soldiers, they have planes. We see the jets diving high in the sky. The clouds try to get out of the way, but they don't move fast enough. The water tries to escape to the ocean, but can only go at its own speed.

"Everything, everyone, is the white man's; all he has to do is stake his claim. They claimed us. They claimed our land, our water; now they have turned to other places. My uncle, who knows the history of our people, and of the United States, says it is a sad time for others; but when my brother began to worry about the others, our uncle sighed, and said: 'At least our turn is over. Don't be afraid to be glad for that.' They are not really through with us, though. They come here — the police, the red light going around and around on their cars: visitors to our reservation from the great United States of America. 'There they are,' my father always says. He tells us to lower our eyes. I have stared at them and their cars, but I will never say anything, I know that. If their President came here, I would stay home or come to look at him, but not cheer. I have seen on television people cheering the President. In school they show us pictures of white men we should cheer. I never want to. I don't think the teachers expect us to *want* to; just to pretend. So, we do."

Pretense is hardly the same as indifference or withdrawal into self-preoccupation. The Hopis are indeed a quiet, thoughtful people; and they take pains not to offend even those they do not especially like — their neighbors, the nomadic Navajos, and their "protectors," the United States of America. A cousin of that girl's, a boy of the same age, told me that white men are just that: "They want to be protectors of everyone, all over the world." Was he making a politically critical remark: the imperialist West, up to its various tricks? Not really, or at least not wholly. He was trying to explain to me how "very strong" white people are, and why: "My father left the reservation; he went to Denver. He said he lived with white people, and he knows them. They are fighters. If they see something, and they want it, they go get it. If anyone is in the way, that is too bad for him. They are very determined. We are not so determined. We stay here; we are determined to remain here. The white people go everywhere, and show how strong, very strong, they are, and soon the people they meet agree, and then the white man is happy, and he wants to be of help. That is how the Indians got the protection of the Bureau of Indian Affairs; and maybe the BIA is right: without their protection, we would have troubles we don't have now. The Navajos say: let the BIA stand aside, and we will settle with the Hopi. My father says the Hopi may be a bird that is dying out. The white man will not let himself become that kind of bird. There is a difference between the white man and us."

A rather complicated response, that child's, to the political authority of this nation. He is both detached, yet rather eager to take notice of a people, a nation, which he can't, in any case, avoid coming to terms with. America is for a few thousand Hopis not only an enormous empire, but a constant presence in the smallest details of everyday life. Sometimes anthropologists, describing Indian culture (Navajo, Hopi, Pueblo) manage to convey the philosophical and psychological distinctiveness of a people, yet fail to account for the inevitable mixing of two worlds that comes about — the time, for instance, in a child's mental life when he is not only a Hopi, but a Hopi who lives in the state of Arizona, one of the fifty states. Unlike their white middle-class counterparts, the Hopi boys I have met don't draw missiles, don't crave airplane models, don't collect scary "horror" toys, and so on. They don't ever play "war": Hollywood notwithstanding, there are no feathers on their heads, no bow-and-arrow encounters, no effort to defy invisible cowboys. They do play other games — a version of hide-and-seek is popular; they also help herd sheep, and they walk and run and climb. They are not averse to teasing and taunting one another, however "peaceful" they are taught to be; and they learn, thereby, that they are Hopi *and* American, however incongruous the combination.

The result is quiet accommodation, a version of the Hopi's quest for peace — an attitude that has to be contrasted with the intense struggle that black children, say, or poor Appalachian children wage in their minds as they year by year come to see what the future has in store for them. Blacks were brought to America forcibly, made slaves, kept tied to the white man's home and place of business. For black children that historical fact has become an occasion for smoldering resentment, often, out of necessity, somewhat concealed. Poor white children, in the mountains of West Virginia or our city slums and near-slums face the injustice of an economic system. Sensitive to rights and wrongs, and the discrepancy in power between themselves and various adults, children don't fail to notice when their parents are given the brushoff or kicked around by a company like Duke Power, told to clear out for some other part of the country if they don't like the treatment they're getting. In contrast, Indians sit back on *their* land, go through *their* ceremonial experiences, and seem to express the knowing, introspective confusion they feel with a collective shaking and scratching of the head.

In a pueblo north of Albuquerque a twelve-year-old boy tried hard to put such a response into words, aware as he spoke that the effort itself was somewhat alien to him: "I've been living in Albuquerque for a year. The Anglos I've met, they're different. I don't know why. In school I drew a picture of my father's horse. One of the other kids wouldn't believe that it was ours. He said, You don't really own that horse. I said, It's a horse my father rides, and I feed it every morning. He said, How come? I said, My uncle and my father are good riders, and I'm pretty good. He said, I can ride a horse better than you, but I'd rather be a pilot. I told him I never thought of being a pilot.

"Anglo kids, they won't let you get away with anything. Tell them something, and fast as lightning and loud as thunder, they'll say, 'I'm better than you, so there!' My father says it's always been like that. My grandfather remembers the Anglos and their horses; they had them for the soldiers. They'd ride through our reservation. Now they have Air Force bases in New Mexico, all over, and they have their atom bombs stored in the mountains. You go near the places where they do their atomic tests, and they tell you to get away fast. Maybe that Anglo kid will be a pilot, like he says. He asked me if I'd ever been in a plane, and I told him no. He thought I was ashamed, but I wasn't. I told him I'd love to ride our horse as fast as my father does, and never fall off. But he said he could fly across the country in the time it would take me to ride on a horse from the reservation into Albuquerque. And I told him he could go that way, and I'd stay with our horse Sam, and he said that was a deal; but, you know, he came back and told me not to get the idea it was a tortoise-and-hare story. He'd told his older brother, and the brother said: Watch out, the slow man can sometimes win. So, I told him no, I knew he'd get in first, but I'd still keep riding our horse, so long as we can feed her all right and take care of her. A horse takes care of you and you take care of the horse. That's what my mother kept telling us when we were learning to ride."

Nolo contendere, I suppose he is trying to tell his white school-mate, though not because he may feel guilty and want to put himself at the mercy of some court. It is hard, though, to get such a message across to someone who has his own reasons not to hear. A plane is a noisy place, and its pilot has to be self-preoccupied. But then, a man on horseback has to keep alert and attentive, as the Pueblo Indian child knows; if his mind wanders from the de-mands of riding, he can fall or (just as bad, Indian children are taught) become self-indulgent or careless to others. As for the subject of "political authority," Indian children have no trouble taking stock of this nation. By the time they have reached sixth grade, in what we call our elementary schools, Hopi and Pueblo children have achieved a complex and sensitive vision not only of their future, but the country's future. The Indian child is content to go his own way, and doesn't quite understand why the white child won't let the matter rest there. The Indian child hasn't developed the firm sense of property, of ownership, that his white friend has. The Indian child doesn't worry about time, and seems to regard himself as a mere part of a landscape, both human and natural, rather than the master of it. A white child in Albuquerque, not unlike other Anglos who lived in America a century ago, talks of crossing the continent, and the faster the better. His Indian classmate wrinkles his forehead and wonders why the hurry and the greed: the miles of land regarded as a distance to be conquered or done away with, rather than accepted as part of the universe — a territorial presence, a companion almost.

The Indian is not really angry or envious of the white child; maybe in awe of his future power, maybe afraid of it — even as the white child can't help wondering whether somehow, in some way, he has missed out on something, and may end up "losing." I do not believe, however, that the Indian child feels that the white world (its advanced technology, its competitiveness, its acquisitiveness, its absorption in various kinds of swift conquest) is evil, whereas his world is the good one. That boy and his brothers, sisters, and friends have watched supersonic jets, carrying God knows what on practice missions, streak across the clear, vast New Mexico sky, and remarked with astonishment at what others can manage to do. Let those others do as they wish, one hears Indian parents *and* children say: only let us be allowed our rights and privileges, too.

The Indian boy will learn to bow to America's power, even as his grandfather did: Horses are not Sky Hawks and Phantoms, and those noisy, fast-as-lightning planes are yet another version of Simone Weil's "the spectacle of gladiatorial games." The Indian boy will only smile and shrug his shoulders when asked about presidents, congressmen, governors; they exist, he knows, but they belong to others, not him, though he has not the slightest doubt that the decisions those leaders make will affect him. Unlike black children, who can act reticent, fearful, and shy, yet eventually utter their dissatisfaction and rage, the Indian children I have met seem to reserve for themselves, on those "reservations," a notion of psychological independence that assumes philosophical and political forms: They are they, we are we; their leaders are theirs, ours are ours; yet, of course, we are all part of some larger scheme of things — America.

One must shun the temptation to leap from the child's political awareness to the adult's political behavior. It is true that the cynicism and resentment one hears black children express toward our political system have, in recent years, become overtly expressed in the civil rights movement. I know from my own work in the South with black children, however, that in the relatively quiescent late 1950s many rural, politically isolated, and inert children had strong suspicions of this country, very much like those more recently uttered; nonetheless most of those children were never willing, as they grew up, to become involved with the civil rights activists they met in the middle 1960s. Fear, intense and strong, prevented such involvement — and perhaps most of all a nagging sense that the protests would subside, the protesters depart for other struggles (or perhaps, to pay attention to the momentum of their own lives). Left behind, as the segregationists of the day kept saying, would be the same old people: sheriffs, businessmen, politicians, and, always near at hand, the Mississippi Highway Patrol. On the other hand, the apparently infinite patience of the Hopis, their children's astonishingly high acquiescence, in the face of this world's trials and limitations, their continued veneration of so much that is, inevitably, a bulwark to political quietism, may one day, in a flash, give way to widespread social unrest or protest, even as the Pueblo boy who is reluctant to fight it out with his white classmate nevertheless makes it clear that, pushed hard enough, he stands quite definitely on certain ground (literally and symbolically) and is not averse to self-defense.

The attitude that children take toward political authority, toward those who rule them, possess power over them, is but one element in their developing lives. As the Pueblo boy makes quite clear, one can be perplexed by or find oneself alien to a whole culture, including its political authority, yet learn enough realism to know what is not possible under given circumstances. We are left, naturally, with the knowledge that only *one* element in a growing child's life is his or her political awareness — some of it destined to be "forgotten" as the demands of a society exert themselves with ever-increasing urgency. Not everything, though, gets shunted aside into those "deeper" layers of the mind that psychiatrists study. The poor, the racially excluded, the subdued (who work, "quaintly," making rugs or jewelry on their reservations), the constantly exploited or humiliated who live in North America, South America, Europe, Asia, and certainly in every part of Africa, have had a way, history shows, of holding on, as Freud says people do, to their earliest impressions, and treating them, in later years, as important reference points — a means, actually, of interpreting "reality."

Those of us who want to understand how children grow up to embody the political and ideological variations of this planet — revolutionists, loyal soldiers, restive but apparently obliging "natives," troubled men of property, confident proponents of one or another government — would do well to recognize that, like adult sexuality, a political inclination has a "developmental history." There are, of course, all too many psychological determinists; one winces at the thought that "developmental history" will quite soon be read as "developmental imperative." In fact, both clinicians and historians have reason to know that in the lives of individuals and nations alike there is simply no way of knowing at what moment an apparently unremarkable, even unknowable set of feelings or attitudes will suddenly appear, to everyone's surprise, as utterly critical and persuasive in the life of a person or community of people. Or, as a Hopi girl of thirteen put it, blending a child's political awareness with a culture's wisdom and a citizen's practicality: "The news of Watergate is a dark cloud. The sky was clear, and the hunters ran wild; then dark clouds gathered and rain fell, and the hunters stopped for a while. Will we soon get more hunters, just as greedy? Or will we learn to control greed, so that we don't just pray and pray for bad weather to stop the hunters in their tracks?"

We in America could perhaps profit from such a metaphor, made by a "culturally disadvantaged" person, a mere child, who has yet to become as "politically socialized" as her parents, never mind "the people with a long reach," as some Hopis, with only the thinnest of smiles on their faces, refer to some of our leaders in Washington, D.C. As for those Indian children who fall back upon the tribal imagery they have learned, and represent that political authority in the form of a fierce mountain lion or a nondescript but large, toothy, hungry animal — somewhere in this universe the spirit of Simone Weil, mindful of her essay on Imperial Rome entitled "The Great Beast," must be attentive indeed.

The passage of another decade does not find that Hopi, now a woman and a mother, worried about quite the same greed. In 1983 I visited her, met her husband and small daughter, who had just had a first birthday. The baby was crawling everywhere; she had yet to stand up and claim that moment of developmental achievement. The mother was watching her intently, rejoicing in her vitality, her explorative energy. We had been talking about the Hopis and their long territorial disputes with the Navajos. Suddenly the mother was moved to reflect upon her child in this way: "I suppose countries are like children — they want to grow and get bigger, and they want to be able to see a lot, and they think the land is for *them*, and that no one should keep them from it."

Her niece was nearby, a twelve-year-old Hopi child I'd come to know in occasional "follow-up" visits to New Mexico and Arizona. The niece took issue with the aunt, reminded her that the baby itself seemed a bit frightened when it moved (crawled) too far from its mother. Soon enough the child wanted to be nearer by. Then the niece dared extrapolate: "There is a heart to a country, and it beats only so strong — my grandfather says. When a country tries to take land that doesn't belong to it, there will be trouble. A heart can't work for a second body, only for one body, he says to my mother and father. The Navajos want a lot of land, but once they got it, they would be in trouble. Their hearts are weak — too much work to do. Their hearts are cold. We're in good shape; our hearts are fine. We don't have a lot of land, but we can smile. This land is our home; the Hopi heart is beating strong in us, in our home. Even if the Navajos get one of those big Anglo bombs, the nuclear ones they told us about in school — even then they won't turn our land into their land. If they drop the bomb, there'll be no land left; it will all be poison. If they don't drop the bomb, the land will still be ours; we'll be here, on it, and they'll be far away, wanting more and more, but living where they are, strangers to us, to *our* land."

I wasn't sure her logic was all that good, but I began to see what she (and her wise old grandfather) was trying to say — that people have a sense of what land is theirs, and what land belongs to others, and that conquered land is not necessarily felt to be one's own in some psychological or spiritual sense. Moreover, her reference to the possibility of nuclear extinction, worked into the everyday conflict between the Navajos and the Hopis was also helpful — was, in fact, quite edifying. Yet — not for the first time — I'd been made to realize that the response boys and girls make to the major political issues of any nation's life is somehow also connected to their particular experience. Even as black children in rural Mississippi have told me that they worry, once in a while, that the Ku Klux Klan might get hold of a nuclear bomb or two, and God help the black people of America if such were to happen, so too this Indian child could think of the danger of a nuclear war only by resorting to the concreteness of a traditional conflict in Arizona between her kin and an assertive Navajo nation much larger and stronger.

In *The Moral Life of Children* I tried to understand what different American children think about the presence of thousands of nuclear bombs in our midst — if indeed any moral thought is given at all to the subject.[12] This Hopi girl's spontaneous way of considering the threat of nuclear annihilation prompted me to examine with a fresh eye some of the comments my wife and sons and I have heard from children in the United States and in other countries about the nuclear bomb — and trace them to the apparently minor and irrelevant political events that offer a context for boys and girls to consider this most apocalyptic of modern subjects; hence the last chapter of the present book, wherein the greatest "beast" of all is examined through the eyes of children: nuclear bombs wielded by one or another political authority.[13]

II

THE HOMELAND: PSYCHOANALYSIS AND THE POLITICAL THOUGHT OF CHILDREN

IN a long conversation with Anna Freud about politics and psychoanalysis, several of us were solemnly warned: "This is an extremely important matter, and it requires careful research. The danger when you write up your work will be the same danger we face all the time now in psychoanalysis: everything we write or say becomes quickly heard — then forgotten in the worst way by being turned into a cliché."[1] We had just been talking about the manner in which a nation may be regarded by its citizens (or, alas, subjects); we had been using words such as "motherland" and "fatherland," and the one I use now, "homeland." Miss Freud had been reminiscing about her childhood, her youth — the Austro-Hungarian empire and its last, monarchic days. She smiled broadly, then became, suddenly, quite intense: "This is something so *obvious* — and yet we have failed to address it: what children make of their nationality and (don't forget!) what parents encourage them to make of their nationality." Soon we were all excited, but fearful, hence her warning — fearful of leaping straight from the obvious to the banal.

Still, as Miss Freud had warmly encouraged us to do, we went ahead — and in response to her suggestion kept asking various (and quite different) children the *most* obvious questions possible. Up to then we'd been trying to avoid the temptation toward the trite by a series of indirections. As we talked with children, their parents, their teachers, we would speak of the nation's flag, its currency, its social and cultural history — hoping, thereby, to hear what, say, the people of Northern Ireland, Catholic and Protestant, thought about their political situation. What ideas might young people have about being Irish or English or from Ulster? About being Catholic and in Belfast or Protestant and in Belfast? About being a teacher or a parent and hearing children speak of their present-day (national) place of residence? When we heard a child or a grown-up use the word "motherland" or "fatherland," and become (as often happens) misty-eyed, quite sentimental, we would edge nervously away. We felt at first that we had to get beyond the stereotypical phrases and ideas to the deep meaning each person carries about his or her nationality.

But sometimes the stereotypical, or "the obvious," is for millions the intensely personal, and we will find no way around that convergence. A Protestant child of ten in Belfast, sitting under a picture of Queen Elizabeth, told my wife and me that "the Queen is our mother; she holds all her subjects together, my Granny says, and if you're not one of her subjects, you'll be a girl who has lost her mother, and that's the saddest girl in the world." The child's next comment (if she had been in an office, rather than her own living room, it might be considered by the doctor to be an "association"!) went like this: "So, we have to stay part of Great Britain; it's our homeland, my Granny says."

Stray, anecdotal remarks, spoken in the midst of a discussion of Ulster's "Troubles," are instructive reminders that at times the "clinical ear" has a problem that is not one of attention, but of judgment or proportion or context: What, precisely, is the significance of such observations? For one thing, the observer (while listening) must remind himself that the child across the room is *not* depressed, has had no cause to see a doctor, has a good appetite, sleeps well, is in no danger of being abandoned by her parents, or her grandparents, all four of whom are to this day alive. Nor is her "Granny" an unstable soul, overly "involved" with the

British Royal Family out of reasons psychiatric rather than nationalist, cultural, religious. Still, both the elderly grandmother and
the child barely a decade old revere that London lady, the Queen,
with all their heart, their might; and too, speak of her as if she
is — well, what "Granny" once said she is: "the mother of all of
us."

By "all" is meant, of course, only *some* — those who live nearby,
in a particular, Protestant, Belfast neighborhood, and then, the
additional millions known also to be "subjects of Her Majesty."
What about the rest of this earth's people? After successive months
of acquaintance, after three years of visits, one can wonder out
loud with such a question, and hear this response from the child:
"I think they're the people who cause trouble here." One then
persists, tries to get the discussion away from Belfast, from Ulster,
even from Great Britain itself: "I mean, the people throughout the
world who just aren't English — or British, or who like the Papists."

The child, next, ponders the answer she has supplied. She seems
to be searching for a further response that she herself can find
convincing, appealing. She says, at first: "I don't know about all
those people, why they bother us." Then, silence — broken by
her decision to say that, really, she *does* know something about
"those people." She knows this: "They're not as lucky as we are.
There's a lot of trouble all over the world, not just here. A lot of
people don't live in good homes. Their families are bad, you know."
She is prodded a bit on that score, asked what is so "bad" about
those families: "Well, the father might drink, and he might not
give his paycheck to his wife, and he may just disappear." And
the mother? "Oh, she could be just as bad," the girl casually
opines — then waits for her mind to collect its psychological
knowledge more concretely, specifically: "If the mother cares nothing for her children, like some do here in Belfast, in those bad
neighborhoods, then the children become daft. That's how we have
wars — people lose their senses, and it's because they haven't
really got their senses in the first place. My father gets upset, and
wishes we were across the [Irish] sea, and home in England with
our people everywhere and the others nowhere around, he says.

That will be how God fixes things for us when we go to see Him in His Home, in Heaven, I hope, unless we make a bad slip and He says no — and then we'll be with the bad people, and they're the most, I hear; there are more of them than the good. The Queen said she prays for us, or it was the Queen Mother, I think; it *was* her, and she's my Granny's age, and my Granny says with the Queen Mother praying for us, we can't go wrong, and we'll get there, to England, or to Heaven one day, all of us, and no [Irish] sea to keep us apart!"

The themes are not obscure — and surely are recurrent: the saved and the damned, the good and the bad, the lucky and the nameless, faceless ones, countless in number, who aren't deserving of an elderly lady's Buckingham Palace intercessions. Other notions also appear — a girl who worries about being separated and lost, and whose family, and those who live nearby, speak in a similar vein. Sometimes, as I have listened to her, I have wondered what I would make of this child if she were talking this way in my (American) office — until I catch myself noticing how widespread an imagery can be. When I shared some of these statements with Miss Freud, she gave an ironic, wry smile: "The directness of symbolism — we must not make too much of it; or too little, either."

Elderly wise people (as I mentioned in the Introduction) can remind one of the Delphic oracle — all-encompassing and elusive at the same time. I wanted to hear more from Miss Freud — yet I knew I'd been hearing quite enough from children like the one whose words I've just summoned. There comes a time when one's jaded professional and cultural experience begins to hinder rather than help one's understanding of a scene. Best to try to recapture an early, twentieth-century innocence and say, without an embarrassed apology for the trite: England and her Royal Family and even her territorial waters are a continuing maternal force in the lives of this Belfast child, her parents, her grandparents.

Here is someone, after all, who remembers being sung the British national anthem as a "wee baby" — so early in life that she offers a "screen memory" of sorts: "I was very small, and I can't even see my father, but it was he, I know; I think I know because I smelled his [pipe's] tobacco on him, as I do now every night when I kiss him before going to bed. I am in his arms, and he is singing to me, and I say 'again,' and he sings it again, 'God Save the Queen,' and then he gets up and he walks with me, and that's the best treat, and he sings it 'again,' and finally he gives me a big hug, and I know I won't be hearing the song for a while, and my mother comes with a goodie, a sweet, and that's all I remember, I go to sleep, I guess. It's mostly the music I hear, and the tobacco I smell — that's what I remember: the first thing in my life I can recall now. My Granny said the Queen would love to know I was her subject so soon in my life — hearing my father's singing of the anthem."

The anthem — music and tobacco: as powerful instruments as any of Proust's evocations of "things past." With a little more "remembrance" — the child's, that of her "Granny" — one hears about a little flag held dear by a three- and four- and five-year-old child, and of a doll of the Queen, no less dear. "Transitional objects," as we say in psychoanalysis — enduring in their significance. A child, and those who nurture her, holds on tight to some nationalist paraphernalia, as she makes her (normal, gradual) separation from her earlier, highly charged life as a baby. The literary expression is synecdoche: a part stands for the whole. A blanket, a doll, a flag, a teddy bear, help children move from a continual attachment that is "whole" or "total" or utterly unyielding, to one that, being partial, is much more provisional.

This same girl had further comforts attending her departure for school. She recalls the first day: "I wanted to turn right around and wait until my next birthday. Mother said no, I must go with others my age — else I'll be 'slow,' and I won't want that later, when I'll be older, and I said I'd do as she wished, but there I was, suddenly, sobbing, and she had tears in her eyes, too. I remember seeing them as if it was yesterday and not years ago. Next, she told me to cheer up, and I wasn't sure how I was to cheer up. Father said the Queen would be there, to cheer me up at school — her picture on the wall in my schoolroom. I wasn't cheered up, though. Then he told me of his brother, and how he fought in the war against the Germans, and he was on a boat, and they all began the day saluting the flag, and ended the day saluting the flag, and the Queen protected them, and no submarine got them. He was far away from home, but he is glad he fought in the war, and now he tells everyone he was never happier than then, when he fought for England. So, I forgot all my worries, I guess, because I just said, 'goodbye father,' and I said, 'goodbye mother,' and before they could say anything to me, I said I'd be all right, and I knew I would be. I recall seeing a picture of our Royal Family in the school before I even got to my classroom — the one of the Queen and her husband and the children, the one we have in the hall, as you enter."

As you leave, too: Each day she said goodbye to *two* families, and really, thereby, said goodbye to infancy, even as she was about to begin experiencing the opportunities and vicissitudes of another kind of daily life. For her a distant but powerful family, whose members she'd yet to see in person, was a powerful ally. No wonder she told me she was sure that England would never lose a war: "I think God knows our country is good, and He won't let us down. He wants us to keep strong, and He knows we've been brave all the time, and so we deserve to win. There were times when other countries had more men, to go fight, but we knew how to fight better, and we worked hard, and we didn't get soft. England is not soft, father says, and he is sure England won't become soft."

Toughness, discipline, self-control — qualities a child has been learning at home, and will soon learn in school, have lasting symbolic incarnation. Her father's picture books of World Wars I and II give major prominence to the Royal Army and Royal Navy and Royal Air Force. *His* early childhood memories recall Belfast blacked out, the fear of air raids, and even of invasion, the terrifying hysterical voice of Hitler on the radio. But the boy had been reassured by visits to the vast shipyards of the great port city, and the equally comforting words that accompanied the spectacle: "My grandfather held my father high up, on his shoulder, and he showed him all the boats they were building, and he told him they'd save our England. And they did! My father said he knew no other country could beat us, because we made the best boats in the world, and we still can. If there was more of us, the English here, we'd be more on top. We're on top here in Belfast because we don't spend

all our coins on one sweet, then another. We save, and we remember tomorrow, not just a tooth that wants pleasing."

Such a casual lesson in a family's history (her grandfather was a
foreman at a Belfast shipping yard) connects, certainly, with all
sorts of social values, not to mention a nation's political and military
history. How intimate are the connections a child makes between
the larger world's stories, customs, values and the child's own life
as it is lived out, then (later) remembered with nostalgia, with
alarm, with apprehension, whatever the feeling may be. By the
time this girl was ten and eleven, she knew the names of some of
England's great warrior ships of the past — words such as *Invin-
cible, Indomitable*. I was never sure that she had her facts straight,
and I had trouble at Queen's University in Belfast verifying the
accuracy of her claims. I tried not to check them when talking with
her parents and grandparents because she prized her privacy and
her right to talk with me alone (she was a feisty, proud lady even
at nine, when I first met her). But as Miss Freud knew and told
us — as we knew and told ourselves — the point was not which
British cruiser or aircraft carrier or battleship was named what,
but how a child used a nation's assortments of traditions, legends,
historical experiences to construct her own personality.

If one keeps this child (and of course, many others) in mind,
aspects of psychoanalytic theory come strikingly alive. Compara-
tively little fieldwork, unfortunately, has been done to document
the everyday, common habits of children; to see whether they
illustrate the truths child psychoanalysis has obtained through clinical work, aided by the proposal some empirical English psychoanalysts have advocated — that ideas be a response to "direct observation," rather than the obverse, the habit of confirming theory
by a selective "reading" of reality.[2] Nationality is a constant in the
lives of most of us and must surely be worked into our thinking
in various ways, with increasing diversity and complexity of expression as our lives unfold. As soon as we are born, in most places
on this earth, we acquire a nationality, a membership in a community. Our names, often enough, are recorded in a roll, made
part of a government's records. The infant knows nothing of this
event, but the parents certainly are aware of it, and what they

know and feel, as citizens, as subjects, as comrades, is communicated to the child in the first years of life. A royal doll, a flag to wave in a parade, coins with their engraved messages — these are sources of instruction and connect a young person to a country. The attachment can be strong, indeed, even among children yet to attend school, wherever the flag is saluted, the national anthem sung. The attachment is as parental as the words imply — homeland, motherland, fatherland. It becomes subject to the same fate as other attachments.

Nationalism works its way into just about every corner of the mind's life.[3] The energies of the id, the instincts, certainly become connected to nationalist sentiments, if not passions. The tears, the goose-pimpled flesh, the shouts and cries of adults are not lost on children — many of whom, at school, are eager to show their own strong and deep love for their country. "I love my mother, my father, and my country," an eleven-year-old boy told me in Boston as I interviewed schoolchildren, in order to gauge their worries (if any) about a possible nuclear war. I was struck by the intensity of his avowal. He had lost an uncle in Vietnam, and his mother had never forgotten this loss of a brother — hence her son's repeated mention of that war, that death. He had an American flag in his room, a picture of his dead uncle in his room, and also pictures of his parents. His love for his country was evident, sentimental, fierce; it was a love that mirrored, I began to realize, the differing ways of his quiet, kindly mother, his strutting, prickly father. The boy sometimes spoke of America as a great, big, generous country — full of good things to offer its people. He knew by heart the words to the song "America," and he loved talking about the "amber waves of grain." He had seen his parents cry, singing that song, and he did so, too, when it was played. As I heard him once reflect on his country's greatness, I thought of the "oceanic experience" Freud mentioned — the sea as the great maternal presence among us: "I went on a trip with my parents, and we were all happy, because there's so much to the country — it just stretches and stretches, and it's all the best land in the world, and you can't go wrong here, if you give your best to what you're doing, because this is the great country of opportunity."

But then a shift: "You almost have to want to fail here, my dad says, otherwise there's always ten chances waiting. It's worth dying to protect all we've got. No wonder people try to sneak in here; no wonder they challenge us: they're all jealous, I think. You have to be careful, when you've got something good; people will want it!"

If one attends his imagery, that of children all over the world, the constructs of psychoanalysis once more come to life — a nation's continuing life becomes enmeshed in the personal lives of its children. Among the favela children of Rio de Janeiro one hears the country of Brazil connected to those early hopes, expectations, anticipations so many children sustain, despite their actual circumstances. "I pour what I have into the children who stay alive," a Brazilian mother told me, the specter of infant mortality and the grim economic prospects of her family a constant shadow upon her. Her daughter (at nine) affirms that outpouring: "If you look at the city down there, you know there's some chance for you. My brother says he always makes enough to eat. If you have a good eye, you can meet the person who will give you a good tip, he says. People come here, to this city, to Brazil, from everywhere in the world. Brazil is getting bigger — I mean the buildings and the roads and the stores and the restaurants: more and more! My mother says she remembers when there was land and land, and now there are stores and stores and stores. Our country will be first one day. The priest said so, and my mother said she hopes so, because then *we'll* have more and more!"

I suppose such children, so many boys and girls in so many nations, are giving unwitting evidence of an urgent, nationalist morality — the nervousness of their true condition balanced, at least temporarily, by a conviction that to have survived so far is a considerable achievement, and augurs fairly well for the future. Because a child's mind, like that of a grown-up, seizes symbols, craves a general explanation for a particular set of experiences, a nation's name, its flag, its music, its currency, its slogans, its history, its political life all give boys and girls everywhere a handle as they shape and assert their personalities.[4] Anyone who has seen children store up collections of coins or reenact aspects of a nation's history (the military battles, the political confrontations, the exploratory expeditions) will recognize that the so-called oral is, indeed, followed by the anal and the phallic — meaning that the "character" traits psychoanalysts have described connect rather readily with a child's sense of his or her country's political history.[5]

But psychoanalysts have, for nearly a half a century, emphasized not only the vicissitudes of the id, of eros, but the manner in which those other two "metapsychological" (Freud's word) structures, the ego and the superego, come to terms with the instincts.[6] Children quite early show themselves capable of using those "mechanisms of defense": projection and introjection, identification, denial, and, eventually, sublimation in conjunction with their developing political sensibility. "They are the worst people in the world" one hears a child in Belfast say, or Johannesburg, or Rio de Janeiro, or Warsaw, or Managua, or the United States — recognizing the maneuvers of children who have learned to follow their parents' lead, to become in their heads and hearts not only members of this group, but opponents of that one. The more experience one has with such children, the more one appreciates how pervasive nationalism is as an instrument of the ego. The Ulster child of Protestant background, as her remarks show us, had already, in little more than a decade of life, managed to link herself decisively with one neighborhood, at the same time turning another one, psychologically, into a place of monsters and madmen. She would not allow for exceptions — a measure, perhaps, of her apprehension that she might, just possibly, be in error, factually and morally: "There isn't one of them that's worth even a pence of the Queen's money."

In Chapter III, I will try to show the contours of such a "political life"; here I want simply to offer a more clinical (or psychoanalytic) point of view. This girl, who has learned to be especially scrupulous about how many coins she has been given as an allowance, and where they are kept, and how they are kept (in small stacks, according to size); this girl, who worries that her father "gives more" (attention as well as money) to her brother, scarcely a year older, is the same girl who heaps unremitting, unqualified scorn on children she has never seen, except at a distance, but whose "worth" she is sure she knows all about.

The Queen, in all her majesty, her power, and her privilege, has become very much the inside property (so to speak) of this same girl. How good she feels about herself when she announces the company she keeps with the Queen! She does so not only through the poster, and the old doll, still there in the bedroom, but again, the coins: "I have two coins that are new, and they bring good luck. I don't spend them. They are shiny, and there's our Queen, and she's with me, and no dirty Fenian will get me." Such magical confidence bespeaks a powerfully felt bond, long established. As one watches this child, one notices her straightening up, her body responding to her words. The head tilts down a bit as the body stretches and the eyes turn slightly wider, while a hand comes to the hair, to pat it, to set it straight: as much of a regal bearing as one youngster can manage. Later in life, at fifteen, at sixteen, she will aspire to an English university, will share idle fantasies of meeting a young court-connected aristocrat, rather as some of our American youths dream of encountering movie stars. But these fantasies are not easily separated from the almost fierce intellectual determination of a person who has made it quite clear to everyone, especially her schoolteachers, that she is resolutely determined to leave Ulster, to find a better life in England.

One hastens to insist that these identifications and projections and sublimations and introjections are by no means necessarily pathological. In fact, they are devices commonly if not universally used — the homeland as a place where one gets one's bearings; where one takes in a part of the world, keeps another part at a distance, and learns how to use one's given attributes with some sense of achievement and satisfaction. The homeland as a "security blanket," as a source of nourishment, as a place that gives sanction to some of one's urges and strivings — while enabling one to discard others as foreign, as belonging to one "them" or another. The homeland, also, boosts one's forceful side, one's urge to forge ahead, make a mark upon the world. Once a young patient asked me this: "Where would I be if I wasn't an American?" I wasn't sure how to answer his question, because I wasn't really sure what he was asking. I replied with a request that he explain himself. He was a bit bold, if not sassy, at times, and this was one of them: "Well, I mean, where would *you* be if you weren't an American?"

I replied, carefully, that it was hard for me to answer that question and thought that I'd been properly, cleverly evasive — out of the clinical imperative, I assured myself, that requires a strong dose of reticence in the doctor, so that the patient can speak not only freely, but keep fairly free of the tug of the person who is there to listen and learn, and only later to explain. But the boy, twelve years old, the child of an electrician and a nurse's aide, had no great trust for a doctor apparently unwilling to state convictions — the starting point, actually, of his message: "If you weren't an American you wouldn't be able to say what you think. Only in this country can you do that. People forget, and they just take our country for granted. That's lousy, when people don't stand up and thank their lucky stars they're American! If you hide your love of your country, and you don't stand up for it, and say you love it, then you're not being loyal. My father says he's glad he had a chance to fight for this country [in Korea], and he'd do it over and over and over again. I hope I get a chance to show how glad I am to be here, and not anywhere else in the world.

"I just hope I don't get the eye trouble my brother has. If you want to be a pilot, you have to have perfect eyesight. I'd like to be a pilot. I'd like to do patrols, to protect our borders. I'd like to go to Colorado, to the Air Force Academy. If I was born in another country, I'd never have a chance. Here, everyone has a chance, if you have the guts. My dad says there are a lot of people, they don't appreciate this country. They wouldn't even fight for it, if there was an enemy, and he was out to get us: the Russians! America has given us everything, and if you don't try to return the favor, then you're in trouble. Dad nearly died in one battle, and he tells us it's the one time in his life he didn't mind dying. He says he wasn't scared, because he knew he'd be giving his life for his country, and that's the best way in the world to die. He says if he got sick, though, if he had cancer or got a heart attack, like his uncle got last month, then (oh boy!) he'd be scared, really scared. People say to him: Look, you've had bullets coming right at you, and you charged ahead, and you won medals for bravery, and every time you get an ache and pain you worry. Dad says he's no coward, but he's seen a lot of people in his family die of cancer, and now his favorite uncle died suddenly, with no warning, and it's scary. But he says he'd sign up tomorrow, even if a messenger came from God and told him he'd better not, because it's a hundred percent certainty he's going to be killed in action — because that's what the United States of America deserves from its people. And I sure hope I'll be the same way. I'll enlist when I'm old enough, I'm sure."

Such remarks, condensed from a meeting that lasted a half hour longer than the traditional fifty minutes, are not too surprising — if, that is, the doctor is seeing children from a working-class neighborhood whose residents, in home after home, have known combat in Asia or Europe, and hold on to those memories with determination, and with nostalgia rather than regret. This boy was telling me that his nation (its international postures, its military confrontations, its geopolitical struggles) is very much on his mind — part of his thinking life, his dreaming life, his effort to organize himself, to plan for his future, to weigh what he can and will do. This boy was also connecting his love of country with his class background — suggesting that my class background might well be responsible for a tragically diminished nationalism. The consequences for "transference" and "counter-transference," for our ability to get along with reasonably clear pictures of each other, were quite obvious.[7]

Whatever the word "ego" means in theory, in no way (one feels, upon listening to this child and others very much like him) should such a psychological construct be thought to exclude the capacity for a sustained and compelling political consciousness. I am referring to the persisting integrative function of a political ego — a part of a child's awareness that incorporates into both the intellect and the emotions a range of nationalist values, sentiments, ideals, and uses them to shape a life: its commitments, its purposes, its practices, and not least, its espousals. The vocal intensity that nationalism inspires in children the world over contrasts strikingly with what a child psychiatrist is used to meeting in his clinical work — silent, fearful boys and girls, who are (understandably) loath to "open up," to get those talks going which enable a festering wound at last to drain.

Having mentioned "ideals," any psychoanalytic theorist would be immediately moved to consider that special colleague of the ego, the influential superego — and its political side. It is obvious that nationalism generates mandates and prohibitions — that nations normally claim to stand for something and make a strong, visible, almost daily attempt to impress upon people near and far the specifics of that "something." Nowhere on the five continents I've visited in this study has nationalism failed to become an important element in the developing conscience of young people — an element so important that I had to separate a discussion of the political psychology of childhood from its companion volume, *The Moral Life of Children*.[8] Who can listen to children, of any nationality, and not hear the political superego constantly exerting its requirements upon eager and vulnerable minds? I refer not only to the indoctrination one sees in totalitarian societies, but also to some of the agitated jingoism, the hateful chauvinist invective, the arrogant nativism that one may find in democracies. Clinical observers of children, pediatricians as well as child psychiatrists, get used to hearing occasional remarks that, in common fact, are but fragments of an all-too-enduring tradition. A Belfast pediatrician, for example, makes this not surprising observation: "I will be examining a child, and making small talk, and as if the paramilitary people have sent a signal, I hear a burst of vile talk: the dirty, filthy Brits, and their whore the Queen, and Thatcher the pig — and much worse. I think to myself: This child is saying what he thinks 'a good Catholic' should think, and 'a loyal Irishman' should think, and he is saying it as a confidence to me, 'a good Catholic,' and 'a loyal Irishman.' And I am simply appalled! I do not think we yet know what such talk does to these children!"

We both had to remind ourselves that the answer to his implied question is, actually, rather observable: What happens to "these children" is that one day they will become the grown-ups — the ones who, as he put it so aptly, send "a signal" every day to *their* children, "world without end" as the religious phrase goes. These "signals," these politically energized admonitions, injunctions, exhortations, these vociferous calls upon boys and girls to say this, believe that, become in their sum an important part of the mind's house, maybe the hallway that connects the various rooms yet is never really considered to be a room. That same Belfast doctor told me a week later: "I have read my fair share of psychology texts, and I find no mention in them of this terrible vice of nationalism — I mean, what it does to our children. I am sure that this is not the place on this planet Earth for a doctor to claim objectivity about this matter, but I am convinced children in other countries are as much persuaded by this virus as our children here: it is an unconscious you fellows don't seem to have analyzed! Think — stop and think — of how many assumptions we pick up by virtue of living in the country we call 'our country.' If I had more time . . ."

He never completed his sentence, but then, he'd already said rather a lot. There is no point in overstressing the psychology of politics, as it bears upon the mental development of children, but the psychoanalytic texts and journals have clearly succumbed to no temptation to overdo. A relatively modest theoretical literature is devoted to this question but a real paucity of clinical field studies. To some extent, as my colleagues keep reminding me, this lack is explicable. I quote Miss Freud once more: "Our work has always been centred in hospitals, in infirmaries and clinics. It is the *troubled* children whom we have seen, and that is to be expected. But I agree, we have an obligation to leave our offices and learn how children are doing elsewhere by getting to know them elsewhere. Eventually such work becomes 'clinical,' too — not because the children turn out to be sick; no, not at all — but because what we learn from *those* children helps us with our thinking about the children we treat."

So many conceptual thinkers debate "Freud and Society"[9] — debate the proper way in which psychoanalysis ought be formulated with respect to what is "internal" and what is "external," what is "drive-bound" and "familial" (oedipal) and what is "social" and "cultural" — and yet, at some time, we need to know whether all that "thought," whether those "ideas" have any connection to this world's concrete reality. Freud was indeed a great thinker — but his abstractions were meant to explain experiences he'd had in his office: suppositions prompted by a doctor hearing things, seeing things, and trying to comprehend *them* through what those who read his books call his noteworthy reflections, his psychological principles. If we are to hope that a psychoanalytically informed political psychology may develop, to complement the social psychology of politics mentioned in Chapter I — we clearly need to place ourselves *in medias res,* as the expression goes; to hear, for example, what a youth of thirteen who lives in Hattiesburg, Mississippi, and is almost ready for high school, and of solid Anglo-Saxon heritage, has to say about his nation, and yes, the vicissitudes of the superego: "I don't know why I get teary when we salute the flag. I guess it's because I know my father near died in Vietnam. He never talks about what happened there — no, never. He is quiet about a lot of things. Once he said to me: 'Sonny, there's only one thing I positively believe in, and that's the United States of America.' I was surprised, I guess, at what he said, because I asked him whether he didn't believe in God, too. He answered me funny; he said he wasn't really sure about where God is, but he was mighty sure where America is, and that's why, he said, there's only one thing he 'positively believes in'!

"Then he told me this country is what's made him good, because he had a lot of trouble with his own daddy, and they fought like hell, and his mom would just cry and cry, and she was weak-willed, and whatever her old man wanted and said, she'd go along. But my daddy took argument with his daddy and there was lots of trouble. I mean, my daddy was the first one in his family to call a nigger Mr. and call a nigger Mrs., and he's been their best friend in this part of town, and they know it. You want to know how he got to be their friend? I'll tell you: through being in the army, and through realizing that's what America is all about, including our state of Mississippi! The Stars and Stripes, they're meant to be for everyone, daddy says. He saw a colored man save a white man's life over in 'the Nam,' and he's never forgotten what he saw. He says this country is way bigger than any damn problem we have.

"I see on television the news, how people live in other places. Maybe God has put us here to test us, like our minister says — put us in the U.S.A. so we can have a good chance to be good; and if we fail, then we're headed straight for the worst part of hell, that's for sure! My mother says you need *spine* to be good, and what gives you the spine is the flag out there, reminding you of the country and all who've fought for it, your daddy included, and there's the pledge to the flag, and there's singing the songs we do. In school the teachers make sure you know the words, and we have to write compositions on them, so you don't forget *what* you've been singing while you've been singing! Then, they have us memorizing from the Declaration of Independence, and if you can live as good, be as good, as those guys who wrote that, then you know you're on your way to God. My daddy said God has His favorites just the way anyone would, and we shouldn't brag, but look at America, and we're better off than the rest of the world, everywhere, and that means it's God giving us that extra boost. If you can remember that He's been looking out for you, for your country, then you'll try to be good — I mean, live up to the best that's in you. That's how I see it."

As one feels the strong emotion prompting this boy's words, and sits in his home and gets to know his parents, his extended family (called "kin" or "kinfolk" in the South), one begins to appreciate — in an ordinary, rather quiet and reticent family — the strong eloquence of a patriotism become for each member, and certainly for this boy, an abiding, politically mediated, moral influence, which works in many ways. Nationalism, even a militaristic kind, softens a socially transmitted racism. Nationalism props a populist egalitarianism that otherwise might have to be fearfully set aside, lest the charge of "communism" be dragged out. Nationalism encourages social commitment to a neighborhood, a willingness to exert oneself toward civic tasks. Nationalism also energizes the entire moral life of a child, his parents, his relatives — gives them all a structure on which they can hang a range of oughts, noughts, maybes, ifs. Nationalism prompts a range of (often inconsistent) precepts, teachings, opinions, and surmises that, added up, keep in motion both the superego and the ego ideal, the stern, reproving conscience many of us know well, and the high-minded side of ourselves we occasionally regard with awe, with anxiety, with irritation, with the resigned despair of the wayward one, but at moments with the conviction that a good step has, indeed, been taken.

Colleagues of mine, more comfortable with generalizations, have asked me after a presentation at hospital grand rounds or psychiatric and psychoanalytic seminars, to pull together some of the themes the boy I have quoted here manages after his own fashion to convey. One colleague has spoken to me of something he calls the "political imago" — a consciousness that develops in children and possesses its own day-to-day mental energy, a segment, putatively, of the superego and ego ideal both. It would not be hard to slip into a particular language, even draw a diagram or two, propound upon the "political imago" as it fits into the topography of psychoanalytic theory[10] — and yet, I believe I worry less about losing the reader than losing myself. "Perhaps, right at this point, we can continue to make our direct observations," Miss Freud has said — and added: "only later may we want to try to fit all the pieces (all we've seen) into a larger picture." As the Mississippi boy's daddy would put it, has put it: "You don't make a federal case out of something until you're good and ready."

That word "good" keeps coming up, as one hears him, his son. How embattled their goodness feels to them — how much in need of the "spine" they mention! They are not of psychopathic or sociopathic disposition, and so the issue is not the relation of an enfeebled conscience to a body of beliefs and rituals that doesn't exact more than lip service. These are, again, plain people of no excess learning, not impoverished, not down and out. They are churchgoing Methodists, white-collar people in social background, and of a region known for its strong military and national pride. Their religious life, one notices, merges with their political life, as does their regional and working life. They believe that God had His preferred child: America. They believe that the South has made its moral mistakes, but that America has the ability, still, to redeem those mistakes. And personal redemption is dramatically, convincingly, unforgettably evoked in a Vietnam battle scene —

so that America's political life (including the decisions that made
for another of the world's sad and bloody wars) has endowed a
resident of a south Mississippi medium-sized city with "the most
important time" in his life.

He meant moral time — an awakening of his conscience. He
meant political time, too — an awakening of his sense of how his
city works, his state, his country. He meant that his affections were
now to be less rigidly split (blacks no, whites yes), and that his
frustrations and angers, his "aggressive drives," were also now to
be less rigidly split (blacks yes, whites as a public rule no). Some
highly cherished moral and spiritual values are in question. A
nation's history becomes a family's history, becomes in turn a
child's apparently idiosyncratic conscience: "I'll hear my daddy's
words, and then I'll be nice to one of the colored, and sometimes,
you know, you'll hear one of your own people saying something
bad about you, and you worry, because like my mother will say
to us, you have to be in step with your own people."

The boy wasn't altogether clear or decisive, one notices. But
then, who *is*, when the issue has to do with a family's choosing to
show moral and political independence — without money, power,
social status, or educational achievements to support them in the
likely event of criticism, even ostracism? Fortunately for this family, the entire state of Mississippi was being compelled, at the
time, to undergo a political reconsideration — given new federal
laws, new Supreme Court pressures, and above all, new economic
goals that favored the end of segregationist stone-walling. But I
am not bringing this child's witness to these pages in order to
discuss *southern* politics — rather, that thoroughly complex matter of the relationship between a society's general politics and each
individual's (here, each child's) personal politics. Without question
Freud saw the Oedipus complex as a familial phenomenon — hence
social in at least a small sense: as the various alliances and enmities,
open and concealed, of several individuals, who if lucky are also
bound to one another by love. That which is social is also, in some
ways, political — the negotiations and arrangements that adjust
power between these individuals. Few psychoanalysts would question the capacity of children to take exceedingly accurate stock of

that kind of politics! Indeed, the essence of child psychoanalysis is the recognition, based on day-by-day clinical experience, that children constantly assess power, gauge who rules whom, weigh dodges, ploys, deceptions, distinctly political enticements, as one or another figure in their microcosmic *polis* takes front rank, retires to the rear in fearful ignominy, suddenly recoups his or her fortune, and just as suddenly is once again isolated, seeming to be powerless or stranded.

When children describe these transactions in our offices today, we are not dumbfounded or skeptical. We are actually surprised when they are unable or unwilling to make such psychological *and* political comments about the people intimately around them. "Ask him who runs the family," a supervisor of mine, a fine child psychoanalyst, often told me — his rather blunt language deliberately chosen in order to get to the heart of things, and thereby (I was learning) reach the child more effectively. The look of hesitation, maybe slight embarrassment, that came to my (then) young and perhaps self-satisfied face was the supervisor's clue: Best to break through, first, the doctor's "resistance," his plain inexperience and ignorance, so that the child, who knows better out of the natural rhythms of his ten-year-old citizenship (so to speak) in a six-member city-state, will begin playing some important cards. Finally, half-choking on the words my supervisor had suggested, I nevertheless uttered them — and heard an immediate "my mom." What to do with *that?* Nothing, the neophyte helplessly concludes — only to hear, a week later: "Ask him how his father gets back at his mother — what deals he makes to even the score, who his allies are." More hesitations, if not qualms, but the apprentice obeys — and finds himself talking about power and submission, talking about arrangements and agreements. (To talk about "deals," one can always gossip with *another* supervisor about the way "some supervisors" work with their trainees!)

In time all this procedure becomes second nature to the doctor — recognition that children have a lot of political knowledge (about family matters) on the tips of their tongues — and another recognition: that psychoanalytic training centers are *also* families of sorts, and not without *their* politics: power being exerted, feared, resented, and often, alas, embraced with utter and eager self-denigration by young initiates whose lack of personal dignity may well match that of their even younger patients, known as "children in psychiatric treatment." Still, some theorists tell us that such a political life, for the young, stops at the door of each family's home.[11] Once the child leaves his or her house a dumbness or indifference is supposed to settle in — perhaps modified, occasionally, by the child's ability to make a necessary estimate of neighborhood politics or school politics. Years after these supervisory experiences had ended, and I was, as we say, graduated and on my own, I recall hearing a mother tell me, at length, how shrewd in some ways her somewhat anxious and phobic son was: "He's constantly trying to figure out who's the one he should team up with. Then he becomes a slave to that person. Before I ever thought of getting treatment for him I began to realize that he was scared out of his mind a lot of the time, so naturally he'd be a clever boy, when it comes to analyzing the other kids, and deciding who is the one to tie your fortune to! I wish I had his intuition! In my office job, I never have been able to pick the right one — the guy who's going to be the winner, who'll have the bonus money to hand out!"

A few seconds later, when I asked her about her son's possible interest in current events, in the news television offered, in politics, I was greeted with this expression of surprised perplexity: "Politics, I don't believe my son even knows what the word means! He's only thirteen! How *would* he — I mean, he's interested in how automobile engines work. I think he'd like to get in a car, on some days, and just drive away from all his problems! I don't think he knows a thing about all the mess this country has got into [Watergate, the Vietnam War]. I don't even know whether he'd be able to tell you who's our President; and I'm not sure I care to know myself, these days, even though I voted for him. I guess children don't interest themselves in politics. That's the curse of growing up — you have to bother with all the terrible news that you hear. I try to block it out, but sometimes I don't succeed, and that's a bad day for me!"

All very breezily conveyed, with an edge of mordant disgust

familiar to many of us Americans, who have read Mark Twain and H. L. Mencken (or all the journalists who emulate them) and who have heard extremely successful politicians, some of them Presidents of the United States, rail against "big government," and "lazy bureaucrats," and "dirty politics" — suggesting that everyone in office is suspect, save for *them*. But her son was not as unobliging as she had predicted, were I to be so fatuous as to pursue my line of inquiry: "I couldn't help knowing about Nixon; everyone knows what he's done! He's ruined himself. He may be the first President to be impeached. I feel sorry for him. Everyone's after him. But he brought it all on himself. I don't know why he didn't just destroy those tapes of him talking with his friends. Can't you just get someone to go erase them, or burn them? Maybe we could do better in this country if the President had more power, and he didn't have to keep explaining himself all the time. My dad says Nixon was good, and now he's scared, and so he's no good. I fall apart when I get scared. I don't even remember the silliest little things — like how to get on my bike and pedal and pedal, until I'm safely away from trouble. I just freeze."

A pause. I prepare for a new question — but he has a few more words, and these are self-scrutinizing, but also cautionary for others: "I guess if you're in trouble, you can't react — because you're afraid you won't do the right thing, anyway. That's me — when my nose sniffs danger, I turn stiff as a board, and then all I do is stare ahead, hoping some buddy of mine will show up and get me out of the mess I'm in. Maybe that was what happened to old Nixon. He lost his cool, like I do. A President should keep himself protected, or all his enemies will get him. I think Nixon must have forgotten that a lot of people were waiting for him to stumble just once. I know that if I start to show even one person I'm 'chicken' — then, I *am* 'chicken'; I mean I get 'chicken,' because the guy moves in and treats me the way you do when you're with someone who is 'chicken'!"

By no means could this boy do analytic justice to all of Watergate's many intricacies, but he certainly made a thoughtful, psychological beginning — and as I heard him talking about the way people "freeze," the image of Nixon so doing didn't seem implausible at all. In any event, I call upon the lad here because he was my patient rather than someone whose political ideas or convictions I was trying to understand, and so (even allowing for my interest in the subject, an interest that often doesn't result in any talk of politics whatsoever with patients) our discussion was — I suppose — incidental. Yet, a mere political innocent, as his mother would have him, was already a citizen of sorts — alert to what the nation, his nation, was struggling to get through, and sensitive to some of the personal nuances that have always been part of any nation's politics. Such awareness, of course, was not at all truly "incidental" but rather the result of a young person's prior political learning; what was learned in a family, in playgrounds and backyards, in school classrooms and nearby athletic fields, and in the town life of shopping, eating in restaurants, standing in line to enter moviehouses.

"Whatever you do," observed this boy, ever conscious of the strengths and weaknesses in other boys, "you have to remember there are others, who might step on your toes." All politics is not quite that grim, one tries with determination to believe, but the boy had put his finger on a large lump of political reality. The source of his knowledge is not a textbook, a school's course, a teacher's clever asides, or even some television docudrama meant to explicate the inscrutable for the supposedly inert: teaching millions of naifs, children or grown-up, a few seamy facts about how people get, hold, lose power. Rather, a boy moves from a sense of his own frequent powerlessness (and his fervent interest in power, and his comprehension of its immediate uses and its eventual limits) to a closely reasoned, if informally rendered, analysis of a political scandal that had seized his country at the time of our conversation.

I doubt Sigmund Freud would have been surprised at the outcome — he who saw political ambition, after all, as a further elaboration (sublimation) of oedipally derived energies.[12] Certainly Anna Freud was quick to tell us, during our informal seminars with her, that she had heard similar political keenness from some of her young British patients.[13] She did point out that her experience had taught her to expect that "broader knowledge," she called it then (at other times I've heard her call it "social knowledge") to be offered in a form of questions: "I have found that the most astute of the children I see (some of them turn out to be more astute than I had initially thought them to be!) are not given to lengthy remarks about the world — but they do indicate their interests or curiosity with very pointed questions, which they don't ask with any expectation (I've decided, after years of hearing them) that they be answered by me or anyone else. They are asked as we may ask them of ourselves, in our frustration or irritation. But the fact that they are formulated and put into words is well worth our acknowledgement, and our research effort, I admit."

When pressed for an example, she recalled a girl of nine or ten who wondered aloud why England "needed a King and a Queen." The girl also asked whether a King or Queen isn't a "parent higher than all other parents,"a blameless parent, one no one should have cause or wish to scorn or vilify or bitterly dismiss and try to oust. Miss Freud, in turn, asked us what we thought about the child's questions, which were, really, statements, and what we had in mind, generally, meaning about our subject of "children and politics," the title we'd given our interests in correspondence with her. In response I shared with her a question I'd heard in 1975 from an English girl who was living in Northern Ireland, because her parents taught there at the university: "I've asked my mother and father if you can elect a king or queen, ever, and they say no, it's blood that makes you royal. Do you think there ever were some people, and they fought, and one became king, even if his blood wasn't royal?" I thought the answer was yes — and of course wondered whether the child had ever asked this question of her father. I asked her if she had, and she said, "I keep forgetting to ask him." I pursued the matter no further; anyway, the mother arrived with tea and delicious, honeyed cakes and flat, but sugary and tasty biscuits and lots of jam. Miss Freud smiled as I told her the story, and we all searched through our knowledge of history for specific answers to the girl's question, until Miss Freud reminded us that a child wasn't asking, really, for this kind of actual survey, but rather, for consideration of the question of political legitimacy, not to mention parental authority — whereby derived, through divine right or through everyday struggles? If the latter, did even a child have the right, perhaps, to join the fray?

This child had never read Plato's *Republic* or Aristotle's *Politics* or Hobbes's *Leviathan* or Freud's *Group Psychology and the Analysis of the Ego*, but the politics they all ponder is the politics she was capable of at least questioning. How to rule? Who is to rule whom? What emotions prompt the ruler to do his or her work — and the ruled to go about their obedient business? Plato argued for a hand-picked royalty — a chosen community of specially educated individuals. They would stand apart, responsible for the state's sovereignty. He saw, in other words, the possibility and desirability of a politics freed of family ties, never mind royal blood — a chosen elite turned into a caring political leadership devoted to the common good precisely because they would be free from the bonds of individual and family life. Aristotle said no — we are too cravenly personal: Even with the early pedagogical instruction necessary to Plato's notion of an ideal ruling caste, a powerful streak of the self will always find its own private preferences and purposes. Have your dreams, in effect he said to Plato, but here is how we mortals are — bound by our nature, our day-to-day entanglements.

Those entanglements, of course, have not gone unnoticed by political theorists over the generations, even as children notice them constantly. Hobbes and Locke, for all their differences, knew how much egoism (instinctual energy) we all possess, hence how solid a political structure must be established, lest the jungle in each child become the collective jungle in all people — undeterred by the agencies of a government. But egoism need not be only a matter of greed and murderous rivalry (thanatos). The passion may be that of an ardent desire for others, the child in pursuit and emulation of mothers and fathers, endlessly it seems: The brothers and sisters whose family love energizes a communal inclination, a dedicated commitment to link arms, share a political cause (eros). Again, boys and girls, sitting in treatment or simply walking the streets of a city, war-torn or delightfully at peace, are capable of their own kind of pointed apprehension of such traditional philosophical issues, the very heart of political and moral inquiry. Their imaginations are charged by continuing participation in family politics, and their inclination to go from that kind of world to the larger one is no different from Plato's, Aristotle's, Hobbes's, Locke's, Freud's — all of whom did so, with differing conclusions, of course, as to what distinguishes these two realms of experience.

The word "homeland," of course, ineluctably combines both of those worlds. One emphasizes the psychological connection between "home" and "land," made all the time by children, yet reminds the reader (and oneself, and one's colleagues) that the administrative corridors, or the legislative amphitheaters, or the judicial chambers of various countries are not simply families writ large, "homes" on public display in a particular "land." Rather, they have their own all-too-subtle, often bizarre psychology, something Kafka surely knew,[14] and something those of us who use psychoanalytic analogies too readily or glibly have yet to learn. The politics of the homeland is not necessarily the politics of the home, though each person involved in any nation's politics has, of course, a home life to add to the pool of shared insights and experiences that, in their sum, most certainly do influence (though there are other "variables") how political decisions are made.

Nor is even this increasingly knotty level of political and social thinking beyond a child's ken. When a boy of Mississippi knows that his father may have learned to like black people personally, yet watch his step in public lest he risk his job, his social standing, his neighborhood friends, and even the respect of some members of his own family, he has (at the "mere" age of twelve, as the condescending expression goes) learned to juggle what theorists refer to as different "levels of abstraction." The child's language may not be the palaver of a journal article or a book — it may even be better, because as earthy and strongly suggestive as can be: "Inside our home we say one thing, and outside we say another, and so there's two people in me, and my daddy says there may be some other people in me, if you want to keep careful count!" We are, in these pages, trying as best we can to keep count — or at the very least, to add the "variable" of political thought to the enumeration of what takes place in the minds of children.

III

RELIGION AND NATIONALISM:
NORTHERN IRELAND

B ELFAST is one of the world's great port cities, all its children
are quick to say. Belfast is situated at the mouth of the Lagan
River, and often those same children add a legendary comparison:
The city resembles a lobster, with claws holding tight to a lough —
and beyond, the sea. But only Catholic children (and by no means
a majority of *them*) are likely to remind a visitor that the city bears
a Gaelic name: "the approach to the sandbank." Long before the
seventeenth century, when English settlers began to build in earnest, Irish people had given a name to the place — land and water
especially well joined. A Protestant teacher who dipped into that
bit of pre-Norman factuality in 1976 found herself heckled roundly
by a classroom of twelve-year-old children, all Protestants themselves. She has never chosen since to go quite so far back into her
native city's maritime cultural history.

The history has been set down in dozens of books and hundreds
of articles[1] — the continuing religious strife, the ancient royal confrontations, the various battles won and lost, the ethnic suspicions
and antagonisms, the economic and social history, the ups and
downs of a struggle waged by some for independence, by others
for loyalty, above all loyalty: "The U.K., hey hey, let's stay." Those
words were assembled by some Protestant children from the Shankill
area, a Belfast working-class neighborhood where Catholics are
feared and hated. It was not a very good slogan, the boys who

coined it decided; they abandoned it. Why not get to the heart of the matter with a few familiar swears — "dirty Taigs," or "filthy Fenians"?

As for the object of these slurs, Catholic children were not without their own epithets: "Orangies" or "Huns" or "lousy Prods." Any reader who wants to understand what both Catholics and Protestants of Ulster call "the Troubles" must know the etymology of such swears, which remind us of William III of Orange and his victory (in the Battle of the Boyne) over the Catholic King James II (1690). The same articles and books tell about the Irish Republican Brotherhood, otherwise called Fenians, and their long, painful struggle against the Crown. The expression "Taig" is less likely to be a subject for written explication, but there are knowing "Prod" children who can detail a derivation: *Tadgh* is the Gaelic form of Teddy, and it's a common name among the Catholics of Ireland, North and South.

The North — Ulster — was born late in 1920, when England's rulers decided to yield to the Irish Protestant (Unionist) demand for continuing citizenship in Great Britain.[2] The Parliament building for that new principality of the United Kingdom soon took on the name of its location — Stormont — and no Belfast child seems without an opinion of the place. For some, Stormont is the lovely spot where an executive and legislative body rightfully dominated not only a view but the whole six-county area, which was thereby "saved" from a foreign country (often called "Dublin"), not to mention from something abstractly called "popery." For others, the word "Stormont" tells of British scheming, of divide and conquer, of a relentless bigotry that has not only a religious but an economic side, providing power and money and jobs for Protestants, a life of poverty and subservience for Catholics.

Since 1968, Stormont has existed only in political memory. Britain returned to Ulster in 1968 because Ulster split in two. Sometimes, to hear Belfast children talk, the only neutral ground left in the city is to be found on the higher slopes of Cave Hill, the public grounds to which both Catholic and Protestant children are often brought for frolic, for games of luck or strength or canniness.

No one can give us examples of good cheer and harmonious play, among Ulster's children, across religious lines. War, violence, hatred generate their own literature. A moment of relaxed time for young people of both religious backgrounds is impossible to conceive — a dream of hopeful philosophers, naive social planners, or romantic poets. One summer, I boarded a bus each day with two adults, one a Belfast Catholic, the other a Belfast Protestant, counselors in a summer program aimed at bringing together children from both Protestant and Catholic neighborhoods. As the bus gradually filled with first Protestant and then Catholic children, the historical and sociological explanations of religious rancor and loathing would come repeatedly to mind. Every morning, all the way to Cave Hill, insults filled the air. On the way back, however, there was invariably a considerable spell of silence; only as the bus gained proximity to the Shankill, and to the Ardoyne, a Catholic neighborhood where unemployment is endemic, did the scolding and revilement and invective assault the ears again: the high-pitched, singsong, preadolescent noise — a brutal legacy claimed without embarrassment or shame by minors now glad to reaffirm an old enmity.

But why the silence — so long, it would always seem until abruptly terminated by the first catcall or slogan? In fact, the silence that entered the bus with the children had been earned by a day of activity. When the boys and girls got off the bus in the morning they soon enough found things to do, or responded to our initiatives: games and walks and races and hunts and picnics and explorations. Such cliques as there were usually had to do with sex rather than creed. At lunch, when one might expect a lifetime's sentiments and experiences to assert themselves in fresh antagonism, the children remained at ease, grouped according to one or another "activity." This was our banal, self-important word, but suddenly "activity" possessed a mysterious magic: the power to dissolve the nastiest of misgivings, connected to one of the most lasting of historical fights.

Because we went, at first, only to Cave Hill, I began to invest the place itself with a mysterious, healing authority — grounded in the city's past. Below the public playgrounds, the lower seaward slopes of this hill have been inhabited for generations. Well-to-do merchants long ago staked out a "park" here or there, and now the "parks" are collections of red-brick houses, the suburban residences of middle-income or comfortable working-class people, mostly Protestant. To them and their children, Cave Hill represents the enterprise and prosperity of Protestant Englishmen. But Cave Hill has meaning for Catholic children as well. They conjure up a time of fishermen and fowlers, imagine Gaelic nomads putting burial cairns atop the remains of their dead, or shouting in triumph at the discovery of good cutting stones. Those same children know that the caves of Cave Hill sheltered the native Irish from the insistent intrusions of the Vikings and the Anglo-Normans. They know the hill as a source of peat, and as a place of outdoor prayer on Christian holy days.

Its double past seemed to grant Cave Hill a moot neutrality — hence (I reasoned) the children's ability to shed years of animosities there and play together. But we tried other places, and those trips (over to Bangor, down to Newcastle, up to Ballyclare, and thence to Larne) were no less amicable. The bad language stopped, we discovered, not only when we got off the bus at Cave Hill, but in the countryside beyond Belfast, or along the shore, once the great port city was no longer in sight. No place, though, however attractive and pleasure-giving for the day, could prevent that final burst of bad blood upon our return to the two neighborhoods. When I asked a Catholic child or a Protestant child for an explanation; when I pointed out what I'd seen and heard, and then asked why, I was always treated to this: "Well, now, we're going home, aren't we!" In order to understand why a child will, under some circumstances, suspend his or her truculence and antipathy, one has to hear the child out, learn the specifics of what seems to be an enduring prejudice, and thereby the possible grounds of hope that a change of behavior, if not a change of mind and heart, might happen.

Tony, for example, is a ten-year-old boy who lives in the Ardoyne. His father has been jobless for three years and is on the dole — yet another poor Catholic who finds himself to be an ironic beneficiary of the British welfare system. As a young man, he worked in construction, but there is precious little of that in Belfast these days. His son is well versed in the economic aspects of the Troubles; over the months I talked with him the youngster gave me a full account of what it is like for a Catholic man — what it will one day be like for Tony and others like him unless a great many political and economic reforms take place. "There's no future for us, unless we get our rights. The way it is now, Belfast is run by the Brits, and it's the Prods who own everything. The owners of the stores or the factories don't like us, because we're Catholic. The union people, they're against us for the same reason. My father tried to find work for a year, then he gave up. He got sick; his stomach went sour. It's in his head, my mother says. When he was a boy, he wanted to work in a cigarette factory, but they told him he could sign on their waiting list, to clean the floors. No Catholic makes the cigarettes! They never called him. He says he hates the dole, but what can you do? If it was fair here, he'd stand a chance of finding a job. Our priest says we shouldn't lower our heads; we should be proud, and remember that they owe it to us, the money — England and the Prods here — for all they've done to us.

"The soldiers drive by and they call us 'dirty Fenians,' and they say we're pigs, and we should go south. We wave our Irish flag at them! We have to use our heads; they're waiting for us to make mistakes. They'd like an excuse to be rid of us. They'd as soon kill us. They'd as soon drive us across the border to the Irish Free State. They want no part of us, nor we of them; that's how it is, and it's been like that since so long that you might as well say forever. This is one island, and it should be one country. But England made sure we'd be split, and there's been trouble here in Belfast ever since, and no one has an answer."

Not one speech that; I have pulled together remarks made over several weeks. Tony is a bright lad, but the teachers despair for him, and others like him. He lacks "motivation," for reasons he himself mentions — a shrewd appraisal of his likely prospects. When asked about hopes, wishes, the future, Tony remains silent. When asked again, he replies tersely: "The IRA [Irish Republican Army]; I'll not be a stooge or a slave." A feisty boy, not yet ado-lescent, indifferent to education though possessed of sharp intelligence, ready moral indignation. At age seven he began carrying messages from one house to another in the service of resistance to both civilian and military authority. Ulster for him means a hostile Protestant majority, determined to stay part of an empire that only sixty years ago granted another part of Ireland independence. He can't forget the low esteem those Protestants have for his people — a fearful arrogance and condescension he's heard described by parents and grandparents, aunts and uncles and cousins, priests and nuns, neighborhood adults and a host of friends his age, older, and younger. Every day, moreover, he sees his father idle, watching the telly or standing outside and talking with others like him: men without work; men angry and confused and resentful about the way their time on this earth is being spent.

One day Tony took crayons in hand and made a picture of the Ardoyne. (Figure 2.) We had been talking about what he'd like to see happen — a notion of a better life. He wanted to let me know what had to come first, the essentials of a transformation. He drew for me a vicious battle scene. He posed the Irish against the British and declared his Catholic Church (however imposingly drawn) essentially off limits, hence irrelevant to the street encounter that meant so much to his future and that of his people, so he firmly believed. A grim, dark, terribly bloody scene; and one in which he himself figured — a tall, red-headed soldier, wounded, yet still firing away. For flag (Irish) and for Church, one gladly risks death. As for the Orangies, they are no less inclined to do the same, he stresses. It is a fight to the finish, the boy declares afterward; and he feels no sympathy for England, the Protestant minister Ian Paisley, or "them over in the Shankill." But he has an afterthought: "If only some kids my age, Orangies, could be told the truth!" Meanwhile, death utterly dominates a drawing.

Still, in this bleakness there are qualifications. The Church does require at least a nod to charity. And of some, maybe passing, influence is a child's capacity to dream, to imagine persuasion at work (even as he has been, himself, won over, day after day, to a cause by the talk of others). When Tony met his Protestant counterparts from the Shankill, he was stunned: there they were, on the same bus, and ahead stretched a whole day's activities, all to

be shared. He was able to give a charming and instructive account
of what crossed his mind: "The Devil come down to earth! I'd seen
them from a distance. I'd walked the Shankill Road! We try to stay
clear of them. We have all we can do to fight the Brits. On the
bus they swore first; but if they hadn't, I'm sure we would have
started! We may be outnumbered in Belfast, but we aren't going
to lie down and wait for people to step on us. When we got up
the mountain, we left the bus, and the counselors had us playing,
and everyone forgot the Troubles, and we wanted to win the game,
and they split us, so we weren't Catholics against Protestants, you
know. So we had to forget everything for a while. Then, you're
back on the bus, and you remember. My mother asked me if I
ever talked with any of them, about the Troubles. No. They don't
like us any more than we like them. But if we had it fair in Belfast,
we could live with them, like we played with them this summer."

A Protestant boy from the Shankill, George by name, eleven,
has his own way of describing and picturing with crayons what is
happening in Belfast, and what took place that summer up in Cave
Hill and elsewhere. "We have a big problem here in Ulster: the
Catholics. They're all Fenians; they want to drag us down. If we
didn't keep them in their streets, and watch them, they'd try to
take over the city, and those six counties would be owned by
Dublin and the Pope of Rome. We'd be living like pig farmers.
We built up Belfast; it's our doing. We built the ships and the
factories. They don't have the mind, my dad says; they drink and
they have ten kids to a family, and even more. Then they shout
'poor' and 'unfair.' If we left it to them, there'd be us, doing all
the work, trying to keep our streets clean, and inside, our houses
clean — and then there'd be all of them, more and more and more
of them. We'd have to leave, or settle for the Mystery Shop running
things."

He pauses for a minute; he is asked to explain that last reference.
The Catholic Church, he willingly insists, is full of "mumbo jumbo."
His grandfather tells him every day that Catholics are "superstitious," and that inside a Catholic church one finds "a zoo." The
boy doesn't want to explain, he wants to declare. He hasn't actually

been inside one of those churches; he never will find himself in a sufficiently curious mood to take the necessary steps — but his grandfather did, once, and the boy tells about what was seen and heard: "They were falling down and they had candles, and there was a funny smell, and they didn't know what was going on, and they swallowed stuff, and they went and talked with the priests, and they were told what to do and what not to do, and there were the nuns, wearing those robes. They're not like us, not in the church, and not in the way they live, and they will breed and breed, and one day, Ulster will have a bigger problem than now. We think the Fenians should go south. They should be with their own, and we should be with our own."

There is no more to say on that score. But George is willing to draw a statement that conveys his ideas, his worries, his notion of what ought to obtain in Belfast. It is an us-against-them scenario, grimly presented, even extended to an apocalyptic warning. Like Tony, George can use the foul language of bias with no apparent scruples. Like Tony, George can present himself as a ruthless warrior, a tall and gun-wielding defender of Queen and country. In George's picture (Figure 3), the Shankill is a place besieged by the dregs of society. Catholics are messy, scattered, ratlike. Protestants are stoic, clean, neatly arranged. Armageddon would appear to be the razed, rubble-strewn no-man's-land between any Protestant part of Belfast and its nearest Catholic center of population. A high red-brick wall should separate all such neighborhoods, the child insists — and does so with a red crayon.

Yet Cave Hill worked a bit of magic on George, too. He explains why, and so doing, reveals a side of his thinking hitherto not put into words, or drawn with crayons: "On the mountain we had some good times. I wish we could live there. I told my mother, and she said we can't leave here; my father doesn't make enough money. He's lucky to have a job. He works in a store, and when he comes home, he's tired of being nice to customers. The owner lives in Waterloo Park, up toward Cave Hill. When my father has a drink he says we're never going to see an end to the Troubles, and a lot will die, and you can be sure it's going to be the poor Protestants and the poor Fenians who'll do the dying. There are some rich

Fenians, and they drink a bottle to every glass our people take, and they don't lose a man in a fight. We do, and the poor Fenians do. We have our rich; they live up on hills, and they have big homes. In Lisburn there are fine homes; my father has seen them. He had to deliver to a relative of the owner. We were glad as the Fenian kids to be up there on the hill, and see the city below. 'God save the Queen,' my friend said; 'God save Belfast,' a Fenian said, and I told him he was right, and I hope he was right, and I hope God does!"

Ulster populism, or at least a thread of it:[3] a boy's struggle to make sense of social and economic inequalities as well as the learned assumptions of religious intolerance. George has not forgotten what apparently it takes a little liquor to make his father remember and repeat: that the issue is not only the Pope and England's Royal Family and pride in Scottish ancestry and pride in Irish ancestry, but the matter of money, with all the consequences that go with its abundance or scarcity. Protestants who live in the Shankill are having a rough time of it. Many are jobless; no luckier, when it comes to facing bill collectors, than the Catholics of the Ardoyne. Indeed, one often hears a sense of failure deviously acknowledged among some in the Shankill and other relatively impoverished neighborhoods. Outbursts of pride in the past, exclamations of a glorious tradition, can cover an abiding doubt about a social predicament — so George's father, and George too, seems to know, at least sometimes.

Perhaps desperation prompts me to mention the effect those daily Cave Hill expeditions had, at least temporarily, on a busful of children. There is no question at all that many of Ulster's children, responding to the grown-ups around them, are full of wrath. After my talks with child after child in home after home, the all-around soreness, the endless name-calling, begins to wear on the listener. Belfast offers continual support to Freud's emphasis on "aggression" as an inevitable psychological element in childhood, to say nothing of the "adult personality." These are children who have been encouraged to say nasty things about others. Moreover, these are children who go well beyond words. All the time one witnesses boys and girls caught up in street violence. They imitate their elders, curse enemies, pretend to shoot them, crow merrily over imagined victories. They light fires, throw detested flags into the flames. They spot a person who is a stranger, who looks a bit different, who may be known as one of "them," and in a flash ranting, heckling, physical assaults take over. They assemble and march, like their elders — combatants eager to display their devotion to a cause. They watch the telly, gloat at successes, get glum over defeats, savor some deaths and mourn others with an intensity that reveals how intimately the Troubles have worked their way into the emotional fabric of the young.

True, children everywhere pretend at cowboys and Indians or war or cops and robbers. But occasional games, connected to imaginary events, or distant historical ones, or those enacted on television or in movies, are not to be confused with games that are meant to copy an immediate life. Nor is that distinction, alas, the only one. In dozens of instances, almost daily during periods of unrest, Belfast children actively assist Protestant and Catholic paramilitary groups, the IRA on the Catholic side, and the UVF (Ulster Volunteer Force) on the Protestant. I have seen children throw rocks not in play but in dead earnest — at British soldiers, at shop windows or house windows, or at individuals. I have seen children carry messages, run interference, try to be objects of distraction, set fires, stand as lookouts, reconnoiter and spy, and send danger or safety signals of various kinds. I have even seen children wield guns, use knives.

Not a list of activities likely to be recommended by specialists in what is called "mental hygiene," and without question a child psychiatrist eager to document psychological disturbances in children will find plenty of evidence in the Ardoyne and the Shankill and elsewhere in Belfast. A Belfast pediatrician who has worked in England and America on research stints tells me this: "It is true, we see plenty of trouble here — especially symptoms of anxiety: fast breathing, squinting eyes, hives, indigestion, a lot of crying and scratching of skin and temper outbursts. We see phobias — if you can call them that: youngsters who worry they won't survive the week, or have to touch every other lamppost, lest some bombs go off! But I'm not sure most of the children here don't manage, on the whole. And what strikes me is not only their seriousness (I suppose you psychiatrist chaps may find that worrisome!) but their consideration for others. These are thoughtful children: they have seen people struggling and dying for something they very much believe in.

"The other day, I saw a girl who lost her brother to the IRA. He was shot dead as an act of revenge, in full view of his entire family. The child was upset, tearful; she'd been repeatedly vomiting, had her parents in a bad state on her account. They thought she had appendicitis; a few years earlier they'd almost lost a son to peritonitis secondary to appendicitis that had been ignored too long. Later they lost him after all — to the guns of the IRA. I examined the girl and I told her she was all right. She quieted down and she was a dear child. She thanked me. She said she wished her brother was alive, but she knew he died 'a good person.' I was struck by that phrase. I asked her what she meant. She said that the lad believed in Jesus Christ, and was a loyal subject of the Queen, and tried to be helpful to their parents, and every day visited both sets of their grandparents, who lived nearby in the Shankill. And then she added, as if I might have some doubts: 'Billy even felt sorry for the Fenians. He said they belong to Jesus too.' I couldn't help it; I had to question her further: I asked her what she thought her brother meant by that statement. She didn't pause for two seconds: 'Billy meant that the Lord creates all of us, and we may fight, but we should pray for those we fight with, and if we don't, we're going to be in a lot of trouble when we meet Him.'

"I call that remarkable — a girl of only nine, and with a lot of cause to be full of vengeance. She loved her brother, and she mourned him. She loved Jesus, though, and remembered his teachings. These can be pensive lads and lasses, even the wee ones of five or six. They ask me tough questions for which I'm not sure Socrates would have easy replies.

"A Catholic boy, only eight, asked me one day why the Prince of Peace didn't come and make peace, just like that — and the child snapped his fingers. I told him I didn't know, but I wished

He would. The boy promptly said that maybe God can't do all He'd like to do! I believe theologians are still sweating over that one! I turned to him, and wondered where he'd heard that — at Sunday school, maybe? Or in the regular church school he attends? No, the lad said he and his brother, a year older, saw a cousin of theirs, older and about to go off and become a nun, get killed by a stray bullet. The two boys decided, right then and there, that God had seen the tragedy (because He sees everything) and must be crying and was helpless. They told a priest what they'd concluded, and he told them to stop being so 'thoughtful.' That's the word he used; the boy told me. On the way out, as I was dispensing some cough syrup and an antihistamine, the boy stunned me: 'Do you think, maybe, there are two Gods, one for the Catholics and one for the Protestants?'

"I told him I didn't think so. (I didn't dare tell him that I am not altogether sure there is even one!) I told him he was 'thoughtful,' and his brother, too. Well, such a modest child, such a gentleman: He thanked me, and said that he wasn't the only one who had such ideas; he'd heard others come up with similar speculations. You'd best be careful when you feel sorry for that boy and his brother, and their friends; or for the others over the line of faith, in the Shankill. Don't go back to the States and have everyone crying for these wee ones! I saw plenty of children there in America who never saw a soldier shoot a gun, a tank rumble down a street, a bomb go off, a loved one injured or killed — and who didn't strike me as the finest souls this earth has seen."

A banality, maybe — that neither hardship nor its opposite necessarily makes for the development of virtue. Even happiness, Freud kept emphasizing in *Civilization and Its Discontents,* is an entirely subjective matter, hence not something an observer can correlate with scores on a socioeconomic scale. The residents of the Ardoyne and the Shankill are not people to complain of their impoverished situation; and in fact, many of the families of both neighborhoods seem ablaze with both fanaticism and, as indicated, an abiding sense of purpose. It is possible, I suppose, to regard such individuals as strangely in luck — able to distract themselves from the objective misery of their situation by the diversions of a religious and military struggle. Apathy and self-pity yield to the excited flush of fighting enemies to the death. A strong sense of history, a fervent religious commitment, an attachment to neighborhood and to nation (be it Britain or the Irish Free State), all combine to make individuality less prominent. Among children, pictures of the self are painted with great reluctance; among adults, egoistic display is rare. These are people who feel solidarity with certain others, and have an enemy to help define who is a friend.

All this distraction from the self is no small psychological asset, as a Catholic mother surely knew when she offered these comments about her children: "They don't have the best life. If we'd emigrated, like my cousin, to the States, to New Jersey, I know we'd have more — a car, a washing machine, better food. But she has a lad of sixteen, and he got arrested for speeding, and they found drugs in the car, and he doesn't want to do anything but own a motorcycle; that's his goal in life. I told my son, and he's the same age, and he said he's glad we're here, and we have the Orangies to stand up to! I asked my children once if they thought we should leave here. All the pain, the Brits and their guns, the Prods and their terrible hate of us, the fighting, every day the fighting — should we kiss it all goodbye? No! said all of them in chorus. No, they said over and over — not for American porridge, and not even for a motorcycle. We're not a spoiled people; and our children aren't spoiled. They may swear a lot at the Orangies, and they may be tough, even with each other; but they're not brats, they're not out for themselves, each for himself. They're for each other, for the Ardoyne, and for a united Ireland!"

The politics of the nursery, the sociology of the playground, the psychology of the family — these are not at all beyond the ken of a six- or ten-year-old, even a four-year-old. But we are rather more grudging and skeptical about other kinds of judgments. A child's moral life is stereotyped, dominated by reflexes, derivative, imitative, various social scientists insist — as if the ego can be endlessly manipulative (the suave, knowing negotiator), and the id cleverly insistent, unashamedly sure of what it wants, and what it will, at all costs, manage to get, whereas the superego is doomed to be a mere dangling object, its motions and purposes blindly responsive to particular parental voices. I do not believe psychiatric theorists have done even conceptual justice to the operations of our consciences; and I believe a place such as Ulster offers the empirical evidence that ought to help us understand better how our children learn what is "right" and what is "wrong," what is believable and what is absurd, even dangerous, and not least, what they will stand by, even fight and die for, and what they will never be willing to embrace, no matter what constraints are imposed upon them.

During the years of my visits to Ulster, for instance, I was constantly told by both Catholic and Protestant children — sometimes as young as four or five years old — that they could always tell their "enemy" among their own generation. How can that be? I wondered and asked. Gradually I began to get answers. I was being educated by boys and girls — lessons in sociology and anthropology and history, lessons as well in moral values, in one or another philosophical point of view. Now I know that Catholics play hurling, with a hurley stick, and Gaelic football, whereas Protestants play hockey and soccer; that "bat" is an *English* word, not used in any *Irish* sport; that in Belfast the *Irish News* is a Catholic newspaper, the *News Letter* is a Protestant one, and the *Telegraph* acceptable, mostly, to both sides; that clothes tell the man, so to speak — plaids or tartans of green and brown for Catholics, red, white, and blue for Protestants; that names bespeak creeds — Seamus as against James, Sean as against John, Cathal, pronounced "Cahal," as against Charles; that pins on a lapel are a giveaway — Gaelic clubs, religious medals, as against (for the Protestants, of course) the crown in miniature, or the red hand of Ulster, harking back to a historic migration from Scotland.

It was a nine-year-old girl in Derry who first let me know, defiantly, that citizens of Northern Ireland can hold either Irish or British passports; that Catholics choose, most of the time, Irish passports; and that no one in Ulster need serve in the British Army, in accordance with an agreement made in 1920 at the time of Partition. It was a seven-year-old boy in Belfast, Protestant, who quickly let me know that Catholics are excluded from entire factories; that the two religious groups have quite separate and distinct musical traditions, different folksongs as well as different military ones; that the schools are thoroughly segregated, and that he could tell in an instant whether a home is Catholic or Protestant. On what street is the building located, and inside, is there a "bleeding heart" or are there "crucifixes and statues," or is there a picture of the Queen?

In Derry (as Catholics call it; Protestants prefer the full name, Londonderry), I was given a tough, vivid lecture by a seven-year-old Catholic girl, Nora: "Never say Londonderry here in the Bogside. You'll be killed! Everyone will think you're an Orangie. Maybe if you're lucky they'll hear you say a few words, and they'll know you're an American; but if they don't spot your accent, you'll be wiped out!" A pause. Her naive, proudly open-minded and even-handed listener wants to know why the vehemence, if not murderous venom. She lets loose a blast of historical references: "You see that wall over there? It was built in 1618. The English came here, businessmen from London. They named the city after their capital. They used to stand on that wall and call us 'croppies,' and throw pennies at us. They called us pigs. They said we belonged in huts, and we should do their dirty work, and be honored we had the chance. The bog — they said that's where we belong! Well, let them chase us out of the bog now. This is Free Ireland!"

A child mixes history, specific nationalist confrontations, geographic significations, into a passionately espoused moral statement. Are we to dismiss such remarks as mere rhetoric, memorized at the knees of parents, or learned by rote in an elementary school classroom? Are we to insist that these are declarations of a child cowering in fear at the hands of adult authority, and so ready to say anything and everything, so long as what is spoken meets with the approval of emotionally significant grown-ups? Maybe all that is true; but true for us, even when we become eighty or ninety. The unconscious is timeless, including that part of it we call our "conscience." Voices of approval and disapproval are lifelong companions.

Many of us psychoanalytically trained psychiatrists emphasize in our discussions of children the relentlessly punitive, demanding side of the superego, and some cognitive psychologists hand out questionnaires or make experiments in offices or laboratories, and then talk of a "preconventional" or "conventional" stage in children, wherein they do what serves their ("hedonistic") purposes, or what will obviate punishment, or gain the sanctioning nod of a mother, a father. Those same theorists, however, deny that children undergo the subtler, more compassionate, more ethically reflective "stages" of moral development — indeed, they deny such personal, ethical, psychological, and intellectual progress to many adults as well. Only a handful, we have been told, an ethical elite (Herbert Marcuse's "advancing edge of history," for instance) can free itself of the individual (emotional) and the socially or culturally enforced constraints that blind a truly "mature" ethical awareness. Knowing the vicious persecutory "morality" that has come out of various sectors of the twentieth century's "advancing edge," one wonders what children in Belfast or Derry really have to look forward to possessing, morally, when they become older and, if lucky, more privileged, socially and educationally. In any event, as we wait for that millennium to arrive, boys and girls the world over may not be fashioning psychological concepts, but they are, it seems, struggling hard and long to construct a moral life for themselves.

Here is a Derry mother, a Bogside mother, describing her nine-year-old daughter's confusing behavior: "Cathy teases the Brits. They come on their patrols, and she asks them what they're afraid of. She says: 'We have no guns, and you have so many!' They glare at her. She smiles back! She tries to talk with them; she starts talking about her father, and how he was fired by a Protestant, because he wanted no Catholics in his place, even to do the dirty work. She shouts that 'Catholics are poor, and Protestants rich,' and she asks them is that fair? She got one soldier to argue with her, and he told her, after a while, that she belonged in the House of Commons! No, she said, she'll go to Dublin if she has to leave, but she wants to stay with us!

"I don't know where children get the ideas they do! Sometimes I look at Cathy, and I remind myself she's only a little bigger than a wee baby. But she stands there and tells the Brits that they can point guns at us, and pull the triggers, even, but that won't win for them, because we're right and they're wrong — the Prods, and the Brits. The other day she got another Brit to talk with her. He was a Paki [Pakistani]. Cathy asked him why he was over here, fighting for the old lady Queen, and for Paisley and his gang. Then she reminded him that if he got killed, what about his family, they'd miss him. I told her to hush up. She kept going, though — and he came over and told her she had a sassy mouth. He pulled out some candy, and told her to take it, and maybe it would sweeten her. She did; she chewed on the caramel, and she said thank you, and she gave him a big smile, like she does to her father when she wants to cuddle up to him.

"Next thing I knew, she was telling him she wasn't against him, no matter that his skin was dark, and she wished he lived through his tour here, and got back home safe. He thanked her, and the following day they had a longer talk, and they became friends. He told me I had a nice girl, and I said that I know I do! When Cathy said her prayers, she asked God to spare her Paki friend. Then she decided, one day, that it isn't the individual Brits here who are the enemy — it's the rich Prods, and it's England and the way the English government treated our people. She's always having these long talks with God! And with the priest! Father would say Cathy is truly a Christian. He says in his sermons that our children are close to Jesus, just like He said they were when He came down to us."

One afternoon Cathy came home with a less religious or philosophical line of thinking. Her British-soldier friend had drawn upon his personal life in an intriguing way. Cathy gave her mother the gist of the observation, and the latter, in turn, offered it to me the next day: "The Paki told Cathy he had the answer to our problems in Derry. He said that if a few hundred of his people were brought here, then all the Catholics and Protestants would unite — and hate the Paki people! Cathy said no. I did, too. But at night, cleaning up and talking with my husband, I changed my mind. I think we'd have a lot of unhappy people in Derry, if there was a district filled with colored families. I admitted as much to Cathy, and she asked, 'Mummy, do you mean that the only way we can be nice to each other is to have people around we can point at and not be nice to?' I told Father, and he said Jesus was crucified because no matter who the person was, no matter how unpopular, our Lord stood up for him.

"I asked Father about the Prods. Would Jesus stand up for them today? They've been bad to us, and they still are; we're 'pigs' to them, and they say so, and we are poor, and they own everything. Father said, 'True,' the way he always does, but he said, 'Hate feeds on hate,' and someone has to break the circle, and Christ did that, and if we could only be Christians, we would, too. Of course, I do believe Father wants us to keep fighting for our rights; I know he doesn't want us to surrender. He wants us to stand up for ourselves as Christians, and not stoop to the level of those who've been so bad to us. But that is hard to do, very hard! We're only human; we're not gods!"

No great wisdom there. The everyday speech of common people, uneducated and thoroughly impoverished. Trite remarks, perhaps meant to serve the purposes of self-justification. As for the Pakistani, a British subject serving Her Royal Highness, he has no college education, either. His family took advantage of their Commonwealth status, migrated to London after World War II — another partition the English engineered as they extricated themselves, yet again, from part of the Empire's swollen territory. Did Freud, in *Civilization and Its Discontents,* say any more than that Pakistani soldier? "It is always possible to bind together a considerable number of people left over to receive the manifestations of their aggressiveness." As for "moral maturity," one wonders how many of us who are full-grown, college-educated, and versed, even, in the intricacies of ethics, philosophy, political or economic history, would do much better than "wee Cathy" in her real-life situation.

I remember another girl of the same age. American and black, struggling against mobs in New Orleans during the integration struggle that dominated that city's life in the early 1960s. (She figures also in this book's companion, *The Moral Life of Children.*) This child, only six, of humble and illiterate background, prayed

at night for her white tormenters. I was sure she had "other feelings" — located (where else?) "underneath." My wife asked me
one afternoon whether many of those who knew the workings of
history's dialectic, or were versed rigorously in one or another
philosophical "system," would ever have survived the mob ha-
rassment, let alone implored the Lord on behalf of the bewildered
and the pitiable (white) men and women who assembled every day
to threaten those who defied their sense of what ought to be.
"Maybe," she pointed out, "more sophisticated people might have
found 'good reasons' to pull out, save their necks." Poor Ruby, all
she knew was standing firm during the day, and praying to God
at night! "And," my wife asked, "why keep pointing out the obvious, that Ruby is 'really' scared? Don't you think she knows that
you want her to 'talk about it'? Maybe her only chance is to keep
quiet — hold on to herself. Why should people say what is on
their minds all the time?"

Condescension is a constant danger to people bent on finding
things out, wrapping the world up in wordy formulations, explanations. A clever mind, stuffed with facts and buttressed by theoretical underpinnings, can miss the very essence of a people's
situation, their sense, quite well known by children, of what must
at all costs be done. For Cathy, a child of Derry's Bogside, distrust
and animosity were qualified by a capacity to stop and reflect —
even cast doubt on her own passions.

One cannot, unfortunately, attribute Cathy's perceptiveness to
her schooling. She herself chafes at the narrowness of the nuns
she knows: "They'll not let us say what we think!" As for Ulster's
Protestant children, they read references in textbooks (for example, *Britain 1714–1851*, by Denis Richards and Anthony Quick) to
"unambitious Irishmen."[4] True, the young people also learn that
the rents people paid "went in all too many cases to England to
keep absentee landlords in luxury." But moral judgments are being
made in these texts, if one follows their associational thrust: "Those
who could not pay their rent were evicted, and Ireland was no-
torious for thousands of wandering beggars who had given up hope
of regular work and spent many of their nights in the open. This
was the general countryside scene over much of Ireland. In Ulster,

however, there was some prosperity. Here the population was
Protestant, with many of Scottish descent."

What in God's name will be the end of it all? The phrasing is
Irish, and whether Catholic or Protestant, the Ulster men and
women and their children ask the question. A million Protestant
people who consider their religion and their connection to Great
Britain an extremely important part of themselves do not want the
island to be one country, with Dublin its capital. Half a million
Catholics loyal to another religion, and with quite a different attitude toward Great Britain, want precisely that — the "last" six
counties returned to the Irish Free State. The library shelves
contain millions of published words — the sum of which tells how
those ancient animosities persist with undiminished intensity. If
ever Freud's phrase "narcissism of small differences" applies, it is
in Ulster, where people have learned to look hard in order to find
a distinguishing blemish in their neighbor — his or her name or
way of speaking or, of course, manner of worshipping Jesus Christ,
supposedly the Lord of both Ian Paisley and his paramilitary supporters and of members of the IRA.

The issue in Ulster is not only religion; the issue is class — the
poor fighting the poor, and neither getting much for all the anguish
endured. In the more comfortable parts of Belfast, near Queen's
University, or in the suburban towns, such as Lisburn, one finds
Catholics and Protestants able to live quietly — maybe not with
great affection, but without the kind of brutish everyday violence
one sees in the poorer sections. In some of the rural parts of Ulster,
even now, for all the religious polarization of the past decade, farm
families or small-town families of both creeds manage to get together. The explosions of religious hate have been fueled by a
deteriorating economy and a sharpened sense of inequality, not
only between the two main religious groups, but within them as
well.

"It is a consolation, the meanness our children learn," a Catholic
great-grandmother of eighty bitterly, proudly told my stunned
children. She has lost one son and two grandsons to the thrill of
dynamite and bullets. She knows their futility — and yet; one has
to add that qualifying phrase. In his memorable documentary film

on Ulster's Troubles (*A Sense of Loss*), done almost ten years ago, Marcel Ophuls gives us Conor Cruise O'Brien's explanation, hardly prompted by affection, of the strange hold the IRA has on people in Ulster, in the Republic of Ireland, in America. When everything seems hopelessly muddled, endlessly complicated, thoroughly bogged in the futility of a political stalemate, the smell of gunpowder offers a lure, even to those who customarily shun the call of rebellion by force.

Nor is it fair to denounce the IRA single-mindedly. The violence of a social and economic order is often not dramatically visible, but is no less insistent in its day-to-day presence — as all who challenge, in desperation, a political authority come to realize: our own colonial forebears in the eighteenth century; the labor organizers of the nineteenth century and early in the twentieth; the civil rights activists of more recent times. Demagogues are everywhere, waiting their chance, like bacilli: the mischievous, porcine, hysterically foul-mouthed brawler Paisley and his ilk on the one hand; on the other, many thugs in the ranks of the IRA — individuals who blackmail and terrorize their own people, as well as others, and who mouth twisted ideological fantasies as unreal and self-serving and mean-spirited as any dished out years earlier in the name of Stormont, the Royal Throne, and Free Presbyterianism.

Sometimes, in an off moment, one hears, even from street fighters ready to die for a cause, a few words that connect their exceptional circumstances to those of our own. The elderly lady mentioned a few paragraphs back was heard to ask her son, a member of the IRA: "What would we all do without you people?" Then she explained her line of reasoning: "It would be an even sadder life. We'd sit and stare out the window, and wait for the excitement of a bad storm!" One remembers that comment as one watches Mr. Paisley scream at, hector, implore, and admonish his Sunday flock — offer them the bewitching, enormously satisfying illusion that they are combatants in an apocalyptic confrontation worthy of the last book of the New Testament, the Revelation of St. John the Divine. "I go to hear him [Paisley] and I come back and feel I can go on another week. He makes us feel there's something to live for — and there's an important fight going on, and it's ours, and we'd better take care to be the winners!" The words of a carpenter, proud of his old brick Victorian home, spotless and a touch austere — all he wants, all he ever wanted, and threatened, he is sure, by a swirling, grasping, uncontained, and vengeful horde: the eternal "them," the disowned "I" each of us tries to be rid of, though some have lives that equip them to do so more gracefully and privately.

Something to live for; one doesn't forget those words in Ulster. As often happens where there is a worrying social climate, gifted individuals respond to it — reflect in their poems and stories, show on their canvasses the same sense of irony and ambiguity, the same quizzical apprehension as an old Catholic lady, or a Protestant artisan, keeps on transmitting. Ulster, in this century, has given us C. S. Lewis and Louis MacNeice, and Forrest Reid and Joyce Cary and Brian Moore and Benedict Kiely and Michael McLaverty and that great bard of our time, Seamus Heaney.[5] Ulster has given us a notable artistic tradition: William Conner's shawled mill girls, the street pageantry, the slightly rebellious children; James Craig's evocation of a pastoral life, sweeter than the one portrayed by the great nineteenth-century Irish novelist William Carleton, but not without a reminder or two that calm country surfaces can all of a sudden become menacingly troubled; and Frank McKelvey, and Colin Middleton, and in recent years the artists who have used aerosol as well as ink or paint — the graffiti, the handbills, the cartoons that make up a war's propaganda, as well as the satire or melancholy response of watercolorists (George Campbell), painters (Joe McWilliams, Brendan Ellis), and sculptors (F. E. McWilliams).

In the poem "Belfast," published a half-century ago (September 1931), Louis MacNeice[6] sang of "The hard cold fire in his basalt." In his mind's eye the poet seemed to be glimpsing the Lagan River from the vantage point of Cave Hill: "Down there at the end of the melancholy lough / Against the lurid sky over the stained water." He knew that he had to make reference to Catholic life, the moments of superstitious desperation: "In the porch of the chapel before the garish Virgin"; and to Protestant life, its moments of extravagant, bullying pride: "The sun goes down with a banging of Orange drums." But in Belfast, among the anonymous people of those flats, inside rows and rows of red-brick homes, separated by thin, cluttered concrete alleys, is a far less eloquent but not unknowing vision, worthy of the one MacNeice tried to offer in "Day of Returning": "They call me crafty, I robbed my brother, / Hoaxed my father, I am most practical, / Yet in my time have had my visions, / Have seen a ladder that reached the sky." A Belfast girl, not yet ten, stunned her Protestant teacher, and parents, by drawing a boat (an ark, of course), putting "everyone" on it, then announcing that "all Catholics and all Protestants are sinners"; she added that "we'd better well board this boat and pray that we are taken to Him, because God's love is our only hope."

Meanwhile new political episodes in this endless and savage struggle suddenly appear — and the children are always watching. In 1981, the lives of many of Belfast's children were touched significantly by the hunger strike at Maze Prison.[7] I heard Belfast's eight-and-ten-year-old Catholic children asking mothers and fathers if they might begin a sympathetic fast. One candy-store owner (in England and Ireland, places like his are very special institutions where families gather to talk and exchange news as well as to eat) told me about it: "The poor little ones come here more often than usual. They always love sweets, of course; but now a lot of them are hungry, rather than here to have extra dessert. They've tried to show their mums, at mealtime, how loyal they are to the men in prison. I've had a few mums come in and tell me to feed them extra, even if their children lack the money, and they'll pay later. I asked one boy — he's ten or eleven — what good it will do, for him to eat less. He gave me a cross look. Then he eyed me as if I might be the enemy! I've never seen the people here so hurt. The reporters measure by crowds and noise and violence. The police do, too. They're all wrong. It's the quiet that I find strange. There is a hush over the families, a serious look I'll even see in a lot of our wee ones — as though we're all feeling a terrible sadness inside our stomachs, while the men die in that prison: one, then the next, and then the next, skin and bones. I've never seen anything like it here, and I'm over two-thirds of the way to my first century of life!"

Among the younger children in the Ardoyne, the Catholic neighborhood of Belfast I know best, questions about the hunger strikes abounded. Boys wanted to know the biological and medical facts: what happens, as willful abstinence yields to malnutrition, then the awful wasting away, the deterioration of first one bodily function, then another. Boys also mentioned, again and again, how much determination is required to complete a fast to the end. During those months ten-year-old Jimmy Foley had been more serious than his parents or relatives have ever seen him: "If you're in a battle, you hold your gun tight, and keep firing. You have to be brave. But if you are lying on your bed, and you are hungry, and they bring you food, and you say no to them, then you must be tougher, even, than the soldiers in a bloody, bloody war. I'd want to steal me a bite; I'm afraid that would happen. Then I'd be ashamed. I might cry. In the movies you see soldiers cry. But I'll bet not one of our men has cried, even if his stomach hurts, and he knows he's going to starve unless he takes the food."

The girls seemed more horrified — almost as if the laws of nature were being challenged. They were asking the old existentialist questions, which children have always asked during moments of danger or confusion. Jimmy's cousin Maureen was born exactly two weeks before he was. She didn't quite keen over the ten dead, whom she often referred to as "lost to us." But she spoke with decided earnestness, and she kept brushing her hair away from her forehead. Her mother said: "The girl is truly upset. She's taken to pushing her hair away from her eyes, but I'm afraid she still can't make much sense of all this suffering."

In fact, Maureen's eyes were by no means clouded. She looked intently at the telly as it brought news of the latest death by starvation. She looked at the freckles on her arms. Suddenly she said: "I remember my old aunt [great aunt] telling me that I have the freckles of her father, and he was the most kind, the most very kind man in all Belfast. If he saw someone in trouble, he'd go and help; but he died crossing the street to reach a woman. She'd fallen down. But a car struck him, and he never made it alive to the hospital. My aunt said the last thing she looked at, before they closed the coffin, was his freckles.

"If I was in the prison taking no food, I'd keep looking at my freckles, and I'd think of my aunt and her father! My mother wonders, 'Where do those men get their strength?' My father says, 'They've got purpose in them — more purpose than the Brits thought.' My mother says, 'More purpose than *we* thought!' I ask all the grown-up people we know where you get that purpose from. They shake their heads. Even the priest shakes his head. He says we must pray hard for the men. My best friend and I, we both asked him if God will take all our men right to His heart. When I eat now, I think of our men starving themselves, and then I ask God to take them to His heart. We have a picture of His heart here, in our front room [titled "The Bleeding Heart of Jesus"], and I look at it more than I used to. When will God decide to stop all the Troubles, and make *everyone* good, not just some people? That's my question!"

Some of her friends wondered aloud, as she has upon occasion, whether they might try a "bit of starvation" themselves. They did not mean to sound self-centered or vain or frivolously personal; they surely didn't mean to mock the dying prisoners. They were doing what we all do, connecting the personal and the everyday with life's "bigger" issues, so-called — social and political matters: "It's good to lose weight, but it's hard," one of those friends observed. Then she continued: "My mother always is slimming, but she doesn't lose much. When she does, she is happy; but she's back up again a few weeks later! Now she talks with her friends, and they all say we could do with a little of the discipline our men in prison have! I've tried skipping a meal. I wouldn't mind slimming down myself. But I get so hungry, I eat two meals in one when I go to the table and start eating again. I pray for the will, but so far I don't have it.

"I think of the prisoners all the time. One day I'll hope to have their purpose. Some *girls*, some *women* should show they can help. I asked my mother what would happen if all of us stopped eating, just like our men in the Maze. She said, 'Wouldn't *that* shake the whole world!' My father says he's not sure *what* would make the Brits budge. But if everyone took no food, and got weak, I think we'd show we're the equal of all the guns the Brits have."

Such speculations were not confined to the Catholic population. In the Shankill, a working-class Protestant neighborhood, the anger and contempt directed at the IRA in general (and at the dying, and dead prisoners) was unsurprising. Yet in many homes one could feel other emotions: apprehension, surprise, consternation, the creeps, the jitters. And the questions from children and parents alike suggested to me that, ironically, the struggle had inspired a similar response in many, on both sides: a unifying, if episodic shudder. In the Ardoyne, in the Shankill, the question was the same: "How can people do that?"

Every day one heard Protestant parents asking that question — often with disdain, but with genuine curiosity as well. Protestant children followed their parents in paying close attention to the news from Maze Prison, in going through the motions of denunciation, but in showing alarm, skepticism, incredulity. Young Peter Allen was tall for a twelve-year-old (a boastful five feet three inches) and an avid follower of the BBC reports of Ulster's summer crisis. He was ready to fight, when grown up, for continuing allegiance to the Crown. He insisted the matter was one of life and death. But variations on that last phrase were used by him in a quite specific way: "Those men choose to die. They'd rather die than live, and that's proof they're not very smart people. They're being used. They're like sheep, being led by dogs. I can't imagine going with no breakfast, and then no lunch, and no supper, either! If I miss one meal, I'm in a bad state. I want my food! It makes you wonder — ten of them!

"At first we thought they were putting on an act; but they're serious. It's death for them! Well, we're rid of them. But new men step in. We'll have more and more trouble if we don't stop them. How, though? My father says they're not behaving like human beings."

On both sides, initial disbelief soon gave way to thinly disguised fascination: "How long will it last?" Another question: "How many men will hold fast?" *Hold fast:* an expression that lends itself to both a literal and a symbolic approximation of what Ulster's people continue to ask, because it was a *will* that struck admiration or fear in men, women, and children — a voluntary assertion of self-control that seemed to defy comprehension and made ten or so men appear above (or below) their fellow creatures. No wonder so many Catholic children looked at those familiar (and heretofore generally ignored) pictures of the Last Supper in their homes with special regard — no wonder so many Protestant children responded to the Reverend Ian Paisley's talk of the Devil, of Satan, with special enthusiasm; it was a common inclination to seek Biblical imagery, a common feeling that normal human limits had been transcended. A Catholic teacher, no friend of the IRA, found himself perplexed and amazed, pointing out that "even Gandhi never went the whole route, and now we're to have a dozen, maybe two dozen, doing so."

A painfully haunting quality to this prison drama strongly affected the region's political life, and, very important, its social and psychological climate. One kept expecting the hunger strike to falter and end. The families of four men had second thoughts, but others seemed implacably set to die, or to watch their sons, their husbands, their brothers die. No matter what the past legal (or criminal) record of the suicides, no matter what the methods or designs of the IRA as an organization, a dramatically unsettling, even eerie selflessness was at work. These men were proving their point: they were indeed different from others confined to Maze Prison — willing and able to demonstrate a perseverance that tests and stimulates everyone's thinking. And their potential suicides had given children and adults alike cause to stop and think — had given yet another boost of moral meaning to lives often sad and burdensome. Then, suddenly, the fasting ended. One man, then another, chose life — no matter how unyielding the British continued to be. Again and again I heard children ask this question: "Can you blame them?" No one did — not even the IRA people in the Ardoyne.

Sometimes those children did blame themselves, however. It was a dramatic example of the manner in which the energy that religious faith supplies to a child's conscience can prompt that conscience, though preoccupied with nationalist enthusiasms and mandates, to turn against its possessor with lacerating vengeance. Take the response of Kerry, a Catholic lass aged thirteen, to the decision of those in the Maze to end their hunger strike. *They* had the "right" so to decide, she kept telling her friends, but she wasn't at all willing to be so understanding toward herself: "Maybe if we'd prayed harder! I asked one of the nuns if our prayers might have given the men more strength — if we'd said them more often than we did. She said she didn't know; she said it's all in God's hands. My friend Mary said it's in our hands, too, because we're supposed to pray a lot, and then He hears you, Jesus, and His mother. The nun heard Mary and she told her to pray, but not to be fresh, and she looked real cross at her and said if she talks back and disagrees with a sister, God will hear *that*, all right!

"My brother Tim thinks the only thing we can do is get guns and fight; but he is the littlest one of seven, and he doesn't know that it's the Brits who have their jet planes and atomic bombs. My father says they could wipe out all of Belfast! That means us! I pray every night to dear Jesus; I tell him what's happening, and I say we don't have the planes and the big bombs, but we're on His side, and we just hope He's hearing the right story. Our sister teaching us religion said we must never forget that the Prods are going to school, and they're praying to Jesus, just as we are, and so it's up to us if Jesus is going to help us out, and if we fail Him, and say a quick prayer, and go on to chewing gum and watching the telly, then He'll not be with us; He'll turn to the others — and then we'll be in a bad mood, and it'll serve us right! So, I keep saying my prayers, and my Hail Marys, and I think He *is* hearing, because I can feel Him in my head, I really can. I don't know how to say it, but He's there. I can't see Him, and I can't hear Him, but He's with you, He's with me, and I feel Him, I sense Him near me.

"I think He must have decided to keep our men in the Maze alive because they might have some more work to do one of these days. Why else would He let them start taking the Brits' food? Mary says she'd *never* take their food; she says she'd die rather than eat what they served. But that's 'talk on the cheap,' my mother says. My mother wished we'd find a way to leave Belfast. She has a sister in the States, in Rhode Island, the smallest one of all of them, and they call us two or three times a year, and when all this prison trouble started a few months ago, they called, and they said we should just get away, as fast as we can, because it's getting worse and worse and worse. But it's not — it's the same. If the men had died, all of them, then maybe the Brits would close the prison, my mother says, but there won't be a change until the Brits pull out, and they won't let our starving prisoners push them out.

"But if God wanted, He could change the Brits. He could make them do what *He* wants. That's why it's too bad our men didn't hold out longer. No one can blame them, but you can picture yourself there, and wish it had been you. I wish it had been me! I heard our IRA people saying that: If only it had been me! But someone said 'you never know,' and my mother got upset, and she scolded them, and said 'you *bet* you never know,' and we shouldn't be talking as if we *do* know! I never told her that I didn't eat my lunch. I gave it away to others. I pretended I was sick at supper. Everyone said I was losing weight. But I said no, I wasn't. I said they had the men in the Maze, and their hunger strike, on the brain! But I thought if I could lose weight, then the men in prison would get some strength from me. I thought God would know I was going down on the scale, and He'd tell them, and they'd say that if the girl over there in the Ardoyne can do it, then so can they, and they'd keep up their courage, and never, ever give in. That's what Mary hoped, too."

Mary was at the time her closest friend — the same age, a neighbor, too: "three doors down" on a street of row houses. I had best present some of Mary's statements on the same subject, condensed (as Kerry's are) from a summer's many conversations: "I told Kerry we should try to get God to pay attention to our prisoners; we should pray as soon as we get up, and pray during the day, and pray the last thing — before we go to sleep. My father says you don't have to pray, because He knows what's happening, God does; but He can't keep watching everything going on, even if He is the Almighty. Besides, there's talk of a women's IRA, and I'd like to be a member! Besides, I can't just eat and eat, and think of my cousin [one of the prisoners] sitting in that Maze, and turning his face, every time a dirty, dirty Brit comes with a tray of their dirty, dirty food. Besides, if I was in that place, and saw myself getting weaker and weaker, and losing my muscles, I'd sure like to know that there was at least one person there, in Belfast, who was with me all the way, until death takes both of us — that's how I'd feel.

"I get sick when I see people stuffing food into their big mouths these days. My mother is fat; she's so fat that she could stop eating for a year, and she'd still be fat. I know, I know — it's not true! But when I see her frying all the potatoes, and I know there will be leftovers, and she'll eat them all, and then blame us because we won't 'save her' by eating everything she cooks, even though she *knows* she's cooked too much; and when I see her eyes glued to our plates, just waiting for us to get up and put half of what she's dished out to us on the counter; and when I think of my cousin, and of his friends in that Maze — then I want to take all the food we have in our kitchen (the food my mother *hasn't* cooked) and throw it to the dogs, or throw it in the faces of those Brits when they're on patrol here. Let them shoot us for messing them up with our fried potatoes and our buttered bread.

"When they gave in, our men in the Maze, I felt my stomach burn. I wish I could shoot a gun! I wish I knew how to aim, so that when I pulled the trigger, the bullet would go right where I want it to go! I went outside when I heard the news on the radio, and I walked and I walked — until I realized I was getting near the Prods, and I thought to myself: If I had a gun, I could open fire, and I'd take five or ten of them before they got me!

"Yes, yes, I'm just unloading the garbage in my head. Kerry said I have a bad case of the nerves, and I should go to the infirmary and rest! I'd like to go to Maze Prison and rest! I'd like to go there and sit and stare at the Brits and dare them to try to make me eat. If they put needles in me, and tried to feed me that way, through my veins, I'd pull the needles out. I'd cut the vein with a knife. If I had no knife? I'd use my fingernails! I'd push them into my skin. It sounds as if I'm upset, I know; and Kerry has told me I'm headed for a real bout in bed. But I've decided I don't want to grow up and be like my mother; she smiles at the Brits, and they like her, and they've even given her some of the food they took from the IRA people. I know it was their doing; it was left at our door, and I told my mother she's not fooling me. She says it was owed her by her sister; but my aunt said my mother uses her 'as an excuse.' My aunt won't go further, but I know. My mother was always telling us when we were kids to forget all the politics of Belfast — but we never obeyed her. Our father was our hero; he said the truth all the time! He fought the Brits all the time. Then he got run down by a bus. It was driven by one of Paisley's people. He said it was an accident. He was a liar! They all lie, all the Prods. Now, my mother has been without him for three years, and she's forgotten him, I know. All she has her mind on is money and food and getting a nice dress. I think she'd take up with one of the Brits, if she could. She knows the IRA would kill her — right away they would. So, she flirts, and only we see her flirting. Some days, I'm ready to turn her in myself. But I worry what would happen to my small brother."

These are terribly sad and unnerving excerpts, and I present them at length because they enable us to see in the expressed worries or sympathies, the angers and boiling rages of these children, so political in content, an astonishing self-arraignment, an intensity of self-laceration, that makes the word "masochism" seem frail. I have not heard one boy talk in quite this way, so conscious of food — even though it was men who were on a hunger strike in 1981. I do not claim to have seen a wave of anorexia among the preadolescent and early adolescent girls I knew in Belfast, but I did watch a substantial number of them become enormously preoccupied with their eating habits in response to the Maze Prison episode.

The pediatrician I have mentioned reported similar experiences to me — "a bit of hysteria, mini-hysteria," he described it. Because I knew Kerry and Mary rather well, I pursued with them intensively their ideas and plans — so that I was getting to be as informed about their mental life, I would estimate, as I'd ever been with the children I've treated at Boston hospitals and clinics. *Not* that these girls were hospital patients — or striking others as in

need of "treatment." They were members of a community thoroughly aroused and agitated by one phase of a long struggle with
others of Northern Ireland, not to mention an occupying army of
young men, constantly marching up and down the street with guns,
or driving by. Perhaps the entire community might be described
as subject to hysteria, or pathologically obsessed by religious and
nationalist ideas, values, expectations, anxieties. For one talking
with a Mary, however, or a Kerry, the issue comes to this — stated
by the Belfast doctor I've been mentioning: "I don't know what to
say, but that every community has its standards of 'normal' and
'abnormal,' and so does this one; and the IRA might well be regarded by you or me as a collection of psychopathic individuals,
or madmen, but that is not how they are seen here, even by many
who disapprove of their methods, so it's hard to know what to
think and how to characterize these young ones, when you hear
what's on the top of their minds!"

On the bottom of those minds, too — I replied immediately to
my colleague, and then played some grim excerpts on tape and
followed that listening session with some striking drawings and
paintings by children. Mary's drawings were especially dramatic,
fiercely determined. Had I not known her for five years I would
have immediately declared them to be worrisome, indeed. In one
(Figure 4) she is a modern Joan of Arc, waving a rifle as she
singlehandedly assaults a building that houses a British Army bar-
racks. Her goal, she announces when she is almost through with
the drawing, is the flag she had put on top of the building. She
has worked long and hard on the building, and particularly, the
flagpole, the flag. I am, frankly, curious, even a bit amused, as I
notice this patience, this care extended Her Majesty's outpost.
Finally, I try to broach the subject — the irony, I guess: "Mary,
I've seen you draw flags before, but this one has really challenged
you."

She looks at what she has done, then gives me a quick, knowing
glance — as if to let me know that she's quite able to pick up my
cleverly evasive and provocative comment and needs a few seconds
to come right back, as she surely does: "Well, those flags I drew
were for your collection of flags. This is the Brit flag on the Brit

headquarters, and I'm trying to get to the cursed building so I can tear the dirty thing into tiny pieces. God save the Queen when I get my hands on her bloody red, white, and blue dishrag — there'll be nothing left of it before you can say 'Orangie.' And if any Brit tries to stop us, we'll fire away. They all belong back in their London."

It is hard to see where the red of her Royal Highness's flag ends, and the blood of her subjects, the British soldiers, begins; or for that matter, the blood of Mary and her far less distinct followers also begins. She is, quite evidently, leading a bold insurrectionary assault upon firmly entrenched police power, a visible bastion of an alien political power. So doing, she is willing to die; and she is far from reluctant to take others with her to the grave. The scene is not only full of violence and death, it lacks even the slightest pinch of pictorial hope: no sun, no blue sky — no sky at all — and no grass or trees or flowers or watching animals. The girl who drew this has a charming lilt to her voice, and is still a child rather than a young woman in her body; she hasn't relinquished her collection of small dolls and a miniature house near which she keeps them, and books about horses, Irish workhorses and racing horses and ponies. This lass loves making cookies, and eating cookies, and digging up new recipes for cookies. For years she has told me she would like to be a nurse, would like to nurse sick children, not to mention the five children she wants, one for each finger of her right hand, she jokingly announces, three girls and two boys, whom she'll "love all the same," with no preference as to sex or order of birth, and feed with "the best of food," if she has to "beg for it" from the nearby grocer. This girl loves to say her prayers, and has wondered what Mary, "mother of God," felt "when she saw her only begotten son, our Lord, nailed to the Cross." She knew that Mary "must have cried and cried, and wished people would stop being so mean," and she has impressed her nun teachers by her "sweetness" (they describe it). But *she* is the one, here, who has a "stomach for murder."

When I heard her say that, I asked her, please, to repeat what she'd said. I claimed I'd not heard her. She knew better. She didn't raise her voice (a sign of belief), but rather, lowered it a notch, I thought: "They have a stomach for murder. They don't want to sit around in the pubs any more, wishing the Brits would get out someday. They don't want to go hiding from the Brit tanks, and from the Brit friends, the Prods. They don't want to sit and talk and get soaked with beer, and give in to them. They want to fight, and they want to win — and it means shoot to kill. There's no other way. The only chance we have is to go on the attack. The Brits suck up to American guns, and too many of us in Belfast, the Irish people — we suck up to the guns of the Brits. Let the Prods do that! I'll march on them, and if they kill me, that's the price you pay if you're a soldier. I know three of our best boys who got shot and killed fighting them, and I hope I get a chance to show them what *we* can do. My mother can't have it her way, because we're going to be different, and the Brits will be scared. They'll leave. We'll show that Mrs. Thatcher!"

There was a faint smile on the child's face — for which I felt grateful, considerably relieved. I'd begun to worry as I saw the anger build up on the drawing, and in her comments. Mary seemed about to go through a psychological transformation: from childhood to adulthood in one fell swoop — to become a military leader eager to kill, willing if not eager, one gathered, to lose her own life. Her smile acknowledged that she was not yet the formidable prime minister's equal, but it reminded me (who needed the reminder) that a substantial "reality" colored these extravagantly stormy, riotous, and rather gory drawings she had been doing, reaching a climax in this one. I think I turned less pale. She relaxed, as she made her first concession to humor in an hour or so with the charming announcement: "Well, it's intermission time." She put down her red crayon; set all the crayons aside, picked up the drawing and put it, also, very much aside (on top of a bureau) and then asked me what I thought of Mrs. Thatcher.

As I fidgeted, she easily read my mind, saved me from making one of my all-too-predictable rejoinders, told me what I wanted to hear — *her* candid appraisal of an enemy who was also, in a way, a bit of an inspiration: "She doesn't care about anyone but the Queen and the Royal Family. People *like* that, at least the top dogs in England do. She wasn't a top dog when she was my age;

she was just anyone you'd see on the street, but she was star-struck, our teacher said: She wanted to mix with the rich, and you do that by becoming rich yourself, or you win the election, and then you rule everyone, even the rich people. She's a smart one. She's perky. She knows who butters her bread, but she won't get down on her knees for you and me, just for the Queen. I'd like to have a pistol nearby, if I was bargaining with her! But she'll fool herself one day, because she's thick with the worst people in the world, the rich snobbish ones, and they'll sink her, somehow they will.

"I hope she takes a lot of that royalty down with her: I hope when there's a shoot-out that she isn't killed until some of those English Lords and Ladies get popped off. If I was going into a battle with her, I'd offer her a chance: surrender and be with us. You're not so bad you can't join us! I'd tell her that. My uncle says he has no time for politics, but he thinks Thatcher is better than most English politicians. He thinks she's tougher, and she'd kill her best friend if she had to — she'd throw in her husband and her son, too. You know where you stand with her! She doesn't talk one line, then another. She's just our big enemy, and no fooling! I'd not want her shot by us [the IRA]. There'd be too many tears in England, and we'd be in big trouble here; they'd arrest every-one, and they'd kill us on the street, and blame us for starting trouble. We have to figure a way to get Mrs. Thatcher to say she's tired of us. She'd order all her men home, if she had to send them someplace else!"

This extended fantasy of sorts, interrupted in the telling by the eating of crackers, the watching of a telly news broadcast, and some inconsequential asides (neighborhood gossip, and a coming sports match), offered yet one more reminder that at least some of Belfast's children are not only intensely, shrewdly, and forcefully political, but also much drawn to the political side of life as a means of settling all sorts of personal and familial scores. Mary rarely mentioned her father, dead three years before, and I had met him only two or three times in all the years of visits to their home. He had held down a job at a pub, sweeping floors and clearing tables. He was an alcoholic. Mary loved him very much, she told me often — and I fear she romanticized his drinking — but usually she shunned even an indirect reference to him. She spoke all too eagerly about her mother — with the relentlessly critical eye (at twelve and thirteen and fourteen!) of a self-styled revolutionary leader. At ten, Mary had already told me she couldn't abide the complacency of her mother, who was (I couldn't help but notice) a thoroughly devoted parent, trying to care for seven children, of whom Mary was next to the oldest. (Mary's older brother had little interest in politics, and instead was a champion runner. He dreamed of migrating to America, of working as an athlete, then becoming an athletic instructor in a school — like her hero, his coach.)

One day, when Mary was only nine, we talked about families — mine, Kerry's, then hers. I pull her lament together here from remarks more rambling than usual: "He isn't alive much, our father. He is so upset at what is happening here, that he drinks a lot, a whole lot. He cries. I hear him coming home, and it's late, and he cries a lot when he comes into the house. Our mother won't even go to meet him. She sleeps through the night, and when we ask her if he's come home, father, she says: 'go and look, then come tell me.' I hate her when she talks like that. I hate her. He must hate her, too. She cares about bread and milk and cheese and eggs for us — and my father would be starving for the boys in the Maze, if it would do them any good at all. He wanted to fight the Brits when he was young, I know he did. Then he just gave up, and that's when he started drinking too much. I only wish the IRA could find something for him to do. If I was drinking that much, I'd get some dynamite, or a bomb, and I'd use it. I'd tie it to myself; I'd sacrifice myself. The sisters told us people have done that. They say in the States people were so upset about a war America was fighting — in Asia someplace — that they burned themselves to death. I've wondered if there might be some way for Kerry and me to do that. Kerry thinks I'm fooling, but I'm not. I've wondered if my father would want to do that. He'd never let me do it with him, but I would. We could show those Brits! We will, someday!"

Such talk is not easy to hear for a doctor familiar with symbolic "associations" in his patients — not without feeling his brow furrow, his eyes widen. One takes new stock of the child, then remembers that a cousin of hers (true, a boy) died hurling a firebomb at a British patrol. He was a runner for the IRA — a tough street fighter on its behalf. He was fourteen. He'd been throwing fire, literally, at others for a year or two. He died when others fired back — and Mary actually claimed to rejoice in his death: "It's better you die fighting them, than live and become a coward who kisses the ground they walk on."

She'd picked up that kind of talk, those phrases, from her IRA friends and mentors — an important fact for me to know, lest I attribute such a vivid and unsettling image exclusively to the exertions of her own mind. Mary has constantly heard talk of murder, self-imposed starvation, arson: stories or plots, and not least, assassinations in which a member of a family pays for wrongs he or she has done, or pays for wrongs done by others. Anyone who knows the Ardoyne, and other such neighborhoods in Ulster, knows of such intrigues, all with murderous consequences; knows, too, that such acts are constantly being discussed in front of children, submitted to their muster prior to the making of decisions: "What do you think?" That's the question Mary knew her cousin was asked just before he and others resolved to "go ahead"; and so, no wonder she, next in line by age, and dreaming of being next in line as an activist, was herself ready, in an instant, to say yes, without qualifications, yes: "If they came to me and said 'Now, Mary, will you help us?' I'd jump and say yes, and I wouldn't even want to hear what they're asking me to do. No, we must all join in the fight. The sisters say to pray, and my mother says to get by the best you can, and keep your friends everywhere, and my father is gone, but not my cousin and not me and not Kerry. She is still scared, but she'd be a brave soldier, if it came to her being needed — if it all depended on what she had to do. I hope I'll be brave, when the right time comes!"

A year later, at fourteen, she was not quite the Mary who spoke the words quoted above. Her mother took ill with cancer of the breast, and Mary learned that the mother had known she'd been ill for some time, but had refused to go see a doctor. Her bachelor uncle, a heavy drinker, who lived with his widowed sister and her children, drank even more when he learned this news, and became violent at home — breaking glasses, kicking the family's small dog in the early hours of the morning. Mary went through highly emotional conversations with her mother — one after another "heart-to-heart" — and with each exchange her political interests, her fiery nationalism, diminished noticeably. She became, now, interested in her younger brothers and sisters. She learned how to cook — in her words, "at last." She began to worry about how she looked to others, and wore (more and more) dresses rather than dungarees. She spoke out, tentatively at first, against the IRA's recruitment of young people, such as herself: "Let them fight, the older ones, and let us be left alone! It's not fair that little boys and girls be left without their fathers and mothers — all the murdered people we've known here, and all the funerals we've gone to, and all the tears!" Even as I write these words I know her to be a young woman (we'd call her an "adolescent") who has bravely stood in her recently dead mother's shoes, wanting to help those more vulnerable than herself grow up with some sense of a family's psychological stability. "I dream of peace here," Mary told me on my most recent visit to Belfast (1984); and she meant, by "here," the noisy kitchen, where children had their usual "upsets," and where her uncle (four months sober) sat all too glumly and silently, sipping tea endlessly, smoking endlessly, eating nothing, losing weight. "A pity, the thinness in him nowadays," she remarked — and I couldn't help thinking back four years to the days of Maze Prison and a younger Mary's yearning to shed pounds on behalf of a united Ireland, free at last of Brits and no longer in fear of the oratory of Ian Paisley.

As for Kerry, she moved with her parents to Dublin, where an uncle lived (and had a good job as a waiter in an up-and-coming restaurant). But I got to know another friend of Mary's named Kate, and though the two were "ne'er as close" as Kerry and Mary had been, there was a strong bond of respect and affection between them — one that grew stronger as Mary came to realize all that Kate had endured as a child. They were the same age, went to the same Catholic School, shared the same IRA politics. But Kate was bolder, sassier at, say, ten or eleven, and had twice been taken into custody by the British during the summer of 1981 for teasing British soldiers, for "disturbing the peace" of a city's street, for speaking "swearing words, in a fresh and vulgar manner" to the local constabulary. What Mary dreamed of doing, thought about doing as she talked or drew and painted, Kate actually did.

She was, at twelve, tall for her age, with lanky legs and utterly straight brown hair, with a slight hint of red. The hair came down almost to her shoulders. When she got anxious or angry, she put her hands through her hair repeatedly, or lowered her head abruptly, so that the hair suddenly all came forward, covering much of her face. She wore a crucifix on a chain around her neck, and often played with it, sometimes stopping to look down intently at it. She was "deeply religious," the sisters told me: "Kate might become one of us when she's older, for all we know. She may have a vocation. She may!"

As for Kate's idea, at twelve, of her vocation, it went like this: "If I could choose what I'd be, I'd be a surgeon! I'd be in a hospital someplace in Belfast, and I could help take care of our men, who get hurt. If I went with them, to fight the Brits, I could sew anyone up, who got hurt. If I saw a Brit, and he needed to be sewed up, I'd just walk away. I'd never give any of them help! They look down on us, and they never listen to what we say. If I could *really* have my choice, I'd be a soldier! I'd be in the Irish Army [that of the Republic, not the IRA], and we'd cross the border and fight the Brits and beat them. Then we could tell the Orangies: Stay here, and we'll be nice to you — nicer than you've been to us — or go back to your Scotland, if it means all that much to you! They've taken me in for being a 'public tease' to their soldiers, but if I was a soldier, I'd not get upset when some kid, a girl like me, starts saying what I said. I'd stop and listen to her! I'd ask my friends to listen."

She stops there. She has begun to notice my incredulity — and maybe her own. She pulls back somewhat, acknowledges that it would be an exceptional soldier who would be that honest and open — even to a child. Anyway, she admits, she isn't exactly a child: "The Brits say we're all grown up — that's what they say when they arrest us! They told me I'd go to jail next time, and it wouldn't be a camp for little girls; it would be a jail, and I could spend my time talking with crooks — women who killed, too. The men [of the IRA] told me I could learn a few good tricks, and they thought I could break out easy, real easy. To escape from prison for men is much harder."

She doesn't intend to go to prison, though. She is a very bright and able student; the nuns constantly encourage her to work hard — thereby to get a good chance at university education. She is not incapable, even at twelve and thirteen, of severe moral and political anguish, as I began to realize first when I heard her talking about her people's struggles, and later when I condensed her statements into the following excerpts. How sensitive and thoughtful children can be! How alert to ethical issues, to matters of contemporary social significance, to the political conflicts taking place around them, and to religious values they may have heard espoused, at home or at school, by their friends and their neighbors. Kate will always remain for my wife and me, for our sons, a vibrant spokesperson of young political and moral intelligence at work: "I don't want to be knocked around by the Brits all my life, and I'm sure I will be unless we all teach the Brits one big lesson, that they can't treat us as if we're dirt, for their boots to push here and push there. I try to shout at them. I hope just one or two will hear me. My sister says they won't, and she's fifteen, and she used to shout, like I do, and then one day she just gave up. I remember; I was eleven, just over my birthday a week before. Maggie came home, and she was hoarse. She said her throat really hurt. Mum told her to take a candy, a mint, and to take lots of water. Then Maggie started crying, and mum sat down with her, and then Mum started crying, and then I did. Maggie was upset because two of the Brits stopped and they listened to her; they did. They argued with her. She thought she had a chance to win them over. But they argued with her hard, and she said she couldn't do anything but stop talking; and then she came home. Mum told her she was wasting her good head, and she should study in school and learn the best answers for any Brit who comes to Belfast, and that's what Maggie has been doing this past year.

"I want to be like her. I feel dumb out there shouting at the soldiers. But the [IRA] people think we should, and they're the ones standing up for us. They say when I get bigger I can stop — but for us smaller kids to shout at the Brits is important, especially if a reporter comes here, or one of the telly men. I know we're being a help somehow, but there are days when I just want to go home and watch the telly, and not stand there hoping to be seen on it! My mother says she prays that those two Brit soldiers will argue me down, the way they did with Maggie.

"I feel a little sorry for those soldiers. I hate to admit it, but I do. They looked scared to me. I told one of the [IRA] men what I thought, and he said no, they're not scared, and that's why we have to fight harder, to make them scared. The good Lord, He must have made them, as He made us. He must be upset by the 'Troubles' we have here, and He must wonder how we all got to be such enemies! I've read the history books they give us in school, but I *still* don't see why we're ready to kill each other — *now!* God won't interfere with us, the sisters say; but He must be very upset with us, and He must be trying to figure out if there isn't something He can do to stop this. I believe the IRA men when I hear them talk, but then I remember the parts of the Bible the sisters have us memorize, and I just know our Jesus wouldn't want us to be killing each other, and He probably will be very upset with me, for all I've said to those Brits, when I go to meet Him.

"My favorite sister says you have to be loyal to God, but what country you live in — that's not important. But it was the Roman Empire that put Jesus to death, we learned, and so it *was* important — even for Him. I told this to the sister — my opinion! — and she said I was being 'a bit too clever.' She asked if I'd got my ideas from the IRA. I told her I said the truth — not an 'idea'! She smiled and told me I may have a vocation to be a teacher! It was the same afternoon that I tried to be friendlier with the Brits when I talked to them on the street near the stores. I told them we weren't put here by God to hate each other! One of them stopped (the first time that happened) and said 'you're right, girlie.' I didn't like the way he called me 'girlie,' but I thanked him. Then he wanted to give me a stick of his gum! He reached into his pocket and took it out, and he handed it to me, and I couldn't take it. I could feel myself getting red. My friend said later I was as red as the red on the Brits' flag! I kept my hands to my side. The soldier took back his gum, and he told me I should listen to my own words, and not preach to him. Then he left us, he and his buddy, and they both were laughing. I decided I should have taken his gum and kept talking with him, but I wasn't sure what to do, and what more I should say — and I was scared, real scared. If the [IRA] men saw us, they might be very angry. My friend said we should ask them what to do. I think I may stop helping them [the IRA], and let some of the younger kids go after the soldiers."

She heeded her own words, thereafter. She was summoned by older children, by some of those "IRA people" she often mentioned, to a meeting, and asked why she had withdrawn from her "station." She was silent for a while. They told her they wanted her continuing help. She said yes, she would gladly offer that — "but not with the Brits on the street." Why? She replied that she felt herself unable to get their attention. That didn't bother her interrogators. Finally, she succumbed to tears. They told her she would hear from them. She went home frightened, disappointed in herself — and strangely unable to forget that soldier, his gum, and not least, her own persuasive admonitory and morally urgent message.

She told her mother, days later, that she'd been having dreams in which the soldier figured. The mother told her to forget the soldier, forget the dreams, too, and above all, forget the IRA and its street activity. Kate wanted to comply with her mother's suggestion, but she also missed her chance to exhort others. Her dream in which the soldier appeared was a momentary, nighttime chance to have her say, and listen to herself. When she had told me of her dream, she was quite willing to explain it, in her own way — as if the significance of dreams was something she had a sovereign emotional and intellectual right to pursue. There was, in fact, no one dream, she pointed out to me, simply a recurrent theme in many dreams: "I won't always remember the dreams I have, but lately, when I've had the one with the Brit in it, that soldier, I know as soon as I've waked up that he's been in a dream, and I've had another argument with him! I've wondered if he ever dreams about me! Probably not! I'm not sure why I can't get him out of my mind! I don't usually think of him in the daytime. He may be 'a friend in disguise'! There was a story the nun read to us a few years ago — I forget most of it — but I remember the nun telling us one person in the story, he was 'a friend in disguise.' She said that God sends messages to us through the people we meet, and that's when they become 'a friend in disguise' to us. After a few dreams with that same Brit trying to be nice to me, I decided he was my 'friend in disguise'! I told the sister who's my favorite in school about my dream, and she smiled and said that 'God has his mysterious ways with all of us.'

"I began to think *He* might be sending the soldier to win me over to the Brits' side! But I know God would not get Himself into our 'Troubles'; He must be so smart He can see way in advance why He should stay clear of them! In my dream the Brit tells me I should practice what I preach; he says that — 'Kate, practice what you preach.' Then I take his gum, but I don't open it and use it, because I'm scared if they should see me, the men who spy for the IRA. Each time it's the same; I'm walking down the street, and I stop and try to get some soda pop, but I don't have the time, because I'm to be at that corner, and start teasing the Brits. So, I run. Then I'm there, and I see smoke, and that means we've planted another bomb, and it's gone off. Then I see the soldiers coming, and they're rushing to the place where the bomb has gone off, but this one Brit stops, and it's him (my friend!) and I'm starting to talk with him, and I tell him this is a place that God must not like, because of all our fighting here, and he smiles and tells me I'm a 'wise one,' just like the sisters will tell you sometimes, if you say good things in your composition. Then he does it; he says, 'let's you and I change it all here.' I don't know what he means — what that's supposed to mean. But he says that if he could trust me and I could trust him, that would be a start, and it's then he gives me some gum — asks me if I want some; and it's then that I get nervous, and I always wake up then. It's as though the IRA is watching me in my sleep, but so are the nuns, because when I wake up I think of them first thing."

I suppose she has yet to join us who conceptualize experience, who move from words such as hers to others: a girl with split conscience, struggling to reconcile conflicting religious and political mandates, and perhaps negotiating between a sternly commanding superego and the beckoning nod of the ego ideal, that morally refined part of many lives which occasionally influences them. But she knows the tug going on as she sleeps, knows the meaning of her slightly excited, even feverish feeling in the early hours of the Belfast morning, as the light summons her to another day. Sometimes, when I am asked what children of ten or twelve or fourteen "really" know about a subject such as "religion and nationalism," I think of Kate, her street confrontation, her chosen withdrawal from further street activity, her dreams, her thoughts about those dreams — and wonder what more we might ask of ourselves in the way of political knowledge or religious introspection. But Kate would not want herself to be used in this way — as a (faintly disguised) scold. When she was a bit older, just turned fifteen, she was so "confused" she thought of migrating — not to the Republic of Ireland, not to England, not even to the United States of America: "I'd like to go where there aren't any of us Irish living — not the Prods, and not us, either! Not the English — we've had enough of them! I've never been out of Belfast very far, a few miles, so I don't know where to go. One sister at school said she thought the place for me would be Italy. I'd be near the Pope then. But I'll bet a lot of Irish people come to see him!" But she never left Belfast, and in 1984, at age seventeen, saw little likelihood of ever seeing the Pope.

In fact, when Kate became fifteen, she began to lose all interest in politics — not an unusual transformation in Belfast, but one that contrasts sharply with the "political socialization" of children in the United States, where in late adolescence interest in politics is often just beginning. Kate was now able to look back with some amusement at her earlier recurrent dream. The soldier was "a handsome devil," she came to say when she was sixteen and going out steadily with a young man of nineteen who lived not far from her. This young man was ambitious intellectually, hoped to go to Queen's University in Belfast on scholarship, hoped to be a teacher. Kate had every intention of working on his behalf, if she could get a job. It was on such matters that her mind concentrated, though she was obliging enough to look back: "It all seems so long ago, that I was on the street shouting at those soldiers. Some of my old girlfriends are still with them, the IRA, but a lot of us just got tired of them and of all the fighting. I will admit that if that one Brit showed up here today, right now, I could pick him out of a crowd, I'd have no trouble doing it; I still see his face when I think of him, and I now realize he was a pretty handsome fellow! No wonder I was having those dreams! But I'm not doing bad, thank you, with my Gerry; he's a real sporting man, and he's smart, and if anyone will make it out of this street, he will be the one and I'll be there with him, you bet! If he and I had our way we'd never once think of our 'Troubles' again. I hate to say it, but I think Jesus Christ must be wishing He'd never let these churches get going in His name — all those Prod churches, and our Catholic one. There are Sundays when Gerry and I don't even want to go to church. We hate any news on the telly about the 'Troubles,' and we won't read the news stories, and when I hear the priest talking, and he's getting us all going, with his tough speech, I want to leave. I want to pray to Jesus Christ all by myself — I mean, just Gerry and me, and in his parents' home or mine. Lately, we've been going on weekend picnics, and we're never happier than when we're away from the streets here!"

So went the swift midadolescent evolution of a one-time warrior into a youth with high personal hopes for herself and for her boyfriend. She can't be considered "typical"; few in the Ardoyne even aspire to college, or become girlfriends or boyfriends of those who do. But I have talked with a number of children (about a quarter of those I've followed) who do gradually, in their teens, lose interest in the urgency of Belfast's religious nationalism. Perhaps they become exhausted, and "burnt out" — can't indefinitely submit to the constant, wearying stimulation of rage. I went to Belfast in order to learn *whether* children do become knowing about, attentive to a political scene. Yes, one learns conclusively, they certainly do become decidedly political children — but some of them go full circle, turn into exceedingly apolitical youths. Kate, speaking not only of herself, but others she knows well, described this psychological turn briefly, pointedly: "You can live your whole life here within a few months, or a year or two. You start out like a baby, then you learn everything; you see people you know — you see someone in your own family — die. You become a soldier. You're willing to die yourself. If you don't, you may keep fighting; and because jobs are so scarce here, there's not much else to do! Or you may just decide one day that something in you has died, but you're still alive. So, you start living, but it's not the same life as before."

Such a youth has not lost her political knowledge, or for that matter, her political interests; she has withdrawn from a political life, perhaps sacrificed it. Others of her background and age don't. In the Shankill I spent the same number of years I'd given over to the Ardoyne watching Protestant children assume *their* political birthright. Anyone who has attended one of the Reverend Ian Paisley's Sunday church services knows what that means — a thorough mixture, indeed, of urgent Biblical assertiveness and militant nationalist sentiment. Alice, at only eight, had committed most of the Reverend Paisley's terser pronouncements to memory — I often wondered whether she had even the slightest comprehension of what her voice kept uttering. But as I questioned her further, hoping to hear *her* view of things, not a word-for-word acknowledgment of what she'd heard in Sunday School, I began to realize how earnestly (and sometimes, ingeniously) children can make the pronouncements of the adult world very much their own.

In Alice's case a congenital defect aided such a psychological development. She was born with a left hip and leg destined never to be normal, so that her right leg not only carried the major burden of her gait, but was noticeably longer and sturdier. "We took her to the doctor when she was small," Alice's mother explained to me, "and the doctor said there was something wrong with the 'growth centers' in the leg, and she didn't even have all the muscles she needed — they just weren't part of the body the Lord sent us." Not every parent, needless to say, would phrase this child's medical difficulty in such a manner. Nor do other children choose to think about their situation quite as Alice did at eight years, six months: "I go to the doctor, yes; he's a nice man.

But he says there's not much they can do. If I went to London or to America they might be able to change my leg around — I mean, do an operation that would make it stronger. But it's 'only a maybe,' he says, and we'd have to be rich, and we're never going to have much money. My father says that even if he worked twenty-four hours, day and night, every day and every night, we'd never be able to get together enough money to travel all over the world, and see those doctors. Besides, there's one doctor who's the best doctor in the world, and He's the only doctor who never has died, and He never will, and if you trust Him, then you know there's nothing that happens, no sir, nothing, that isn't *meant to be*. My Granny, she's told me that God is watching us from the first second we're born, and He has a plan for us, a separate plan for each of us; and you never know what the plan is, the whole plan, until the last second of your life. What's meant to be will be, and He's the one who knows what's meant to be — that's what Granny says.

"My father says Granny has a 'talk' with God twice a day. As soon as she wakes up, she kneels by the side of her bed, and asks Him to do what He wants with her for the rest of the day. Then, when she's ready to go to bed, at night, she thanks Him for 'giving her the day.' She always says to me: 'Thank God for giving you the day'! I try to remember to do just what she does. I forget a lot; but I'm getting better — my father says 'much better.' Granny says my bad leg will become my good leg! She says: 'Alice, you'll see.' She says: 'Wait until you're as old as I am, and then you'll know about God's plan.' Sometimes I wish I could see way ahead, and His plan would be there, and I could find out what it is, so I'll know. But a lot of the time, I forget all about my bad leg; I do what everyone else does. I go to school, and I try to help my parents, and I mind my little brother and my sister, and I go to church, and I help my mum with the shopping. But after that bombing, mum gets nervous before she goes to market."

A year later this girl was herself a bit "nervous," but not because she was afraid that a bomb might explode as she was helping her mother choose vegetables or meat at a store. She had become a not-so-unwitting "messenger" for a Protestant paramilitary group — specifically chosen, I would eventually learn, because her limp,

her obvious vulnerability and fragility, made her the least likely
subject of suspicion. Not that she did anything illegal. She carried
envelopes, with pieces of paper inside them, from one person to
another. That is all she did, and at the start of this career, she
knew little of what she was doing, or why she was doing it. In
time she became outspokenly proud of her job, and by no means
reluctant to explain to anyone her sense of her own place in the
complex mosaic of nationalism: "You have to help your people,
when they're being attacked. If we don't fight for our streets, the
Pope will come here, and he'll have all the people from Dublin
up here, cheering him, and they'll push us out, and we can't go
anywhere. We're here, and we're going to stay here! My Granny
says she'll go and fight with us, if the Fenians show up. She says
she can pull a trigger, even if her arthritis is bad. Her eyes are in
good condition; she says she can see a long way into the distance.
It's only reading that gives her trouble. If the Fenians get *that*
close, she said she'd pick up the biggest rock she could find and
throw it at them.

"They asked me last year to help carry letters 'back and forth.'
They said they don't trust the telephone. I said I'd be glad to help
them. I never asked them anything, no. I know the people; one
man is my uncle. He's a very nice uncle, too. He always gives me
a big, big birthday present. He's the one who told the people that
I could help out. I told him it takes a lot more time for me to walk
than some kids I know; they can run so fast they're in your sight
then out of sight in ten seconds flat. But my Uncle Rod [Roderick]
said that's just perfect — they want a slow, slow walker, and I'm
the one. So, I said yes.

"I *do* know more than I did last year — I mean, I've heard
everyone talk, since 'the Troubles' here got worse, and I hear the
men talk, while I wait to get their letters. Even if I wasn't carrying
anything for them, I'd be hearing my father and my mum talk,
and all her neighbors; and I'd hear in church what's happening,
and how we could get wiped out, that's how bad it's got, this last
year or two, Mr. Paisley says. He's very worried, Mr. Paisley is,
my father says, and Mr. Paisley is the one who knows everything

about our bad, bad 'Troubles' here, and if you don't listen to him, you're putting a cloth over your eyes, and you're blind!"

She makes an illustrative gesture with her handkerchief, takes it out of her skirt's pocket, puts it up over her face, the upper half. Quickly she pushes the handkerchief back in her pocket, then she begins to talk louder, even as she is emphasizing the strength a one-time weakness has come to be: "We've all waked up. Granny says when she was my age she was asleep; she didn't know what the Fenians were doing — having their huge families, and trying to get all the people they knew from Dublin to come up here, and to push us, so we'd surrender. They want us to give them everything! They want us to join the Irish, be part of Ireland, that country. No sir, never; we are the Queen's subjects, and we'll fight for her to be our sovereign. The Queen is our sovereign, Granny says, and my father says she always will be."

A complete stop in that train of thought; accordingly, I begin to phrase a new question or two. Suddenly there is this afterword: "My mum says she thinks we should sit down with them, and have a big argument, and then sign some agreement — but she knows they won't be fair. She says they're not very smart people, and you have to be charitable. But she says they've done *so many bad things* — it's just too many for us to forget: the bombs, you know, and the shootings, and the fires they set. She agrees with Mr. Paisley, that you have to pray to God to protect us from them, or we'll lose everything. But she thinks some of them aren't so bad. She knows a butcher, and he's a Fenian, but he married someone my mother knew when she was a girl, my age, and she's one of our people, and she's very nice, and he converted from the Catholic Church, and he's all right, mum says. She thinks he didn't get a very good education, and his speech isn't good, but he is polite, and he'll give you a little extra meat, if he knows you, and he'll never forget to say 'please' and 'thank you.' "

She has noticed over the years that children and grown-ups alike are friendly to her, and exceedingly polite. She hears others experience rudeness (and, of course, display it); often under such circumstances she stops and wonders why she has immunity from

similar lapses in civility. But she also reminds herself of the truly
awful, even frightening insults she has heard. Her Granny, who
in a way is her confidante, her best friend, has discussed this
puzzling phenomenon with her, tried to explain what might be at
work: "If Granny is right (and I think she always is!), the people
who are very nice to me feel sorry for me; and the people who
say bad things, they're just bad people. Most of the people here
in the Shankill are good people; they stand together, and they'll
fight together. There are some rotten eggs in our basket, though;
Granny knows a few, and she says they should be sent to live in
Ireland and leave our church. Remember — Jesus was betrayed
by a man who was one of his closest friends. You can't think
everyone you've known all your life and thought was a good fellow
is going to turn out to be a good fellow all the time. Sometimes
people get caught by the Devil. Mr. Paisley, we hear him tell of
the Devil, and all the people the Devil owns. The Devil owns
them the way someone does a house, or a store. So you don't hear
him, and you don't see that he's been here, but he has. The Fenians
are a sneaky lot, my father says, and he knows; he watches them
when he's downtown, and they steal a lot from the stores, he's
sure. They have their arms full of things, and they take those taxis
of theirs back to where they live. We don't know how to be rid of
them!"

On occasion she has wished she were "all better" — and she
has corrected herself, usually, when she uses that phrase: "I mean,
not chosen by God to have this trouble." Mostly, such a qualification heralds a spell of emphatically stated thankfulness; God has
selected her, out of all the others He might have chosen, for a
quite unusual fate, and she ought to say hallelujah now and then,
rather than singling herself out for pity. But we do forget ourselves — human, all too human. Soon we remember, though. Once
we have remembered, we become joyous, and we think of what
might well be, someday — surprises, excitements, bonuses, rewards, awards. Who can know? Ours but to wait — and always,
have trust in Him, thank Him for that most important of all gifts,
to be a member of His flock. Saved — that is it, this is what counts:
to have been saved. And above all, saved from that Devil: "If I

catch myself with a tear in my eye, no matter why, I stop myself
and pull out the handkerchief, real quick. Dry your tears, Granny
says; and she dries her own, she tells me a lot. Think of Jesus on
the Cross. He died so we can smile. You can't forget Him and
think only of yourself. If He didn't like you, He'd have sent you
here to be a Fenian, and you'd be living with them and the Pope
would have you in his hand, and whatever he told you to think,
you'd think, and whatever he told you to say, you'd say. That's
what Granny knows, from being told by Jesus to stay here and
teach us all she's learned from Mr. Paisley and from others she's
heard preach God's true words."

Such sustained arias of gratitude do not always follow the laments
of a girl who (for instance, at age ten) had seen her friends take
part in a bicycle race, and be rewarded with "sweets." She knew
that "sweets" were always available to her — that, in fact, the man
who ran the bakery, and the man who ran the confectionery shop
were always eager to give her "a little something extra." Usually,
she declined to respond to those offers — simply shook her head
with the confident no of the well-fed girl she was. (Her father was
a clerk in a downtown department store.) But that day she'd been
seized by her "sweet tooth" even before the race had begun, and
had, in fact, fairly gorged herself during the race. When it was
over, she'd felt "sick" — quite ill enough to go home immediately:
"I was sick to my stomach." She knew that she should acknowledge
her own complicity: "I ought never to have eaten all those candies."
She also knew enough to connect the race with her own condition:
"I kept looking at my leg, the bad one, while I was there; and I
should have been watching the race, instead. I was feeling sorry
for myself, and that's a very bad idea, my Granny says. But you
can't be perfect! She says that, too! I always remember her saying
that when I know I've done something I shouldn't do. It's just —
well, it's just that I get tired of this old leg of mine some days,
and I wish I didn't have it. I told my mum once that I'd be better
off if the leg was just taken away from me. Then I wouldn't try to
forget it, and try to be like everyone else, and try to hope for the
best to happen every day.

"Usually *nothing* happens! I don't tell Granny that! She can always sit me down, and by the time she's finished her questions, she's found *something* that's happened — a good sign of God's smile, she says. Even if I'm not sure she's one-hundred percent right, I know it's best to agree. She's old, and she gets cross if you argue with her. But later, I'm not feeling so good, and I talk with my mum, and she says if you don't feel good, you should not feel good, and why should you whistle in the dark, if you want to stop and cry? So, I do! The other day I saw on the telly a boy, he was just born, and they said he'd need an operation, and they'd take him to London, and they might make him better, there. I was ready to cry then, too. But I heard he was from the Falls Road, a Catholic baby, and I thought: He'll have a lot of trouble, anyway, even if they *do* fix him up, those doctors in London.

"I asked my father if an English doctor would agree to see a Fenian from Belfast. He said probably, yes; the English have forgotten what the Fenians are really like. But my mum said a doctor should see anyone, and it doesn't matter, the religion of the patient. I know they don't agree sometimes, mum and my father. If I was the doctor I'd see the baby, even if he was a Papist. A baby isn't to blame for the mistakes of the parents! When you get to be older, then it's your fault. I've seen the Fenians, and all the trouble they've given us. Mr. Paisley says: You reach the 'age of reason' and you've got to stand up and ask God to bless you! So, we do! I've got over the 'age of reason.' It's seven, I think, or eight! But when I was a baby, I didn't know anything. Maybe if my mum had taken me to London, they'd have tried to fix my leg. Maybe there's a doctor someplace who can do something. The Fenians believe in all these bad superstitions, Granny says. But what if there was a doctor, and he was a Fenian, and he was the one who knew the most about a bad leg like mine? I think he'd see me and try to help. I think that many of the Fenians, they don't know better, but they're not as bad as the IRA, those murderers. The Fenians should leave Belfast; they should go to Ireland, and they'd be happier. They wouldn't live the way they do here. They'd probably take better care of their houses. We'd have peace then, and none of our 'Troubles.' Everyone would feel safer here. The Fenians would feel safer, too. They wouldn't always be complaining that we treat them bad; that's what they say on the telly. They say they want to be equal with us. But if you're not equal, you can't be equal. You can wish and pray, but if there's no miracle, there's no miracle."

Then Alice (just turned eleven) changed her slightly rambling train of thought abruptly. I'd been saying things, as she talked: minor phrases of agreement, or words meant to help her (I believed) to explain what she clearly was trying to explain — to herself, I couldn't help but think, as well as me. I think I wanted to push her a bit further, prod her to make connections I thought she *had* made a bit below the surface of her mind. She ignored my nudges, however. She wasn't willing at all to be hurried by me toward — well, *her* 'Troubles.' Instead, she would approach her own difficulties, then veer toward the Troubles of Belfast, of which she spoke easily, and sometimes, with a child's all-too-ready sarcasm, learned well from the grown-ups.

Finally, Alice eyed my red shoulder pack, where (she knew well) I kept my crayons, paints, drawing paper. She asked me how I'd been doing at the school I'd been visiting, and as I heard myself giving her an account of it, I began to realize I'd *not*, in fact, "heard" her — not picked up her inclination, at that moment, to move beyond words. Tardily, I began to move in my mind toward the desirability of having a drawing session, not our first. But she was the one to ask: might she "try painting"? She'd never before used paints, had claimed them to be foreign to her experience: "We only use crayons or colored pencils in school." Now, she was venturesome — and set to work.

A half hour later we could both view her first painting (Figure 5). She had been very busy. She had taken obvious delight in using paintbrushes, paints of various colors. Part of the scene was a pastoral landscape; but abruptly, city buildings appear, and as the eye moves from left to right the character of the buildings changes: at first, flimsy housing, all of a piece, and clearly inadequate, if not squalid, then individual homes, neatly arranged, of obvious individual dignity. In between is the dividing line or Wall — Belfast's separate neighborhoods, obviously, with their intermediate zones of barrenness or corrugated metal or abandoned dwellings, their windows and doors all cemented, a testimony to people split decisively from each other. But the artist wants to populate her carefully wrought world, and does. In the humble section of the city are to be found small people, whose features are not distinct. Their hair is uniformly dark — as is Alice's. One or two have a missing arm, a missing leg — as if the author had hurried too much, or wanted to indicate that these individuals may not be fully formed, may blur into one another: a social group collectively malformed. No flowers or trees are anywhere in sight.

In the other street or neighborhood, grass is really abundant, as are flowers and trees — the interrupted continuation, really, of the rural countryside to the far left. The sky that has clouds only where the less impressive dwellings are found now resumes its former bright blue, sun-suffused presence. The men and women here are distinct individuals, brightly dressed, and with no apparent infirmities. They have red hair, blond hair. The title of this painting: "A City."

When Alice has finished her project, she puts it down on a table between us, does not hand it to me, as she often has the drawings she has done — of herself, her Granny, her school, her favorite playground. I ask her if I may come and take a look. She says yes, and I do. "Which city is this?" I ask. I am sure I know the answer, and I wonder why she hasn't provided it more explicitly for the viewer, why she chooses to put the evasive article "a" before the word "city." After a silence of about ten seconds — as long as *I* could stand without discomfort — I ask another question, entirely suggestive: "Is this Belfast?" More silence, until our eyes meet, and then from Alice a thin, wan smile: "Well, sort of." I'm not quite sure what to make of that comment. I scurry around, mentally, for some further (leading, prodding) question. I wonder about a sudden, quite new psychological quality in this girl I've known several years — coyness, evasiveness. Then, she ends another silence herself: "I guess I got the idea from living here in Belfast, but it could be other cities, too."

I await her amplification. Surely she has something in mind. She seems to be struggling for words and so I make an effort to restrain my intrusiveness. Finally I am told this: "Mr. Paisley said last Sunday that there are the saved and the damned. He said God knows who's who, but we have to wait to find out. Then in Sunday school they read from the Bible, and I kept remembering that the first will be the last, and the last first — it says in the Bible. You have to watch out, or you'll be way on top, but you'll lose your way and get in trouble. Mr. Paisley thinks the British government, a lot of people in it, have gotten lost. They're 'on their knees before the Pope of Rome,' he said. And the only thing that will save us, he said, is ourselves — even if we're not in London, running the government for Her Majesty the Queen. But what if God came here, and He looked around, and He saw some people who live in good homes, and they are strong and have everything, and He saw other people, and they are in trouble — then what? A kid asked our Sunday school teacher that question, and he said God knows who's worth saving and who isn't. The kid still wasn't sure what the answer to his question should be, and so he asked it again, and the teacher told him to stop bothering us. When the boy said he only wanted to know, the teacher warned him of the Anti-Christ — that he could come and claim any of us anytime. So, we all bowed our heads and we prayed hard. Granny worries about the Anti-Christ. My father says he's not sure who the Anti-Christ is; and mum says Jesus was a good, good Lord, and He won in the battle with the Anti-Christ, so we all can be saved. But I told her Mr. Paisley said there are the people who are damned, and she said yes, she forgot. Then, she had to go shopping. Before she left she said prices have gone so high this last year, she's sure the Anti-Christ may be the people who own the shops where we get our food and our clothes!"

Other such comments followed, vivid in their theological suggestiveness, and reminders that not only Alice is "evasive," the word I'd used earlier in thinking of her. As for me, I began to realize that sometimes it is *my* mind that is "evasive" in its own way — unwilling to settle for a complexity, a thickness of psychological texture, eager to utilize a more categorical mode of analysis: this means that, and that means this, and no blurring. Meanwhile young Alice, just set to enter adolescence, had reminded me that for her the city of Belfast, its nationalist and religious confrontations, was not a single-minded obsession, but related to other confounding matters. Why the suffering of Belfast, and why the kind she had personally experienced? Why, too, the Bible's reminder that lowly, pain-afflicted people may attain the top rung of the spiritual ladder, and that fit, affluent people may be in for a great fall? Moreover, as one waits for that day of judgment, so commonly mentioned in church, what does one do — try to displace those who are poor, weak, infirm, and hurting, in hopes of a future inheritance of bliss? Try to convince oneself that even if the neighborhood one claims as one's own is rather nice, this relatively comfortable life is a measure of one's proven humility, one's clear-cut spiritual worth? If, too, one has a bit of lameness — what *then* does one do: claim on its account a destiny of heaven, because Christ so obviously ministered to, cared for the lame, the halt, the blind? But how does one do so, and avoid pondering the judgments accorded the Fenians — whose down-and-out status is declared by one's family as *prima facie* evidence of deserved damnation, rather than a sign of an auspicious future?

Alice was not one to answer such questions, and she has learned to be wary of her own natural, impulsive curiosity. The last time I met her, when she was sixteen, and a bright, able student who dreamed of becoming a doctor one day ("I've known so many, and they have been nice to me"), I noticed no diminution of that curiosity, though it was, as always, kept under careful wraps. She never forgot that one painting she had done, and told me this about her present thoughts about it: "I still don't know whether you stay as you are, or you change a lot — when the next life comes. Granny told me before she died [a year earlier] that she'd soon be 'in God's presence,' and there's His city, she said, a city where we go. I wondered if it's like Belfast. I guess we'll only know when we get there!"

I recall hearing, in that statement, the phrase "a city." When I did I thought back to that painting, and back also to my impatience with a younger Alice. Now I began to realize that yet another "child" had been yet another teacher to me. Our "a city" had been rendered in paint, by a knowing observer of this world's ambiguities. She quite properly has abstained from the clear-cut certitudes pressed upon her endlessly at her home, in her church, in one part of "a city" (Belfast) that is, in turn, a small part of yet another, larger "city" (the world). Why shouldn't a child exposed to a physical impairment that puts its mark on her, and to an arbitrarily and passionately and murderously divided community, and to a religious faith that emphasizes a someday cleavage of good and bad — why shouldn't she settle for "a city" and leave the question of which city up to time itself, and her mind's eventual, further effort at reflection, rather than the whim of a doctor who wanted to press her, then and there, for an unequivocal interpretation, a conclusive designation?

On days when I want that inclination of mine appeased, however — going for the jugular of the absolutely definite, precise, unqualified — I think of a girl I also met in the Shankill, Bea (Beatrice) by name, the oldest daughter of a former athlete and soldier who had struggled for years with a severe drinking problem, and of a former schoolteacher who has described herself, rather often, as "English," thereby distancing herself not only from Belfast's Catholics, but from its Protestants as well. When Bea was thirteen she explained to me, during many talks, her complex family background — and the way in which her religious life mixed with her nationalist sentiments, loyalties, antagonisms: "My mother was born in Yorkshire, and her father was a minister in the Church of England. He met King George VI and our Queen Mother. She is the most wonderful person in the whole world; she's over eighty, and she still makes you feel so proud to be one of her subjects, when she waves and smiles. My grandmother, my mother's mother, ran a tea shop for a while. She was a schoolteacher, too, like my mummie. They both taught English history. My grandmother died many years ago, and mummie doesn't teach now — except us: she says we're her 'class,' my brother and me.

"Mummie has a lot of trouble with daddy's drinking, but it's much better now. They met in England; he's from Belfast, and he was a soccer player. His family is from Scotland; they're Presbyterians, but they don't go to church much. Daddy had terrible fights with *his* daddy when he was growing up. My grandfather was the treasurer of a cigarette company here, and for a long while they had plenty of money and they lived in a nice part of the city, near the [Queens] University. But Grand-daddy got very sick, and he died. He had a bad time with gambling, my daddy says. He left the church because he was ashamed of himself. My daddy ran away to England, to play soccer and go to school and try to be happy. It was very sad at home, with his father so sick, and in big debt. I guess he swept my mother off her feet, when they met: he's always been a good looker, and he had 'charm' then, mummie says; and he still does. He can whistle, and the birds come running! But mummie's family knew he wouldn't amount to much, but even so, she stuck by him. She says if she had it over, she'd marry him, still, even with all the heartache. Even with our troubles over money: Daddy has lost a lot of jobs in his life! But he's been *trying* lately; he's *really* been trying!

"Mummie takes us to the Cathedral [of the Church of England, in downtown Belfast] and she says it's like going home, every Sunday. Sometimes she cries a little during the service. She says she has her 'memories.' Daddy never goes. He says he's a Protestant, but he's not fit for church yet — until he 'licks liquor'! He says the Church of England is 'too much' for him, anyway. He says 'big shots' go there, or the people who want to be 'big shots.' His drinking friends were always talking about 'big shots' who have moved out of the Shankill. One is an American who was from here and has come back, and he's the one who thinks all the Anglican types are 'big shots' or 'four-flushers,' daddy says: putting on the dog! Mummie laughs, but she doesn't mind being called 'the Queen' or 'her Highness' by daddy. She loves the Royal Family; that's why we have so many pictures of them all over. Mummie has a brother and he works in the Morgan Bank in London, and when we're in a slump, Uncle Jimmie wires us enough to tide us over. It may sound 'bold and brassy' of me, but I'd like to go to London and work in that bank. My uncle could train me, maybe. I'd be much happier in London than in Belfast. I just wish daddy would say, one day, that he's had enough of living in the Shankill, and fighting with his 'temptation to drink,' and enough of all these dirty Irish people, and their bad habits, and he's ready to leave. Mummie believes daddy 'caught' his drinking troubles from the Irish, the Papists here. They all drink as though beer and whiskey are pure water or the milk from the cow in a pasture nearby! If you live near people, too close, you'll catch all their bad habits and diseases, even if you start out good and strong, unless you have the most terrific willpower in the world, and not everyone does!

"If I get to England, to live there, I'll be back with my proper ancestors. It'll be like a big escape, my uncle says; he thinks we've all been pulled down by the Irish. Here in the Shankill the people are Protestant and they love the Royal Family; but it's not England. The Catholics are the worst people; they have no manners, and they don't know what the word 'clean' even means. The biggest thing in your life is your country. If you're Irish, you belong to a poor country that's never done anything but send people to other countries, Mummie always says when they're talking about 'the Troubles' here on the telly. If you're stuck here in Belfast, but you're from England originally, then you're like a fish out of water; you're not where you belong, and that's the worst, the absolute worst that can happen to you. Mummie should have got daddy to go with her to England. If she'd put her foot down, he'd have come. She's too 'soft,' my Uncle Jimmie says. He's a great man: He makes lots of deals, I think. He's not way up top at that bank, but he's a banker, and he lives in London, and that's the best life in the world, to be English and have a good job. It's not far from his bank to Buckingham Palace! I'll be visiting there again, one day, and a whole week before we go I won't be able to sleep, just like the last time; I know it'll happen. When I saw the guard change at the Palace I wanted to cry. I told my brother, if I was him, I'd want to be a guardsman for a while, and then get a job like Uncle Jimmie has. What luck, to live on the *other* side of the Irish Sea! What bad luck for us, my daddy's troubles!"

Even this would-be English lady of manners and means, of Anglican worship and monarchist sympathy, has to stoop to the same inclination other Belfast children have — to connect Belfast's "Troubles" with their troubles. Even as Alice, physically somewhat vulnerable, struggles with an underlying compassion for other vulnerable souls, so too Bea, whose overriding passion is migration to a maternal homeland, connects her "troubles" (meaning exile

and all it entails in her mind) with Belfast's "Troubles." For Bea
a people (the Irish) and a city, a country (Belfast, Northern Ireland)
are a nemesis. Whenever Bea talked about the friction between
the Catholics and Protestants of Belfast, her own family's discontents surfaced soon thereafter. For her, Ulster means the sorry
state of a family's social and economic life; England means promise
— even a proper pride. I do not think Bea will, in future years,
be much drawn to the kind of self-criticism that such church fathers
as St. Augustine found necessary.

I find myself doing her an injustice, maybe. She has always been
an outspoken, forthright girl — however pretentious some might
find her social and religious and nationalist views to be. In fact,
she impressed my wife and children as quite the bluntest child we
met in Belfast, and a candidate for the title of bluntest child we'd
met anywhere on this planet! She had none of the (manipulative?
ostentatious? deflecting?) guilt one sometimes hears from children
as they share their ambitions and prejudices with a friend, visitor,
inquiring foreigner — the mode of self-representation that couches
one's wants in the masking language of self-effacement, or in asides
meant to ensure one's status as an egalitarian, or a Bible-reading
Christian. "Bea wears her heart on her sleeve," her mother once
told us, and she was, surely, quite correct.

No one could meet this girl (we first met her when she was ten)
and not see the meaning for her of the Queen Mother and the
English flag and the Anglican church service and England's history — its battles, its empire, its institutions. Hers was a passionate nationalism, religiously sanctioned, which enabled her to feel
strong and optimistic enough to face down serious, even quite
ominous family difficulties, not to mention the everyday struggle
her neighborhood waged in an economy plagued by recession and
unemployment. Many in the Shankill find great consolation in the
conviction that the one irreplaceable virtue is a Protestant heritage.
When all else fails, that remains. Such a heritage also invokes
England as its source, its protector. But many in the Shankill, like
Bea's father, and the Reverend Paisley, also feel betrayed or scorned
by England, or inferior to its people, by virtue of what Ulster
means, they think, to those very English whom they admire. And

so, finally, what can Ulster mean to the so-called Ulsterman? This continuing and seemingly endless dilemma — the symbolic meaning that nationalist affiliations take on in the minds of young and old alike — was not lost on Bea, who said to my wife: "I'd like to flee Belfast so I can forget all the flags fighting the other flags and cozy up to one flag, and know it's mine, and like the rector says, 'no ifs and buts.' " Her nationalist longing connects with her effort to find out which set of parental ties and commitments matter: the flag or the nation as sources of energy in a child's analysis of her past, as explanations of her present, as a means of anticipating her future.

IV

IDEOLOGY AND NATIONALISM:
NICARAGUA

No one can spend much time in Belfast or other communities of Northern Ireland and not be convinced by boys and girls themselves of their strong, religiously connected nationalism — a firm sense of being Irish and Catholic, or Protestant and part of Great Britain, a sense Belfast schoolchildren develop in the earliest grades, and which is a constant (and constantly mentioned) presence in those young lives. Just so, the Nicaragua of recent years, since the downfall, in 1979, of the Somoza regime, has offered dramatic evidence of what a revolutionary educational program, given strong and unwavering support by a government, can mean to the psychological lives of boys and girls — be they six or sixteen.

I had been working in Northern Ireland for a number of years before I went (in 1983, with two of my sons and a wonderful translator) to Nicaragua — to visit Managua, Masaya, and León.[1] I no longer felt any need to "prove" to myself that politics can be an influential aspect of what we call "child development," but I'd often wondered how a nation which calls itself "revolutionary" and is unabashedly influenced by such Marxist-Leninist countries as the Soviet Union and Cuba, *and* which takes a strong interest in the education of its children, might go about the task of reaching the minds of those boys and girls, and to what effect. Even stern critics of the Sandinista government have not failed to praise the Literacy Crusade, an impressive effort to teach thousands and thousands of men, women, and children how to read and write. I was especially moved by talks I had with young people from well-to-do homes (their parents no Sandinista enthusiasts) and who were attending private (Church-affiliated) schools, but who remembered with great excitement and pride *their* involvement in this Crusade.[2] For these youths, now sixteen and seventeen, that had been a time of unusual nationalist feeling. One sixteen-year-old, whose father is a lawyer, told me: "I never knew much about my own country, my own people, until I went with my friends into the countryside and helped some peasants and their children learn the alphabet, and showed them how you put one word together, then a second word. It was a strong pride of my country that I felt for the first time: We are all Nicaraguans, whether rich or poor, whether we live in the city or live in the small towns and work on the land. My parents always looked to North America, or to Europe, to Spain and France. We knew nothing of our own country's history. I was ashamed. I'm still not sure what reasons made Somoza have no interest in building up support from all the people — so they'd feel *together*, so they'd feel themselves to be a *people,* a *country*. But that's how we all began to feel when we worked in the Crusade, and it was the best time of our lives.

"Now, it is no good here — lots of trouble. I wish the Literacy Crusade had lasted much longer. Maybe we'd be better off. Maybe *we* needed the Crusade as much as the people we were there to help! I told my father that, and he couldn't understand what I was trying to say! I agree with him, though, that these Sandinistas aren't just trying to teach the poor how to read and write! They are indoctrinating them. No wonder they have their own people, their teachers, their soldiers, going everywhere, in the schools and in the neighborhood centers they've built, even out in the fields, where they have meetings — going to teach people, especially the young, like me, and like my younger brother and my little sister: teach them what to think and what to believe.

"True, I admit it, the Church teaches *us* what to think and what to believe — and our teachers are part of the Catholic Church; they work for it, and belong to it, and they *do* preach, I mean, indoctrinate, if that is the word. Yes, I agree, if I use the word with the Sandinistas, I should use the word with the Church. But the Church is indoctrinating about heaven and hell. The Sandinistas are indoctrinating about here, this place — Nicaragua: our country."

A bright, sensitive, quite shrewd youth, he helped my sons and me, from the start, to contemplate the interaction in children's minds between ideology on the one hand, and nationalism on the other; and also to compare the Catholic nationalism, whether in Northern Ireland or Nicaragua, with the Marxist nationalism that the Sandinistas have been eager to promote.[3] As this youth indicated, though the Sandinista assumption of power, with its strongly reformist programs, heightened the political awareness of the educated young, boys and girls like him, he claims to have been "worried" when Somoza left the country — not out of respect or admiration for him, but out of a fear that there was no one who could replace him. (His parents had become increasingly disaffected from the "Somoza people," but because of what they themselves called their "disinterest in politics" had not risked either open disagreement with the regime or active support for its numerous enemies. A skeptic might credit their desire to keep on making money, or their desire to avoid jailing, torture, death.) I heard from several youths of similar age and background an account similar to that of the youth just quoted: "We all wondered what would happen in the country. The Somozas *had been Nicaragua*, my grandfather kept telling us. He thought the country would dissolve — that 'without the leader,' he kept saying, 'there would be nothing but chaos.' My mother and father were a little more hopeful. But they worried about a dictatorship of the left. They thought there would be a Nicaragua, yes, but it would become so different no one would recognize it. 'It won't be bad like the old Nicaragua; it'll be bad in a new way — a new country, but not really Nicaragua any more.' That's what my father kept saying.

"But suddenly we were all talking about our nation, our Revolution, our new government. Suddenly the word *Nicaragua* was on our lips — not a story about Somoza, or some new gossip everyone heard, or the latest deal between one of Somoza's friends and some foreign company. We *did* become more patriotic; I mean, we became more aware — how do you say, more *conscious?* — of our country. We thought about what was happening to it — to us. I remember long talks my parents had, and their friends, each person with a different opinion, it seemed. I remember, once, my mother said that under Somoza she had 'forgotten what it's like to feel part of a country.' The reason I remember is because I asked her what she meant, and she started to cry, and she said — well, this was what I remember her saying: 'Under Somoza, it was not a country, it was dog eat dog, and we were high up — yes, top dog — but we were always afraid. Someone could snap his fingers, and we'd be in exile, in prison, or dead. No one thought of Nicaragua. Everyone thought of dealing with the boss, and with his cronies.'

"The words, true, are mine, but my mother gave me that message, and I kept wondering who would replace Somoza, when he left. When the Sandinistas wanted us to go into the villages to teach the poor, I thought this idea was very strange, and I asked my parents what *they* thought, and they agreed: very strange. My father said, 'maybe we have a country now!' Then he added, 'maybe' again. Now he's *sure* we have a country, but he doesn't like it. He thinks the Sandinistas betrayed their own Revolution. To answer your question, I don't know what I think. Most of the time I think two ways. One way is that my father is too old and too prejudiced to be able to see the clearing; he looks at every tree and worries or gets angry. But sometimes I think I see only the clearing, and as my mother says, it may be a *picture* of a clearing, supplied us by the Sandinistas! Who knows what will be the outcome — for Nicaragua, for people like us, for the campesinos?"

I wish I'd been in Nicaragua in 1979,[4] to talk directly with children of his age, then, about the "consciousness" he now describes as appearing almost overnight and so dramatically. His memories, and those of others whom I heard, tell us, at the very least, that for late adolescents of today's Nicaragua, a much stronger nationalism is at work than before, and that the ideological aspects of that nationalism are significantly a part of the thinking, the imaginative life of such individuals — even their dreaming life. (The young man I've been quoting has had what I suppose could be called "anxiety dreams" of a forced departure for him and his family. He calls those dreams "exile dreams," or more specifically, "the Miami dream.") Still, for today's observer who aims to understand what is happening to children through "direct observation," the recent leap in nationalist sentiment among children of various social circumstances must be comprehended not through reminiscence of those no longer "children," but through interviews with Nicaraguan boys and girls of the middle 1980s.

Such interviews offer striking evidence of how children think when a major part of their instruction is, indeed, ideological. Even in the day-care centers, boys and girls of four or five can be heard referring to their country, to its new-found "freedom," to its "future." In the schools, political slogans are everywhere to be seen. Almost every aspect of the curriculum (from reading and writing, to arithmetic and science) has been explicitly connected to the Sandinistas' political and economic point of view — a proclaimed "democratic socialism." *Freedom, justice, liberty, equality, fraternity,* those mainstay words of Western democratic capitalism, are constantly mobilized in classrooms; so too are evocations of past *class struggle,* continuing *class struggle;* and so too are words such as *imperialism, exploitation,* with the inevitable attribution: *North American,* meaning the United States of America. No wonder, then, that a visiting doctor, talking with these children, finds that even the Belfast boys and girls whom he has known much longer and better than these Nicaraguans are far less preoccupied with nationalist ideas, slogans, reveries, dreams. In the middle 1970s I thought no children could be more intensely political, more nationalist in their passions than those I was getting to know in Northern Ireland. In the early and middle 1980s I began to comprehend, for the first time, what a recently institutionalized revolutionary government, intent on shaping the education of a nation's children, can achieve with respect to their "political socialization."

In a Managua barrio, for instance, I talk with boys, with girls, with individuals, with groups of nine-, ten-, eleven-year-old children, and they always mention their country, its struggles, its victories, its obvious jeopardy, almost immediately. "Citizens" they call themselves, "citizens of a liberated nation." I ask them for details, and I certainly hear and see many — faces alive with eagerness to recite, to narrate stories, to list past wrongs, to enunciate plans and expectations for the future. In classes teachers make *their* recitations, articulate *their* (quite long) lists, enunciate what they hope confidently to see in a decade or so. One child, Alfredo, whom I get to know well (gratefully, for the group rehearsals, the group exclamations are not very useful to a psychiatrist who works best with individual children), is quite enamored of his country, and tells me why. When I hear him say that he's glad he was born when he was, I express interest in learning about the reasons for such a declaration. "I wouldn't be alive, maybe, if I'd been born before the Revolution. I'd have died. We kept on dying then. The rich lived, their children lived. We died. That was the doing of Somoza; and he had his buddies, those killers. What diseases didn't do to our parents and to us, Somoza's men did!"

He pauses, and I find myself suddenly aware that he is "only eleven." I also begin to think the boy has been "rehearsed," has been all too overwhelmingly "indoctrinated" — because he uses phrases, entire sentences, which he has clearly been told to memorize, to use in school drills. Do American children, do my children, did I as a child, learn in a similar vein implicitly or explicitly political stereotypic notions? I also notice myself wondering: Is it fair to compare the relatively vague and occasional references "our" children (referring to their nation, its history and values and purposes) make during their ordinary lives to the insistent lessons that I sense are being taught Nicaragua's children?

Alfredo is ready to go on, does go on, and I listen, ask brief questions, get ample if not strikingly voluble replies from a boy who is not especially loquacious. Not usually loquacious, I hasten to remind myself at times during our conversations: "We have finally woken up. It wasn't a sleep; the teacher told us that to sleep is natural. We all sleep. (I love going to sleep when I'm tired!) It was something else; we were drugged. Somoza held a gun to our heads, and we stopped thinking. We were slaves. There wasn't a true Nicaragua; there was only Somoza and the people who played with him and got their rewards. He was *not* an animal; no animal wants to kill just to kill. An animal will kill to eat; Somoza killed to keep us slaves. He killed people every day, just to keep us as scared as possible.

"I'm lucky I didn't die when I was a baby. There were no 'shots' for us, then; we died all the time — every day, my mother says, babies died. I almost died many times. I guess I was lucky. I was lucky to live — so that I could see our Revolution happen, before our eyes, with our ears hearing the people fighting the Somozistas. Then they left — but now they're trying to come back. Our country is being attacked by them. They are like the diseases we all got in the old days; they will destroy us if we don't fight back. We'll be like the doctors we see now, the doctors in our barrio, and the doctors in our new [children's] hospital [in Managua];[5] we'll keep our Revolution really healthy — we'll make sure it doesn't get a bad disease and die.

"The disease is the North Americans — your country. Not its people! The teachers tell us to know the disease, and to remember that in the United States people are sick, too, just as we were sick for so long. Do your children know how many years your country ruled our country? Do your children know what happened to us when we tried to be a free people? Nicaragua was not a country for the longest time; it was an idea. That is what Augusto Sandino wanted — that the *idea* of Nicaragua become the *country* of Nicaragua. That is what happened in 1979. That is what we achieved. That is what we'll never surrender, our country. It is only the North Americans who won't let go of us. All over the world people are glad for us; they congratulate us; we have our country back again. Our priest is one of us; he said that Jesus Christ was alive, and then He was betrayed, and killed, but He came alive again; and it's the same with Nicaragua."

Without question the child has learned his lessons well. A rhythmic pulse punctuates his speech, his statements: they are declared, one after the other, in an exclamatory manner, and if the listener is from the United States, the condemnatory theme is heard quickly, noticed constantly. Still, Alfredo was kind, affectionate, acting hospitably as an individual toward us as individuals — and he was enormously curious about the United States. He also had his skep-

tical side — a willingness to abandon Sandinista ideology in favor
of a boy's natural interest in strangers, and just as important, a
boy's interest in the might, the power of their country. This line
of discussion proved extremely interesting, provocative — perhaps as significant as any I've encountered anywhere in my multinational (so to speak) research. In effect, a boy had "heard" an
ideology well, learned its admonitions, its principles, its aspirations, and indeed, put them all to phrase-by-phrase memory —
and yet, he had also asserted his own self's inquiring spirit as
though he held it as a right. As we heard him ask questions and
make comments on our answers, we realized how important it is
for a totalitarian country to squelch this instinctive human aspect
of a child's mental life, lest rhetorical pieties (many of them justified
in morality and historical fact, I hasten to add) be put in jeopardy
by the ironies and complexities of a historical moment. Listen to
this brief word-for-word, unedited exchange:

"When will you be leaving Nicaragua?" (Alfredo asks this of me.)
"In a few days."
"Will you come back here?"
"Yes, I hope so."
"So you like our country?"
"Yes, very much."
"I'd like to visit your country, some day."
"I hope you can. What would you like to see there?"
"Oh, I don't know. Maybe, your buildings, and your planes.
Maybe your boats, your big boats."
"What do you know of our buildings and our boats?"
"We have seen pictures of your navy and your air force, and
pictures of the buildings where your owners live."
"Is there anything else you'd like to see in America?"
"Yes, your McDonald's places."
"Have you seen the McDonald's in Managua?"
"No, but I've heard about it; my brother saw it."
"What did he think?"
"He has a friend who had some money, and he got some french
fries and gave my brother some."

"Did he like them?"

"Yes, they were good — very, very good!"

"If you came to America, would you want to see anything else, or go someplace else you've heard about?"

"My brother [he is two years older] says there are many McDonald's, and that there are lots of [video] games and televisions. Here there's only the one McDonald's."

"Would you like to see more of those here — more McDonald's restaurants and more television sets?"

"Oh, yes."

"Do you think the government wants to see more of them here?"

"Yes. Maybe. I don't know. The government wants the people to be fed. I know that."

A pause, then Alfredo asks: "Do you go to McDonald's at home?"

"Yes, sometimes."

"Do you like it?"

"Yes, but not as much as I like my wife's cooking."

"Yes, I see."

Another pause, then Alfredo says this — after a glance at his mother's small stove, newly acquired, and at the provisions the family has just obtained, with the help of the Sandinista "block leader," who distributes staples such as sugar and flour: "My mother used to have nothing for us on certain days — 'little or nothing to eat,' I remember she said. She'd always have something, a bit to eat, but she'd tell us 'nothing,' because she knew we'd expect much less to be there after we'd heard her say that! Now, she reminds us of how bad it used to be. We have our food now; some days there's more than other days, but no more do we hear 'nothing'! That is gone!"

Another pause. I try to figure out what question to ask next, but Alfredo has his own agenda: "My mother doesn't like the lady who gives us sugar [the block leader], but it's no great sweat to go there and smile. She wants us to join the crowd every once in a while, so we do."

"What do you mean, 'join the crowd'?"

"I mean, go to the rallies, when the people come, the Sandinistas. We cheer them!"

"Do you cheer all the time?"

"Oh, yes."

"Do you like everything you hear?"

"Sometimes we can't hear them at all. The noise is loud, but we can't make out the words!"

"When you *do* hear the words — what then?"

"What do you mean?"

"Do you always like what you hear the Sandinistas say? Does your mother like what she hears? Your father, does he go to the rallies?"

"I don't follow all the speeches. Maybe I watch the people too much, so I don't hear the words coming from the platform! I'm trying to see which of my friends is there, so we can play!"

"Well, when you do hear the words and pay attention — then what do you think?"

"I think the Sandinistas are our friends. My mother says, your friends are the people who try to help you. Before the Sandinistas, no one cared if we were alive or dead. Today, Nicaragua cares for its children!"

"Did you learn that phrase, that sentence in school?"

"Yes, and it's true! Look at our clinic; because of it my sister is alive, and because of the hospital, where she had to go. They bring food here; they want us to eat. My father says this Revolution is for us. He saw the Somoza 'Guard' kill people all the time. They would drive up, pull someone out of the house, shoot, and drive away. If you asked any questions, you'd get shot, too. Where were the North Americans when all our people were being killed? Now, they're making sure more of our people get killed! My uncle has just gone into the army. My mother worries. She cries. She wishes there were no more armies in the world!"

"Including Nicaragua's army?"

"Including ours, yes. But we need an army to protect ourselves. We need an army."

"Alfredo, I'm afraid people in every country say that — and their leaders, too."

"Do the North Americans say that?"

"Oh, yes, sure."

"Your country has one of the biggest armies? Yes?"

"Yes."

"Why does your country want to harm my country?"

"I hope my country *doesn't* want to harm your country."

"Do you think it does, or it doesn't?"

"I think some people in my country don't like your government, and some don't know much about it, and some like it — or like it much better than the one before it, Somoza's."

"Well, what about you and your sons?"

"Good question! I like it better than Somoza, but I see mistakes being made here by the government, that's my opinion as a foreigner; yes, as a North American — that the government is not doing some things the way it should."

"What do you mean?"

"I mean, that the government isn't as free as it could be."

"What do you mean?"

"I mean that what you read in the newspapers or see on television is controlled by the government. And the Miskito Indians, on the Atlantic coast — the government itself has admitted mistakes, pushing the people to obey government rules they don't like."

"I'm sure if the government admits a mistake, it's right!"

"Yes, I agree!"

"But does the North American government make mistakes, big mistakes?"

"Yes, we've made them, bad ones. Then, we criticize each other, we argue about who made them, and why."

"That's good. It's good to argue, until you find who's right."

"Sometimes we don't; we just keep on arguing and arguing!"

"That's good! We can argue here, too."

"I hope so."

"So do I! The *commandantes* aren't the only ones with the answers — my brother said that before he went into the army! He's fighting for Nicaragua, not the lady who gives us sugar, the block leader! Not for Somoza, and not for the *commandantes;* only for Nicaragua! But let's have no more North

Figure 1 (p. 37)

Figure 2 (p. 84)

Figure 3 (p. 86)

Figure 4 (p. 110)

Figure 5 (p. 131)

Figure 6 (p. 153)

Figure 7 (p. 154)

Figure 8 (p. 164)

Figure 9 (p. 176)

Figure 10 (p. 177)

Figure 11 (p. 189)

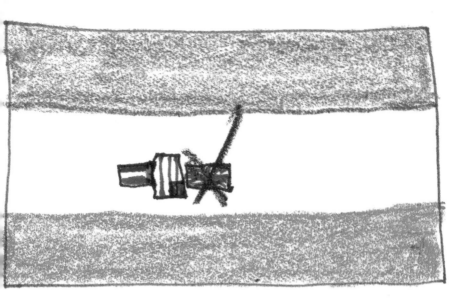

Figure 12 (p. 196)

Figure 13 (p. 199)

Figure 14 (p. 204)

Figure 16 (p. 206)

Figure 15 (p. 204)

Figure 17 (p. 206)

Figure 18 (p. 218)

Figure 19 (p. 218)

Figure 20 (p. 228)

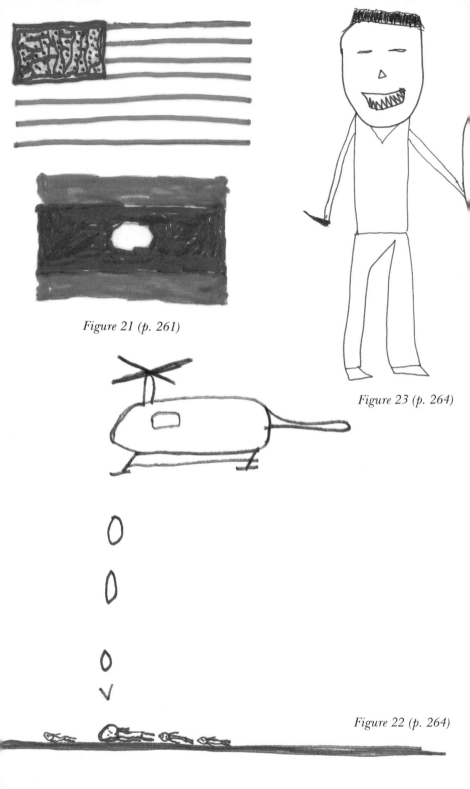

Figure 21 (p. 261)

Figure 23 (p. 264)

Figure 22 (p. 264)

Figure 24 (p. 265)

Figure 25 (p. 281)

Figure 26 (p. 281)

Figure 27 (p. 284)

Figure 28 (p. 285)

Figure 29 (p. 290)

Figure 30 (p. 295)

Americans on our land, bleeding us! Only visitors, like you people!"

"Thank you!"

This spirited exchange had us North Americans curiously excited, and also rather exhausted. The boy more than held his own: he had an ear for *our* ideological assumptions, even as we took note of some of the political slogans he had thoroughly assimilated. We also noticed his mind working independently, regardless of the ideological pressures acting on him as a student, just as we were trying to stake out for ourselves some minimal clarity of vision, some way of regarding Nicaragua's contemporary situation in a way that would not be merely reflexive — another moment of "North American" arrogance, smugness, condescension.

Without question Alfredo was drawn to the United States, interested in it, eager to know more about it than he is likely to learn from the *commandantes* and their employees in Nicaragua's schools. Even though he comes from a poor background, he has heard of America's famous hamburger chain, and knows of its one Managua store — a real hot spot for the children of the city's bourgeoisie.[6] He knows, too, of pizzas and Cokes, of electronic games, and of course, of television sets, one of which his parents own. He knows poverty, yet also is aware of some of the goods and services a country such as the United States offers its citizens. He is as interested in our blue jeans, our strong leather belts, as the Russians are or others who live in avowedly socialist or communist societies. He has been educated in recent years to read and write, to know his country's history, to comprehend (in a specified way, of course) the social and economic situation that obtains in Central America, and in other parts of the world, too. My questions to him, moreover, did not strike him as surprising or unique. His teachers have carried on what one of them described to me as a "dialogue" with their children — asking questions, helping their students to prepare answers to them. Alfredo, with his answers, would not have done so well in a test, but then, the teachers know that — know how willingly children respond to their efforts at "political education," but how "unpredictable" they can sometimes turn out to be.

One of Alfredo's teachers was quite blunt with us: "It is our job to help our children understand what has happened to our country. They want to understand; they want badly to understand. Our courses in political education are very successful. The children are animated — yet solemn. They don't make disturbances. In other classes we'll have to raise our voices to tell them to be quiet; here in this class they need no reminders from us. They want to hear every word we speak! This is *their* struggle, their parents' struggle. We don't teach them big ideas that have nothing to do with their lives. We teach the story of Nicaragua, their country — and what happened to it. They tell us what happened to *them* — how so-and-so was shot dead by the Somoza police, and how they saw their father die, because there was no doctor to see him, or their brother, their sister die, for the same reason. And meanwhile, Somoza and his cronies raped our country of all its wealth.

"Of course the children are tempted by the bourgeois life! Who isn't? We are not as surprised as you seem to think we'd be! Here, we have a longer job ahead of us as teachers. We have to earn the trust of the children. We must have many conversations with them — 'a dialogue over time,' as one of the *commandantes*[7] has put it! We must reach to these young ones, and by sharing the truths we discovered in our long struggle with Somoza and his North American backers, we will win the trust of this new generation, and our country will be stronger that way. But it takes time — always; and only in the last few years has time been on our side, thank God."

He uses that last phrase, even though he is bitter about the Catholic Church, whose struggles with the Sandinistas are well known both in Nicaragua and the United States. Those struggles are also known to the barrio children he teaches — whose parents are, often, quite religious, and at the same time devoted to the Sandinistas. A number of barrio children attend both "religious-education" classes under the Church's sponsorship (in the weekday evenings, on Sundays) and the above-mentioned "political education" daytime classes in the public schools.

Alfredo was one of them, and his drawings indicated how imbued he was with both Christian values and Sandinista values — even while North American, materialist values have also continued to be a force in his life. Moreover, he is a boy who enjoys playing with other children, who loves to have his say, who doesn't take even parental constraints easily, and so his teacher is right, indeed: a certain individualism, a certain privatism that is utterly ordinary and human appears strongly evident in him. As one of Nicaragua's leading pediatricians told me, while we walked through the country's major children's hospital (a new, modern facility, the pride of its patients and doctors alike): "Nicaraguans are a genial and informal people. Our children are easygoing, mostly. I have traveled to your country and to Europe, and I think the people here are as friendly as anywhere, friendlier than in most countries." We continued with an informal discussion of so-called national character — the pediatrician was a firm believer in it. I was (am) reluctant to embrace the categorical aspect of such a theory — a proposition that has X nation populated by people of Y personality, due to Z factors. Still, I'd been enormously touched by the friendliness of the children I'd been seeing, and as we talked remembered some of Alfredo's drawings, so warm and open and hopeful.

In one of them he portrayed a barrio landscape, somewhat softened by tropical flowers and trees (Figure 6). The sun shines brightly in a clear blue sky. The Sandinista flag and the national flag are hoisted high over the homes, on top of a gentle hill. A church proclaims its insignia, a mighty Cross, by no means intimidated, hidden, or apparently, rejected — for people stand near the building's entrance, even as they could be seen in the barrio. It is a scene Alfredo himself described in this way: "This is our country, with Somoza gone. We're going to build a new school right here; for the time being, we use the land as a playground. Our houses will get additions to them, or be torn down, and new ones built, they say. Our priest tells us God is smiling on us, and the Sandinistas say we're one of their best barrios, to show visitors. If you can't be proud of your country, you have nothing left to honor! The teachers say they don't even want to think of how bad it used to be for us under Somoza. There was always a funeral here, every day, and on some days, several funerals. People were shot; people died because they were sick and no one cared if they got better. Now, our country cares for its people! This picture is our country — the people here, our flag, our church, our old school, and the land for our new school, and there will be a clinic here, too, so we won't have to travel far to get to see a doctor. I'm glad I had the good luck to be born here in Nicaragua, after the Somozas left!"

In another drawing Alfredo is more ideological, in a manner of which the Sandinistas would approve (Figure 7). He draws a picture of a wealthy, fancily dressed girl, says she is "spoiled," that her father was a "murderer who worked for Somoza." What precisely did he do? He was a general in the dreaded police force the dictator controlled. The girl seems lifeless, a mannequin. There is blood on her hands and her shoes. Dead bodies, poorly clad, lie at her feet. (She sits on a thronelike chair.) A black sky is overhead — with no sun. There are no trees, shrubs, flowers, grass. A cemetery is a short way off, a grim spectacle. I ask the boy who the girl is. He says he has been shown photographs of Nicaragua's former ruling elite, has been told stories about them in class. They murdered not only individual people, he has been told, he firmly believes, but his country. This picture is about Nicaragua's death — and even the rich girl seems dead.

I prod him and suggest that under Somoza, no matter his wickedness, many Nicaraguans (and not only the rich) were far from dead: they had families, did their best to live halfway useful and self-respecting lives. After all, there is the example of his own parents, his aunt, his two uncles, his one remaining grandparent. These are good, strong, vibrant, shrewd people, endowed with (among other virtues) a sense of humor, as well as fatalism, which made me laugh, my sons laugh. They taught Alfredo to laugh *before* the Sandinistas took power. Is it fair to draw, both literally and symbolically, so unrelievedly morbid a picture of the former Nicaragua, for all its sorrows and gross (if not obscene) injustices? He listens, gives me my point: "Yes, I see. Yes, our people have never died. It was the *country* that had been killed. We needed to get rid of the Somozas, and then we had to build a new country."

Fair enough, I think to myself. Who am I to hold a monopoly

on symbolic understanding? To take the longest and most complex
of views on what is happening in the world — while expecting
others, children or adults, to deny themselves the pleasures of
making larger statements, or rejoicing in a sweeping historical
statement? And what of my reservations and qualifications, important as they may be in any complete analysis of what did and
did not take place in Nicaragua under the Somozas, or for that
matter, after they departed? For Alfredo, for other children we
met, even among the strongly anti-Sandinista schoolchildren we
visited in two private (Church-run) Managua schools, Nicaragua
as a nation has become a relatively new and quite energetic reality,
inspiring or frightening, but in any case, very much a presence in
children's lives: a moral presence, correctly reproving or suddenly
flawed; an idealized presence, or a formerly idealized one, now
tragically betrayed; a presence that inspires passionate devotion,
or prompts equally passionate melancholy or scorn; and in plenty
of young minds, a presence not only noticed and admired, but also
questioned and suspected.

Even the most ardent Sandinista children worried not only about
the outsiders — the Contras, the North Americans, the "bad Church
people," the CIA spies who are supposed to be anywhere and
everywhere, but they worried about Nicaragua, the new object of
their relatively constant attention. Alfredo's cousin, a "Young Sandinista," said to us on his fourteenth birthday: "I'm not fourteen.
I'm really only four! For ten years of my life we all were in hell.
My father told us when we came back from Church: 'hell is here —
and Jesus Christ is someplace else.' We'd ask him where Jesus is:
Please tell us. He'd say nothing! We'd ask again; we'd keep on
asking until we knew he'd either hit us hard with his hands, or
shout at us to get away and stay away for a long time. Every time
we got him to answer us, but the answer was always the same:
'He's *someplace*, but I don't know where. He's nowhere near us!'
Then the next time would come and we'd be asking again, and
our father still had no idea where Jesus Christ was, even though
the priest told us He was inside our stomachs, because we'd just
swallowed Him, or we were going to swallow Him. So He must
be someplace inside the Church building, we figured.

"Then, one day, our country was born, just like Jesus when He rose up — and my father now knew where He was. He told us, without our asking him, I still remember — he told us that Jesus was right here in our Managua, in Nicaragua. He'd been very busy going to other places, but now He had time for us, and that's been our good luck. That's why everyone comes here, from all over the world. The North Americans, suddenly they're here, all the time they come here. Some of them know Jesus has touched us, the way my father says, and they're glad; and some of them are afraid He's been here with us, and they're worried; oh, *are* they! But they shouldn't worry! Nicaragua wants peace! Nicaragua wants justice! It wants to be left alone, so it can grow and be a good country, not a place where everyone is being killed or dying like people did here, so many, all the time, dying."

He knows; he lost his mother, four of his six brothers and sisters, to illnesses that might have been readily cured, had medical assistance been available. But he knows, too, that the Sandinistas feel hard pressed, that his nation is hurting (at least many in it are), but it is also happy, relieved, newly hopeful. He fears army service, though he also looks forward to it. He will "die for Nicaragua, gladly"; but he also has seen "too much death already." "I hate the thought of seeing more," he willingly acknowledges. Still, if there has to be sacrifice, Nicaraguans will offer it: "For the country, you say yes: take me." Then he turns to Alfredo: "Right?"

The younger boy nods, declares himself in complete agreement: "Our country can't be destroyed, not again. The North Americans won't do it this time, won't get away with it. We are on to them; we know them the way you know people when you've learned your lesson so many times that there's no way you can be tricked. If we won't be tricked, we won't be beaten. We'll keep fighting until up there in Heaven Jesus Christ says: Enough, leave these people alone, because they belong to Me, and not to the North American generals and the big companies that run that country. Enough! And when Jesus says 'enough,' and Nicaragua, its people say 'enough,' then there's no way, no way we can be turned into a slave again, like we were last time, a slave."

An entire country is regarded as a one-time slave by one of its children — who has learned to regard his life itself as a particular beneficiary of a historical event he has a clear memory of witnessing, at least in the way someone bears witness who is in a cheering crowd of thousands upon thousands of people. We place great stress, we "North Americans," upon the telling and formative effect of incidents, accidents, or crises upon the mental lives of children — "traumas" of one kind or another that won't let their grip go. Why need these troublesome experiences only be, for all children, familial — connected to the troubles parents have with one another, with their children? Is it not possible that a nation's various tragedies and successes can also work their way into the conscious and unconscious lives of its citizens, so that what they think and do, years later, gets some of its propelling energy from this kind of remembered human involvement? Anyone who has seen a political crowd in Managua, weeping over deaths inflicted by Somoza, hailing the Revolution's new day, will think twice, speaking psychodynamically, before dismissing such moments as "superficial" or "tangential." Anyone who hears an Alfredo talk, or his cousin, or the well-to-do youth whom I quoted at the beginning of this chapter, will surely have a hard time consigning nationalist enthusiasms to the less-than-compelling category of childhood subjectivity.

A priest in Masaya,[8] Nicaragua, who is no dear friend of the Sandinistas, told us that he has seen children in that city speak of their country as if it was an "eternally watchful new friend," one who may make mistakes, but one who has to be embraced, and if necessary, protected with the sacrifice of one's time, energy, even life. So the children we met seemed to say — no doubt pressed to do so by their ideologically zealous teachers, but also engaged by the "existentialist" aspects of revolutionary life. "The Revolution Lives," a child says with chalk on a cement wall, and saying so, he is not alone. This statement means, too, that the individual child who bears the chalk also lives — a statement of affirmation no less significant than that of a writer, a teacher, an orator, a philosopher, a preacher. Such a declaration is especially significant for children who grow up in families whose members traditionally felt like neighbors to death by virtue of their medical, social, economic, and political vulnerability. We psychiatric theorists, in the comfort of our democratic society, in the comfort of our privileged membership in that society, talk and write about a "death instinct" or "thanatos" or the "aggressive drive"; we refer to sadistic forces at work in individuals and families and one or another kind of "group"; we talk about irrational phobias that paralyze children, about terrible anxieties or nightmares some of those boys and girls have reported to us. It is well that we should. Yet, there are worlds (and Nicaragua was one of them for decades, the Nicaragua so many of our Presidents, Democratic and Republican, regarded as our friend) in which death is not a speculative "drive" in the lives of children, but a continual, concrete, highly visible, utterly memorable part of everyday living; and so too are sadistic soldiers, murderous policemen — all of which we ought to keep in mind when we come to talk about "aggression" in the lives of boys and girls. Some young people have nightmares that are not only the work of an evening's imagination, but are images that each dawn brings to one barrio after another: "They came here, they shot him dead, they drove off — and my mother said we're lucky they didn't finish us off, while they were here."

One of Alfredo's friends, a thirteen-year-old boy who remembered so very well what Somoza's "men" did to his father, spoke those words tersely, and with no apparent emotion, only eyelids lowered. One noticed the right shoe moving, arclike, back and forth, in the barrio's hot, dusty earth. No wonder, a few minutes later, as the subject of the revolution came up, the subject of Nicaragua's future, that the same boy said, "Nicaragua cannot die." He said "cannot," not "will not." Then he added yet another emphatic statement of his country's immortality that is, also, a bit of an explanation: "Nicaragua is our fatherland, so it cannot die. The Revolution will live." His father is gone; his country is here, right here, in his life; and he, though he be "indoctrinated," an observer concludes, though he has become "ideological," the same observer adds — the boy, one also notices, reaches out to his nation for the healing assurances strong fathers can offer their sons. What one nation took away, another offers. No wonder this boy, like so many children in Managua, is at such pains to refer to "the Somoza regime," as against his "country, Nicaragua," which he describes as "just born a few years ago." He believes in "Nicaragua" as his new benefactor, regardless of the doubts some may have or the doubts others may not so far have the heart to entertain.

V

LANGUAGE, CULTURE, AND NATIONALISM: FRENCH CANADA AND POLAND

A NATION'S children may perceive nationalism in a hundred ways. In Belfast some perceive it as a last-ditch stand for Queen, Country, and Jesus. Others, just across town, hear its note in a yearning for union with one's "brothers and sisters of the Holy Church," the "blood relatives who belong to the Republic." In Nicaragua the child may perceive the nation as a new voice, a new ideology that tells him at school how the Idea, the Truth, the Revolution, see history, money, power, and justice. A child, too, may identify his nation with its language, with speaking and hearing one's "own" language rather than a "foreign" tongue. The child learns that a language carries an entire cultural tradition made up of stories, poems, legends, myths, and social memories — to which the child will one day add his or her share.

Yet, although nationalism may be perceived in any of these ways, the love of country (and conversely hatred for those who do not belong to it) is part of a seamless web of experiences, loyalties, convictions, suspicions, antagonisms — to which language, culture, religion, social values all contribute. The Church we attend, the brand of politics we have preached to us in school, on television and radio, the language we use to express ourselves, the cultural values we have found ourselves inheriting — one or another of these "variables" becomes connected in our minds with our sense of what a particular nationalism is meant to stand for: Catholicism, Protestantism, the House of Windsor, one dialect, another dialect, the Sandinista program, in Quebec the French language, in Poland the Polish language or the Polish cultural tradition or even the history of the Catholic Church in Poland. That last-mentioned item adds to an already increasing complexity — the way in which nationalism affects religion, even as religion can help shape a number of the world's nationalist enthusiasms.

In Quebec I got to know some Canadian children.[1] They live only a few hours by car from my New England home. They are not unlike my own children, reasonably well-dressed boys and girls, their parents neither rich nor poor, who have all grown up taking the comforts and opportunities of the Western capitalist, democratic countries for granted. They are children who can expect to vote, as a matter of course, when they are grown up. They are children whose parents and grandparents and great-grandparents, and even great-great-grandparents have been born in Canada, have been glad to consider themselves Canadian — and yet, in the mind of Alain, who is nine, something sets such young people and the older people in their families apart, "something" that he describes: "We're not the Canadians who wave at the Queen and tell her we love her! We speak French, and they've been trying to get us to speak English ever since we came here, and they haven't won, and now we've won, and we can speak our French, and they don't like what's happened, but that's it, that's the outcome, and they can cry until no more tears are left, and still we'll be speaking our French."

I hear about "our French" from him again and again, and I also hear about those others, the "they" he keeps mentioning, and I realize that I don't have to travel across the Atlantic to Belfast, if I wish to hear children inflamed by their devotion to one variant of nationalism, by their concomitant enmity toward another. Here is how French-speaking Alain moves from mention of the French language to consider what is at stake more generally for many thousands of people: "If you're one of the Anglophones [English-speaking people], you think you own Canada, and you think you're not really Canadian unless you speak English; and I think many of the Anglophones want us [Francophones] to get out. They don't say 'go back to France' to your face, unless they're a gang, a teen-age gang. But you know what they think. My father remembers how he was treated; he says, if you spoke French in the old times, you were treated like dirt. They wanted to wipe their feet on you, and if you didn't let them, they'd make you pay. They owned a lot of companies. They still do — they're rich, a lot of them. They think they're the best people in the world. They make you want to go and get a gun and fight — or you can go home and feel bad, bad."

I know of these tensions, these accumulated grievances. I am aware that the author of one book,[2] and many of its readers, have compared the fate of Canada's French-speaking people to that of the black people of the United States. As I sit and listen to some Francophone families I think of the confusions, the perplexing questions, the ironies connected to this vexing historical conflict, one that persists today. I find those two words,[3] Francophone and Anglophone, so commonly used now by Canadians, more than a bit jarring — and they themselves remind me that language can help create a new political or social reality. How paradoxical, for instance, that the French language, regarded as extraordinarily subtle, "refined," aristocratic by so many English-speaking people all over the world, should be regarded by Alain and his family members as a one-time mark of oppression, a sign of inferiority in the eyes of others. Yet, as I listen to Alain, and his older sister Annette, who is twelve, talking about their Francophone life, their sense of what Quebec is like, as opposed to Ontario or British Columbia, I begin to wonder whether the issue, really, is language, or a number of other matters, collectively subsumed under the polarity Anglophone-Francophone.

Class surely is a consideration — the long-felt grievances of peo-ple who haven't had as much economic clout, as high a social position, as others. So one hears from Alain, and from his sister, who can be gentle and soft-spoken one minute, then quite stern and sharply sardonic the next: "My brother doesn't say what has to be said — that the British have ruled this country for a long, long time. They think we belong to an Empire, *their* Empire. This is not the United States. We never got our freedom from London! Only now are we putting the British [she says *les peuples de la Grande Bretagne*, not *les Anglais*] in their place. We had to organize. My father knows; he was one of those who helped start our drive to establish our own power here. We'd had enough of the rich British who come to Canada looking down their noses at us, and fleecing us every chance they get. They are the bossiest people in all the world — and now they complain if we don't bow to them, even when we've been elected by the people to run our own province, here in Quebec. What a nerve! That is Great Britain for you! I tell Alain, it is fine that he knows some nice English people; but he hasn't heard what they say about us, the French, when they close their doors and sit and cry because their flag is not the one we bow to, and pray to. My father wishes General de Gaulle had come here and been our leader, and that we'd split from British Canada, and become French Canada — *Le Canada Français!* I say we should still pray for that to happen. Let it happen! Long live the idea that there will be a French Canada!"

The reader will notice my effort to adhere, at least somewhat, to the French syntax as I translate. I tried to be my own interpreter in the interviews I did in Canada — only to learn how rusty my skill in this beautiful language had become, and how much easier for me it is to read than speak and understand spoken French. Anyway, the tape recorder gave me a second chance to make sense of what I'd heard — and often the children, from parents I can describe only as intensely French, as fervently nationalist Francophones, spoke in an urgently exhortative manner, therefore requiring little in the way of encouragement from me. I noticed occasionally that they did not expect or demand my exact understanding of their remarks.

The pictures these children made were exceptionally vivid and stirring. Alain loved battle scenes, and it was he, actually, who reminded me that the issue between two Canadian language groups is not only "class," but as in Ulster (where wars fought centuries ago are still mentioned as if part of today's conflict), a matter of historical experience. "You forget," Alain's teacher tactfully reminded me, "that for Canada the major struggle was not between farmers and King George III, or between slave owners and those opposed to them." He waited a second or two, then moved my mind northward: "The big struggle here was between the British and the French — that's our great memory, Canada's; so, that war goes on, you might say, just as your North and your South weren't on very good terms for a long time after your Civil War had been fought, and a nasty war *that* one was, yes!" Alain portrayed, in several of his pictures, Canada's early war between the two colonial powers, and, in several others, an updated version of that earlier confrontation. Once, he supplied both sides with airplanes, and ominously wondered whether both sides might be destroyed, given the hard feelings involved and the modern dangers of military technology.

The picture was, actually, his depiction of a struggle for height, for prominence (Figure 8). The English side had tall buildings, and, nearby, an airfield, whence planes took off; and at the airfield's edge, a missile site. The French side was more nondescript, some lower buildings and a smaller field. Hills seemed to enclose the entire French scene, whereas the English world was one of imposing substance — ordered urban commercial and residential growth. Still, the French made up in determination and courage for what they lacked in wealth and military power. (They had no missiles, I began to realize as Alain was finishing his work with crayons and color pencils.) The English had more planes, but as in a war movie of the 1940s, they had become complacent: a solitary French plane had dropped its cargo of bombs, devastated the grounded aircraft. Other French jets soared; the English jets hovered near the city, "protecting it," Alain told me. They achieved that aim, interestingly; anyway, he told me the French pilots had no wish to destroy a city with people. Their purpose, Alain's purpose, certainly, and maybe the point of much that is called French nationalism in Canada, was described for me in a poignant declaration by this not yet teen-aged boy: "I must tell you, the French over here [he points at the right side of the drawing] have been insulted until they no longer can sit back and receive these blows to their pride. They don't declare war, no; they rise, to fight back. When the British were stepping on the French, no one called it a war; when the French said *no more,* and stood up for their rights, then it became a war. So, we fought — and we did pretty well; that is what has happened.

"You see here, this plane, all by itself, knocked all those planes out. You see, these planes are flying higher than the British dare fly. They're afraid. They've become soft. Our men will take chances. My father says: 'We haven't got anything, *anything,* to lose!' So, why not! We don't want their streets, where they live, for ourselves. We want to keep them from telling us what to do. We want to speak our language; it's a much better one than theirs! Let them learn to speak French, the way they've made us learn to speak English. What is fair is fair! We're trying to even things out: Liberty, Equality, Fraternity! Our pilots are rising to defend us — so we won't disappear. Is it wrong to fight against people who work to make you be exactly like them? No, sir! As you see, we are not their equal with equipment, but we win because it is our pride that is working for us!"

In this mixture of particular exposition of a drawing and a more general rhetoric that he has heard all his life, a Canadian boy informs his listener about a fusion of sorts that has taken place — the linkage of a spoken tongue with the personal pride of people who fear extinction if their language were to vanish. Precisely what kind of extinction, though, do such individuals face, or better, fear that they face? When Alain talks of "disappearance," what does he mean? Surely the English-speaking people of Canada intend no such (literal) outcome; and surely the Canadians who speak French have no interest in a return to France (one way for them to "disappear"). No, they stay alive and end up living in a place where not everyone speaks French and where the Tricolor is not the uncontested national flag. I mention these two extremes because I have heard children in Quebec broach them, only to dismiss them. It follows, of course, in our talks, that they strive to figure out why their parents, and they along with them, feel so threatened, so vulnerable — by contrast, say, to hundreds of thousands of English-speaking people of humble background, who also struggle hard to get by, and feel in continual (social, economic, even political) jeopardy.

I never heard Alain address this matter directly, but his sister Annette, wonderfully proud of her native tongue and her city of Quebec, and not shy with her political and social opinions, even at thirteen, had an interesting way of discussing "the difference" between relatively poor or so-called working-class Anglophones and the Francophones of Canada (some of whom, by the way, are rather well-to-do). "It is not good to be poor," she said, "but to be poor and listen to people say bad words about you in another language is to be doubly poor." She pursued the subject further in this manner: "Our country is very big, and it's not as crowded as the States. My teacher says there's no comparison between Canada and the States, because we have a few big cities, but we have lots of land where there aren't many people; in your country, there are hundreds of cities, and many, many more people. Maybe if there were more Canadians who came from other countries (besides Great Britain and France) we'd be more like the States; we'd be a 'melting pot.' Our teacher says the States, they are a 'melting pot.' Here there are the Anglophones and us. They speak their English, and they remember their Queen, and they won the wars a long time ago, and when people speak their language, they've had a real big advantage. The rules are in their favor. They're the insiders! You open your English mouth, and before you know it, people are listening! They've decided you count; you mean something; you're not just sending Indian smoke signals out of your mouth — you're speaking, and you're 'the kind who's important.' My father remembers an Anglophone teacher who used to tell him and his friends that they shouldn't 'waste time' in school. You know why? She said they weren't 'the kind who's important,' and so there's no point in studying. You know why they weren't 'the kind who's important'? One guess! They spoke French! They were French! If you want to be important, you've got a lot in your favor if you're an Anglophone and a lot against you if you're a Francophone — that's what my father learned, and that's what he says we should never forget. All the time, all the time, he says we should never forget.

"It's getting to be different, now. No question! We have made Canada *ours*. It used to be part of Great Britain — that's what the

Anglophones have thought; but now it's *French* as well as *English*. My mother and father, they sometimes say they can't believe it's all happened — that our beautiful French language is just as important in Canada as the English language. In Quebec, we can speak French and not think we're strangers or that we're bad, and belong in some home where they take care of dumb people who can't be on their own. My mother said, in her day (when she was my age), to speak French meant you weren't 'really' Canadian; you were a foreigner who hadn't given up the old country and joined the new country. But now to speak French is to be Canadian — that's what the sign says on our street! *'Parler Français Est Être Canadien.'* "

The time comes when one simply bows before such a phenomenology[4] — the statements and drawings of children and the existence of such signs present a collective "appearance" (as Husserl and his disciple Edith Stein[5] would put it), which has its own definite significance. From a more "existential" point of view, this identification of language with nationality, and of both with "being,"[6] may also be one of those irreducible psychological givens. To be sure, one can move from the philosophy of Husserl to psychoanalysis and see in the swift current of a sensual French tongue all sorts of symbolic possibilities — the "oral" and the "maternal" side of life continually possessing a mouth with its utterances. So I heard a pediatrician friend of mine in Quebec, eager to affirm what he was sure I believed, and wanted him to confirm. I told him that French was, of course, a language of great power and nuance — a marvelous instrument of human expression, and no doubt, for millions of children in Canada, not to mention France, associated with the earliest of memories: mothers using words, and fathers, too. Still, in French Canada the French language has become the foundation for a contemporary political struggle — a reason for people to try to come to a new set of terms with their history, their present social and economic situation. I doubt whether the psychology of language use, in itself, can be quite the major issue for Canada's children.

Canada's Francophones have, indeed, been somewhat isolated over the decades — as it is harder for Americans of any background to be, in our much more crowded nation, our socially mobile, polyglot population. For Alain and Annette, for their steadfastly French-speaking, conservative Catholic parents, Quebec *is* another country, when compared with, say Ontario, which for them is a hunk of America that just happens to be called part of Canada. Children like these show a visitor that they *are* the language they speak, not only because using it makes them human beings (the creature that, through words, obtains a foothold upon consciousness, upon reflection, upon the self as an object, as some have put it), but also because its use enables them to make particular human claims on behalf of one segment of one nation. "If we didn't speak French, we wouldn't be Canadian," I heard Annette say one day, and at that I really took notice: What could she *possibly* mean? She saw me readying for the question, the feigned impassivity a cover for a surge of incredulity — and responded with this: "Oh, we'd just be people who were conquered by the British who came here and we'd be like them, and they haven't gone back home yet, but if they did, we'd be like them, and not a proud people."

I didn't even bother to explore the meaning of that "yet." Her "reality testing" is excellent; she is no fool about Canada's social and political history; she knows that Vancouver, Toronto, Ottawa, and a host of other cities and towns are not about to be depopulated by a mass, trans-Atlantic migration eastward to London, Yorkshire, or Dorset. She knows that nationalism is both a political and psychological fact, that one lives in a country, is a citizen of it, has voted or will vote in it, possesses sentiments and attitudes about it. But nationalism is also (she is saying) an almost spiritual matter — of the pride one feels, or fears losing. To continue to speak French, I was being told, means to have resisted becoming a beaten remnant; means to be proud survivors who will eventually triumph, who can wait and wait, outwait history itself! Now, smug pride is our most universal, human companion, the most grievous of sins, and the most likely one to confront us, minute after minute, in our lives. Vanity, vanity, all is vanity — including the way in which we want to appear, to be heard speaking, to be described by others. For Annette, for others, the French language offered a chance for distinction, for remaining alive, even, in the spiritual sense, the psychological and social sense — no matter the risk of proper pride turning to sinful pride. There was no other real choice, she and others seem to feel, in a country with Canada's history, geography, cultural composition — so she told me, time after time. She also let me know, as had other children elsewhere, how cogently and tenaciously children can take the measure of the world, make its (nationalist) *raisons d'être* their own.

In every totalitarian country the government is quite aware that children can become explicitly nationalistic when prodded, whether at home or school or because of events. Nicaragua has the Young Sandinistas, even as Fidel Castro has his Isle of Youth, to which come young people from all over the world — or, rather, that part of the world which is proudly "Marxist-Leninist." Perhaps (I've been saying at occasional moments in this book) some of us who live in the capitalist democracies fail to notice how our own children learn political values — but I shall come to that matter in Chapter VII. Here I want to emphasize how hard the Polish government (like the *commandantes* who run Nicaragua) has tried to persuade its children of the virtues of Communism, but to little effect.[7] In fact, the words one hears from Polish children, even those whose parents are intimately connected to the Communist Party, encourage one to realize what a farce indoctrination with nationalism can be among children or within families. For some forty years the Polish government, with all the power a highly centralized regime can muster, has attempted to teach two generations of children a version of history, economics, politics, and not least, social ethics — to establish what a society ought to be like, as against what societies have been like. But this persistent educational effort has been rewarded by obvious failure — for children by the millions have clung tenaciously to *their* political and moral view of things. *What* view do they hold to? one asks — knowing full well at least some of the answer from even a cursory reading of Western newspapers: the view of the Roman Catholic Church, and that of a traditional Polish culture, passed on for generations.

Yet, such correct responses don't quite exhaust an educational issue that turns out to be extraordinarily complex — the way in

which a host of influences have worked upon a population, sometimes supporting one another, sometimes at odds with one another.
Much neglected in some analyses, I believe, has been the Polish
language[8] itself — and yes, the view Poles have had of other languages, such as French and German and English, not to mention
Russian. As with the children of "French Canada," Polish children
have been taught to make so much of their spoken tongue that
one wonders if any language could be expected to bear so heavy
an (ideological) burden. A boy, Josef, just turned thirteen, is at
pains to tell an American (in Warsaw for the first time) about the
"special" qualities of his country. As he begins there seem to be
no surprises — the usual references to geography and history —
but soon the language comes up: "We've been a big country once,
and we've had to keep the Russians out, and it was always hard.
But we prayed and fought — that's what you have to do. And we
talked! My grandmother always tells us to remember that every
time we open our mouths to say something, we're telling the
Russians we're *Polish,* and the Germans, and anyone who's listening. It's *our* language, not theirs. Their missiles won't wipe out
Polish — and they can keep talking their [blankety-blank] Russian,
and the Germans can keep talking their [blankety-blank] German."

I have deleted his expletives, as the saying goes — the boy's
curses upon the Russian language and the German language. His
mother requested that I do so, lest her son's reputation be tar-
nished! But the boy only said what many other Polish children,
not to mention their parents, can be heard saying, repeatedly,
about the languages used by their nation's two powerful, historical
antagonists: the coarse ugliness of the sound of German, the tire-
some and stupid, if not animal-like sound of Russian. Beauty, lying
in the eye of the beholder, lies also in the ear of the listener —
as one tries to suggest, occasionally, to a bright child in Warsaw.
But Josef, at thirteen, would have no part of an American's effort
at objectivity: "We know these people. Your country is far away
from the Russians and the Germans. Here, we are next door to
them. The Germans want to eat you up, and so do the Russians.
Poland has always turned to France, my father says. French was
our favorite language. [His father is an engineer, knows English

and German, but prefers French, and would never speak German or learn Russian!] French is a beautiful language. I wish I could learn it some day. [What irony! The superiority of French asserted in Poland — while Josef talks about Polish rather in the way French Canadian children sometimes talk about their language, with the apprehensive stubbornness of those who feel themselves under attack, in dire straits.]

"I wish, to tell you the truth — that I could go away, live in Paris or London. There is a future there. Not here — there is no future here. I have seen that train come, from Paris to Moscow, and from Moscow to Paris. Everyone in Warsaw, including the people in our government, would like to get on that train when it's headed West. No one wants to go East. In Paris we'd be free to say what we want. We'd be free of stupidity — that's what my father says is the *real* problem here: a stupid system, and stupid people running it. Poland wasn't supposed to end up like this! We're not stupid: we don't sound stupid, the way the Russians and the Germans do — the noises they make, talking. It hurts. We hold our hands over our ears!"

A surprisingly sharp tongue, for a boy who is quiet, a bit withdrawn. The interviewer is primed with questions about the Church, about political indoctrination in the schools — only to hear, yes, militant espousal of a nation, but directed at the words its people use, the sound of those words, the sense of fluent authority they convey to children who think of other languages as rapacious, bestial, and, at the least, thoroughly grating to the ear. Moreover, a bit of mysticism works in Josef's mind as he reminds his guest (and himself, too, carried away with enthusiasm for his own idea, once he has heard himself express it: a true intellectual in the making!) that Latin for centuries was the Church's language — and so, says this young social and cultural and political critic, "Poland was twice saved."

Would he please explain that terse remark? Yes, most certainly: "My father is not very religious. To be honest, I'd have to say that he's a scientist, and he doesn't know if God exists, or if He doesn't exist. But he never misses Church; he loves to go to Church. He says he sits there and remembers his mother and father sitting there, with him, when he was a little boy. My grandfather was a cellist. I think of him, sitting on his favorite chair, holding the cello, and playing his favorite music, Bach. He died a year ago, of a stroke. He was sitting at the table waiting until his tea was strong enough, and suddenly he put his head down on his arms. My grandmother thought he'd fallen asleep, then she heard little noises in his throat; they were gurgles, she told me later. He had died in a second or two — after the attack made him lower his head. Everyone said: I should die that way. Everyone but my father: he wants to be able to say goodbye to people. He told me he'd like to make his last speech, with all of us around to hear, and then die while listening to some of his father's favorite records: Bach, Mozart, Chopin, Debussy! My grandfather had wide taste!

"My grandfather would go to Church a lot — but my father says he wasn't the most believing one in the church on Sunday. He used to tell my father that he loved to listen to the music, and he loved to hear the Latin Mass — more music! I remember him telling me and my two cousins that the Russians have no idea what Latin means — that you can say anything in Latin and know they're too ignorant to understand; and the Germans, many of them aren't Catholics, and the ones who are, they are the same people Caesar defeated, and he describes them in his *Gallic War:* they are *bellicosi*, warlike, and they are *barbari*, barbarians, and the lesson is: History doesn't change, it just brings all of us here to learn the truth, and then we die. My grandfather said that; he wrote that, in his last letter to his sister. My father made me memorize the letter! It was mailed after the old man's death. My father copied the letter before sending it on to the old sister, my father's aunt, who lives in London. Her husband was there during the war. He'd been in the Polish Army; he fought Hitler, and Stalin, and escaped to England, through Sweden, I think. He never wanted to come back here, and yet he told us in his letters that he'd die Polish. He learned English in London, and so did my father's aunt, and they spoke English sometimes, when they had to — but mostly they spoke Polish. My father's aunt said that her husband spoke only Polish the last year or two of his life. He refused to speak English. When they went to France on their vacation he refused to speak French. He was a true patriot! That's what the award said, that he got from the English government, I think, a long time ago. He was called 'a true patriot of Poland.'

"My father says that in Church, hearing the Latin, he could forget about Russia and Germany and Czechoslovakia, and he could think of Jesus and the disciples, and the Romans and St. Paul, trying to convert them and the Greeks, and the time when we had our land here without armies, occupying armies, on the land. We've always been Poland. The priest tells us our nation is our Polish people praying in our Polish language to God; but father says our nation is our Polish people remembering our Polish history, and speaking Polish, and being glad that Latin is still known by the priests and the bishops. My father taught himself Latin, and he's going to teach me Latin when I'm a little older. Those Russians, they could never learn Latin!"

Which Russians does he have in mind? one wonders. There is no point in quibbling with a boy who aches for his beloved country's sad, grim fate. Still, he himself is neither sad, nor grim. He truly loves Poland, the Polish language. He thinks the Polish Catholic Church has been given a special human authority by the people that transcends even its divine, transcendent purpose and so he loves the Church, too, as does his agnostic father: "The Church is keeping the torch of our country going, and that's the best thing it could be doing. My father says he doesn't only sit in Church now — the way he used to — but he gets down on both his knees and says 'Thank you' ten or twenty times. He's not sure who's there to be thanked! But he thanks Him, Jesus! Jesus helped save Poland, and we're going to keep saving our country."

He repeats himself, reminds anyone within hearing distance of his voice (which here is raised a bit) that the mere act of flexing those vocal cords in the particular way that enunciates the Polish language is an act of assertion, of national endurance and preservation, of defiance. He repeats himself with the spoken animus of a child, a Polish youth, inveighing against his nation's traditional, conquering enemies. He declares a skeptical contempt for the bureaucrats of Warsaw who run the government: "They think Russian. They kneel to the Russians. If they speak Polish, it is in order to hide the truth. They are not our people; they should be living in Moscow, or Kiev; they belong, better, in Siberia."

Perhaps this boy is exceptional, I think — until I think better of it. Surely most Polish children aren't so conscious of their language, their superior cultural traditions — or so I insist to myself as I try to describe in my notebook what he would have me believe about his countrymen: that they are decent, thoughtful people, intellectually accomplished, musically sensitive, heirs to Rome and Galilee, to the entire Western religious, scientific, artistic tradition. Yet, if many Polish children lack his kind of national pride, they are not without their own equivalent of his loyalty to the language, to the historical memory, and to a Church that is the repository of so much of a nation's hopes.[9]

"I know we'll win; I know they'll never take our country from us, even if they invade us," a boy who lives next door to Josef announces with clear conviction. His name is Stefan, and he is of much less educated background than Josef. Still, the twelve-year-old boy is full of delight as he talks about Poland, about its past, its soldiers who fought bravely and well, its people who have suffered much, but have never groveled at the feet of those who (through mischief and an ill-deserved superior might) conquered a great people's earthly territory. That is the point — Poland's pride! Perhaps Stefan's very insistence bespeaks the vulnerability, the repeated defeats, the many betrayals, hence the constant apprehensiveness of these children, attentive listeners to their parents' melancholy stories. These are children who draw and draw and draw what they say and say and say: Poland lives in its people's words and songs and unforgotten tales of yesterday, and in its humor, some of it lighthearted, some bitterly shrewd and sardonic: "Reagan is surrounded by one hundred bodyguards; there is one traitor and he doesn't know which one. Mitterand has one hundred lovers; one has VD, but he doesn't know which one. Jaruzelski has one hundred officers; one is intelligent and he doesn't know which one."

This is not a child's joke, but the girl, Sophia, whose father tells it, can laugh with great enthusiasm at hearing it one more time, and she is a mere eleven years old — weary, too, about the prospects for her country, and eager to figure out a way of affirming its life for the entire length of her life: "I know some of my friends wish they could go to your country, the United States, but I don't want to leave here. I wish we could get those packages from Chicago, like my friends do, but my mother is good at the stores. She can figure out which line to join! She leaves one line and starts standing in another. It's her nose, she says. Some others follow her, because they know her luck! She told us the secret: When her corns hurt, it's time to move. My father says she knows when to make her corns hurt. If she moves around, they don't; if she stands still, they do. Her nose dictates to her feet! There's still no law that says you have to *stay* in a line — but some do; they get paralyzed, my mother says.

"She prays and she sings our country's songs, and sometimes she knits. She says we enjoy our food better than we'd enjoy Chicago food; but she says not to believe every word we hear come from her these days! When she feels low, she takes a flower to the Cross in the Square. Let the soldiers keep taking them away! We win! Our crosses won't always disappear. We can see the Cross of the Church, and the Cross of Flowers will be there as long as we want it to be! When I grow up I'd like to grow flowers for my country, and food, and I'd give it to my friends, and not to the government. There is always something you can do for Poland!"

She tells *her* joke, meaning one she hopes "the others" (her friends in the Warsaw apartment house where she lives) haven't been telling: "Why is there no underground subway in Warsaw? Because the underground is already full!" She goes further, insists that it be told, what she has heard grown-ups and children her age alike say — how *rich* the Communist Party members are, how insolent and exploitative, the red bourgeoisie: "Do you know that these are the people who have become the enemies of our Poland? They are crooks. My mother says they take all the good things, the food and the clothes, and they kick around the Polish people; they are agents of the Russians. They must never sleep! They must be afraid of the worst nightmares!"

She had once had a few nightmares of her own, she says. They were worst during the early days of martial law. She thought her

country would disappear; but no, her parents reassured her constantly that such a catastrophe would never take place. After sharing that information she gladly obliges a request to draw a map —
to show her country on paper. She draws Poland, big and pleasing,
with stretches of green, with the sea to the north and mountains
to the south — and no other nation there, only the thick black
borders of her own country (Figure 9). She explains: "I don't want
to draw 'them': they are all bad ones, and we pray God will tell
them what the truth is. When Jesus comes here and starts settling
His scores, He'll make sure our Poland gets what we deserve, and
He'll get rid of those other ones, I know He will. He may be kind,
but He won't be kind with the people who have been so greedy,
and tried to take our land and our food and turn us into their
servants and kill our people."

Sophia's map is that of a country surrounded by thick black —
in mourning, perhaps. The boundaries, in their extraordinary
thickness and apparent solidity, mark a nation's territorial reality.
Words are absent, even those which designate cities. It is obvious
what country this is — but in case of doubt, one is given symbols:
the crosses that designate the eternal meaning of Poland, along
with its agricultural land, its ocean front, its hilly stretches. A sun,
full and beaming, is placed directly over the country. No clouds.
A mixture, it seems, of a nation nearly quarantined but specially
blessed.

Through all the barriers of language and martial law, of fear and
anxiety, these Polish children prove themselves to be marvelously
outspoken and dramatically confident. They are, indeed, in love
with their country, conscious of its politics, eager to serve its larger
(if you will, eternal, or transcendent) purposes. Their Church is
their protector in a very special way, and they know it. We in
America have *read* all this, too, and we *know* it — and yet, to hear
boys and girls of ten or twelve, declaring in no uncertain terms
their *amor patriae,* their never-ending loyalty to a church, a language, a long tradition of folksongs, holidays, architecture, is to
be reminded how vividly and energetically nationalism can take
hold in the young. "I speak Polish," the boy Josef could say with
such conviction and joy — and then declare: "No one can ever

stop me from speaking Polish. Even if there was a missile with a nuclear bomb on it right next to us, here on this street, we'd still be speaking Polish, and we'd still keep our flowers coming [to the Cross of Flowers in Victory Square, Warsaw, a symbol of Solidarity's struggle, the Church's struggle, Poland's struggle]. My friend's grandmother says that when we die, God will take us, and when He hears us speak Polish, we will quickly go to Heaven, but before we go, He says to us: 'I know you've already suffered, you've had your hell with those Russians and those Germans, so it's all sunny days ahead, now.' I hope that's how it ends! I don't know."

Josef does know, however, that there is great vitality and thoughtfulness in many of the people his parents know, in some of his teachers, who, though they pay lip service to a pitiable state bureaucracy, slip over all sorts of clever and funny and deeply touching messages to the students entrusted them. There is no point in turning sentimental about the Polish nation's predicament. It is not very auspicious now or in any foreseeable future. Nor ought millions of people to be described with easy words of praise — a puzzled and saddened visitor's gratuitous farewell. But the visitor experiences not *only* regret and deep worry for these Warsaw children. They hold their heads up, go about their days, find their pleasures in games, in a ride on a streetcar, in poking fun at political leaders or their servants and visible representatives, the police, the military. When a child such as Josef proclaims not only his solidarity with Solidarity, but his commitment to a nation, it isn't whistling in the dark, regardless of the geopolitics of any coming decade, or century. He believes in the power of a language he is sure will not perish from the earth.

In one macabre drawing Josef even extracted a measure of survival for Poland out of speculation that Russia and the United States would rain missiles upon each other, and Poland, in between, would be spared (Figure 10). When he finished this project — a virtual arch of missiles, dozens of them, stretching from Moscow to Washington, he took a moment to contemplate the Warsaw, the Poland he'd marked prominently between, and he began to pull back from the scenario: "I wouldn't want to be here if the whole world, in every direction, was destroyed. But as long as the rest of the world is around, we'll be around, our Polish nation. The priest told my friend last Sunday, after Church, that he is sure Jesus has learned Polish, because we pray harder to Him, and more often, that others do. I hope so. We need all the friends we can find — and if they can speak Polish, that's the best." He is raising his arms in a gesture of national affirmation, and his voice, too — that Polish voice he has learned to treasure, to connect with one country's beating, pumping heart. True, the heart can pound, become arrhythmic, bleed, give out altogether. But Josef has seen pictures of "The Bleeding Heart of Jesus," and heard references to "Poland's Bleeding Heart," and he will tolerate no cautionary medical reminders. A nation's heart doesn't stop, ever, he reminds the visitor — not as long as he, Josef, can refute nihilism and fear by using bright, solid, flowing Polish words.

One problem, however, does continue to trouble him and other Polish children — how to handle the scorn, the vigorous contempt they so often feel toward other Poles, the hundreds and thousands who are Communist Party members, government functionaries, policemen, and soldiers. They, too, speak Polish, are Polish. If the Polish language and the culture it bears are to serve as marks of distinction for a people who fear disappearance, then that language must prove to have a magical, compelling grip on those who use it. No wonder, then, the vehemence directed at state functionaries by so many Polish children. Josef not only calls them "traitors," as his parents do, he goes further: "the worst traitors in the world"; and then, with a fierce look of disgust, and also with angry futility, he announces that no word in Polish is suitable for such people. They are beyond his moral imagination, he insists, their motives are incomprehensible to him. "If it were greed, we'd understand," he says, but he rejects this prosaic impulse as not sufficient: "Worse than greed." The American suggests what he's heard other Poles say, "murder." Yes, that will do — "murder of a people." The Polish language just barely accommodates such a pronouncement, and Josef, saying it, lowers his head noticeably.

In all the years of this research, I comment to myself — including work in South Africa where a government has decreed blacks noncitizens — I have never heard the equal to the fierce, intransigent estrangement of these Polish children from their own government. Their "political socialization" serves a people's spirit, a language and cultural legacy, a beloved Church, rather than a national state, with all its guns, planes, tanks, with its control over all the secular institutions.

VI

RACE AND NATIONALISM: SOUTH AFRICA

For more than a decade I have been working in South Africa, and even now I find it painful to distill what I think I know into words — not only the frustrations, the inadequacies, the melancholy, the outrage such a country inspires in visitors, but the feelings I sense in its own people, as I hear them (Alan Paton's chosen verb) cry,[1] and cry, and cry. An Afrikaner by ancestry, a teacher who has broken with his fellow Afrikaners, with his own family even, on the question of apartheid, says: "There are no tears left, only the saddest feeling imaginable in the gut, an emptiness that means all hope is gone." It might be best to begin with him, with those Afrikaners, with their children.

On my first visit, in 1974, to that beleaguered, tormented, utterly perplexing country, I was introduced to a black South African who had been "banned" for two years.[2] He could receive one visitor at a time, under specified conditions. I was driven to his home, in Cape Town, which was, in effect, a continuing prison. (He could not leave it.) I sat there with him for several hours, and he was brilliantly knowing about not only his own country, but mine. He asked me many questions about how black people were doing in the United States, about Dr. Martin Luther King, Jr., and Robert F. Kennedy, whose visit to South Africa in 1966 he well remembered; and he kept asking me to ask him questions. I put to him the first-time visitor's usual ones (I was then trying to learn how the crazy apartheid system got going in the first place) and I was offered the usual answers, though with patience and consideration. How boring the effort must have been! Another of these ever-so-sympathetic whites, oozing compassion and moral indignation but lacking any notion at all of what either he or anyone else might do!

I made my nervous, guilty declarations and avowals, which included a determination to stay longer, to return and document what is happening, to tell others in "the States" what was seen and heard. Meanwhile, he listened and listened, this stoic, soft-spoken, shrewdly watchful man, with a broad smile that covered (I would later begin to realize) years of terrible pain, torture and more torture, and no doubt, smouldering rage reserved for — whom? I suspect, from what I've heard him say over the years, that even the dreams *he remembers* preclude direct expression of that rage. Once, with a wry turn to his smile, and after posing some questions to me about dreams, their nature and purpose (and thereby awakening my professional curiosity, of course, as to *why* these questions), he made an end of that segment of that day's conversation with a brisk wave of his right hand: "Then the dreams we don't remember — they are the ones that protect us!" I didn't know what to say. Besides, I realized that he wasn't asking for one of those smug nods that we psychiatrists occasionally peddle to our eager consumers. He was telling me something I hadn't thought about — maybe even giving me in a sentence a dramatic new theory of the significance of dreams for millions of this planet's humiliated and betrayed people: the dream as the last island of individuality, the dream as the one repository of secrets no torturer can extract, because the victim is no more privy to them than the bloodthirsty jailer.

This gentle South African man and gentleman (a man regarded by the government as "a dangerous Zulu revolutionary communist"), this learned, carefully discerning talker urged me, strongly and again and again, to get to know the Afrikaners, to talk with their children first, to learn what was happening in their lives. I asked him why, expecting the observation that it is important, so to speak, that the enemy's mentality be known. But he had his own, unforgettably original way of framing explanations. To begin with: "You see, there is a lot for someone like you to learn here from the Afrikaners. They are in constant psychotherapy, you know." Silence. I tried to figure out what that generalization meant, to remind myself that I'd heard quite the opposite before I left for South Africa, that Afrikaners had no great interest in psychiatry and psychoanalysis. Finally, I surrendered with a request for an explanation. He quickly obliged: "We are their psychiatrists. Without us, they'd be in great despair. How lucky for them that we don't see them only by the hour or the week. We see them constantly, all the time: twenty-four-hour therapy! We treat them for everything — feelings of inferiority, worthlessness, inadequacy; feelings of envy or rivalry; feelings of anger and bitterness and jealousy and depression. Whatever their 'problem,' as you people say it, I believe, one of us is there to give them the needed lift, to listen to them, to supply them with an 'outlet,' to help them get a 'perspective.'

"I have a friend in Cape Town who is a psychiatrist, and I've read his articles. Whenever he describes his troubled patients, and the treatment they need and get, I think of my mother and my father and my uncles and aunts, and all the 'treatment' they've been giving the Afrikaner families they've been 'seeing' for these many, many years! Do you think, one day, when apartheid ends, the South African Medical Association will grant us, millions of us, our accreditation as psychotherapists? Of course, accreditation is not our biggest problem! Actually, our 'problem' is not unusual, I know. I've read that many doctors, many psychiatrists can do a good job helping others, but damn it, can't seem to do a thing for themselves! That is our major difficulty, and I see no immediate answer for it!"

It took me some time to shake off this image — the blacks of South Africa doctoring the mental ills of their Afrikaner patients! Meanwhile, my interlocutor kept pressing me to go see "them"; and finally, I said yes, I'd do so — whereupon he warned me it would not be an easy matter to arrange such a project: "You'd have trouble getting into Soweto [the great black district of Johannesburg], because foreign white people aren't supposed to be there, except with the administrative permission of the government. But we can always get around *that* obstacle. Once there, with your experience in the American South, you'll hear a lot from our children; and you'll be moved, I have no doubt about it, and you'll go home, and you'll tell what you observed, and you'll move some of your countrymen, I have no doubt about it. But I really do wonder whether your countrymen need this report of yours — unless for *their* therapy: to hear about how awful it is 'over there,' and so to feel better for being where they are, and of course, *who* they are! No, I think you and your countrymen would profit more from any knowledge of our Afrikaner people you can obtain; I think we'd all like to know a bit more of what it is that is happening inside *them*.

"I've had them beating me — beating the living shit out of me — and I've held on to my sanity, I swear (if, indeed I have; I leave that for you to decide!), by asking this question, precisely, of myself: Who are these people on this, God's earth, and how did they ever get to be as they are? So, you'd certainly be satisfying my curiosity — or maybe I shouldn't be happy that you might do so! *Then* what would I ask myself, the next time around, in one of those jolly torture 'sessions' they call them, 'interrogatory sessions'? Well, leave *that* to my ingenuity! I'll come up with a question or two! You — well you go ahead! Try finding an answer to my 'torture question'! I'll be much interested, believe me! But as I've said, it would not be so easy to do this sort of work. It's easier for you to talk with a banned black man than any Afrikaner, walking freely on Jo'burg's [Johannesburg's] streets!"

I wasn't quite sure, at the time or later, as I thought about this challenge, whether the "you" in that last sentence meant anyone who might want to become acquainted with Afrikaners, or someone such as me, an American, a psychiatrist who worked in the civil rights movement during the early 1960s, a presumed critic, antagonist. As my wife listened to the tape, she felt strongly that this eloquent and discerning black man, who had spent years taking the measure of apartheid's power, both in South Africa and abroad (where South Africa lives or dies, economically, by virtue of its complex involvement in the gold and diamond markets), was simply stating a fact of life — that the Afrikaners tend to be distrustful even of their English-speaking fellow white South Africans, to say nothing of us outsiders who they know are opposed to their racial and social policies, and who they know would naturally be more disposed to talk with, say, the black people of Soweto, or their strong white allies, such as Helen Suzman,[3] at that time (1974) the only real opponent of apartheid in the South African Parliament, or any number of students or professors at the old, distinquished, and liberal University of Cape Town. Still, I wondered what the point of it was — to attempt meeting with Afrikaner families, and especially, their children. I would hear the doctrines of apartheid upheld, surely — and I wasn't sure how much of such talk I could stomach. Nor was I in the least convinced that I could build up trust among some Afrikaner families, even if a few of them did agree to let me come and visit with them when I next came to South Africa.

I went through the motions of establishing contact with Afrikaners[4] — but with small enthusiasm; and I was ready at one time to abandon the project altogether. But I met yet another human being whose moral authority, whose utter decency and thoughtfulness, whose courage quite overwhelmed me. This man was born in the rural Transvaal of deeply pious and conservative Afrikaner stock.[5] At twenty-three, while attending Witwatersrand University, he had gone through an agony of ethical reflection and self-arraignment — had turned solidly against apartheid, had given his considerable energy and intelligence to working with interracial groups daring to oppose the government's policies. The result was almost complete estrangement from his own large family, which he still dearly loved. He was such a modest, self-effacing person, so tactful and considerate, so lacking in self-righteousness, or the arrogance to which some of us fall prey as we denounce others, and preach our own beliefs — that I was jolted when he suddenly became quite firm with me, almost like a schoolmaster in the way he addressed me: "I wish I could take you to some Afrikaner homes, to the children; but you had better make your own way. You can — and you really should. You must! It is too easy for us, the 'liberals' and 'progressives' of this country, to write off the Afrikaners. The

English have been doing it, I'm afraid, ever since they came here. Their smugness has not helped our country at all! I notice that people like you, who come here from the United States, are quick, too quick, to call Afrikaners 'fascists' or 'racists' and much worse — never having really talked to an ordinary Afrikaner at all. Look, I don't defend what has happened here; but I think you owe it to yourself to understand this country's social and economic history; and you owe it to yourself to learn what my people have to say for themselves — *not* what others will tell you about them, including me. I get so overcome by bitterness and hate, that there are days when I wish every single Afrikaner in this country could be shipped off — sent to Holland or France or Germany, wherever we belong. But of course, we *belong* here — so we're taught, starting with the first words we learn!"

There was a good deal more, powerful in its populist sentiment — a well-to-do intellectual frankly stating his people's fateful nineteenth- and twentieth-century predicament, not in order to defend the present government's program, quite the contrary; but to shed light for a stranger upon various betrayals, deceits, condescensions, manipulations — history's dubious gifts that preceded the electoral triumph of the Nationalist Party in 1948, and with it, the onset of apartheid as the latest assault (by no means the first) perpetrated on colored and black people in South Africa. By the time I'd spent an afternoon with this man I had no doubt that I'd try, at least, to hear what I could hear from people he still regarded as his.

I must admit that at times I heard remarks all too painful and sad — not totally unlike comments I've heard in Alabama and Mississippi, and, indeed, in Massachusetts and Connecticut and New York and Illinois. There have been moments, in fact, when the sentiments, the resentments and frustrations, have sounded all too familiar. In schools, in homes, in churches of South Africa I have been asked to heed all the worries and fears I heard expressed in the segregationist South of, say, 1960, or in the Boston of 1974, when school busing began.[6] I suppose the urgency is greater in South Africa — but I am not so sure, really. As my wife and I play the tapes, read the transcripts, make our comparisons, we have to conclude that we've yet to hear Afrikaners come up with a racial statement we can't, alas, match with its American equivalent. On the other hand, and very important, today's United States government is not today's South African government — even as the racial difficulties each country faces are, in many respects, quite obviously different.

Best, now, to turn to Petrus,[7] a charming Afrikaner lad whose father is a high school principal in a small town of the Orange Free State. When I first met Petrus he was only seven. He is now, at this writing, in college. When I met him, as a child, he had all he could do to keep quiet during the long Dutch Reformed church services his family attended every Sunday. Now he goes to church eagerly on his own. For a while he thought of being a minister — and a professional soccer player as well! Now he is "headed" toward the law. For a while he was a fractious child, hence subjected to his father's tough disciplinary action, including use of the belt to the boy's rear. Now he stands ramrod straight, is polite without being obsequious, outgoing without being an overtalkative hustler. He is, really, a notably courteous person, ready always to make a visitor feel at home, eager to help him or her get to see a countryside he knows well enough to appreciate. For a while, too, he made all sorts of nasty, spiteful remarks about colored and black people. Now he is reticent on that score, and, like his father and his mother, acts thoroughly formal with their servants, and with other black or colored people. I do not think my presence makes any difference at all, in this respect — because after a decade of acquaintance, and after the wide range of behavior I've seen in words or deeds toward black and colored people, there seems to be no point in putting up one or another pretense. Besides, I have sometimes watched the boy and his parents without being known to be present; and most significant, I have talked with black people who know Petrus and his kin in the special and highly instructive way in which whites are known by blacks.

I find myself poring through a decade's notes and tapes and wondering where to begin, wondering what deserves prominent mention. I decide, on my most recent trip to South Africa, to talk with Petrus about this matter. When I do, he is a bit nostalgic as he peruses all the drawings and paintings we did together. (When I tell him of the consternation these have caused the South African customs authorities, who are not usually bored or indifferent, anyway, as they go through the belongings of entering or departing Americans, he is amused, even excited. He wants to know what they thought, what they said. I tell him they never told me what they thought, only wanted to know *whose* pictures I was carrying — and *why*. Fortunately, I had an explanatory letter from a prominent South African pediatrician — and Petrus made me promise to send him a copy.)

Here are some remarks of Petrus when he was twelve, on the occasion of the third anniversary of the Soweto riots. He still stood by them, now that he was eighteen: "The children there, they are being used. Why should boys and girls go and fight the police? That is not natural. There is a lot of trouble with our black people. They are tribes, and they fight their tribal wars. We have tried to keep them from killing each other. Do the Americans know that our tribes are not the same as their Negroes? My father says our country is to blame for the bad things people say about us, because we don't go abroad and explain this country — to the Americans, and the French, and the English, and the Italians, and the Portuguese. You know, we're getting lots of Portuguese here; they've moved from their past colonies, because the colonies are now communist countries; and they tell my father that they kept hearing bad, bad stories about South Africa, and they all were lies, they've found out now, after they've moved here.

"We don't know how to keep the blacks from fighting each other. They're very bad in their neighborhoods; they steal a lot, and they cut one another up. My uncle is a doctor and he saw terrible things when he worked in a hospital, when he was in training. He said that if a white man did to the blacks and the colored what they do to each other — we'd all want him jailed. He has taken pictures, but my father says the press in America wouldn't publish them. We get a bad break all over the world. People like to talk one way, and if you check up on them, you'll see they aren't living up to their word. That's why everyone wants to come here and get all the bad news they can find about us, and then go running home to spread the word about the terrible, terrible South Africans!"

At that, I reassured Petrus that it was, indeed, necessary for *his* thoughts to go on the record, so to speak — and he proceeded to repeat in slightly different language much of the talk immediately above. Then he told me (not the first white South African child to do so) how "outnumbered" the white people are in this country, and what such a state of affairs meant, in both the short and the long run. Even today, I recall the moment when I asked him how many black people lived in South Africa, and how many whites. This boy, usually so precise about what he knew or didn't know, told me without so much as a moment's hesitation, with no hint that he might be a little in error, that there were about a hundred blacks to every white, "maybe more." I asked him what the population of his country was. He said "about twenty-five million." I asked him how many whites there were. He said "about two million." [The number is five million.]⁸ I asked him how many blacks there are, and colored people. He said "all the rest," and then added this: "They cross our borders all the time. There are millions of them in those countries to our north. They are starving, and they envy us our country. They want to take away what we've got here. We know how to grow food, and build our cities and our mines, and they want to walk in and take it all away. We'll never let them get all of our cities, and our farms. Anyway, they wouldn't know what to do. They're not up to our level."

What does he mean by that comparison? I ask him for particulars. He says, tersely: "There's a big difference in intelligence." He won't elaborate. I press: "What do you mean?" He repeats himself, almost word for word. I try not to act or look critical, but I am sure that he senses otherwise — and finally, I change tack. I suggest we go back to drawing — something he likes to do in school, and in our meetings. I ask him what he might want to draw on that day, a Saturday. He has no ready response. I say: "Petrus, why don't you draw a picture that I can take home and show to others your age, and say, *here*, here is a picture a South African has drawn about his country, about its people." I know I am being vague and elusive, but I've given this speech to other children, in South Africa and my own country and South America and Europe, and sometimes it works rather well. The child sets to work, with an idea in mind — and soon enough, or not so soon, but in due time, I am handed a drawing or a painting: maps, national flags, people doing one or another kind of work, a landscape, words taken from coins or paper money — in sum, children's remembered national scenes, signs, symbols, slogans. Such representations have told me, rather quietly, what children have to say about their political life; and that morning Petrus was willing to join the ranks of those boys and girls, with an ambitious canvas.

He worked with paints, and proceeded efficiently with his project (Figure 11). It started out, I thought, as a simple memoir of South Africa's coastal life. As he was doing that phase of his work, I recalled that his family had taken him to Cape Town a few weeks earlier — hence the chosen subject this morning, I confidently concluded. But soon I began to see that Petrus had a fairly comprehensive agenda in mind — and eventually, I found myself thinking of Gauguin's monumental Tahiti triptych (1897):[9] "Where Do We Come From? What Are We? Where Are We Going?" The boy wanted to show me, pictorially, a history he had learned of his people — his version, perhaps, of the Voortrekker monument in Pretoria, a massive memorial to the Afrikaner experiences that culminated in twentieth-century South Africa.[10] For Petrus the beginning was in European trade, English and Dutch ships lusting after Asia's riches. Eventually the English turned on the Dutch settlers, hence the "war between the whites," as he called it. (He did *not* call it the Boer War!) He made sure I knew — and how *many* times Afrikaner children have told me this — about the British "concentration camps,"[11] which he painted with detail and a strange if grim magnificence, as if to remind me of a people's suffering, a people's endurance, a people's rise from slavery: "Don't you see, we were attacked by the British. They were dishonest, and they tried to take everything they could find — gold and diamonds and our land. They built the world's first concentration camps; that's what they called them. They rounded up our men and they treated them like animals. We had to march inland, and we went farther and farther, but they wanted more and more, and so they chased us. It wasn't so long ago. My grandparents heard all about it from their parents and their grandparents. It all took place in this century! We must never forget! In this world, people want to forget all this; they want to tell us we are wrong — about the black people. But no one wants to know what the British did to us; and the Zulus, the tribes, they were wandering around, and they were as poor as they are now, but they didn't want to see us settle and show the world what you can do if you work hard! That's the big trouble: The British are very good at getting others to do their dirty work, and the natives, the blacks, they don't know how to do much on their own. We have to tell them what to do."

After his concentration camp, he offers the viewer the productive power, the visual majesty of the veld — a boy's valiant attempt to evoke the land that is so very attractive, stunningly so in places, in his nation's countryside. He would explain this third part of his painting in these strong, even haunting sentences, some of them, I would later learn, first heard in Sunday school and remembered well: "We came here, and there was the bush, with wild grass growing. My father says the hills must have wondered who these strange people were! But we showed the hills. God had the sun smile on us. God told the skies to give us the water we needed. God asked the land to be kind to us; it took our seeds and gave us back our crops. We worked all the time, no vacations, only Sunday to pray to God. This is our country of South Africa — where its heart beats. We love our Fatherland; and we'll fight for it, and we'll die for it. In the [veld] school, my brother said he learned all about our history, and he learned songs, and he's taught them to me. I'll be going there in a year, maybe two. We learn about our ancestors, our people. Don't forget this part of our country when you return to America! The planes land in Jo'burg, but it's here that you see what's happened to South Africa since our people [the Afrikaners] first came here, a long time ago, to stop on the way to India!"

His triptych is exactly the kind of historical survey,[12] culminating in a celebration, which he and other Afrikaner boys of thirteen and fourteen are encouraged to make in the veld schools — a periodic retreat of a week, or longer, in which children learn "love of country" (as Petrus's father put it), patriotic songs, history and geography lessons, a military analysis of South Africa's contemporary situation with respect to its neighbors. Not least, the children are given constant instruction on the necessity of remaining true to their nation's "important values." What are they? I wonder aloud to Petrus. He is not slow to respond: "It is our people, the Afrikaner people, who will defend the country. The English, many of them, would flee. Not us. We want to keep all this the way it is [he moves his hand in a semicircle, pointing toward the stretch of fertile farmland outside the window, the small, lovely village beyond, and farther the gently sloping, lush green hills]. If we don't stand tough, South Africa will become a desert. You want to know what? [I nod.] I'll tell you: These tribes — if we left, the white people — they'd plunder everything, and then they'd leave. They wouldn't even stay here. There'd be no South Africa, after a few years. They'd retreat into *their* Africa, where the jungle is."

I interrupt, ask him as gently as I know how, whether it's really possible with any accuracy to make the kind of prophecy he's just offered. He looks sharply at me; he gets right to the point: "I know you don't believe us. You have to live here to understand our natives — these tribes, and the way we try to help them. They come here from all over; everyone wants to come to South Africa, from all their countries and homelands, because we've built the richest and strongest nation on the continent, and people get very jealous, and they want what we've got. But how did we get it? Not by complaining that the British were beating us up! They did! They are still full of themselves — very full. They hold their noses way up. But we laugh! It's our country, now, and they know it. They tried to turn us into their servants, but we left and built our own country, and finally, they surrendered and said: You're the leaders, and we'll do what you say. If we hadn't been here, the English would have left South Africa, the way they left Kenya and Nigeria and Ghana — and look at what those countries are like. They're the biggest mess in the world! But we are here! My father says, we're the backbone of the white people, and the British are the soft, pudgy flesh, the fat mainly!"

Still, I want to hear more about those "important values," and so I ask Petrus what they are, once more — hoping he won't merely repeat what he has told me so many times before, often with an assist or two (in the form of a quotation) from his father, who is a school principal and a small farmer, or from his minister, but never, I noticed, from his mother, a stocky, hardworking woman who cooks and cleans and prays and is usually shy to the point of uninterrupted silence. I hear this: "We must never have a second battle of Blood River [in which a handful of Boers killed more than a thousand Zulus, or so Petrus has been taught].[13] You know, our people made an agreement [a "covenant" it is called in many South African textbooks] that the day would be holy, if they won that battle, and they did. God was with us. He will always be with us, if we worship Him. Without His support, we'd disappear. All those tribes, the Zulu and the Bantu and the Xhosa, they'd swamp us; they'd bury us; they'd push us into the Atlantic Ocean and the Indian Ocean. It would be terrible, because they multiply like animals, and our big hope is that even though the Russians are sending them guns and tanks and lots of ammunition, they're just not smart enough to use what they get. Look what's happening in Rhodesia [he doesn't know, he says, the new name, Zimbabwe]. Without the white people, there'd be wild grass on the streets of Salisbury, and soon the UN would be shipping in food, because the blacks wouldn't know how to grow it — and they'd be asking for our help. We help a lot of African countries, but they won't admit it publicly."

He stops, and he can see that I'm ready to open my mouth and try to press him, yet again, to talk about "the really important values of his people." He abruptly stops talking about the rest of Africa, and returns to his native country, its discontents, its bright future, though — or so he believes it will be: "We have trouble here, but we have given the Kaffirs a better life than they'd ever dreamed they'd have, and I think they're grateful to us. I talk with them. I ask them questions. They are polite. They are good workers, if you keep after them. They speak our language. They are Christians — some of them, anyway. The trouble is, they have their own tribal customs. They're a strange people, our blacks. I wonder why God made them!"

Another pause, then another shift of direction: "You want to know what we believe in, my people? We believe in God, and in our Fatherland! We believe in being strong, working hard, and building our country — making it one of the greatest countries in the world. God gave us the land, and our gold, and our diamonds; He gave us a lot. If He hadn't liked us, and wanted to help us, He never would have brought us here, and given us all this. It's our job to be loyal to Him! We must say our prayers, at every meal. We must bow to Him, always. The worst trouble will come your way if you forget God. That's when a country goes to ruin, when the people forget Who made them, and why He made them; when the people stop going to Church, and only want to enjoy their vacations and their new clothes and they don't want to save, they just spend, they buy whatever they see that they like, and they don't ask if God would want them to buy that, or if they're doing what their Fatherland wants them to do. They just do what they want to do, and that's the beginning of the end of your country, when people are like that! You have to say your prayers and love your country. You have to ask God to protect your country. You have to sing our national anthem, and know the words, and remember our history, and be proud, proud as you can be, of being here, in the Orange Free State. We're the heart of our country, my father says, and our minister says, and we must remain as tough as we can be, and keep our army strong, and go and fight, if we have to fight; because, if we don't prepare ourselves, and stay ready all the time, we'll be drowned, and that will be the end of one of God's best experiments."

He sees me perk up when he uses that word "experiments." By now he is aware of ideas that elicit my attention, I begin to realize. He does not await the inevitable question: "My father says everyone in his school has to write a composition, before they graduate, on why our country is a great experiment of God's. The answer is that He has given us one of the richest countries there is, and He has the different people here, and He hopes we can all do what He intended us to do, and not disobey Him, our God. People in other countries [he looks directly at me with a lingering gaze] should try to understand our experiment here, but they don't. They call us all the bad names. They never think that they may deserve the names more than we do! My father says the world is full of hypocrites; they are people who claim to be better than us, and say we're evil people, but if you take a good look at them, you'll see — well, you'll see what a hypocrite is like! A hypocrite is someone who does the same thing he criticizes other people for doing! We had that word in school, and the Americans and the British were the examples the teacher gave us!"

He wants to pursue Europe and the United States with his newly acquired word, one he clearly enjoys possessing and using. He gives the standard speech about the grim fate of blacks in today's Britain, and about the long, sad, disedifying history of slavery in the United States, culminating in our Civil War. He knows the essential contours, as well, of our Reconstruction Era, and the early decades of the twentieth century, with a powerful Klan, and a much harassed, impoverished black population. I have ceased, by then, being surprised at this almost meticulous scholarship, about a foreign country,[14] in a boy yet to enter what we would call high school. His father is an amateur historian, I remind myself — though his field is "continental history," meaning France, Holland, Germany of the nineteenth century. But the truth is that I have met many Afrikaner children, boys and girls, on various visits to the country, and not one of them, it has turned out, doesn't know much more about American history that just about all my college students, even those majoring in history, know about South Africa's milestones, battles, political events. Petrus is aware of this important characteristic of his, of his fellow Afrikaner schoolchildren. Actually, I must say that the more we talked about the United States, the more complicated and subtle his interest appeared to be, I gradually realized: "Our minister tells us that everyone watches South Africa because everyone knows we're honest, and other countries tell lies — they talk about how nice they are to black people, and then treat them very poorly." Those words, spoken when he was fourteen, were followed by these: "We are trying to give the blacks their own countries. We're giving up our land, so they can have their land. In America there are Indian reservations, and here we have homelands. Our homelands have more freedom than your reservations, I know — our teacher explained the differences to us.

"I wish I could go to America. I'd never want to live there, but I've seen the movies and the pictures, and I know America is the strongest country in the world. America makes mistakes, big mistakes, but if there wasn't an America we'd all be in the worst trouble you can imagine. The Russians would have all their nuclear bombs, and we wouldn't be a match for them. They are building a big fleet of nuclear submarines, we've discovered, and they'll be outside our cities, trying to scare us. We've got to have help from the United States, because their navy is the strongest, and as long as they keep strong, the Russians will watch their step!

"I've heard that America has lots of farms, big farms, like we have; and they had gold, but most has been dug from the earth; and they have deserts, like we do, and big cities, and more television than any other country: there are programs on all day and all night! I'd like to see Hollywood, and the tall buildings in New York. I'd like to see the government buildings in Washington. I understand your roads are first-class — and you can drive on them from one end of the country to the other. I've always wanted to see the Eskimos. We had two classes on them, and we saw many slides. They seem like very good people; they stay to themselves, and don't go bothering other people. The worst thing to do, is to trouble people and not stay where your home is. If the English hadn't given in, and let all our black people go anywhere they wanted, we'd have things better here — the country wouldn't be in trouble. But we've been in worse trouble — and see, we've done well. [He points yet again with glowing pride to the rich, fertile agricultural land, and then to the town, a delightful and cozy place.] We'll be fine, here — so long as God gives us strength to stay together and fight for what we believe. Even a *billion* blacks — we could take them on, and win, provided we're united. If we fall apart and fight, Afrikaner brother against Afrikaner brother, then that's the end of us. My father doesn't worry about the blacks and the colored and the Indians. He doesn't worry about the English, either. He only worries about us, our own people. So far, we're together; but there are more and more arguments among our people. That's the scariest thing in the world — for us to split!"

I am surprised at his rather cavalier treatment of the English-speaking whites of South Africa; not at the obvious grudges and even outright contempt he bears toward them, but by his dismissal of their significance in a potential racial showdown, something discussed in Dutch Reformed homes and churches, where the Apocalypse of the New Testament, with its Armageddon, is considered worth sustained reflection by a people steeled for a last-ditch struggle with numerous potential antagonists.[15] Not that I hadn't heard a similar attitude among other Afrikaner children, perhaps less explicitly stated: The English are weak, divided, complacent, godless; in a real crisis, they'd flee to *their* homeland, England. Afrikaners have no such possible place to which they might repair — they have none and they want none. Afrikaners, that is, have "given" themselves to South Africa — so I hear it put — whereas the English simply live in South Africa, as a matter of convenience and great profit. No wonder Petrus draws the South African flag, again and again, with the two insert flags of the Transvaal Republic and the Orange Free State prominently featured, and the Union Jack treated like a footnote. If he had his way the Union Jack would be banished from this flag — and indeed, in one of many such flags he drew for me over the years, he crossed out the Union Jack with the black crayon available to him (Figure 12). Other Afrikaner children (one of them his cousin, a boy his age, in the same village) have simply left it out.

Some forty percent of South Africa's white people are of English ancestry,[16] and to talk with some of them is to hear no racial views very different from those one hears from Afrikaners. It is a foolish myth, the notion that the English are more "easygoing" with respect to black and colored people. Most English, so I've heard — mostly from other English! — seem readier to give a bit of ground here and there, yet are far from ready to share the franchise with blacks. Most Afrikaners, so almost all Afrikaners say, are ready to say *never,* on that subject. Yet, I have met, on my own, two dozen men and women of Afrikaner ancestry who detest apartheid, and are fighting in every way they know for universal suffrage — including all colored and black people; and I have met, I have to say, some people of English background who make Petrus, his cousin, their Afrikaner friends, seem somewhat more honest and moderate about their intentions and beliefs.

George Orwell, in *The Road to Wigan Pier*,[17] seems obsessed with the "smell" of the mine workers, not to mention bourgeois families whom he met in his journey north to Lancashire and Yorkshire. In *Down and Out in Paris and London*,[18] of course, he was even more explicit on that score — the odors among the poor, which he couldn't help noticing, and later, describing in his essays and books. I kept thinking of Orwell as I listened to South African children of English ancestry talk about black and colored people — an endless recital, it seemed, of their "body odor," the "stink" that emanates from them, "the ugly smells" they emit, the "foul air" one encounters in their presence. I heard such comments in Cape Town, in Johannesburg, in Durban, in villages along the Cape Peninsula and the Indian Ocean, until finally I began to realize that, in the absence of the Calvinist justifications and explanations that so many Afrikaners summon to support their unique system of racial segregation, many English must make do with a more personal code — with simple prejudices unbuttressed by God, by History, by Fate.

One boy, named Brian, whose father teaches at the University of Cape Town, and whose mother is a high school mathematics instructor, and who is only one week younger than Petrus, told me many times that he has "nothing against them, the Kaffirs" — meaning, he explained, in case I didn't know, "our black ones." He simply couldn't stand being near them, because he has asthma, and he often takes in deeper breaths than most people do, and "I tell you, it can be awful." I knew what the antecedent of "it" was, but I thought I'd better, nonetheless, ask "the question" that would prompt "the reply" — and I got one, all right: "You know, they're different. They don't react the same way — they don't think the same way. There's a different metabolism. They're slower. I don't know how to say it — they plain smell. Always! I've never got close to one that didn't; and the colored, too, even if they're lighter!

There's something that makes me want to vomit — so I keep my distance; I have to, because I don't want to get sick!"

A few minutes later Brian has turned to the "Yoppies," a name many English call Afrikaners. Another term Brian and his friends use is "Hairy backs." I ask him for the derivation of such expressions, get a blank look. I ask other children of English origin, get similar blank looks, shrugs of the shoulders — and I decide, rather than pursuing this etymological matter, simply to sit back and hear these children talk about Afrikaners, about black and colored people, as Brian did: "They're not smart, our Afrikaners; they mean well, but they're like stubborn children, my dad says, and if you cross them, then hold on tight, because they'll never forget it, and they can drive you mad with their complaints. They're sort of simple-minded — but they're good for our country, because they love to fight, and we need to be strong, and a pity to the native who dares challenge them. They'll die, rather than give in and say let's have a talk, chaps!

"My grandfather detests them. He says they're devious, and they love to play 'follow the leader.' They'll turn our country into a dictatorship, he's absolutely sure. My mother and father disagree; they think the Yoppies are exactly the right people to run the country now — until we've settled this racial thing. You need people who have *nerve*, who have *guts*, if you're going to keep our country from falling apart. That's what we're afraid of, you know, everyone: that there won't be a South Africa much longer, that we'll fall apart, split wide open. My father keeps money in London. His aunt lives there, and we could be out of here in twenty-four hours, he says, if it came to that. But with the Yoppies running the show, there seems no trouble in sight! Every time we get into trouble, they dig in, and the next thing you know, we're riding high again! You have to hand it to them!"

I was intrigued by the emphasis I'd heard him put (and other children, too) on the possibility that South Africa might fall "apart" — a telling use of that word, when you think about the doctrine of apartheid, apartness, which is meant to keep the country *from* falling apart. I asked Brian what he saw ahead in his lifetime — a

South Africa such as it is, or a "multinational" state, in which blacks and colored people would be independent of white sovereignty. (He'd used that phrase, "multinational state," as had other children, to describe the goal they believed apartheid was meant to achieve — a so-called homelands policy.) He scratched his head, said he had "no idea" what even a few years would bring, never mind a decade or two. That day, a bit later on, he drew his version of the South African flag, and it bore little resemblance to the flags I'd seen done by Petrus and other Afrikaner boys and girls. The Union Jack dominated the South African flag, and the two "Boer flags," as Brian referred to them, were rendered in a thoroughly sloppy technique and merged, as if unworthy of serious notice (Figure 13). I kept on seeing this inclination among children of English ancestry — not a very surprising finding, to be sure, yet a distinction in one nation's children which, yet again, reminds us that boys and girls of, say, ten or twelve do indeed have definite nationalist loyalties. More particularly, they know of their national background, understand its distinguishing symbols and are able to represent them on paper, or indeed, put into language what they represent.

To Brian, the Union Jack meant this: "It's Britain's flag, and it stands for our country's civilization. Without the English here you'd have no University of Cape Town, tops in the country. You'd have no hospitals — no first-rate ones. You'd have no big businesses; we're the ones who built up the banks and the oil-trading companies, and the insurance companies, and the mining companies. It's all British know-how. The Afrikaners — they're good clerks, Dad says. They have a good eye for detail, but they have no imagination. They have no contacts abroad, either. They're really a one-track people: they want to hold on to their farms, and their jobs in our companies. And they want to hold on to the government, too! What can we do? We sit back and relax, and we're doing all right here, thank you! If we have to go, we'll go — leave for Britain. But my dad says we'd never live as well in London as we do here. He loves this country, and so long as we can go about our lives in peace, we'll stay. You mustn't become panicky, and run. We know people who have left, and then, a year or two later, they regret it, and they come back. That's something to remember!"

One summarizes: an English pragmatism, perhaps, as against the back-to-the-wall Dutch-Huguenot Calvinism of the so-called African "white tribe," the Afrikaners, whose unique language (a mixture of English, Dutch, German) and strong collective memory both work their way into the nationalist awareness of children. To study the political life of South Africa's white children, English and Afrikaner both, has been to observe them singing the national anthem ("Die Stem"), visiting their country's countless monuments, and not least, listening wide-eyed to dozens of highly charged, sentimental, idealized stories and accompanying illustrative pictures, all meant to tell generation after generation of boys and girls about a nation's history. On the one hand, the divergences are apparent and already mentioned here — the distinctive Afrikaner language, culture, religion, the religion a special contrast with the Anglican Church, and even the dour Presbyterianism (which, I've noticed, Cape Town and Durban seem to insinuate with their easygoing, port-city ways). Finally, there is an ideology the two white "sects" now share — apartheid: a way of seeing the world, backed by power and force willingly exerted, which comes to be connected to a boy's, a girl's nationalist awareness.

Though the English and the Boers live on, in different ways, I think their children are more alike in their nationalism than either group of them (and either group of their parents) is likely to acknowledge. To this outsider the Afrikaner political and social ideology, the *racial* ideology, has triumphed among all white children. Race, rather than language or culture or religious tradition, is the true mainstay of nationalist sentiment. In the end, all the white children of South Africa stare at black people, or at colored people, and invoke apartheid. This is, they claim, their ultimate and particular fate, their greatest challenge, their everyday task, their utter necessity, their blessed patrimony (and matrimony, though children rarely mention mothers as they do in other countries); and this is, finally, their future itself — to live in a country whose essence, as they see it, these white boys and girls, is that of their separateness from darker people, Indians and Chinese as well as the blacks, the colored. Petrus: "We won't be a country if apartheid ends; we won't be here; we'll disappear — I mean we'll have lost the war. But we won't lose a war: never!" And Brian: "It's impossible to imagine a country like this without some separation; there has to be separation. We can't just mix completely; we're different. Our country will keep us as we are — but there will be some changes, I'm sure. If there are too many — well, you see, it'll no longer be South Africa; it'll be like Rhodesia turning to Zimbabwe, and Salisbury to Harare. Where will we all go? We'll leave and be South Africans abroad; but the *country* — then it would be dead!"

These are instructive comments about nationalism among the young. Nearby lies quite another world, distant beyond the calculation of miles: that of black and colored children. Rarely did the white children I got to know in South Africa stop and think about these darker-skinned age-mates, these fellow human beings — think about how they might regard the world, how they might feel as they move through this life, day after day. It can be uncanny, to sit in a Dutch Reformed church in the Orange Free State or the Transvaal, to sit in an Anglican church in Cape Town or Durban, hearing the words of Jesus directly quoted, as He went about his ministry, comforting the sick, healing the injured, feeding the hungry, offering His love to the exiled, the unpopular, the imprisoned, the forsaken and abandoned — and to realize that all the while no parent or preacher is asking these white children, sitting in these comfortable pews, to connect what Jesus did in ancient Palestine to what they might do, today, in South Africa, in His name. One Afrikaner child, an eleven-year-old girl, briefly *did* ask, did wonder — ever so briefly: "If Jesus came back to us, I've tried to figure out what He'd want of us. I don't know. I think He'd want us to help people who are in trouble. That's what He did. But most people are doing all right, here [in the village where she lived]. I guess we'd have to 'follow Him,' like it says in the Bible. Maybe He'd go and try to give some help to our black people and our colored people. Maybe He'd change their lives, like He's changed ours."

An interesting theological finale to an introspective moment: A girl nears the brink of a radical Christian critique of an old, gross inequality, only to find comfort in the Christ who "changes" people inwardly — as she made quite clear to me: "If Jesus could get them [the black people, the colored people] to behave better, then they'd be closer to Him, and He'd love them more." I heard, next, a disquisition on crime and violence in the cities of South Africa; but then this strange self-questioning: "You wonder what those people think, the girls of my age in the homelands. You wonder if they read the Bible, I mean, think about it, the way we do in Sunday school."

She would go no further than that speculation — and quickly retreated to Afrikaner mythology: the hard life *her* people had lived, the brutal condescension of the English at the turn of the century, the determination, nevertheless, of her ancestors, and the just rewards that came of it. As I heard her go through this wobbly moral exercise, I kept thinking of the very people she mentioned. Later, driving to the home where I had been staying, I sat with the transcripts and drawings of a girl of the same age as the Afrikaner girl, a girl who spoke the same language, a vigorous, articulate Afrikaans. Her name, Issabell Appelgrym, would also immediately mark her as Afrikaner, and of course, she is not without Afrikaner blood. Moreover, she attends the Dutch Reformed church with her quiet, hardworking, thoroughly fatalistic parents, who earnestly believe that God has His reasons for what He has done, and humanity has no right to question those reasons.

The only distinct difference between these two girls is perhaps best described through the remarks of Issabell herself, who lives in a township on the western side of Johannesburg:[19] "I wasn't sure, when I was a little girl, what it means to be 'colored.' I remember the first time I asked my mother, and she said I shouldn't ask, because there's no answer; it's just a name that means your skin isn't as light as some other people's skin. But her skin is lighter than my father's, and he's colored, too — and so I kept asking questions and more questions that afternoon, and finally she told me to stop, or she'd punish me with no supper. Then I asked my father, and he said to wait until I got older.

"Last year, when I had my tenth birthday, I asked my father, again, and he said all right, and he explained that my mother's father, he was a white man, and her mother, she had white blood. I guess I already knew my mother was light enough for someone white to be in our family. But I started crying when my father showed me the pictures of my grandfather and my grandmother on my mother's side. I'd never seen those pictures. They both died before I was born. I think my grandfather killed his uncle, after a fight, and then he killed himself; that's what my father thinks. My mother won't talk about her family with anyone, not even my father! She's not white, but she's *almost* white. My father says if you saw her with a white man, she'd look whiter than she does now, with us. You take on the color of the person you're with — if you're a light enough colored person."

She stopped talking for a moment, turned away. Her eyes were wet when she looked back in my direction. Perhaps the sad irony of her own observation stopped her train of thought; perhaps she had been undone by this discussion of her topsy-turvy world and its loony commonplaces that pass for a nation's political and social agenda. Before I could offer a remark or pose a question, she had more to tell: "In school we speak Afrikaans, and since I speak very well, the teacher asks the others to listen to me! One girl came up to me after I'd read a story, and she said I was a slave of the white man's. I told her she was wrong, but she swore at me and said I'd be thrown in jail one day. I didn't ask her who'd throw me there! But I told my father, and he started to cry! I've seen him cry before, when his brother died, and his father, only a week apart. They both had infections, I think. They had no room for them in the hospital, and they sent them home with medicine; but the medicine didn't work in time, I think. That's the only time my mother said a bad word against the white people. She said if they'd been white, they'd be alive. She said that white people have everything, and we get any leftovers there are.

"My father said she might be right. He said one of these days the blacks will start a big revolution. They're in worse trouble than anyone, and there are more of them than all the rest of us, and when they start their revolution, they won't be nice to us, because they think we're on the side of the whites, and the whites think we're on the side of the blacks, and we're in the middle, and no one trusts us, and we may be the first ones to be killed, or they'll just lock us up in some big prisons they'll build for us, the colored prisons!"

She had once drawn a picture for me of her house, its immediate environs — a prison, I'd thought at the time. It was bleak and desolate and grim and sunless and ramshackle and strangely isolated from the natural world: no earth, even, let alone grass, flowers, trees, all of which children the world over, I've noticed, even poor ones, will at least occasionally try to represent in their drawings or paintings (Figure 14). I thought of that drawing as I listened to her comments, and as we sat in silence for a minute or so, both of us wondering what more to say. Then Issabell told me a little more: "If only it was true, that you can make a wish, one wish, and it'll happen! I used to wish I'd just turn white, and then I could leave here, and live some place nicer. I told my mother what I wished, and she smiled. She said there's no harm in wishing. My father says God will punish us for trying to look different. He put us here to be His witnesses, and we have no right to tell Him that He was wrong, and we should look different."

Now I thought of another picture, a self-portrait of Issabell's, done two years earlier, when she'd just celebrated her ninth birthday (Figure 15). In the drawing her eyes were an incongruous mixture of red and yellow that resulted in a brownish color (she'd had "pinkeye" a week earlier!), her hair was a tawny orange and long, her dress yellow with a green belt, her shoes red, her body outlined in orange. Even Afrikaner children, for all their racial pride in being white, will use a black crayon to outline themselves. What else — a white crayon? They know intuitively that white is a poor color when "definition" is the issue — to set oneself apart (to use a word!) from the whiteness of the paper. Occasionally a child will then make a point of filling in his or her face with orange — to emphasize whiteness. But most Afrikaner children, like their white counterparts all over the world, simply assume that the paper's whiteness is also *their* whiteness, or the whiteness of the person they are drawing. When Petrus drew himself (as he did many times in the years I knew him, visited his home and school), he always reached for a black crayon to do the initial drawing. So with ordinary American children — no matter their skin color. Black children in America usually color themselves brown — push the brown crayon hard or lightly as they apply it, depending upon the shade desired. I've carried "tan" crayons, light brown ones, and a few American black children have used them; or they've created their own mixture — using orange, yellow, black, brown crayons.

I mention all this because three South African children called "colored" by their government have turned out to be the most color-conscious children I've ever met. That consciousness is especially apparent in their self-portraits.[20] Issabell not only used to outline herself in this drawing, but she applied orange to her skin, and then mixed the orange with white — followed by an application of the "tan" crayon, which offered a dark peachy shade. She never once touched the brown or black crayons. As I watch her at work (with glances now and then; I'm doing my own landscape drawing on this occasion, something I often do while children prepare such artwork), I find myself noticing her skin color — which is what I suppose would be called in America "medium brown." The fact that I should be going through this kind of classificatory attentiveness tells me something, or so I think, as I sit there and sketch, and watch this "colored" girl do likewise.

Her self-portrait is a striking statement — enough to hold the attention for a long time of someone who has been working with children for more than twenty-five years, and so doing, been the recipient of several thousand drawings and paintings. At first I am a bit alarmed — this jumble of colors on this child's skin. Eventually, I will learn from her and others that many "colored" children in South Africa are quite confused about their situation — at a loss to know what to think, or draw or paint, as they try to get their (racial) bearings in this life. This confusion takes explicit form in the ways in which they color themselves colored, in the conflict of colors, actually, one sees in so many of their drawings. I have eleven self-portraits Issabell did for me in three years — from age nine to age twelve. The first one, just mentioned, shows her using different crayons to convey her skin, but settling on no one color. Her hair is made longer than, in fact, it was then, or has ever been. She is close-mouthed, literally; her nose is absent; her ears are rather large, indeed, as are her eyes — a child saying, perhaps, that she hears and sees a lot, but doesn't have anything to say. Because she *does* have a lot to say on most subjects, I assume, as I look at the picture, that the implicit subject of this drawing is race — what she can't discuss, even at home with her own parents, never mind me, but what she constantly tries to comprehend by observing the world and hearing what it has to tell.

When she was ten (and we were more familiar with each other), she relaxed her portrait, showed some teeth, included a nose, made the ears less dominant — but still struggled with the issue of skin color. Now she gave herself a bit of ground — a straight brown line under her red shoes (Figure 16). At twelve, that line was thicker, and she took the trouble to hint at some housing, but failed to complete what she started, and so the structures have a "bombed-out" appearance — not unlike, sadly, the appearance of the old housing development where she lived (Figure 17). Her skin in this drawing is a bit more settled in its brown shading. She has made a point of giving herself a white dress, which she sketches with white crayon. It is rare to use the white crayon at all, and rarer, still, to use it to fashion a dress, for children in other countries, or in South Africa itself. *Except for colored children.* She puts red polka dots on the dress. She makes a stab at a blue sky, but stops midway across the paper, then tells me it's the rainy season, and darkens the heavens with black. No sun is offered.

As I look at several hundred drawings by South Africa's colored children, I begin to realize that this is one of the moments in my research when I feel strangely categorical, when the social-science phrase that usually bothers me, "a finding," begins to come to mind: Colored children are not only troubled by their peculiar situation, caught between two worlds, but they work their difficulties into their drawings and paintings with striking consistency — as if the tensions and worries they bear are not so easily put aside (suppressed, repressed) as are those of, say, American black children. Now (my wife, always skeptical of generalizations, reminds me), one cannot say that *all* the colored children we knew were willing (were impelled) to use their crayons or paints as Issabell did — but enough of them were to make us realize how much the matter of race is on their everyday (conscious) minds. Neither South Africa's white nor black children show so much evident concern about their skin color as it appears in their artistic productions. Indeed, my wife and I began to feel, as we started accumulating these drawings and paintings in 1975, that we could recognize those of a South African "colored" child right away — and now, ten years later, we have not changed our minds.

Nor are the words of these children hard to miss; they have a quality one soon enough recognizes as those of, say, twelve-year-old Issabell: "I have a friend who lives near here, and he's very smart in school, and he's the best student in Sunday school. He told our minister last week that God must have fallen asleep when He made us. The minister didn't like what he heard! Oh, man — he exploded! But we all liked it — we thought the same thing. We don't know what to do — try to be like the white ones, or try to be like the black ones. We're not either, you see. I hear my mother crying sometimes and I know why she's crying; she's heard something in the boss-house [where she works as nanny to three Afrikaner children six days a week, from seven-thirty to five-thirty] that bothers her. Mostly, she won't tell us what is worrying her; but sometimes she does. A few weeks ago she told us that she heard one of those boys [there are two of them, and one girl] tell a friend he had over that all the gardeners are black, and the nannies are colored, and then there are the 'regular people' [whites]! That's the way they could figure things out — between us and the blacks, and between everyone else and themselves! Then, he saw my mother there, in the room, and he asked her if he wasn't right! She told him he was, and she went back to the kitchen. She told us that night [they were eating supper at the time] that she would have put poison in the food she had prepared for them, if there had been any around. But she prayed to God that He forgive her for thinking like that — once in their home, and once in ours.

"If you ask me, God shouldn't make my mother apologize! We're the 'lost sheep' the minister talks about! No, he never called the colored people that — but we are, anyway! You don't know where you should go. The whites don't want us; and the blacks don't want us; no one does — even our own colored teachers. They say bad things about us right to our faces: Come on, you, prove you belong here and not in Soweto! That means we should obey them, and be glad we're not darker! Come on, you, prove you've got some real intelligence in your head! That means, you must have some white blood, so you must be smarter than you're being right now, so get to it, or you'll be called one of their [the Afrikaner classifying authorities'] mistakes! I'm beginning to hate school. Why go to it? For girls, the chances are you'll be a nanny in someone's home, and if you're lucky, they'll not curse you, they'll be polite to you. For boys, there are some good jobs, a few — but only a few. They [the white people] want to have a few of us around, especially when you Americans show up!"

Silence, and she lowers her head quickly. She resumes, seconds later, with a guarded apology ("I'm glad Americans come here; they're nice people"); then she initiates a discussion of her nationality — perhaps, I speculate, because she knows that this subject is my major interest, and for her to bring it up voluntarily at this moment is to apologize even further. In any event, I listen, and keep feeling glum, melancholy, not personally accused, but all too aware of her situation, her future, compared with my own life, my good luck on this planet. "I don't know why the government goes through all this trouble with us," she says. Then there is an amplification: "I wish they'd just carve out a really good piece of land — not too much land, just enough for us to grow some food and build our houses — and send us there and leave us alone, all the colored. The trouble with the homelands is that they're *not* homelands — that's the trouble! They're bits and pieces of the worst land, and they pack the blacks into them; and then of course they try to escape, because if they don't, they'll starve to death. They haven't tried that with us [setting aside homelands], but they'd do it, if they thought they could succeed. [I ask her what she means by succeed.] By 'succeed' I mean get us out of their way, and not have the world shouting at them, especially America. We know here what worries the government: your country. If your country gave us hell, lots of hell, there would be changes. My father heard two [white] doctors say that, where he works [in a garage, as an attendant].

"You're right, I did say 'us.' [I'd mentioned that to her, the choice of "us" in the phrase "give us hell."] We're part of South Africa! We're supposed to be citizens. That's what they say, the Prime Minister and his people. We're supposed to get our own people working for us in the government ["power-sharing"], that's what you hear. They'll never give us anything, not anything big! We're part of South Africa the way my mother is part of that house where she works, and my father that garage. We're people they need to do their dirty work. There are two kinds of dirty work — the real hard kind, where you come home and you're barely alive, and the easier kind, where you come home as tired as can be, but you have just enough energy in you to catch a second breath, and have your supper, and go to bed! If you're colored, you are a South African citizen who is supposed to do the easier kind of dirty work. If you're black, you're not a citizen, not of South Africa, they say — just someone who works like the lowest animal there is, an ox, I guess, and if you even ask a question in a whisper, they'll send you to those big zoos they have, and the whites call them 'home-lands' for the 'tribes.' My father says he won't vote, if they give him a vote, because it won't make any difference: 'We're high-class oxen to them, and the blacks are the oxen you see pulling a million times their weight, and the bugs are all over them, and they're wasting away, because they don't have the right food, enough food. With us, they'll spray something on us to keep the bugs away, and they say they don't want us to die, because we're that important — that they want us to live; and we won't be har-nessed to [carry] the big, terrible loads.

"It's like this: You have the South African people — they're the whites. Then you have us: We're living here in South Africa, and they say we're citizens of the country, but they'll move us to one place, and move us to another, and woe if we talk back to them; then, they'll lock us up and beat us up, the way they do with the black people, and with some of our people, and even with their own white ones, if they take our side; I mean, really join up with us against their own. I heard on television one of them talking [an Afrikaner], and he said your country is a big part of you, and it has a 'soul,' and its soul joins with your soul, and it's like marriage! I thought that was great! He was talking to his people, and I guess they like getting married to their country, and then to each other; I mean, man and woman, that kind of marriage. But he wasn't telling us colored people that we're going to be married to the 'soul' of South Africa! No, sir! We came here — well, it wasn't by a marriage! We came from what they did in the woods, you know, or someplace in the house where no one's going to see and find out. You know what I mean?"

I nod, and she is about to continue, but she hears a plane outside, and it is fairly low-flying, noisy, intrusive. She gets up, looks out the window: it is two planes, South African military jets,[21] the fast fighter variety that zoom and swerve and turn up and turn down, birds of prey doing their tricks with each other, and scaring everything in sight. She waits until they're gone — but by inquiring as to what they were, and by beckoning me to come see, and by standing there and looking and looking, her head upward in a sustained gaze, then her head down, lower than normal, and her shoulders bent more than usual — with all those gestures of mind and body both, she makes yet another statement to me, maybe the most pointed and knowing one possible. I know of no way to get her to put into words what she'd just suggested, implied, by her actions, and when she does start talking she refers to how tired her mother would be at the end of that day, which happens to be Saturday, and the last of her six weekly workdays; and how tired her father would be, for the same reason. Then she tells me she wishes they were better paid — and I remember how meager their wages are. I also begin to realize how tired this girl has suddenly felt, and how forthright she has just been in her declaration of despair: Come, Doctor, look at those planes, if you're interested in the political life of children — think of *their* psychological influence on our minds!

I readied myself for departure and thought of those planes as I did so, their utter power as it came across to us in their high velocity, their rehearsed performances, their din, and the feeble clatter, in response, of a few lonely dishes on an otherwise bare kitchen shelf in this broken-down tenement house: Come all ye, below us, pay attention to us, for a fleeting second; that's all the time we need to remind you, and you need to be reminded — who has what power, and who has no power at all; and don't forget what this means in your lives; don't forget those colors on our planes, those South African insignia, those national statements, those assertions of power by a country! Whose country? Why, the country of those below us who can look up at us, doing our military exercises, with a glow of pride and a sense of security, with a thrill that accompanies the knowledge that those machines are *ours*, and the men in them *ours*, the message of national affiliation a reassuring one to *us*.

No wonder Issabell and other colored children told me, again and again, that they weren't quite sure what the South African flag looked like; and told me, again and again, that they weren't sure where the capital city of their country was. Some knew it to be Pretoria, and some knew it to be Cape Town, and a good half or more knew that there might be two capitals, though they weren't sure what they were; and none knew what almost all the white children knew, because they'd learned it in school, learned it well, been taught a lesson well: that Cape Town is South Africa's "legislative capital," and Pretoria is its "administrative capital," and Bloemfontein is its "judicial capital." The supersonic South African military jets, I understand finally, while driving home, had helped Issabell teach me *my* lesson — that power doesn't only corrupt, as Lord Acton's famous words tell us; power also enforces behavior on the powerless, impresses awareness of their utter vulnerability, recognition that to resist power means, for all practical purposes, to be killed, bombed to pieces. No wonder Issabell slumped in her chair, and in essence, sent me on my way. Still, there was plenty of life in her eyes: she'd made a big point, and felt pleased! And even as those planes couldn't destroy this shrewd girl's comprehension of their particular mission, so too they couldn't destroy her pride, as she reminded me one day, in another conversation:

"If they tried to get rid of all of us, they wouldn't have the land to bury us; they wouldn't even have the bombs and bullets to do the job — and they wouldn't know what to do, in their houses and their offices; they'd be helpless!" The words were accompanied by *her* look of pride, easily a match for any I'd noticed on any white South African child's face as he or she looked at his or her country's planes, tanks, guns held defiantly and in fixed position by passing soldiers on parade.

Near Soweto,[22] which stands for South West Township, a place without any real name, simply one that spells out a geographic relationship to Johannesburg, a place where more than a million black people live, those planes can also be heard; and the black children know, too, of the nearby army bases, and know of what can happen "in five minutes," the boys Vincent Flamini ("eat at night"), who is thirteen, and Selwyn Ndlovu ("elephant"), who is twelve, tell me, as they draw pictures in the dry, dusty earth with sticks, and spell out their military knowledge: "You see, this is us," says Vincent; "and this is where their soldiers are," says Selwyn; "and you understand, they are on a twenty-four-hour alert, round the clock, every day — on account of us," Vincent explains; "with plenty of planes and tanks, and more, if they need them," Selwyn adds, whereupon he kicks the diagram he and his friend have made, so that a cloud of dust rises up toward us. "We'd be hit badly," Vincent tells me. "We'd be killed, a lot of us," Selwyn announces. "They fired away at our brothers a few years ago," Vincent reminds his friend. "They killed a lot more people than they admitted killing," Selwyn lets me know, a downcast look now on his face, and bitterness in his voice. "They have tremendous power, we know that; our leaders always warn us of that," Selwyn continues — then is interrupted by Vincent: "But there are more of us, many more, and we'll get guns, more and more guns, and we'll beat them, one day, we'll beat them at their own game."

In case I have any question what that game is, Vincent gives the military details slowly and methodically, staring without interruption right into my eyes, his own eyes not blinking, I notice. My eyes, finally, blink and then lift to the far-off view (we were standing on a hill) that affords a glimpse of row after row of cinder-block houses, and no trees, and no paved roads, and no grass, and no electricity. Outhouses and a permanent layer of smoke, the result of open coal pits used to cook food, and spaces here and there where a lonely spigot serves water to hundreds, to thousands. A market, maybe, with lots of fat and flour, and those shebeens, all those shebeens (unlicensed bars), open in the morning and open in the afternoon, and even open all night; the beer, the wine, the hard liquor, the men and the women, the sex, the frustrations and outbursts of tears, and the fits of rage, the tempers lost, the knives, the flesh cut, the bleeding, the deaths, every night the deaths, violent deaths, accidental deaths, illnesses gone untreated claiming lives. All this is the everyday experience, knowledge, inheritance of these two boys, of thousands like them, and their sisters: Soweto, a name known the world over; Soweto, a place for me to behold, suddenly, eagerly, rather than withstand those stares; and then this, from Vincent: "We'd never be like them; we'd never kill like they did, in front of the [Regina Mundi, Catholic] Cathedral; we'd never watch over them all the time, and tell them they're dirty pigs and dumb oxen and filthy, filthy and monkeys and apes, all they call us; we'd try to be like what the Sisters [who run the Holy Cross School, in Diepkloof, a part of Soweto][23] say we should be like — 'charity,' they tell us to have 'charity,' like Jesus had, and they say He suffered bad, real bad, and if He had the same deal we have, then He was one big chap — a dude, you people say in the States!"

No more words; smiles now from the two boys. I relax a little. We walk along, headed back to school. We've had a long break, and the warning bell tells us to hurry. The boys have a study period, though, rather than a class, and they seem less eager to respond to the demands of their school schedule than I am for them to do so. They see me for what I am, an old man by the standards of Soweto (where so many children die days or weeks after birth, and most people die well before they have accumulated my fifty years), and still a conscientious student, eager to pay the teachers heed, so that my future will be bright. Vincent suggests we slow down, meaning me. Selwyn explains that even these beloved Irish missionary nuns are not free, they who mean so well, and are so good, and who are sent here by God, and who do their work in a country run by people who claim to be God-fearing above all else — God-fearing and afraid of no one else, *no one, nothing,* not one other country, even the "big two": Even those nuns are watched, curbed, told what to teach, what not to teach, and so, Doc, take it easy, let's talk, we'll get there soon enough, and if we don't — well, are you interested in *our* lives, our assumptions, ideas, expectations, or in living out reflexively your own obedient, academic life, yet again, here in this Godforsaken part of our planet?

The two young men (they are that, fully grown in important respects, I have decided by now) sit down on the dry, cracked earth of the path, rocks aplenty. They notice me being fussier than they are, looking for a place that isn't right there, then settling for what is, the parched and rocky earth, but worried about my nice pair of pants, the link for the moment between me, there, and me from someplace quite else. They joke about "the States," then turn serious: If only they could have been born there — or if only South Africa could be turned into a country that resembled America more than Russia. I am surprised by that comparison, and they shrewdly sense the reason — told me by Vincent in this manner: "The government blames everything on Communism. The people here — we're all called communists the second we stand up and say we're not slaves of the white man. They tell you the communists are dictators — but they're not dictators! No! They are fair — to themselves!

"The nuns tell us about democracy. The United States is a democracy. Is South Africa a democracy? We asked the nun in class. She got red in the face. If she'd been black, like us, she could have hid her shame — no one sees us get red in the face! She didn't know what to say to us. She stuttered. The only other time she stuttered was once when we asked her what she'd do if her government treated her the way our government treats us. Then, she told us God knows there is plenty of trouble in the world, and there are lots of people who don't get treated fairly; but He'll take care of us, some day — when we meet Him. That means, when

we're dead and gone. Too late for us! And great news for the
government of South Africa! No wonder the men in the government love their religion, and always are telling us they're good
Christians! You ask me — if you did — I'd say that South Africa
is a democracy, like you hear the people say on the radio, a democracy for the Boers. For us it's being ordered around every step
we take; it's like Russia. One of our Soweto's leaders keeps asking
why America is supporting a Russian kind of government here, if
your country hates dictator-governments. That's what we don't
understand."

They saw *my* embarrassment: silence. Selwyn started teasing
me — asked me if I'd thought of asking questions of various South
African government officials. I retreated into professional avowals — that I'm a child psychiatrist, and I'm trying to figure out
what *children* think about their country, its values and ideals.
Selwyn was too smart and observant to let my self-protective pieties
stand unchallenged: "Well, you've talked to our parents. Why don't
you talk with the children of our Prime Minister, and then talk
with him and his wife?"

I laugh, and say I would, gladly, but doubt very much he'd be
interested. Anyway, access to the Prime Minister is not something
available to me. They smile, but are not ready to stop this line of
inquiry. How about trying to talk with others, "lower down." I
ask whom they have in mind. They don't know any names, only
that there are functionaries and functionaries, thousands of them,
and one level and another level and it goes on and on — don't I
know? Haven't I learned this important fact about South Africa,
that at every turn there are "people checking you out," then "people checking out the ones who check you out," and then "people
checking *them* out" — until, as Selwyn put it, "you begin to check
yourself out, because you see people checking you out in the
shadows, and then you get nearer, and there's no one there, and
it's not your eyes, man, not your eyes; it's what has happened to
you: you've become part of their system, because they've got into
your head in a bad way, and there's nothing you can do but go to
the shebeen and start with the beer, and finally, the beer will
wash everything away."

When he finishes, Vincent nods, and points to his head, and shakes it, and says "the white man is crazy, and he drives us crazy, too." I think of Kafka, remember *The Trial*,[24] remind myself of a speech I heard Dr. Martin Luther King give in Birmingham, Alabama in 1963, twenty years earlier — a plea to white people to learn from black people, learn how "irrational segregation is," and how it "punishes those on top as surely as it does those on the bottom."[25] Silence dominates us, as I struggle for my stock-in-trade, words, and the two youths stare at me, a mixture (I imagine or maybe hope) of anger and friendly pity on their faces. Eventually they suggest that we get up and go to visit a nearby nursery school, run by social workers, supported by wealthy whites who live in Johannesburg. When we get there, some of the children, three and four years old, are performing a complicated dance, and doing it with stunning coordination. I'm told it is part of a "tribal ceremony." When I ask which tribe, I'm told "Zulu." When the children have finished their performance, cookies and juice are served. My two young friends are impatient with all this, and increasingly eager, I notice, to leave. They also want me to go with them, I begin to realize — and finally they ask me to go into a nearby room, so that we can talk.

"I see you like this, the tribal show," Selwyn begins. I nod my head, already enough aware of *their* opinion to refrain from an explicit yes, though also aware that I'd just been smiling and clapping along with everyone else, and finally, congratulating the children on a production that was, without a doubt, one of the most impressively synchronized I'd ever seen children so young sustain for nearly ten minutes. Vincent now takes over: "They love us to be 'tribal,' the rich whites who come here. They throw their rand at us, if only we'll become Zulus and Bantus and Xhosas once again, and stop bothering them with our demands to be part of *their* country! They'd like us to disappear into the bush, but any time they whistle, to come out and get right to work, doing their shoveling and laying their bricks and lifting anything that's too heavy for them and sweeping their streets and carrying their garbage. And you know, we're 'bush people,' so we make good gardeners for them! My father is one, and he tells us what he overhears — that he has 'magic' in him, because he can make anything grow that they want him to grow, anything!"

When he ends that sentence there is nothing more to say for a while. Both young men are full of scornful rage — and finally, when they settle down enough to begin talking, they pour their rage upon what they regard to be the condescension, the noblesse oblige, the cynical philanthropic tokenism of the white philanthropists who take an interest in Soweto's problems. I begin to feel that I belong to those people, because I am a white, middle-class, professional man, and my politics are basically what Mrs. Helen Suzman, a member of Parliament,[26] would consider her politics — faith in democracy and hope that somehow it will redress this terrible social, economic, and racial injustice. The youths see a cloud over my face, the downcast expression; they urge me to cheer up. They ask how my work is going. I tell them that it is painful work, and that with each visit to their country I get more confused. They notice my words "your country," and seem quite pleased. Selwyn makes this statement: "The white people think this is their country, and no one else's. They're wrong, and one of these days they'll admit it, or if they don't, there will be a war between them and us, and when it's over, we'll all be part of South Africa, and we won't try to drive them out; we'll just settle for everyone here being equal in this country. If they're waiting for us to say we're *not* part of this country, they've got a long, long wait!"

Talk of time — the length of the "wait" — got us thinking of the time we'd known each other. Selwyn asked how much longer I'd be doing my research, and I told him then (1981) that I was well along, though I needed a few more years. We reminisced about our first meetings, and they asked if I still had their drawings and paintings. Yes, indeed! Did I have them with me? Oh, yes — I always brought them along, so that I could compare old efforts with any new ones. In fact, I kept some of them in South Africa, with a good friend at the University of Cape Town.[27] I had their particular collection with me, back in my Johannesburg room. They expressed interest, the next time, in reviewing what they'd done three years earlier, and meanwhile were quite willing to do some additional sketches — when I assured them that I'd be very much interested in seeing them. We talk about the subject — what to draw? I say, "anything." They know better: What do you want this time? I am embarrassed — too close to the bone, to the egoism that is part of a researcher's life. I say "anything" again, but move quickly to something: "Well, how about drawing another picture of yourselves, or maybe of your country, some person or place or situation in this country that you'd like to show me. You could say to yourselves: *This* is South Africa — try to say it with the picture." I was stumbling, but I wanted them to put into their pictures some of the strong emotions they had, and had conveyed to me. (I already had a number of their self-portraits, and Soweto scenes.)

The result was Selwyn's vivid picture (Figure 18) of a frontal assault on a police station by a Soweto crowd, and Vincent's picture (Figure 19) of himself and others standing near a shebeen, but looking toward the Holy Cross School,[28] and beyond the tall buildings of Johannesburg. Selwyn announced that he was describing what would one day occur — a South African storming of the Bastille of sorts, a surge of Soweto's youth (bleeding but undaunted) that would overthrow entrenched power. He said he was not anyone special in his drawing, "only one person" in the "big number" of people ready to die in order to overthrow the police. The South African flag, or an outline of it, without the three subflags, would be captured, he hoped, and burned. He wasn't sure what a new flag of South Africa would look like. As for Vincent, he wanted me to know that he emphatically did *not* consider himself "better" than any of the men inside the shebeen. He was just "daydreaming"; that was what the picture was meant to convey, his reveries (embodied, perhaps, in the black dashes!) as he thought about school, and his future, and too, the future of his country, of his country's biggest, most influential city: "I wonder what Johannesburg will be like, when we become free in this country. Will there be a war, first, and will those buildings get destroyed? What will the nuns do? I've wondered why they stay here. They are not treated very well by the police and the government people — and they have a hard time with us, too, I know!"

Vincent's reflective disposition affected Selwyn; he thought his drawing was "too bloody, maybe." Vincent corrected him: There would be even more blood than the picture showed. The Afrikaners would fight to the last man. Eventually (the boys hoped) the blacks would do similarly — and thereby, of course, win by sheer numerical advantage. The next day, we looked at earlier versions of their self-portraits, their evocations of South Africa's racial tensions. Selwyn was interested in the similarity of his drawings — they showed his continual interest in depicting an assault on the police station. Vincent noticed that he'd always been "curious about those tall buildings in Johannesburg," and had always wondered whether his people, too, would enjoy them one day, even as now they work in them, make them habitable, enjoyable for white people. His uncle (his mother's younger brother) is one of those "boys" who sweeps floors in a bank. He comes home with lots of stories, but wants to tell them only in the middle of the night, a follow-up to his after-dinner shebeen visit: "We don't want to hear his stories. He is all mixed up then — and he makes enough noise to wake everyone up. We pretend to be asleep, and when he sees that no one is there to listen, he starts crying, and then falls off. He cries [I have asked why] because he's tired, and he gets little pay, and he's been pushed around by the black man over him, and he'll beat my uncle up a lot of the time."

I sit there appalled, sympathetic, angry on behalf of his uncle, on behalf of him. He adds this: "When we attack the police station, as Selwyn shows you, we'll also have to go after some of our own." I decide not to ask any more; he has just explained enough to me on that score. Besides, I feel disgusted with myself for wanting to pursue this "interesting matter," this "significant irony," my way of thinking about such a "phenomenon" — of black rage against black bosses, the latter themselves at the constant mercy of higher-ups. Obviously, at some critical moment, when *real* power is the issue, the boss becomes white.

As I have reviewed the drawings of Selwyn, of Vincent, and of other black children who live in Soweto, I have come to see that these South African children have identifying characteristics as artists — and, too, as autobiographical storytellers. They are loath to draw themselves alone. Not one black child in Johannesburg or Cape Town was willing (or could be successfully encouraged) to do that — "simply" (or so it seemed for South Africa's white boys and girls, even for its colored ones) draw themselves, paint themselves, concentrate in one or another fashion on their own faces, arms, legs, clothes, hair, fingers, and toes.[29] The black children always drew a crowd, a group (small or large) of adults and children (larger figures, smaller ones). Then, when asked by me, the child would point to a form, tell me that person is he, that person is she. I don't have a conclusive answer to explain this seemingly dominant (possibly universal) preference among South Africa's black children. A distrust of me? An expression of a culture uninterested in the bourgeois individuality so many of us take for granted? A huddled response by fearful children to an exceedingly overbearing world? Still, I have worked with black children (in the segregationist, rural American South of the early 1960s) who have felt shy with me, and suspicious of me, yet in time been willing to share themselves, so to speak, with me visually — and these children have come from a communal (desperately so) world, are quite vulnerable, in constant jeopardy.

The word "tribal" has been all too readily on the tip of my tongue as an explanation — some "mystery" of values I've yet to fathom. Yet, these children themselves have so often scoffed at the effort of the South African government to call them members of this or that tribe. They haven't otherwise struck me as young tribal members so much as urban blacks living on the socioeconomic margin of an advanced industrial society, *and* as blacks also living in a highly racist political world. I am left with these drawings — groups of adults and children, and none of them distinctly, separately delineated, but rather, a blur of sorts: many faces with nondescript features, many bodies without arms, legs, some without either. A portrait of people en masse. A portrait of people yet to emerge from their apartness, surely — the apartheid of their everyday lives. A portrait of a citizen-less population, unrecognized in that most fundamental of ways: stateless — weak, that is, in an ultimate manner hard for most of us to imagine. No wonder these children seem not only indistinct (merged often into nameless others) but also small, and always, set down in some corner of the paper, never in the center, as if they don't really know what it means, literally, to be the center of attention in any affirming manner whatsoever.

The issue, then, I have to think, is not really my white and foreign status. I have known some of these children ten years. Moreover, I have had the assistance of black schoolteachers in Soweto, who have also asked these children to draw pictures — of themselves, their homes, their friends, indeed, draw anything they may wish. The results have been the same — a seeming "difficulty" the children have in drawing not only themselves distinctly, but their own homes and schools. Soweto's domiciliary landscape is portrayed in a smudged pile of bricks and wood. The children in Cape Town's all-too-well-known Crossroads,[30] a settlement in constant risk of being torn down by the police, were similarly unable to draw themselves alone, or their homes. They did offer sticks and sheets of tin, irregularly placed, a sprawl of inert matter that gives them partial cover from rain. They did offer, I fear, the truth of their concrete lives — a rendering of statelessness, of the individual person, the individual home, lost to a policy that decrees them to be a mass of sorts, a black proletariat to be cordoned off, to be transported, to be controlled, to be identified, stamped almost, like cattle: the cards, the passbooks, paper and more paper, official rules and more rules, functionaries and bureaucrats in charge of this and that and everything, it seems. I repeat the question some shrewd black children kept asking me: Wherein does all this treatment differ from "Communism" — that political and economic doctrine mentioned, always, as the great enemy of the Republic of South Africa?

The longer I have come to know South Africa's children, those who are white and those who are colored and those who are black (I did not work with Indian families), the more I have come to understand how important racial nationalism is for all of them — a nationalism that is possessed, among the whites, and a nationalism that expresses a yearning for what is, so far, lacking. When intense fear is connected to nationalist preoccupations or aspirations, as has happened to all South African boys and girls, a striking intensity of emotion results. White boys and girls (of, say, nine or ten) announce that the Fatherland would be "raped" if there were not constant "police action." One asks what that "action" entails, and hears that "they" are always trying to "destroy the country," or "ruin our nation," or "make our Fatherland weak." One asks in what way "they" are trying to do so, and hears that it is by "breaking the laws of South Africa." One asks which laws, and hears that they are the apartheid laws. Even some white children of "liberal" or "progressive" parents, who are digusted by apartheid (alas, they seem to be relatively few of the white people), even those boys and girls can be heard worrying out loud about the "vandals" in Soweto, who "throw rocks," and "could start a revolution." When one asks a ten- or twelve-year-old child of this background how many people live in Soweto, and how he or she has learned about the vandals, one is told that "there are millions there, I don't know how many millions," or one is told "lots and lots, because it's crowded, real packed — maybe three or four or five million"; and one hears that "the papers" and "the TV" and "the radio" have conveyed "news" about the constant "killing there" and "the children who will throw rocks or use knives on you." Who is "you"? Well, in fact, "you" is "us"; "you" turns out to be "white people."

But do any white people go to Soweto? Here the child is likely to say "no" — and rather correctly. It is against the law, in fact, one keeps reminding oneself, for any white person, save those expressly authorized by the government (even white police, for example), so much as to set foot in Soweto. All right, then — when are rocks hurled at whites, if they aren't allowed to enter Soweto? Some children reply that they don't know the answer. Others figure that the white police or army may have entered and thereafter been assaulted. But two-thirds of the children offer quite another and I believe instructive explanation — as in this reply by a white Johannesburg child of eleven, a girl of English background, her father a lawyer, her mother a landscape architect: "They spill over; they get all excited, and they just start their marching, and the next thing you know, our police have to take notice. You know, there's a limit; you can't let people turn the country into a jungle. You have to have laws — I mean, keep people under control. Otherwise, South Africa would be *engulfed*. My Daddy says that's the danger we face in our country, that it will be engulfed, and there won't be any country left once it happens."

For me, this is a child of "enlightened background." I share with her parents talk of books, ideas, events. We commiserate — this tragedy, that impasse: in South Africa, in Europe, in the United States. We read similar periodicals, admire the same writers.[31] Still, their child carries a terrible fear that her country may soon fall apart — and a grossly exaggerated notion of how many blacks live in Soweto, and Lord knows what they are doing of a violent or revolutionary way to the nation in whose territory they live (and work, work damn hard), though not as recognized members, citizens. Meanwhile, other children her age, colored or black, dream of being welcomed, finally, into this nation, dream of enjoying its quite obvious, tangible, attractive charms, wares, offerings. Those boys and girls all themselves South Africans, think of themselves as South Africans, even dream of themselves as South Africans, no matter what a government says and does and announces it will do. As Vincent said to me: "I woke up last night; it was early in the morning, still dark, but a little light was just coming up. I was shaking, because I had a bad dream. The police were there, in my room, telling us we all had to leave our country and go someplace else. They wouldn't tell us where, though. My mother begged, and finally they did — to Robben Island [where political prisoners such as Nelson Mandela have been kept, off the coast of Cape Town]. Then, my mother was a little relieved — at least we weren't going to some foreign country."

Our country, someplace else, some foreign country — these are the phrases of a child who knows exactly which country is his, a child whose race (however despised by those of a different race) has not in his mind disqualified him from an attachment to a place, a spot on their earth, a given nation-state. What his government denies him he nevertheless grants himself. He is officially stateless, yet he is emotionally bound to the land he knows — tied to it in his daily life, and in his dreams at night. No laws in the world can change such attachments, such dreams. A million new rules and a million edicts, and a million pronouncements from the legislature in Cape Town, from the halls of the majestic government buildings high on the Pretoria hills, from the Bloemfontein court chambers — none of them will alter the tenacious psychology of children, for whom a nightmare can in fact be a moral statement (of what ought be), and a cognitive statement (of what actually is). In Vincent's words: "We're here, and we've been here, and no matter how often they shuffle us, and send us back and forth, we're still here, and they know it, because they're here, too." "Here" is South Africa, rent and embattled to be sure — but its children's indivisible nation.

VII

CLASS AND NATIONALISM: BRAZIL AND THE UNITED STATES

As the car works its way along the streets below, Carlos, eleven years old, stands in a small field, littered with garbage, and points — tracing in the air the predictable movements of the police as they approach the favela. A laugh. A shrug. A look toward the visitor from the United States. In time, interrupted by various asides, he offers a relaxed but forthright explanation:

"They are coming to pay us. They work with us. They protect us. They give us tips — when to do our business. We don't make a move without them. They even bring us our money! We'd be stupid, if we tried to go it alone. The police have their eyes on everyone, and they see everything. They have a good deal going for themselves. They have to be careful, too, but they don't make mistakes. They have their bosses — people in the government. We have our bosses — rich men who have each of their ten fingers in a different business. Sometimes the police come here and they are laughing. Times are good! Sometimes they come here and they curse us, and kick the dogs, and complain that we are no good, we are animals, and we should all be sent back to the villages, the countryside. That means we have to make more money when we work. They are in trouble. Someone is whispering into their ears: more, give us more. Or someone is afraid there might be a news story. Every year, there has to be a story. One of the big government people has to prove he's honest, has to say something that makes the police feel sorry for themselves. When they're in that mood, they become greedier. I can tell what they'll be like by the car — if it moves fast, they are going to give us trouble, and if it goes real slow, they are going to smile and play with us, and even offer some candy. Once or twice they put their lights on and make their noise, and we all hide. They don't want to see us. They're telling us to hide, that way. There's a reporter with them, or a visitor from abroad, or someone who teaches in a university. A show: the favela, and the dirty people there, and the law cracking down."

It takes an hour or so for those words, and many others, to be spoken. During that time, the police car comes and parks at the entrance point of the favela. Its occupants have a seemingly brief, casual conversation with a handful of waiting favelados — eight of them, a man, the rest youths between ten and fourteen, only one a girl. Abruptly, the car departs, going much faster than when it climbed the winding roads to the approach of the favela. The man, young himself at twenty, gives the finger to the police car as it leaves. Suddenly the car stops. The two policemen get out and each defiantly returns the gesture. There are smiles all around — from the favelados and from the uniformed men, about to reenter their car. Carlos observes those final ceremonial moments in silence. When the car is in motion once more he gives it the finger himself, as he moves toward his friends below, to laugh and joke and hear the latest gossip and scandal, always brought by the police on their rounds.

Earlier Carlos had explained the scene below: drugs. He wonders whether one day he won't himself be a messenger, an intermediary, an agent of one or another person who also lives in the favela. "I don't know how it works," he tells a visitor. Then he proves otherwise:

"It's a way to make money. I know one family that had nothing to eat. My mother said they'd die soon, all of them. Then their son, Ricardo, got a job. He is twelve, I think. His parents don't know what he does. For a while, he didn't, either. He was told to walk down the path of the hill, walk down the road, walk by the highway for a few minutes, then stop and wait. A car came, picked him up, and took him to Copacabana. He told me that he ended up sitting on a chair in a room on the third floor of a six-story cement building, painted pink and dark brown. They gave him a briefcase, and told him where to take it. The next time they gave him a shopping bag. He kept doing the same errand, every day. Sometimes they handed him a lunch pail. They said he should deliver the thermos inside to a certain person, then bring back the pail."

For the first time in his life Ricardo began to see 100-cruzeiro notes. For the first time his family had cash; not a fortune, but enough to enable them to make purchases. The young man brought home candy and gum, soft drinks, swimsuits, shirts, sandals. His father bowed to him. His mother told his two brothers and two sisters not to ask him any questions — just to enjoy the provider's largesse. His grandmother prayed for him. She had heard, as his parents had, that a good number of favelados, maybe twenty or thirty, maybe more, spread through Rio's streets, bearing packages for the well-to-do, the rich. "They have nothing else to do," the old lady exclaimed — referring to her grandson and his friends. Then she added this, excitement in her voice: "They play football, I hear, on the beach. They run. They eat and drink. And they count their money!"

In Rio de Janeiro's favelas, the children are dazzled by the sight of money. It is magic, power, mystery. It is as elusive, yet as much a part of life as the workings of the Devil. It is also grace. Carlos dreams of food, dreams of water that is safe to drink, dreams of clothes, dreams of Jesus Christ Himself — and of money:

"My grandmother points to the statue [of Christ, overlooking Rio] and says not to worry, not to worry, we belong to Him, and He was like us. I wish He'd come back and come here, and I wish He'd bring boxes and bags full of cruzeiros! I know He'd give them to everyone. He'd go into every house. Then, we'd go down the hill; we'd go to Copacabana and Ipanema and buy. We'd buy everything. We'd bring everything back here. We wouldn't want to stay anyplace else."

At other times Carlos is less sure of his loyalty to the favela.[1]

He goes with his grandmother to a church about half a mile from the foot of the hill on which his family lives, with hundreds and hundreds of others. He is frank to say that on the way over he thinks of the food he'll be given by the nuns — bread, jam, and juice. On the way back he feels relatively content, thinks of little. Occasionally though, he thinks rather a lot:

"I asked the priest why there aren't any miracles today like in the old days. He said it's a miracle we're all alive! I wanted to tell him that I could dream up better miracles than that! A miracle could move us all to one of those tall buildings near the ocean. A miracle could bring us loaves of bread, jars of jam, bottles of juice, piles of candy, all the water we needed, and the ocean too. We could put on clothes and take them off, then put on other clothes. We would still be good in God's eyes. I'm sure He wouldn't keep us from His sight, just because we had lots of money and lots of food. But we'd miss home, yes. We'd come back in the end."

God's vision preoccupied young Carlos. He wondered whether Jesus "in Heaven" took notice of Rio's Jesus.[2] He wondered whether God paid attention to every neighborhood, every family, every person on this earth. How could He? Does He ever tire of it all, go to sleep? And why was Jesus so poor, back then, almost two thousand years ago, when He might have lived differently? That last question was never answered to the boy's satisfaction, not by members of his family, not by the nuns, not by the priest:

"Jesus was poor, but then He died, and I'm sure He lives better now! If He doesn't, then we won't, I guess! Too bad! I'd like to spend a few days in a big hotel on the beach, and have all I want to eat. God must have wanted to have a good time, too. He must have had pains in his stomach. I asked the priest, I asked the sisters, and they said God isn't one of us. But I thought He was! I thought He watches over us. If He can see, then I'm sure He can get hungry. Who feeds Him?"

Carlos goes further one day. He draws the well-known mountain that holds the statue of Christ on top (Figure 20). He draws another height — the hill covered with shacks and cabins of a favela, his. He draws the ocean, and along the shore, the hotels and apartment houses of Rio's rich. He draws the sky. It is cloudy. The sun is hidden. The ocean seems dark, stormy. But the unsettled weather is of lesser significance, it seems, than a black dotted line that extends from both of Christ's eyes, to Copacabana, then on to the sea. For a moment a startled visitor wonders whether the child hasn't confused his Rio landmarks — put the cable lines that run to and from Sugar Loaf (another landmark) upon, instead, the mountain where Christ stands, His arms outstretched. But no, the child has made no such error. He has drawn his sense of what is happening to the world, and tells this story:

"There is a lady who lives near us. She can put the curse on someone. She is dangerous. Best to avoid her. She stares at you, and you run away, as fast as you can. She can make you sick, and you don't get better. Jesus Christ could do that too, if He wanted. I know He must be looking at us; and He must want to help us. One day, maybe, He'll stare everyone in the face, and then bad people will be scared. But if He doesn't help us, the drug dealers will!"

That dramatic, final alternative presented, with a shrug of the shoulders and a wan smile, the picture is put aside, declared finished. Meanwhile, a cousin, Maria, a year older, a neighbor, is far less taken with Jesus, with His celebrated representation in stone. She calls religion a "business." She calls prayer a "trick" people use to "forget." To forget what? To forget what the police do to the favela, and what the people who own the police do to the favela. At twelve already a woman, Maria senses the urge in people to win others over, to use them, to betray them. She has pictures of movie stars, men and women both, on the unplastered walls of her parents' cabin. She observes that it is win or lose with them: "They have to be smart, or they'll end up old, and with nothing." She has heard stories of such outcomes from older women who read film scandal sheets all the time. She stares at her pictures of movie stars, imagines herself one of them, laughs at the ridiculous content of her dreams, becomes tough and cynical, describes the stars as "no better than anyone else," by which she seems to mean on the prowl, seductive — and very important, smart or calculating, hence successful. Not prone to such wordy descriptions, she says it all with a striking image of her future self: "I won't be a movie star. I won't be on television. But if I become pretty (and I think I have a good chance), I'll try to get a man who will come here and take me away, and I'll stay away. I have to get him, and I have to keep him, and I hope I'll learn how!"

The image needs little explanation — and none is forthcoming from the young woman. She wonders whether she should make a pinup of herself — use her own drawing to inspire herself. No, best stay with the actresses already staring down on her bed, one she shares with two younger sisters. "Better those women than the Virgin Mary," she says defiantly; "better my favorite men film stars than Jesus." Why? Jesus is usually "sick and bleeding and hungry, in most pictures." She adds: "He's dying in a lot of pictures." She is her father's daughter; he talks about the Church with vehement indignation and contempt. He claims that the Church is made up of liars, friends of the rich, shamelessly servile camp followers of the powerful. Maria will be no "whore"; she will resist being called bad names by those who are, she believes, "themselves whores" — ready to do and say what the highest price dictates.

Maria will start out, she hopes, in a beauty parlor, somehow, styling the hair of rich women. There is, in the favela, a young man of sixteen who does lawn work in a home owned by a businessman who owns several gas stations. Maria plans to go to that home, plead for a job, any menial job, get friendly with the woman of the house, learn her vanities, vulnerabilities, and susceptibilities, and somehow win her favor. She has heard older women talk about doing so — the guile, the resourceful listening, the ingratiation one must psychologically manage. She hopes for a contact, then a victory: "You can be a piece of dirt; you can be mud; you can be a dirty cat, a chicken everyone ignores or pushes around — and then a lady makes a call, and you are washing hair in Copacabana or Ipanema. You've won — you can buy good shoes. I'll wear them, one day; I will, if I am lucky and if I talk the right way!"

An entrepreneur, already. A determined observer, readying herself, day by day, for a jungle she has analyzed and is soon enough going to invade, try to conquer. A young woman who attends no church, worships no God, measures her future by shoes, dresses, hair styles. She not only scorns religion in conversation, she hates the very sight of priests, nuns, and the police, all of whom she links as a collection of hypocritical moralists. When the Pope came in 1980 and was moved almost to tears by the poverty of Rio's favelas, he left his ring. Maria commented, bitterly: "I'd like that ring! I'd wear it and be rich; or I'd sell it, and buy diamonds, and wear them for all the world to see." Carlos thought her a "bad person" for speaking such words, but Carlos's religious inclinations were not to last forever. By the end of summer 1980 he offered Maria more understanding: "She says she wants to live; she says it's death here, and everyone knows it. I guess she is right. Take a look yourself."

The visitor demurs, tries to avoid looking, yet again, at the terrible misery of thousands of his fellow creatures. Best to dwell on other observations; best to take notice that the early adolescent favela girls tend to be, these days at least, anticlerical and tough, crafty, resourceful in their urban skepticism and materialism; whereas the pubescent boys, the youths just turning into men, are relatively more restrained, fearful, apprehensive as they get ready to deal with Rio's sprawling blend of commercial expansion, tourist life, and extreme, persisting poverty. Soon enough, one speculates, Maria will face her likely fate: teenage pregnancy, and a different order of work than she dreamed of — a life in the *barracos*, the home-made shacks that make up the sad, dreary, upper, poorer level of a favela. Once Carlos, in a moment of grim observation that was all too accurate, talked of the "babies, babies, and babies" that "descend" on the favela, born to its struggling, hungry, terribly vulnerable Marias. He did not refer to the men who, by their actions — their sense of their rights — keep on ensuring that outcome.

Drugs and sex and movie-star pictures and, amid the awful degradation, the transistor radio with dance music and rock music are eternal aspects, it seems, of twentieth-century favela life. And, too, there are the physical constants: a rustic conglomerate of shanties, wood and tarpaper and sheets of tin turned into makeshift structures with cracks in the sides and leaking roofs and only the slanted earth for a floor. No one makes an effort to control or regulate what is built, where things are built, how they are built; no sewer pipes, no sanitation, really, of any kind; scattered electricity, no reliable lights; and of course, no telephones. In Rio, the favelas are so high up that the hills or mountains might be thought uninhabitable. The lower edge of the favela is often socially stabler, more prosperous economically; houses there tend to be more substantial, and may have conveniences — reliable electricity, television, even a refrigerator. As one moves up the hill, however, things get worse and worse, until one seems near the clouds, above the entire city — and in hell.

All the time motion stirs up and down a dirty, unpaved, narrow alley, through which walk grown-ups and children: the traffic of a hungry, thirsty, diseased population, nevertheless attempting against severe odds to make do. Water is at the bottom, at the entrance to the favela: a single pump. Around the source of water stand the women, washing clothes, or filling up old, rusty gallon tins once filled with olive oil, talking, always talking — not to mention eyeing the coming and going of favelados: the interchange between a city slum and distant, prosperous, urban enclaves. It is an encounter that Carlos and Maria are learning to become part of, to gauge and test and fathom for themselves. From a communal pump to a broken-down shanty higher up is a long, burdensome climb — often the tins of water held on the head: "I die climbing," even youthful Maria says. She dreams of the ascent of those elevators she has seen in the Copacabana hotels. In her mind's eye, she presses a button, operating a hair dryer — but sometimes, while doing so, she falls, trips on the slimy path, lands in a pool of garbage, human excreta. The flies scatter, as do the stray cats and dogs and chickens.

The visitor is intent on more than such documentation — the terrible details of city slum life: a rural existence transported en masse to the hills of the city, where, ironically, magnificent views are available to a people grievously weighted down. The visitor has his own ambitious agenda: What do the children of such areas learn about the moral and political life that is theirs — the favela's life, Rio de Janeiro's, Brazil's? Carlos and Maria have talked to him of their ideas, their thoughts, their hopes and aspirations — for money, for a better way of life, for a degree of personal independence. They show a paradoxical combination of weary cynicism and fatuous optimism, and in between, a terrible apprehension of what, finally, must be. Nevertheless, the visitor lingers. He wants to see more — has his own kind of yet unappeased hunger and thirst to quench. He is still very much *in medias res*, so to speak, absorbed in the issue of "political socialization," the main point of his research. But Carlos once told him this: "Brazil is my country. But this is really my country — my house, and the others here. As for those people you point to there, who live near the ocean, they are in Brazil, yes. But do they think *we* are in Brazil?"

A question not meant to be sardonic, though it may seem so in the context of this essay. A child is trying to figure out what possible (political) connection there can be between the favelados and those who live in luxury. Suddenly a moment comes: "The police, they are the ones — they are the rope of Brazil. They hold the country together," he observes, "like a package my father carries up to our house, tied together tight." Maybe a rough analogy, but not a bad way of putting one's finger on an important element of this nation's political and military life — the power of arms that makes for the binding presence of national life. What else, the boy has reasoned, could keep "together," on the one hand, the brutish favela experience, melancholy, yet in ways hauntingly spirited, and on the other hand, the ostentatious press of the self-important rich who inhabit Ipanema or Copacabana?

"Brazil is guaranteed by its army," said one of the members of the nation's military junta in 1979 — to which a few favelados old enough to be called mere children, uneducated ones, would say yes. Quite correct. Such clear-cut, penetrating social and political intelligence is perhaps denied those whose life is cushioned not only materially but ideologically. As William Carlos Williams recalled, in a letter to a friend, about the Depression in the 1930s: "A few children could rub their bellies in delight — good meals! — and have their daydreams; other children, lots and lots, knew they had to grab apples if they were to eat, even if at the risk of getting nabbed by the cops."[3]

In Rio de Janeiro and São Paulo such children are almost obsessed (I sometimes think) by the police, by the army, too — and well-armed troops are often in evidence not far from major favelas. By no means would every child speak as openly as Carlos. Utterly uneducated, he was bright, shrewd, resourceful, quick of mind, and quite imaginative. I was surprised at the way in which he analyzed the city's social structure, its political situation — and reminded by such remarks that many other favelados are far less blunt, far less clearheaded as they respond to questions meant to elicit from them their ideas on how their city works, on the character of their country's political life. In *The Moral Life of Children* I have tried to indicate some of the ethical judgments a favelado child can hand down — on others as well as himself or herself.[4] These same children continually keep tabs on street power: who has it, who wields it, and in what fashion, over whom. But they don't understand the larger workings (or trappings) of power too well — don't know about mayors and governors and national anthems and flags; don't know who the President of Brazil is, and who runs the city of Rio de Janeiro; don't know what happens in an election (if anything!), and how people become candidates for office; don't know how individuals get to be judges, or for that matter, leading military figures. Rather in Brazil one becomes especially aware of how class influences the political awareness of children.

Class for Carlos and Maria, and for their well-to-do or very rich Brazilian age-mates, is the major force that race is for all South African children, religious affiliation for all of Northern Ireland's children, the French language for Canada's children, Polish as a language and Polish culture as a historical phenomenon are for, say, the Warsaw children I met, Sandinista ideology is for Managua's schoolboys and schoolgirls — a determining element in shaping the life one lives, a means of figuring out not only where one stands in the world, but, very important, what one's country stands for: its values, its purposes, its way of behaving toward its people. Carlos tried to tell me that he knew about his country,

Brazil, in his own (class-connected) way; he knew the connection between a nation as an abstraction (its mottos, its flag, its anthem, the pictures on its currency, its remembered history) and a nation as an everyday aspect of one's experience. Carlos hadn't the slightest idea what Brazil's flag looked like. He knew nothing of the nation's anthem or its military marching songs. He knew nothing of its government — who occupied which position. He knew this about his nation's currency: "I look at the numbers, that's all. As long as I can read the numbers, I'm fine! I can't read the words. I can only read a few words." He is functionally illiterate, has never seen a history book, has never really gone to school. He knows the word *banco* at sight, and *Brasil* at sight (as in Banco do Brasil), and he knows the word *cruzeiro* because he's seen it beside those numbers on the paper money he's sought and sought ever since he became aware of being the person he is.

Am I right to connect this boy's earliest awareness to money, to his sense of its importance? What has such an awareness to do with a child's "political socialization," his nationalist attitudes, if any? When Carlos was thirteen, he told me he must have been born near a bank. I knew he'd been born right there, delivered by his grandmother, in the favela. I asked him why a bank. He answered without hesitation: "The first memory I have was my mother crying, and begging. She was on her knees, and she wanted my father to give her some money. I remember him holding the money in his hand, and she was staring at it, and she was saying please, please, and then he let it go, and it floated down, and she caught it, she grabbed it. I remember the smile on her face. I remember my father; he was angry, but he grabbed her, and she kept smiling. She smiled at me, and she smiled at him. Then they went to the other side of the room. They lay down on the floor together. Now I know why he was angry — not enough of those cruzeiros! He probably wanted to take the money and spend it on wine. That's how he died; he'd been drinking and he didn't see a car coming, and it hit him and killed him. The police told us the driver was even drunker than my father was."

A youth remembers a dangling cruzeiro bill — and more: the way money influenced his mother's life, his father's life, their joint

life. His early life, too: a child who witnessed rages fueled by
money, and also, he later realized, seductions based on money: "I
think my father got favors from my mother with money; I think
she was so tired with all of us, that she had no interest in sex. He
either beat her into submitting, or bribed her!" When I heard that
psychological observation, that "free association" in reference, really,
to an important "screen memory" (an extremely early remembrance — often a series of experiences compressed into one or two
visual images), I remembered that Anna Freud had said in a 1972
case-conference: "We are not yet fully aware of all the various
influences which affect the growth and emotional development of
children." No one could take issue with that thought, modest
enough to sound banal, though she supplied an edge to her remarks
when she added: "The instincts don't exist in a vacuum; their effect
on a child depends on who the child is, where the child lives, what
kind of a world the child has to face."⁵ I remember that progression — from a general statement of individuality ("who the child
is") to specific environmental references ("where" and "world"). I
think those cruzeiros Carlos saw as a child in his father's unsteady
hands were an important element in the formation of his character.
Even as a baby he learned that money controlled sexuality — that
he was living in a world where such things happened. Miss Freud's
progression entered into Carlos's "oedipal development"; namely,
the manner in which he responded to the very triangle he mentions
in his early memory, his father, his mother, himself.

"Why is it," he once asked me, "that the only time I saw my
mother and father talk was when he came home with money?"
The question was rhetorical, of course. Yet, the asking said something about the intimate relationship between a government (Brazil's Treasury) and a family. That same day I asked him something:
Did he know where money came from — all the money in all Rio
de Janeiro? He hadn't thought about money in that way, he said,
and he laughed: "I just try to get a few cruzeiros, as many as I
can. If I knew where I could go get more, I'd walk and walk and
never sleep, until I got there." I press the matter: Who makes
money? He replies: "The people who run the city, the country —
Brazil, they make it." Who are they, I wonder. He doesn't know

any names, but his answer tells a lot about the relationship between the two abstractions of class and nationalism in his life: "In a country the people who make money must be the banks. The people who own the banks own money. They're the rich. I don't know who they are, but they must be on top of everyone else, and if the country gets into trouble, they're the ones who decide what to do. Here in this place [the favela] there are a few men who are tough, and you'd better not cross them. The priest tells us he has to answer to a Bishop. The same with Brazil — there must be a few men, and nothing misses their eyes. They are the rulers, the bosses of Brazil! They must be the people who know about money; I mean, it's on their orders that money is made, I think. You can't just make it yourself! If you could, we'd all be trying, and we'd all be rich! It's a few who decide — who have a lot of money and are the bosses of the banks and the government. The police, the army, the banks — they're all taking orders from these bosses."

Not that exceptionally well-educated Brazilian children, born to privilege, opportunity, luxury, would necessarily disagree with this poor child — who, at times, seemed as sophisticated as any adult. The interviews I had with children who lived in Copacabana and Ipanema, both quite affluent sections of Rio de Janeiro, proved more detailed and specific about "political socialization"[6] — flags were identified and drawn, a government's structure was described, or rather, fairly often, recited out of schoolroom memory, and historical dates were mentioned. But we academic researchers may be as far removed from certain blunt truths about the social order as some of the children I might want to call "overprotected" by their wealthy, highly guarded daily life. When, for instance, I asked Claudia, then twelve, about her country, Brazil, she was quite forthcoming, factually. She knew about the country's capital, could locate it on the large globe in her father's grand study, overlooking Copacabana Beach. She could tell me the capitals of other South American countries, too. (Many favela children have never seen a map, a globe, and can't identify Brazil's capital; nor can their parents.) She also explained to me, patiently, that Brazil would "soon be a democracy, like the United States." There are a lot of people, she went on to tell me, who "don't know enough to be able to vote." When they have been educated, they will be "equal to everyone else."

She had learned all this information in a very strict school. She had learned to make maps, to identify cities, countries. She had learned the names of prime ministers and their dates in office. She had learned that there are "states" in Brazil, each with its governor. She knew, even at her age, about her nation's colonial history, and of course, knew why she spoke Portuguese. She could point to Portugal on a map, knew its capital. Beyond such factuality, however, a more reticent child appeared. Her father was, in fact, one of the bankers the favela boy, Carlos, believed to be a "boss" of his country. She was not at all so certain about that: "My father works hard. People think that a banker is someone who sits and does nothing but count the money he makes! Papa is up so early he can see the sun rise, and he is one of the first people in the bank to be at work, every morning. He's always on the phone, and he has to think way, way ahead — far into the future. He talks with the people in the government, but he hasn't any idea what they're going to do, a lot of the time — because he'll pick up *Jornal do Brasil* [one of Rio de Janeiro's papers, solid and respectable] and he'll read something, and tell us he's very upset by what he's read.

"Mama says she worries about Brazil. So does my father. They have an apartment in Paris, and sometimes they talk about moving there. My mother would like to go to the opera all the time, and the symphony. She says Brazil is backward, compared to Europe. She says the safest place is your country, the States — but she doesn't like it there. She says New York, the biggest city, is a dirty city, and full of dangerous people. They'll rob you, and kill you. We do have bad people here, yes, but you go abroad to get away from them, not to see more and more of them! I'd love to see the States. I've never been there — only to Europe. But we see your television all the time, and your movies; we play them now in our home.

"I'm learning French and English — to speak both. If we went to live in France, I'd be ready to speak pretty good French. Mama says she'd move there if it wasn't for her mother and father. They are both old and sick. They'd never come with us to Paris. She's afraid to leave them for long — they might die, and she'd be far off. Also, she gets homesick for Brazil. It's our country, and your country is your country — where you were born, and where you live. You can't leave it without being sorry; even if you want to leave it, because it's better someplace else — to live.

"The difference between France and Brazil? France is older, and they've got better music, the opera and the symphony. France once had colonies; it tried to civilize Africa, parts of it. France has a parliament, and it's a democracy. We're younger, and a lot of our people can't read or write. We have Indians, and we have a big jungle, and the Amazon, and the tribes there. We have to teach our people how to behave; they don't know about how you live when you're in a modern city, and you have to dress correctly, and be polite and talk in the correct way. That's why Brazil has to wait until we have the same kind of government the States have. Papa says the North Americans are always trying to get countries to have their people vote — but half of your own people don't vote! Is that true?"

I nod; I try to explain. She smiles, she sees us in thorough agreement! And she says: "That's what we have here, too — lots of poor people, and they don't want to work to make themselves better. They don't cooperate. They don't obey the laws. You feel sorry for them; a lot of them don't even know the laws. So, how could they ever vote? It's ridiculous to try to change a country overnight. You have to wait, and try to be patient — understanding: Momma says you mustn't be cold to people, you must *understand* them. But to think everyone is equal — that would be absurd, crazy. If someone can read a poem and listen to the opera, and someone else doesn't know the alphabet and stands in the street whistling and trying to get people to give them money — and for no work — then those two people aren't the same. Papa says: "It's like day and night, how different people can be. We should start with the people who are educated voting, and when the country becomes older, and more of the people have gone to school, then more people can vote."

This girl has obviously relied upon her parents for her political views; she has paid close attention to what they have said, and has shaped their various remarks into a reasonably coherent philosophy. She has ideas about how her country should be run, who should run it, who should have little or no say in who runs it. She also has moral notions that support her political ones — what is correct, what is at fault. It is unfair to view her as no more than a copycat version of her self-serving parents — while exulting in the canny eloquence and the brave resilience, rendered in language, of favela children. The latter boys and girls, after all, obtain their ideas, too, somewhere — from others. I hear young favelados picking up phrases from each other, and of course, from those who employ them or use (or abuse) them in wealthier neighborhoods. There is a strong tradition, in the favelas, of listening — of paying heed to the words of various elders: a boss, a persuasive member of the clergy, a grandparent or parent or uncle or aunt, a policeman who does his fair share of hustling, and who, maybe, speaks moral and political rhetoric out of one side of his mouth and lots of cynical, commercial exhortations out of the other, not unlike some successful businessmen or professional men in Brazil or the United States, or in communist countries, whose bureaucrats have shown themselves not to be beyond high and noble talk one minute, and the crudest, most exploitive deeds (and their justifications) the very next minute.

Brazil has a growing (and highly influential) cadre of engineers, doctors, lawyers, teachers, not to mention officeholders in its public and private bureaucracies. I have tried to convey some of their personal, their moral struggles elsewhere;[7] but here, too, one ought to mention the memories of severe poverty so many of these now-successful individuals can't shake off — because their politics so often lies under that dark shadow. (This condition is less true with their children, interestingly.) The middle class, by definition, looks both ways, so to speak, in every country. But Brazil does not have nearly as stable and dependable an economy as that of the United States — nor the firm social and political institutions the older Western capitalist democracies have. A Rio de Janeiro doctor, one of three physicians who were quite helpful in my research,[8] expressed his chronic anxieties, and their effect upon his political views: "It's hard for me to talk with doctors like you, from other countries — I mean, countries like yours, or the [Western] European ones. Here, we are all scared that what *is* — well, it only *seems to be!* Here, we scratch our heads, and we pinch ourselves, and say: Okay, it's all great — but it won't last, or it'll be followed by some terrible nightmare, and the whole thing, all we've built up, will just fall to pieces! I see by your face — that you don't see!

"If you had been inside my flesh all these years, you'd know what I mean. Here, everything is surprising; we're trying on things for the first time — building a modern country, with a government that is reliable; and it lasts, and it enforces the law, and it isn't replaced, in a few years, by another one, and then another one. Instability is our history, in almost all the countries of South America — and what used to happen in Brazil, one government after another. We can't assume, especially people like me, the way you can, that *what is will be*. The rich, they can always take care of themselves. I know; I take care of them — as a doctor. They've got all their bets hedged. They have money, lots of money, abroad — and apartments and even cars. They're ready to leave at the drop of a hat. No one can destroy them — even a violent shift here, in the government and the social order. Some have their own planes, their own airfields; they're ready to go — faster than you and I could blink, let me tell you! When you do your 'studies' of them and their children, you'd better take what they say with a grain (or two, or three!) of salt. They'll talk a great line about how they love Brazil, but they're not loyal to Brazil; they're loyal to their own survival — and I mean survival as rich people!"

I found it hard to confirm what he said. A number of children I got to know, whose fathers qualified as quite rich, felt "loyal" indeed to Brazil, spoke of it with affection and possessiveness, told me that they were born there, hoped to live there, wanted to die there. To be sure, they mentioned their foreign travels — but these were precisely that, voyages to other countries, the different characteristics of which (in political socialization) these children quickly noticed, and did not easily forget. The girl quoted earlier,

Claudia, not unrepresentative of such children, disliked what she regarded as the "rudeness" of many ordinary French working people. She made a connection between that trait and what she explicitly called "democracy": "In democracy, the people think too much of themselves," she told me. Then she clarified: "They have no respect for people who have done better. That's no good. You have to look up to people." She preferred England: at least there is a Royal Family there. On the other hand, that family is not enough "admired," she said. I told her I thought most of the English felt great warmth toward the Royal Family. She was not at all slow in correcting me: "Oh, yes, but they don't give them the credit that should be theirs!" I wasn't sure what she meant — and so had the interpreter carefully restate it for me. Then, I asked what kind of "credit" she had in mind: "Oh, to see people as the best in the world: *royal*, not just like everyone, but much different, much better — higher, much higher."

How strange those comparative adjectives are to such as me, when used in conjunction with England's royalty — "better," "different," "higher," even "much higher." *My* political socialization has taught me — a white American physician — that we are all, in important political and moral respects, utterly equal. True, we are differently endowed (by nature, by fate, by accident, by luck) and we have a right to forge ahead, establish new distinctions in our life — but as the Declaration of Independence says, "all men are created equal," and each of us has certain "inalienable rights." Claudia was not prepared to see Brazilian politics, or the national goals of Brazil, in that light. She would certainly prefer exile in, say, England, to the dangers a social revolution would pose to her family. She liked Brazil because she felt its national purposes, as espoused by the leading figures in its government, in the daily expression of the policies they pursue, were precisely the purposes and policies she deemed desirable. Thus she expressed satisfaction with her nation, meaning its practices as they coincided with her family's aspirations.

As for my doctor friend, and *his* daughter, Paula, whom I talked with many times, especially when she was twelve and thirteen, she didn't quite sound like her father politically. Just so, there was a surface discrepancy between Claudia's obvious affection for Brazil and for English royalty, on the one hand, and her father's frank acknowledgment (confirming my doctor friend's feeling) that he "always" has assumed that "Brazil can suddenly destabilize" — and so he *does* "keep an apartment in Paris." If he were in exile, would he miss Brazil? "If I were in *exile*," he says, politely but with evident annoyance, "I doubt I'd miss Brazil." His daughter Claudia, however, would "always miss Brazil." Paula regarded these matters in this way: "This is our country, and my father says he'd give his life to make it better, and we should feel just as he does, all of us in my school: for we are very lucky to be going there, it's such a good place [a fine private school in Rio de Janeiro], and the teachers really try to help you and make you feel good, besides teaching you a lot. They teach us about our nation, and they show us all we've accomplished, but they tell us there's a lot more to do.

"We have to open up the country — we have to conquer the Amazon, and make all our people feel *Brazilian*. You know, there are people in the 'backlands' who don't even know they're in Brazil. They are Indians, people belonging to tribes. Even here, in Rio de Janeiro, a lot of people don't think of what they owe their nation. They think of what they can get for themselves, only. My mother says she's learned one thing from talking to my father all these years — that he's right when he says the rich and the poor are basically alike: both of them think only of themselves. The rich are out for everything they can get, and the same with the poor; they think of themselves, and to the Devil with their own brothers and sisters, even. Blood means nothing to them — and my father says some of his rich patients are exactly like that: it's their bank accounts, and no one else's, that they think about all day and all night, every day and every night. But let them all be like that; there are enough of us!

"I guess what I mean is this: My friends, all their parents tell them that we've got to build our nation up, make it better and better, and stronger and stronger, so that it won't get into some of the bad troubles we've had. The rich can escape, and the poor, they don't know what to do, because they're in such a big, sorry mess. (I feel so sad when I pass favelas; I cross myself and pray to God for all the people who live in them.) But as for us, this country has been very kind to our fathers and mothers, and we owe it to them to be kind to the country, and if we're kind to the country, we're really being kind to ourselves, because when the country is strong and healthy, so are we. The rich are always in good shape, and the poor are always in bad shape, but we in the middle can be 'riding high' one year, and in the low, low dumps the next year, and the reason is the nation, our Brazil. My grandfather wasn't much better off than the poor. He had a lucky break. He worked in a store, and the man who owned it had no children, and he gave my grandfather and two others (who'd worked like mules for him all their lives) good money while they worked, and he paid for my father's education. When that man died, he even left money to my grandfather, and so my grandfather could leave money to my father. Since my father has an education, and he's a doctor, he is independent; but if people don't have the money to pay their bills, then my father gets nervous. You see why we have to keep the country strong?"

When she has finished with her lesson, we discuss the country, and she insists it is as "free" as "it is possible to be" — and then adds that important qualifying phrase, "right now." I keep on asking these Brazilian children why "right now" there is no room for "more freedom." In 1983, I am able to mention nearby nations, such as Argentina, where there is "more freedom."[9] Always the answer is the same, and provides some evidence that these children offer me a nationalism very much influenced by the class to which they belong. Paula said: "You can't give people what they're not ready to take. Democracy is for a country where everyone can read and write, and people understand what it means to vote. If they don't know what a vote means, it's stupid to round them up, like sheep or cattle or goats, and put them in a room, and get them to put an X beside some party's name, or a man's name. My father does work with the poor, voluntary work, once a week, sometimes twice a week. He'll come home crying sometimes. He's very upset. He says to make the poor into voters is to trick them! They need to become educated! They need to get the help of doctors, like my father, and they need to eat better food. *They* don't want a vote. They don't even know who Figueiredo is." [Figueiredo was the current President.]

Paula doesn't seem as cynical as her father, when she regards both her nation and the two other classes she, like him, keeps mentioning: "The rich are here; some of my classmates, they are rich, very rich. They'd never leave here. I mean, if they did, they'd cry all the time in Paris or in your United States of America! Brazil is their nation, just as it is mine. When we read our history, we are proud. We are one of the important nations of the world. We have lots of land and people, and we have minerals. We will become stronger and stronger! The rich have become rich through Brazil. They're good, my friends who live in Ipanema! We're getting rid of the favelas [demolishing them to make way for luxury apartment buildings!], and more people are going to school — more favelados. You can't be wearing black all the time! You have to smile, and look for the sun to shine, and at night, the stars to give you direction! My mother says what you hope for yourself, in your life, you have to hope for your country!"

In Paula one sees an ardent, touching (and naive) coincidence of familial and nationalist sentiment. She is, one must emphasize, quite knowing about her nation, its leaders, its economic difficulties, its social unrest, its international negotiations. (She doesn't know about the International Monetary Fund, true, but she knows that "bankers in your country worry about our country" — all of which is, maybe, more than many *Americans* know.) I think it fair to say that Brazilian middle-class children, compared to those of other classes, are far more strongly identified with their country; take more trouble to learn about its politics and its history; speak more warmly, even excitedly about its prospects; defend its alleged failures or wrongdoings more persistently, even angrily; respond more vigorously and affirmatively to patriotic summonses of one kind or another, at home, at school, on television, on the streets (where many demonstrations take place), or during sports spectacles. Among poor children there is indifference and apathy, or unnerving cynicism, skepticism, often accompanied by direct, clearheaded awareness of the economic "facts of life" as they unrelentingly impinge upon the politics of a country — bribes, deals, arrangements, trade-offs, agreements, pressures of all kinds exerted in all places. Among the rich there can be moments, or periods, of intense, alert, knowledgeable patriotism — but there are, also, long spells of naiveté, perhaps the result of a sheltered life. Moreover, even if Paula is absolutely correct in her compassionate apologies for the children of rich Brazilians, I have to add that in my interviews with those children I have heard much that contends with nationalism for their allegiance — including, of course, trips to other countries, whose customs and difficulties may end up competing with those of Brazil's for their scrutiny. Such boys and girls don't always have either the time or the uncommitted emotional resources to offer their nation, and a child's fervent nationalism requires both aspects: a family that thinks to pay homage to the nation, to speak of its virtues, to worry about its difficulties; and also a family whose own life is so intimately connected to a nation's life that — let Paula say it: "If Brazil really began to fall apart, my father says, then *we'd* be falling apart, because it's like the roads in our part of the city: all of them lead to one main road, and if that gets flooded, no one can go beyond that point, and everyone has to wait until they open that road again."

She was talking, in negative imagery, of a sense of shared fate. In other countries, the nationalism in children is more significantly connected to different questions, as we have seen. In Brazil the refracting lens is class, and for the United States, too, I believe.

In Chapters I and II, I quoted from a number of American children whom I've come to know these past twenty-five years. I want to provide, here, some focus for the observations I've made in my own country about this side of "child development" — the "political socialization" of boys and girls who live in the United States. There is no question that American children, like those from other countries, have a range of political ideas and attitudes.[10] Though I have of course always been aware that there are rich people in the United States, and poor people, and people in between, it took me many years to think of using "class" as a means of analyzing what I was hearing from children about their country.

Race, yes, geographical background, yes, experience, yes (as in the school desegregation crisis), but not class, itself. The titles of my five volumes of *Children of Crisis* tell the story: the poor were called "migrants" or "sharecroppers" or "mountaineers"; I wrote of "Eskimos" and "Indians" and "Chicanos"; I spoke of Ruby as one who braved mobs to initiate the integration of New Orleans schools. Though I was constantly describing poverty, racism, the terrible vulnerability that goes with being at the bottom of the class ladder, I didn't go into a close, comparative analysis of attitudes generated by class[11] — contrasting, say, sharecropper children with children of the foremen who run plantations, and with children of those who *own* such plantations. True, an occasional foreman appeared, and true, the last volume was entitled *Privileged Ones*, with the subtitle, *The Well-off and the Rich in America*. And true, I did write a book (in 1970) called *The Middle Americans*.[12] But in neither book did I engage directly, with either myself or the children I was interviewing, in the issue of "class."

We in psychiatry speak of "countertransference" — our own distortions, denials, "blocks," refusals of concern and attention, as we work with our patients. Often we hurl the "blame" on the patient: he or she, with his or her "problems" prompts this countertransference. But, of course, Freud knew that blindness, and a touch of stupidity, and perverse unwillingness to look squarely at some matters — these are missing in no one, including those of us who have undergone years of psychoanalysis, and who "treat" others intensively, and therefore might be expected to be aware of our (and their) difficulties. A substantial literature[13] has yet to appear on the way in which one's class background affects one's clinical awareness — or, Lord knows, on how a child psychiatrist's own class affects his capacity to observe children near home, or rather far away, especially when they differ from him substantially. I did try to touch on this topic in the chapters on "method" in the *Children of Crisis* volumes, and in a chapter titled "The Observer and the Observed" in *Farewell to the South*, but not as searchingly as I ought have done.[14]

Nor do I know whether it's possible now, after a decade of wandering across countries and continents, to do justice to this

question — how the observer, or one observer at least, may overcome the most powerful social or political obstacles toward self-
comprehension. We have yet to establish a mode of psychoanalysis
that systematically engages the cultural or social or political aspects
of a person's thinking. By the late 1970s I'd made enough progress
as an American working abroad to be willing to go back and listen,
yet again, to what I had heard in the past and to conduct new
interviews with altered thoughts and questions in mind. The result
is to be seen here, and in this book's companion volume, *The
Moral Life of Children*.[15]

One may hear, among America's poor, the melancholy resignation, or the shouting outrage, of those who feel they have been
dealt an exceedingly bad hand by fate, and who don't know how
to change that state of affairs — *and* who give vent to their frustrations, resentments, bitterness by taking the most searing view
of their nation's political system. I have been quoting such people
and their children for many years,[16] though with no great emphasis
on the purely *political* side of what they have told me. "I don't
know what politics is," a thirteen-year-old Appalachian boy told
me. I was trying myself to answer him (no easy assignment, I think
many readers might agree if they would stop for a moment and
try to find for themselves and a nearby child a halfway accurate
and suggestive answer) and I was getting nowhere, when he rescued me with this: "You have here the county people, and they're
pretty much big shots when they come up this hollow and start
lording it all over us, and we keep our mouths shut, and say yes
if need be and no if need be; but then you have the people who
are the bosses of these county people, and they're higher up, and
they're over in the [state] capital, and they run things in all the
counties. And you have the business people whispering things to
them, and they [the county officials] have to listen, or they'll get
in trouble and they'll be out of a job.
"That's as far as it goes, I guess, unless you go higher, and I
don't know how that works, I just know about the counties and
our state, because we tried to get the buses to come up here, to
take us to school, instead of the long walk [eight miles!] in winter,

but they told us no, sir, and every time we tried to get an answer from them, they kept on saying Lexington, Lexington, and we asked our Daddy what that meant, and he said, oh, they're tossing the buck upward, and that's how it goes: it's politics, and people dodge, they forever dodge, and soon you're way up there in the clouds, and it's the President of the United States, and who's he but some fast-talking dude who has wax on his shoes and can dance his way around anyone in sight. He's the big boss, the President, but our teacher says they lose, some presidents, because they don't do their bossing the way they should, and they slip and fall, and there's always someone waiting and laughing, and he's ready to take over where the first guy has left off, and that's what politics is, the woods, and the animals in it, the big fry and the small fry, with the big usually winning and the small usually losing — it's no good all around, if you ask me."

I *had* asked him, and though not all these statements came forth in one sustained Appalachian Oratorio, the pith and power of this boy's message, offered in a two-hour Saturday-afternoon exchange in 1981, has been hard for me ever to forget. My wife, who has taught American history to high schoolers, and seen all too many flat, noncommittal civics texts, which she, in fact, has described as "mealy-mouthed" and "full of evasive pieties," sat and listened to that boy's remarks and told our children thereafter that she wished this lad might be asked by some daring publisher to write a civics book — but if such were to happen, the boy might learn what editing can sometimes mean: another lesson in politics, the so-called sophisticated version of Northeast conventional politics rather than the country or mountain variety the boy knows so well.

Some children in the Northeast, however, are as able to take stock of their native land's political life as that mountaineer boy proved able to do. I wonder if anything I included in my earlier work ever matched in depth and scope this political analysis that my wife found in a conversation transcribed in the mid-1970s with a thirteen-year-old white boy in South Boston whose mother was on welfare, having lost her husband, the child's father, two years earlier:[17] "If my dad had lived, we'd have gotten the hell out of here! We'd have moved to Quincy maybe — to some town outside of Boston, so that lousy federal judge (what's his name?) wouldn't be able to get his sticky fingers on us. There are six from my family in school, and he wants all of us to ride one of his buses to Roxbury [a black ghetto] and have a ball at those schools — while the black kids are saying they are lousy jails, the same schools, so let them out, please, and send them to some other schools, please. That judge, he's sure a nice guy! He lives in a fancy suburb, and no one in his family has to go through what we're going through. Our teachers give us these history books, and you read them, and they'll tell you that this is very important, what Boston is going through — hey, let's face it, what *we're* going through, not the rich people who work in Boston during the day and slip away at night, or the ones who live up on Beacon Hill — but none of the teachers and the books they give us really level with you, I mean, put the cards right there on the table, straight up, and no clever hanky-panky! In this country it's all in your bank account, what will happen to you. And it's all politics. That's what it's all about, anywhere in the country: You've got the bucks, and you have freedom, and you can sign on the dotted line, or say nothing doing, buddy, and walk away clean and free. If you don't have the bucks, then you're a loser, and too damn bad for you: Follow orders!

"You ask whose orders? [I had asked.] Well, don't you know? For Christ's sake, the orders of the people who give orders — I mean, that judge, and the people he knows, and the people *they* know, and that's the big shots, we call them around here, the big-shot guys: the governor and the mayor and the senators and the guys who own the banks and the electric company and the gas company and the department stores and the newspapers. Is that enough — is that going to get me an A? [I said yes.] I saw on television a program, a documentary about Chicago, I think, but all the cities are the same; they said there's a 'power structure' in each city, and I thought — right, damn right, and if you don't know that, then don't depend on your teacher to tell you. My dad used to say the priests are good about the holy stuff, but they play it cozy, plenty cozy, when it comes to politics, and the same with the teachers: they're afraid of the top dogs who run the whole show.

"If you want to get ahead and be someone in the government, you've got to have connections. You need to have 'the right touch,' my Dad said — someone who will run interference for you. The government doesn't work like an electric clock; the government is more like a clock you have to wind. There are people making phone calls and dropping in and having their nice talks, and a cup of coffee — and next thing you know, there's a law they want passed. Someone has given a nice wad of dough to someone else! My grandfather swept the floors of City Hall; my grandfather knew. My Dad worked for a contractor, who got jobs from the city and the state; my Dad knew! You don't have to be a big genius who has gone to one of the big colleges to know how it works in City Hall or the State House.

"You ask about the federal government. I don't know anything about it — nothing. But it must be the same — I'd guess. My Dad knew a lot about politics — it's what he heard having beers with his friends. We saw on television a show about Washington, and all that goes on there, and I remember, he laughed; he told us that there's a big difference between what you see on the TV screen, and what's going on inside the offices down there. You have people waving lots of big dollars, and then they come running, the government people. No one down there is racing around trying to figure out what *our* troubles are, here in Southie [South Boston]. We're not important enough. Oh, sure, they come to see us at election time!

"You'll find that the kids here know the same thing I know — that there's a lot good in this country: the freedoms we have, and we're better off than people in other countries. But you'll find we all know that there's a different law for the rich than there is for the poor, and the government grabs all it can from us; meanwhile, it helps the ones who can afford to push and push — and that's how you see it if you've gotten the treatment we've gotten here [a reference to the federal judge's busing order]. If there's a war, it's us who fight — just look at the people from Southie who died in the wars we've had. The people in the suburb, where that [federal] judge lives, their sons don't go and get killed fighting for the country. They get deferrals, or they're the officers, and they tell us to go and kill the enemy or get killed by the enemy! You want to learn what we think about all that — just come and listen to my friends and me talk! We'll show you that we may not be rich and we may not be headed for a college education, but we can figure out what's happening in our country; we're as smart as anyone else. We have lots of guys around here who have fought for America, and I've heard them talk! They know the score!"

This kind of affection for America, tempered by skepticism about its political system — the power of money and social position to influence political decisions — is not at all rarely heard among children who live in poor or so-called working-class neighborhoods. In white South Boston, one also hears vigorous denunciations of "communists," an epithet that sometimes includes people others would consider "liberals," "intellectuals," "social activists." In Roxbury, a black counterpart in many ways, "communists" are mentioned much less often; "whites" and "honkies" who are "in the government" and who "have it in," always, for the black man, much more often. Also, considerably less explicit affection is expressed in Roxbury for the country as a whole, for its general record, compared with the records of other countries. Patriotism bursts forth in Appalachia and South Boston, even as skepticism and cynicism about politicians and their motives (and the rich and *their* motives) also are chronically expressed — along with fierce anti-Communism, based on the fear that hard-won "freedoms" (to say what one thinks, to worship as one likes) would disappear overnight were "socialistic" or "communistic" governments to prevail.

It is hard for the intellectual bent on trying to assess a consistent "ideology," social or political or economic, to make complete sense of all these strong points of view: one moment an uncritical adoration of flag, of national achievements, with Sousa marches and patriotic songs; the next moment a passionate populist egalitarian critique of the corrupt, devious, manipulative ways of power, a crookedness that stretches from the local ward to the halls of Congress, with the state capitol certainly a significant way station; followed the next moment by a spirited defense of "American democracy," *and* of the American military, as the only hopes, really, if the world is not to be "taken over," or "invaded," "or "duped," or "conned" by "atheistic communists" or "dictators," or "all the countries that envy us what we've got" — the phrases vary.

In black neighborhoods one hears a desire for more federal help to the vulnerable, but also a deep suspicion of and hostility toward, "poking into" the lives of the "ordinary working man"; one hears a desire for more social and economic equality, but also an angry pride that rejects "handouts" — especially when they are meant for others; one hears a desire that America protect itself and other nations from various totalitarian threats, but also a suspicion that "the military" is itself corrupt, mischievous, arbitrary, self-serving, and always split along class lines (officers and enlisted men) as the rest of the society is, hence an unjust institution. Yet, such contradictory attitudes yield to the special struggle blacks (and Hispanics and Indians) feel they have to undergo, because of the way in which they feel singled out: a long, historical continuity they well comprehend. "The government is all we've got, like it or not," one Boston black child told me, when I asked him about that federal judge's court order. The boy explained himself tersely: "You can't bad-mouth the hand that gives you food." Still, he could — and did. He had no wish to be bused to South Boston's hostile white territory. He preferred playing hooky.

Of course, blacks and other minority groups do not lack their own class divisions — which, to my ear, are as decisive as they are among whites in shaping children's political thoughts and values. One hears among the "black bourgeoisie" in the South particularly strong denunciations of government ineptitude, deceit, arrogance, duplicity — often the consequence of long years of first-hand acquaintance with local and state officials whose (segregationist) personal behavior has been offensive, indeed. One hears (on the other side of the railroad tracks) observations like this, the written comment (in a school theme) of a black boy of thirteen about his country: "I love my country. It's a good one. But there are bad people in the government. They listen to the rich folks and do them all the favors they need, and us poor folks get the leftover stuff, and we get lectures on being no good. No one lectures the bad government people."

As one moves to white neighborhoods — those more comfortable than that of such a child — one hears children markedly less inclined to mix distrust or scorn with their affirmations of affection for the United States. The flag figures prominently in the pictures such boys and girls draw of homes, schools, shopping malls, playgrounds. At eight or nine these children know of Washington and the Revolutionary War, Lincoln and the Civil War, Eisenhower and World War II; know of their nation as a democracy; know of Russia as an adversary, with a decidedly contrasting form of government — authoritarian and interested in promoting atheism. (The churches as an instrument of political socialization in children, through Sunday-school instruction, have not been given their due by some social scientists.) The eagerness in white suburbs to defend this country at all costs and in all respects contrasts sharply with the previously mentioned scornful expressions that pepper the talk of boys and girls in poorer sections of our cities and in some rural areas. I hesitate to slap the word "rigid" upon such an "eagerness," but I have at times noticed that an effort to probe the patriotic attitudes of these children with even the slightest hint of doubt (as in: "Has our country ever made any major mistakes or blunders?") does not usually make for a relaxed response. So I certainly learned when I talked with Walter and Laura, twins who live in a comfortable town north of Chicago. Here is Walter, at age eleven: "I think we're the greatest, and we're the one country that doesn't make big mistakes, because we're a democracy, and the people vote, and they know, they know what's right. If the President makes a mistake, he doesn't win a second term. We don't have dictators here. The whole world wants to come here. My dad says they'd give their right arms to come here, people from all over. You have to thank God you're here, because if you were born someplace else you'd be in a lot of trouble — the chances are high."

Laura listened carefully to that message, then added this one of her own: "You have to be sympathetic to people in other countries.

It's not their fault, if their government does a bad thing, and they can't stop the government. Our teacher said in Sunday school that we should pray for the Russian people. Jesus will try to save them, maybe. The difference between Russia and us — it's that we don't want to conquer the world. They do — they're out for all they can get, and that's why there's the trouble now. Here we've got a country where anyone can just sit down and say: Look, I'm really going to work, and I won't stop until I've made something of myself, and if I have that attitude, and I don't give up, I'll get there. The trouble in the country is with the people who don't want to work! They're lazy, or they're not too bright, and they have this attitude: Let the government help me, or let the next guy work all the time. I won't, because I'm just not up to it, or I feel tired, and I don't want to hurt myself by working these long hours.

"You know something — my grandfather, he worked fifteen hours a day. My father says he even worked on Sundays — seven days a week. On Sundays he went to Church, but then he went to the store. He always came home late, to eat his supper and collapse into bed! But he did it — he made that drugstore do better and better, and he gambled every penny he had, even my grand-mother's wedding ring, and when he died, he left us enough money so we won't starve, even if Dad loses his job. But he won't! Even if the worst happened, my father would go and find another one. He says he doesn't want the government telling him what to do, and he doesn't want welfare, if he's ever out of work. He went to college, and he worked hard, and now he's an engineer, and he thinks this country is the best — and you know why? It's because you have to work hard here, but if you do, you get your rewards, because this is the land of opportunity. It still is! And the people who don't think so, they're the ones who are always doing the complaining; and you wonder why they don't try some other coun-try, if they're so unhappy. Let them try one of those countries where you can't sneeze without someone from the government putting his hand on your shoulder and telling you that you're out of order!"

This statement is steadfast pride in America — unqualified by populist doubts, by reservations based on injustices seen, mistakes heard discussed or regretted or bitterly denounced. Sometimes there is truculence to such talk; I have heard children like Walter and Laura say they are ready, when older, to go to war against "the commies" or "Red Russia" or "anyone who messes with us." I do hear such talk, sometimes, when my research takes me to some "working-class" neighborhoods, but often with demurrers about America's "fat cats" and "richos," who are bitterly denounced. Among wealthier families a militant anti-Communism is often (not always, however) tempered by a conservatism that is quite literal: those who have a lot are not at all inclined to risk losing it in an apocalyptic war, and besides, "even the Reds" (I heard in a town near Birmingham, Alabama) are no fools, and you know who's got the power and who doesn't. The speaker was an eleven-year-old boy, Gerry, whose father certainly exerts much influence in his city, his state — a wealthy businessman, a lawyer who left "corporate law" to make a fortune in "hospital technology." For Gerry, international crises prompt patriotism, a declaration of nationalist principles — but a wary, cautionary stance, as well: "You love America — everyone does; or if they don't, let them just leave. But if we're going to fight, we have to be sure we can win. Besides, it might be that there's no way anyone can win the next war, if it's the Russians and us fighting, so we have to figure out how to bargain with them. They're in the weaker position, and they need our help; and my daddy says we haven't used all our assets in the smartest way when we've been sitting down with them. We should say: Look, you tell us what you are after, and we'll tell you how we see things, and then we'll find out if there's some way to avoid a war that'll kill us all! My daddy says it's the same old problem: The government doesn't have the best people working for it, and that's usually what happens, you have second-rate guys who can't 'strike the right note'! [His father is an amateur saxophonist!] If we had the kind of brains in our government that we have in our businesses, then we'd be much better off. We'd have a better country here, and we'd do better with the Russians — get them to cut it out, and take what we have to offer them.

"We could help them have a better country, because they can't make the things we can, and they're strong, with their army, but that's all. My father has a friend who went there, and he came back and said 'it's pathetic, it's just pathetic,' the whole country. They're so far behind us that they'll never catch up! When you have a country like that, and you're the number-one country, then you get yourself a strategy: How do you get these poor folks to mind their manners? If you can't get on top of that kind of problem — you don't deserve to be at the bargaining table! Daddy says this country is the greatest one the world has ever seen, but it's not our government people who are the greatest; it's us, the people — our businesses and the people who have the 'get up and go' to start them and build them up! My father says his idea would be this: Get rid of half the people up there in Washington, and turn a lot of the government over to private business. There are lots of crooks, lots of lazy characters on our government's payroll. It's no good. This country can be destroyed from inside, not only from outside! Daddy comes back from talking with people in Montgomery or Washington, and he says that he wants to take a good hot shower and some whiskey and start in all over again! He says there's a lot of 'two-bit frauds on the public payroll,' and we pay the taxes to keep them there, and you want to vomit, thinking of all the waste, and how no good lots of those folks are!"

A noteworthy congruence appears between the children of the poorer and the richer families at times when the federal government becomes split, psychologically or ideologically, from the nation as a whole, from its idealized "traditions" or "history" or "achievements."[18] The country stands for "freedom," the children say, for "opportunity," for accomplishments, often called "success," or "being in first place." But there are "rotten apples" in the general population, and more dangerously, in the government. The country, then, is captive (at least somewhat) to its own government. But where does the country begin, the government end? One presses such questioning on children who themselves articulate this division, and hears about "the American dream," and the "people who don't live up to it"; about "the country the way it should be," and "the America when George Washington was President" (or Lincoln, or Franklin D. Roosevelt, or Dwight Eisenhower, or John F. Kennedy, the presidents most often cited) and "the country now"; or one hears about an embattled contemporary President, Reagan, who is "trying hard," and the various antagonists or worse, "those who want to cut him down, cut him down, all the time."

On the other hand, for many children of solid middle-class background, children who don't ever expect to be either down-and-out or wealthy, this country is seen as virtually unblemished. Such children take a hortatory tone in their patriotic musings — as if they all were engaged in a contest to furnish the best possible statement for the Democratic or Republican National Convention — a statement calculated to win everyone's vote, save those contemptible doubters who can't stomach nationalist pieties, perhaps out of some latent impulse toward subversion. Young Walter, quoted earlier in this chapter, announced to me one day: "There are people who don't like to hold their heads high and say they're American, and we're the best country there ever was — and it's because they have a grudge against the country; they must, and they don't want to stand up for it, and they could turn out to be the 'bad eggs' you sometimes find in the grocery; that's what I heard them called, and they are!"

In years of writing about my fellow young citizens I have, in one way or the other, been writing about their view of this country — their dear and touching love for it, their misgivings, serious or slight, about its ability to live up to its high principles. Anyone who goes "out there," and stays "out there" long enough, in the homes of the people of this country, will soon enough hear our children saluting the ideology of individual political freedom (as incorporated in the Declaration of Independence and the Constitution, including the Bill of Rights, and yes, in Lincoln's Emancipation Proclamation and the commanding rhetoric of our best twentieth-century presidents when they have embraced the eighteenth-century philosophic tradition of the Founding Fathers). Those same children split widely, however, when economic and social issues are discussed — some in favor of a classical economic liberalism of the eighteenth- and nineteenth-century variety (with twentieth-century updates of phrasing), and some in favor of one or another populist, egalitarian point of view, justified by religious appeals, by moral ones of the secular kind, or by the plain urgent needs of hard living. By and large class is, I repeat, the most significant lens through which these many and often contradictory nationalist ideas or values are regarded. As I think I have constantly emphasized in my earlier books, there are exceptions even to this (I hope) tentatively stated generalization: some rich children are much concerned about the poor, some middle-class children are sternly critical of their nation, especially its foreign policy, and some poor children are unyielding in their admiration for their country, no matter how serious their need of assistance so far not forthcoming. I wish, frankly, as I indicated in Chapter II of this book, that we knew our children as political children better — spent more time trying to understand further what their statements about our country tell us about them as our sons and daughters, and about ourselves.

VIII

EXILE AND NATIONALISM: CHILDREN OF SOUTHEAST ASIA

"THEY are good children," said the principal of an elementary school in Arlington, Virginia[1] — a response to an inquiry about how the Cambodian, the Laotian, the Vietnamese boys and girls were managing in their classes. When pressed for specifics, she speaks with assurance and out of conviction: "They are eager to learn. They are considerate and well behaved. They are good citizens in our community." The teachers in the school say much the same things. They emphasize how polite, courteous, obliging and alert these "refugee children" are. In one class, where seven-, eight- and nine-year-old children, most of them originally from Southeast Asia, are learning how to read, the favorable comments of teachers come to mind again and again as one watches the children go about their school day, mastering the spelling of words, learning how to add and subtract and multiply and divide, to write sentences and draw pictures and show a command of English vocabulary. When they salute the American flag, when they pledge allegiance to these United States of America, the boys and girls speak with evident conviction, with a telling earnestness that surprises, maybe embarrasses a jaded visitor, fretting over the hot and humid early June weather of northern Virginia.

The teacher is calm, patient. Her North Carolina accent is soft, inviting, persuasive. She knows, however, that many of her children meet her more than halfway: "They may have suffered a lot, but they don't let the past get in the way of the present. They're eager to do the very best they can. I don't have to raise my voice much." The children are quiet, attentive, awake to every shift in the day's academic rhythm. They are also impressively neat, though not in an uptight way. Dene Symathong explains his reasons for keeping careful track of his school possessions: "If you know where you put things, you save time and you don't worry. Everything goes faster."

He is similarly tidy at home. As he talks, his eyes look right in the visitor's eyes. His hands strive for order. Anything out of place is picked up, put where it belongs. He keeps some pictures of himself, of other family members, in a box, which he opens with great care and then closes gently. The box gets a lingering caress as it is placed in precisely the spot whence it had been removed a few minutes earlier — as if the photographs were sacred reminders of an important human reality, just as pens or pencils in a classroom may be regarded as important instruments of a future life. "I remember when we had nothing," the boy says at another time, but he is reluctant to go any further. Why? "The past is gone."

Actually, in the classroom and on the sidewalks of their neighborhood,[2] many of the children, Dene included, are quite willing to indicate in casual ways how persisting an influence memories can be in their lives. A child draws not only an American flag, but a Laotian one (Figure 21). Another child sketches a rural landscape, and hastens to spell out its location (Cambodia), the former beauty of the country, its sudden hellish transformation: "There it was farms, lots of them. I remember the trees and the huts. I remember my grandfather planting. Then the soldiers came, and they shot people." He loves to evoke the pleasant side of an earlier life; he shuns the pictorial recall of murder — but in a low voice he spells out what he saw: "They came to our house. They ordered my father to go with them. He obeyed. They killed him anyway, right there, while we looked. My mother told us to go inside. She came with us. She told us we couldn't fight back. She told us we might be next. We waited, but nothing happened. They had others to kill. There aren't enough bullets, sometimes, for murderers to kill everyone they want to kill."

With that observation, tragically similar to what other children have told to interlocutors, and offered in an apparently matter-of-fact way, the boy pauses, then asks for the grown-up visitor's sunglasses — perhaps an effort to see what the visitor is now seeing inside his head, having heard such words from an eight-year-old child. In a second the glasses are returned: "They are too big — but one day I'll wear sunglasses." A pause, then another memory: "I never saw them [sunglasses] until I came here." And in case anyone might forget: "We had lots of sun in Cambodia." Then an afterthought: "I mostly remember the rain, and going through the jungle." Like so many others, he'd walked and walked and walked to escape the murderous Khmer Rouge.[3]

Now he does another kind of walking: "We get tired of waiting for the ice-cream man to come to our street, so we go sometimes to try to find him. My mother gives me money on sunny days for an ice cream. When it's cloudy, she says no. Sometimes she changes her mind, just before she leaves the house. I know she works hard; so I am grateful. She waits on people. If they want ice cream, she goes and gets them ice cream. Whatever they want!"

Not far from the apartment house where he lives — many families crammed into small apartments, paying rather high rents — are luxurious condominium apartments, with a large pool for those who live in them. The children from Southeast Asia peer through a fence, but do not become overwhelmed by envy or bitterness: "If we study hard, we can get good jobs. If we save our money, we can buy what we want. My mother says we are much better off here than we'd be if we'd stayed behind. It was worth it, to escape. We'd be dead if we hadn't left. My mother would like to go back — but only to the village she knew when she was a girl. I am glad to be here. I wouldn't mind living over there."

He has pointed to "there," to the new, attractive building, to the spacious pool. People who have it better than he does, are goads to his not inconsiderable ambition, self-confidence, hopefulness — his social appetite. He comes from peasant stock — not from the Cambodian aristocracy, members of which are also struggling to make do in Washington and other American cities, and who often do so as ordinary working people, glad to have jobs like this boy's mother's. He is neither ashamed of his background, nor tied to it. He is an intelligent realist, ready to make the best of his new situation. He is an American. When asked for his thoughts on his recent life in a new country, he is quick to respond: "People don't sit here; they move. I remember my grandfather standing still. Even when he worked on his crops, he seemed still — when I compare him to people here! No one stays still here. People drive cars. Planes always come over us. People have motorbikes. They come home and go jogging. On television the cars are racing and crashing into each other. My mother says everyone wants her to wait on them at the same time. She never sits or stands or walks; she runs from the [restaurant] kitchen to the tables, and then back to the kitchen, and finally the clock has run, too — and she can go home. People run for the bus, and if she doesn't run with them, she feels she's sick, and so does everyone else, even her friends from Vietnam and Laos!"

He himself is rather fast on his feet. He dashes from his home to the ice-cream truck. He is speedy at playing catch. He is no slouch at marbles. He climbs a tree rapidly. And at school his mind runs at a good pace. His teacher is impressed, and a little puzzled: "These children have gone through devastating experiences. They've marched with their parents for miles with no food or clean water to escape death. They've been on the sea for days — the 'boat people.' They've been sick and near death. They come here, to a faraway land, and most of them don't know any English. You'd think they'd be frightened and exhausted. You'd think they'd be suspicious and withdrawn. But they get right to work, and they smile and are polite, and they are determined to build a good life for themselves here, and they are willing to work hard — and if you, the teacher, make them work even harder, they're grateful. I have friends who tell me that there must be something else going on underneath — but I'll tell you, I'll just be grateful for what I see 'on the surface,' every single day, in this classroom!"

What she observes all the time is, of course, an important psychological truth, not to be dismissed as in any way superficial or misleading. Children cannot forever dissemble emotionally. These children are not psychological pretenders; nor are they fooling themselves, so to speak, by constantly denying past hardship and suffering. Their drawings and paintings can be, on occasion, grim and forbidding. More than those of most of the world's children, their pictures recapitulate an earlier political fate — soldiers with guns and itchy fingers, planes with bombs: a terrible political ideology at work, curbing freedom, engendering fear. No wonder a girl draws a helicopter black, and shows its bombs, and prostrate bodies in a field below (Figure 22). No wonder a boy endows a rifleman with the huge, prominent teeth of a devouring animal (Figure 23).

No wonder, too, that child after child, when asked what happened in Vietnam, in Cambodia, in Laos, will mention "bad people" — and when asked to spell out the badness, speak as young Twoc did, while sitting on a low wall, behind his South Frederick Street home: "There was the government. No one could decide anything by himself. My father said we had to leave, because the government would kill anyone who didn't get down on his knees and beg to be a slave. If you asked the government *why*, you'd be on your way to jail, or they'd come and shoot you in your house. They'd take away your chickens. They'd kill your dog. Here the teacher doesn't tell you to 'spit out answers.' She said we shouldn't 'spit out answers.' She says we should ask *why*. Every time I hear her tell us to ask *why*, I think of my father. He died on the boat, but before he did he told us he was happy. I remember — I remember then, I remember asking him why he was happy, and he said because he was sure I'd make it, and my brother, and my sisters, and that was all he wanted, for us to get out. Then he told us how he loved his village, but he was glad we'd escaped; and then he stopped breathing, and no matter how much we wanted him to stay with us, and breathe, we knew he was gone."

Those are sad words; they speak of a terrible twentieth-century tragedy. Yet, they are words that also convey fierce pride, unyielding determination — handed bravely from parent to child, and remembered constantly, it seems, regardless of the thousands of miles between there and here, the thousands of days between then and now. To be sure, these Asian children in America have undergone many moments of anxiety, apprehension, regret, even despair. Boys and girls who have endured persecution, exile, hunger, the loss of a parent, relative, family friend, have lots of mental pain to carry around, day after day. Sometimes they have bad dreams, moments a child may describe tersely, but ever so tellingly: "I wake up and I realize I've been back there, and they're trying to kill us, all of us, the soldiers are." Still, that child soon goes back to sleep: "I'm tired, and so I don't stay awake too long." What of the morning? "Oh, then I have to get up and eat. My mother and father go to work. We have to clean the house, and then the bus comes to take us to school."

The rhythms of a new life are healing to her, to others like her, and for those rhythms she is grateful. She can't imagine, these days, how "anyone" (meaning herself) could live without a McDonald's nearby, or a supermarket or drugstore. She can't imagine how "they" (meaning the people who live in her native Cambodia) manage without television and pizza and that ice-cream truck, and not least, the school she attends, where "if you don't feel good, they find out why." This girl who saw so much death in Asia, had been saved from a serious infection, and quite possibly from death, in this country, by intervention with antibiotics. She remembers her earlier years sadly, but talks with relief and gratitude about her present time. She knows she might have died (of all sorts of sicknesses) in Cambodia even if Southeast Asia hadn't suffered the disastrous wars; and she knows that her chances of survival in this new world are higher than most anywhere else in the world.

She was able to make for me (Figure 24) a colorful rendering of the idyllic side of her past (a bright yellow sun, a pink and blue thatched hut, a hazily remembered dog, tall grass, fruit-laden trees) but she also made a point of reminding me that there is beauty in her contemporary life, of a kind she was eager to draw (a nicely decorated school building, with a grand view of trees, flowers, a beckoning blue sky with a sun no less cheerful than the Cambodian one she had earlier constructed). What did she hope to be, to do when grown up? She replies easily to such ordinary questions —

and her answer offers implicit evidence of a shrewd cross-cultural sensibility: "In the States you can try to get many kinds of jobs. You can't be sure until you're older what job you'll get. You may change your mind. My mother says she never had to make so many choices, until she came here. She says even when she gives people a menu, and they read it, they keep asking if there's more. My mother says a hundred times a day: 'Only what's on the menu.' The customers don't believe her, though. They don't even hear her. They keep asking!"

This eight-year-old child also keeps asking — questions about the usage of English words and phrases, questions about America's history and geography, questions about our flag — the reason for its many stars, its red and white bars. She wonders how old the city of Arlington is, the city of Washington. She wonders whether America has known the kind of political lunacy and evil Cambodia has recently experienced, and she wonders whether one day, in some distant future, her native land will be "more like America." What does she mean by that comparison? She hasn't the slightest difficulty being clear and specific: "There would be more food. You could have a school like this one here. The teachers wouldn't be scared, and we wouldn't be scared, the kids. No one would be scared of the government."

As she is promoted from grade to grade, she will no doubt learn that this country was founded for just that reason — so that those who came here would not live in constant fear of political authority. Meanwhile she enjoys the freedom this country offers, and lets her mind wander — not toward Asia, but toward downtown Washington, it turns out. She would like to see more of the city. She would like to go to college there. She would like to be a nurse, someday — oh, a doctor, if that were at all possible. She has seen lots of very sick people. She seen people die. She would like to be able to "fight sickness," not see it take lives. Her lively, discerning, ambitious mind is altogether remarkable, I begin to realize — and soon I am thinking that I have never seen a group of children, in all the years of my work, who are more resilient and perceptive. Moreover, the parents of these children, no less eager to become adjusted to this country, to enjoy its possibilities, are as industrious and as caring as any mothers and fathers I've seen anywhere in the world.

A boy nearby has been listening and nodding as I talked to Twoc. He makes a declaration: "There should be more friends everywhere." He adds force to his statement by pointing to the map of the world hanging on the classroom wall. With a sweep of his hand he moves over the planet's territory. Then, lest there be any doubt in the visitor's mind, the lad has his right forefinger point to Cambodia.[4] He smiles. He claims his nationality: "I'm from here." Silence. Smiles from the other children. "Me, too," another boy says. "Me, too," a girl says. "Me from Laos," another quite young girl says. The boy who started this series of avowals moves on — crosses the Pacific with his hand, stops at California, hastens eastward across the American West, the heartland of the Midwest, stops at the nation's capital city: "This is us; this is Washington; it is there, across the river." The others nod, smiles on their faces. The boy resumes his comments: "The distance from Asia. . . ." He doesn't finish his sentence. We sit at our table, covered with crayons and paper, and wait. Only a second or two, but some curiosity, even tension. He has found his train of thought, his voice, his words: "The distance from Asia," he repeats, "well, it's long." A pause — then: "It is a big distance, yes. But we are here; we got here." The others nod. The boy goes back to his chair. The children are about to do some more drawing — but the teacher announces that spelling is next, all those English words to master.

"Let's try to get a hundred," urges the boy whose hand had just been touching various points on the map of the world. "Yes, let's," says a girl. Another girl is even then looking ahead: "Yes, we can get all the words right today, and then she'll give us new words." They pick themselves up, move across the room to another location, huddle yet again, and soon the air is once more filled with that lovely southern accented voice, an American teacher saying the words ("apple," "after," "house," "here," "yard") and then using them in a sentence, and waiting for the children to write them down, then look up, ready for the next.

Soon the morning will be over, lunchtime will have come: "They are good children, hardworking as can be," the teacher says for the third or fourth time, as the boys and girls who have come "the distance from Asia" prepare to eat their hamburgers, their french fries, which they all insist, in a chorus of celebration, is the best food anywhere in the world. Meanwhile, I prepare to resume my traveling, reading ways — sit on a plane, go over notes, read an article or two, write observations about a group of Asian children who have a knack of catching a stranger's attention and impressing him with their enthusiasm, however much melancholy they also contain. I ask myself why these children, and their parents, as well, seem so uncritical of this nation, so eager to taste of its every offering. I'd made such an inquiry of them, really, in the indirect way I've learned to find appropriate — and had heard their reasons: a belief that there was no going back, and that America is well worth getting to know. I begin to realize that my puzzlement at their enthusiasm ought probably to be turned back on me — it tells of how much I have learned to take for granted. The observer has once again been forced to face his smugness by those he is observing — and never more forcefully than this time. He begins to realize that the issue is not only "the distance from Asia" of these children, but his own distance from the fierce struggle his ancestors, all our ancestors, waged when they came here in order to make this land their land.

Not that these Southeast Asian children ought be set upon some self-congratulatory American pedestal: they are here, and loving it. Should we all not bask in the glow of their continuing effort at survival, their determination to take on American materialism? The children I have just described are exceptionally fortunate among Asian refugee children — to be with their parents, mothers and fathers who have the psychological resources to keep standing up, keep struggling, no matter what frustrations and disappointments have come their way since they came to this country. Other Asian children have come here "unaccompanied"[5] — been placed in foster or adoptive homes, either American or Asian. Still other children have come here with adults who have simply not been able to withstand this latest assault (the tough task of building a new life in a new country), amid the continuing despair generated by the old assaults — a story of murder, deceit, betrayal that they have told me again and again. It seems newly dreadful (and a scandal to this century's civilized reputation) when children tell me their stories in groping English.

In a section of Boston, Jamaica Plain (less affluent by far than Arlington, Virginia), I hear a Cambodian child, Lon, now called Lonnie by many of his schoolmates. As he talks and talks, I wonder that he is still alive and able to be coherent, never mind attend classes and get through week after week of this life.[6] He saw both his parents die before his eyes at age five. He is now double five — and sometimes, I think, has lived, already, two times two times two lives. No wonder he is tired so often, and guarded, and fearful, and a "problem" to his good and sensitive teachers, who also have *their* "limits," and who, accordingly, expect that a psychiatrist might come up with some new ways of putting into words what happens when unspeakable political tragedies are visited upon those who have to suffer them on the ground — as opposed to those who plan them in the government buildings of countries far removed, including our own. I bite my lip, tell myself it's best not to get upset with the teachers, or with oneself as the inadequate repository of the teachers' well-intentioned or desperate hopes. The teachers have hopes for Lon and for Vo, one of his (Laotian) classmates, also ten, also "in trouble," I'm told.

When were they *not* "in trouble," I begin to wonder? I hear Lon talk, slowly and with constant interruptions; but over the days and weeks and months his poignancy grows and threatens to break the heart: "I can remember the chickens — they were always near our house. I think they must have been right there when I was born! My grandmother used to point at one (it was gray), and she said to me that it was this chicken who made my mother laugh right after I was born. You know why? Because she laid an egg the same time my mother had me!

"I never see chickens here — only the dead ones wrapped in the invisible paper in the market: 'Stop and Shop.' I don't like to eat chicken, and everyone else in my [foster] family, they all want me to like what they like. ["They" are good-hearted Americans, their background mixed, the father Anglo-Saxon, and the mother,

Hispanic; they have tried hard to be of help to Lon.] I wish I could do what they want! I try! I hold my nose tight, so I don't taste the chicken. She has cut it into small pieces, and she puts chutney on it, so I won't taste it, but I know it's there, anyway! I take it in [the mouth], and I try to chew it, or just swallow it right away. But I can't. No matter how I try, I can't. I gag. Then I spit. Then she gets upset. She says it won't help, if she stops serving chicken, because then I'll be 'surrendering' to this 'problem.' I say yes, I'll try harder. And I will!

"I see my house and the chickens even now! I can't see my mother any more — only my grandmother. My mother no longer has a face when I try to think of her. I can see her hands, and her leg — the blood on her leg. I can see her hair — but no face. I can hear her voice, though. I remember what she said, before she left to go to another life; she said we should remember her, and we said we would. I remember that."

He sits and tries to do just that — but ironically it is his mother's last request that he literally can't honor: he can't remember her, or at least the part of her that is most her own, the face. Once, after we'd spent months talking — actually, simply walking and pointing out to each other what interested us (two squirrels being playful, frisky with each other; a lovely cardinal that swooped down and seized its seed and flew away; an old car, built I told my young friend in 1938 or 1939), he announced that he was beginning to realize why he couldn't "see" his mother's face: she had been badly beaten before she died, and he was respecting her prior beauty by blacking out that last assault upon her. Here were his exact words: "My mother had to leave us before she was ready to go. She was called to another life. She was bleeding all over her face. She hoped she'd get a new face in her new life — and I hope she did."

Still, he wasn't entirely satisfied with that line of reasoning, a mixture, I presumed to think, of traditional Cambodian religious thinking[7] and the ordinary devices all of us muster when we're gripped by great pain. He still concentrated hard, in hopes of getting a vision, once more, of his mother's face; and he still seemed sad that he was unsuccessful in his attempt. He continued to speak of her as "happy now," he was "sure," but he was just as "happy" that he had no memory of what she looked like. As we'd become closer I'd ventured more boldly in my remarks, yet I feared becoming presumptuous, knowing this boy's obviously high intelligence, his canniness about his own emotions, his evident resilience, so far. Still, he was ailing in his head; he felt glum a lot, and he stared into space a lot, his teachers told me, even as they also commented on how "nice" he was, and how "cooperative."

Once, after he told me yet again that his mother was, no doubt, enjoying a "good time" somewhere in this universe, and surely was pleased that he hadn't tried to "bother her" by "seeing her face," I remarked that I didn't know his mother, but I wondered whether she wouldn't want him to remember her. Doesn't remembering someone usually mean seeing the person in one's mind? Not a word from him, though I noticed from the corner of my eye that he tilted his head upward and toward me for a second (not his usual custom as we walked) and then quickly resumed looking straight ahead. I let the matter drop. He seemed intent, after my comment, on following with his eyes a boy on a skateboard, as he moved down a nearby street with great speed and agility, and I took his concentration on this pleasant but not necessarily unusual scene as a statement. I also began to realize that the boy Lon had his own journey to make, and (speaking of speed) had to find (and let me know) just how fast he could go during our walking conversations. He brought me no specific complaints about difficulties — as many troubled American children, or their parents, might have done.

Some Cambodian and Laotian and Vietnamese children have indeed been brought to child-guidance clinics in American cities for one or another reason, but no one in Lon's life at home had gone so far as to decide he needed the help of a child psychiatrist. Still, this sensitive, quite frightened, increasingly saddened child did, I thought, need more than what I'd originally thought we'd share — conversations about his views and experience of America, his memories of life in Cambodia. He needed, I began to think, to explore what had happened to his mind and heart during those Cambodian days of his life. (This would not be the first time "research" and "treatment" became, really, one and the same pursuit in my professional life. I have written about this complicated business at some length.)[8]

Some months further along, when we were meeting once a week, Lon and I pursued our discussions about his mother. We often began with talk about Cambodia as Lon remembered it — a comparison of the old homeland with the new American experience. He could be eloquent, with his brief, halting, but ever so pointed sentences; and he taught me an enormous amount about what it can mean for a child living in exile from Southeast Asia[9] to think about one nation, then another, to feel one set of nationalist yearnings and loyalties, then another. Though I condense a number of our talks into one, I ask the reader to watch how remarks about *country* come to be connected to memories about a tragedy, and further connected to the mind's effort to heal itself, to come to terms with an indescribably painful past: "I am glad to be here. I like the country. I wasn't sure I would. I thought when I was coming here: so far away, and what kind of place will it be. But I knew the Americans had been very good to us in the camps [in Thailand] and I knew it would be better that I go to America than stay in the camps. I'd never been in a plane before, and I thought we'd keep going higher and higher, and that instead of meeting America, I might meet my mother! Even when we landed in California, I expected her to be there — but I knew she wouldn't be!

"When I was young, my mother told us our country was in trouble. My father told us we were so peaceful we made everyone want to conquer us, so they wouldn't have to see us being peaceful. He used to look at the quiet chickens, then the chickens that wanted to be the lords, the warlords, and he said Cambodia is quiet, and it doesn't want to be trouble to other countries, so it will have great trouble itself. When he got sick, he told us he could feel our country bleeding inside him, and my mother told us the same thing. She told us you carry your country in you, in your stomach, and where you breathe, in your lungs, and in your blood, it goes through your blood vessels. When the teachers show us how the heart pumps the blood, and the lungs take in air and push it out, and the stomach accepts the food and says all done and sends it down further, then I think of Cambodia. It is there, in all those places, in me!

"I can remember the chickens; they were red and gray and white. I can remember the roosters. They weren't happy until we looked at them. Through their noises, they made our eyes move to them! It wasn't enough that we heard them! If we went and stared at them, they stopped their noisemaking. They looked at us, stared and stared. I remember our trees; they had big leaves, and they weren't like American trees. There were many trees in Cambodia, and many lakes and ponds, and many flowers, lots of them — only we didn't plant them; they were there.

"Our country was by itself for a long time; we were sent here to enjoy a quiet country and bother no one. Others are sent here to other countries, and they want to go and capture land and people, and have their guns, and take down a flag, so they can put up their flag — everywhere! It's like the chickens; both our mother and our father told us: Countries are like animals and birds, and you won't change them, because they've been like that too long, and they've been sent here to be like that. In another life the people of other countries might be different, and the same for us Cambodians.

"It is true [I had mentioned the fact] that some Cambodians attacked others.[10] But we hadn't been like that before the Vietnamese and the Chinese and the Americans — they all invaded us. They came into us, and we weren't Cambodians any more! You can't stop being Cambodian and live in Cambodia! Our father told us that, and our mother. They kept telling us that in those last days.

"I think my father was glad to be killed. He never wanted to stop being Cambodian. He was afraid he'd become a rooster, or a fighting bird, or one that swoops down and kills what it can, and flies away with what it got, blood all over. He smiled — I think — just before he died. I don't know about my mother; I can't see her face. But I think she wanted to stay with him. They thought they'd be here, in this life, longer than it happened that they were. My mother didn't cry when they killed my father. She told us to go near the water and wait. She said if she came back, we'd go with her. She said if she didn't come back, we should go to my uncle's house, and see if he was there, and he'd tell us what to do; and if he was not there, to find some people who are leaving our village, and go with them. So, we went, and we waited. Then I couldn't wait. So I went back, and I saw my mother with blood all over her. I can see the blood. I can see her legs and her arms, but I can't see her. I can see my father's face, his body. I don't think he had a smile by the time he was dead; but he was smiling when the [Khmer Rouge] soldiers first came to our house. They talked with him, and he said nothing. He smiled. They shouted. They never smiled. They weren't happy with all the blood they already had in their bodies. They wanted more and more and more! They weren't Cambodians any more! Cambodia is a country put here to remind other countries that a country can be a place where people come to rest and smile and grow food and pray for the next life they'll have. My mother told us we're here to pray for our ancestors, so they will be proud of us, and we will learn to be proud of them. We must always think of them, and they will protect us, if we try to honor them all the time. That is what Cambodia is — my homeland, where my mother and father still are: I know they are there, watching over our land, and hoping it will see a better time — praying for the country.

"They're watching over me here, too. But they live in Cambodia. Even when you die, you belong to your country. All our ancestors are there, and they are wishing that our country will recover. It became very sick. There was much death. People have gone to new lives; the dead are now gone — but they are still part of Cambodia. My grandmother, I know, must say a prayer every day for Cambodia. She loved her country. When she died (before all our wars) she said she was glad to be going, to meet her parents and her uncle especially (she was his favorite niece); but she promised us she'd never forget our country and us — and we told her we'd see her soon, and she closed her eyes."

For a Western doctor this Buddhist conviction about the hereafter is not always easy to understand, let alone accept without uneasiness, even with a touch of perplexed annoyance. Perhaps I should speak only for *this* Western doctor; others have had no such difficulty. Often Lon let me know, quite directly, that his concern was not for himself but his parents — for whom he wanted to "make merit," by prayers and by living as honorably as he could.[11] I had much trouble comprehending this notion — that one gives over a life to prayers for the dead in hopes that they may prosper in their next (and next and next) incarnation. I wanted Lon to put his energies into *his* life — his *American* life. He wanted to help his parents in *their* life, a new one, part of an incarnational cycle. Yet the boy also insisted that his parents were still in Cambodia, and he with them (spiritually, I suppose; I never pressed him to spell this matter out, because I thought there was no way for his Buddhism and my medical rationalism and materialism to find a common language). And yet, the boy was also very much in the United States — and let me add, loud and clear, that he was not psychotic, not schizophrenic, though I might well have thought so had I not known him so well, and other children like him, known Southeast Asian children, visited their countries, seen their counterparts in Thailand's refugee camps,[12] children who had yet to find a national alternative to the land of their birth. For Lon to be in America, I began to realize, was to take a journey of sorts — even as his parents, now dead, were continuing their journey, so he very much believed. He would always be Cambodian, yet he was also living in this new, strange (and to him) fascinating country. His major trial was his inability to visualize his mother — and this terrible frustration, this occasion of deep regret for him, was a matter he and I could share. We both agreed that it would be better for him if his mother's face "returned" to him. That is the word he kept using: "I am waiting for her face to return."

When I asked him why she might have "left" in the first place (the kind of question someone like me *would* pose!), he lowered his head and had trouble replying. At last he did come up with a substantial explanation: "I think my mother never wanted to leave us during all the fighting; I think it was a very bad thing — that she should be called to her ancestors just when we were trying to stay out of all the trouble in our country. But you were either for or against the Khmer Rouge. They killed everyone they didn't like. Our country has never had such people. My father, just before he died, said the Khmer are Cambodia's murderers, but we'd outlast them, the country would. He didn't want to leave us then, either; he was afraid they'd kill us, and he said we should have our lives to live before we left, and he wanted to protect us. My mother was crying all the time, but she cooked us the best food she could find, not very much, and told us to be glad we had something to put in our mouths. She kept reminding us what to do if she was killed, and my father; she kept reminding us where to go and what to say. But she hoped she'd be with us longer, and we hated to see her taken away.

"She must have decided to go that morning — because she could have taken us into the woods and we could have hidden. We saw her die. She left us, and we were alone. I guess she chose her next life to this one. Maybe they [her ancestors] told her to come, and she did what they said she should do. My sister was very upset. She wished our parents had stayed with us."

The reader will no doubt anticipate what I said in response to that last statement of Lon's. When I did, indeed, ask him how *he* felt, there was no delay to his answer: "I was upset, too." But he quickly added: "My mother had to answer their call [that of her ancestors]." I pointed out that I was sure that his mother, nevertheless, felt torn apart — trying to deal with this awful tug upon her tired, sickly body, and her scared mind, and her soul caught in an agonizing bind. I kept asking Lon to think of his mother's torment, no matter the "smile" he claims to have remembered appearing upon her face at the end. I pointed out that this life can really hurt us, sometimes — and that a smile, no matter how sincere, can't hide the torment we also feel. I suggested that the pull of the past may have been all that was left to his mother and father, in the murderous present, but that each child does have a future, and clearly his mother and father recognized that, hence their instructions to him and his sisters and brothers — all of whom perished on the way to Thailand. As he began to nod, I began to feel more comfortable as I spoke my words — a sign to me that they were being received with increasing hospitality by my young walking companion.

Weeks of similar discussions had their effect — and not only on Lon. As I talked with him I began to realize that the dead in Cambodia really do live — in ways hard for many of us in the United States to realize. They live in the minds of those still here; they live in the deeds they keep inspiring among their survivors; they live in the prayers extended them and in the thoughts about them which Lon was always at pains to express, whether to me or his friends, or his teachers, or his foster parents. I also began to realize that his boy's "ambivalence" toward his mother, his effort to erase her face from his mind, meant he was "repressing" not only an important part of his memory of her, but also his anger that she should have "chosen" to "leave" him — this reality, as I saw it, had to be considered together with his serious, animated *waiting*. A boy whose mother was gone uncannily expected her one day to reappear, as it were. She did, too — four months after our sustained talks about her, the doctor says, with ill-suppressed pride. Lon's account of this event deserves attention as much as my explanation. (My explanation? That his gradual "working through" of his grief enabled him to live more intimately, less bitterly with the knowledge of her death, with the memory of Cambodia, with his mother's presence.) He told me one afternoon: "I woke up and I'd seen my mother already! Yes. She appeared at night. It was a dream. She was standing outside our house. She was waving to me, and she was laughing, the way she did, at our chickens and our pig and our bird in the cage my father built. She said I looked good, and I felt good to hear her talk. [She spoke in Cambodian, he said.] I asked her if she'd be staying for long, and she said no, but she'd be back. First, she wanted to make me some food, and she did. Then we ate, and we walked to the flowers and the trees, and then — I woke up."

When he lay there in bed he found himself recalling the dream, savoring it, enjoying the scene of his homeland, and of course, his mother. He also felt wide awake: "I couldn't go back to sleep. I kept having the dream again — even though I was awake now! Then I did go back to sleep. My stomach was asking for food, but I said no to it, and the next thing, it was morning. When I opened my eyes I saw my mother — I saw the dream again. I was very happy. I know she has decided to stay with me! We'll all meet someday, I hope — there, in Cambodia. But first I want to finish school here, to get a good education. Later, I can go back there and help my country get over all its bad times."

I go into this child's psychological hurdles, which he managed to surmount rather well — becoming an exceptionally able student and a fine, thoughtful youth — because his comments about himself told much about his experience as a Cambodian of religious background, a Cambodian now in American exile. The psychological role of a nation in the lives of children comes across concretely in Lon's offhand utterances, replies, asides, questions: his joint vision of his parents and his country; his general outlook on life as a gift of a nation, a religion, mediated through a family; his memories and yearnings, which are very much an aspect of his country. In a strange way exile for Lon has made him more keenly and resolutely Cambodian — so far. Perhaps his parents' death is responsible for this outcome — Cambodia is the only "parents" he has left, on this earth, anyway. Even amid the American hustle and bustle that fascinates and preoccupies the children mentioned earlier, those who are fortunate enough to have their parents alive and with them in this country, one still sees working in child after child not only a nostalgia for the past, or reveries (which depend as much upon what has taken place as on what the daydreamer hopes will occur) — but serious nationalist reflections. Some Cambodian or Laotian or Vietnamese children have no difficulty in transmitting these to teachers in schoolrooms, to doctors and nurses upon receiving medical care, or, very important, to one another while playing in the neighborhood.

An extraordinary teacher of mine has been Sarann, a twelve-year-old girl who came to the United States from Cambodia when she was eight, after being in the United Nations Refugee Camps on the Thai–Cambodian border for more than a year.[13] Her mother had died in Cambodia, but her father survived, and is a devoted, loving parent to his three children, a boy and two girls, of whom Sarann is the youngest. Sarann has been told by her father that the family will stay in America. In fact, her father had a chance to move from Boston to California about a year after he had taken up residence in the East, but said no, he wanted to stay put, even though friends of his reminded him that California was nearer to Cambodia. Sarann explained her father's reasoning with these essentially moral and political reflections: "My father says he was brought here by the people who run our Church; they worked very hard to get us to Boston, and get us a place to stay. If we left, so soon, they would be hurt, we know that. They are always trying to help us. They ask us if there is something they can do all the time! We try to think of what to ask, because they smile and seem happy when we make a request! It is a gift to them — a question to ask, or a favor to ask, or some advice to ask! They hope we will become American. They say we will make America better! We hope so! My father says he doesn't know what would happen to us if we tried to go back to Cambodia. We might be killed. There is still fighting there, we hear. We like it here, and my father is saving money. He says if there was peace there, for sure, we'd take a trip back, but we'd stay only for a week or two, then turn around and go to Boston.

"When our friend in California wrote, we all talked, and we said to go out there is to leave our friends here, and it would be very bad of us to do that. My father says when he was a boy, everyone in Cambodia was polite to everyone else. Then, no one in Cambodia liked anyone else! Here, people are polite to us. We like them, and we must never turn our faces away from what they have done for us. In California, we'd be in another country, the third one since I was born. I used to think this city, where we live, is a country, but I know better recently! But to cross this big America, even if we're still in the same country, would be like leaving Cambodia; so, no!

"I told my father that no matter what he says, I'm still interested, one day, in going back — but that time will be when I'm all grown up, and I have a job. I'd like to be a nurse, and I think I can be successful with that dream! Our American friends have taken us to see hospitals, and they have a friend who is a nurse, and she has invited me to visit her at work, and I have gone there, and I have tried to help her. In America there are so many hospitals; in

Boston, especially, there are many hospitals. Wherever there are hospitals, there have to be nurses. Without nurses, the sick people are in the worst trouble. It was a nurse who made my mother happy, before she died. Mother was very sick. She told us she was burning up. Her lips were cracked. Her tongue was stiff and dry, and she couldn't hold down rice or even water, but she had to have rice and water to live — and so, she died. But the nurse took care of her. We didn't know what to do. My father took care of us; my mother told him to do that.

"We stayed there in the village until our mother died. It was a friendly place to us, even though we knew no one. The people didn't turn against us, even though we were on our way to Thailand. They said we all belonged to the same country, and as long as they could, they'd help us. We saw lots of people, long lines — people going to Thailand. We'd been going, too; but we had to stop. One man said we could stay as long as we wanted; he said he'd keep us in his house. But my mother told us to let her die, and then keep going. My father was very tired, and he said he would obey my mother's request, and if he died, then we should keep walking: there were so many to follow — we wouldn't lose our way, he was sure! The nurse got some water in my mother, slowly, very slowly. She held her head in her lap. She had some bandages and she put them on my mother's sores. She had something for her lips. It was then that I told myself that I'd become a nurse if I lived to be old enough.

"When I've finished, and have my nurse's cap, then I'd like to go back to Cambodia. My father says 'only to visit'; my older sister and my brother aren't sure. I hope they would come with me! We could bring to our country some presents! We could bring food and clothes. We could bring books and pens and pencils and paper. We could bring medicines. The nurse I know said, when I told her: 'You could bring yourself!' That was very nice to hear!"

Sitting with Sarann and watching her draw and paint is as instructive as listening to her. I have asked her on numerous occasions to draw herself, to draw scenes from her present, American life or her past Cambodian life. I am constantly impressed with the political aspect of this demure and petite but formidably intelligent, conscientious, neat, hopeful girl. She is able to give a running account of a family's flight through the roads and jungle paths of its homeland, threatened by murderous bands of soldiers of all persuasions; but she also tells what she remembers happening to her native country. In one picture (Figure 25), she shows people standing near some houses, under some trees — and approaching are men on foot with guns, as well as, overhead, a swarm of buzzing helicopters. The intention is a massacre, she announces. I don't have to ask for the details: "The Khmer — they wanted to kill everyone who was a stranger to them. They wanted to empty Cambodia of all the people, except for themselves. Even before my mother got sick, she knew we were all going to be in great pain. She'd heard from someone that the Khmer were going from village to village. They were drinking our blood, our country's blood. That is what my father said — they are drunk on our blood, and they won't stop drinking! You see, here [she points to the soldiers she has drawn], they are blood hungry, and they want to see our earth turn red. I recall my mother saying, before she died, that she never believed any people could be like our own people were, the Khmer. That's what happened to us — we stopped being the country we used to be."

She has also drawn the country that "used to be": a pond, trees near it, flowers aplenty, grass, a clear sky, a large and friendly sun, some houses, and near them, rice fields under cultivation (Figure 26). None of this imagery is very surprising or original — merely a child trying hard to retain a personal memory, and as well, a nation's (now) mythic memory: the good days of an earlier time. When Sarann places a touch of gray in the sky of her idyllic picture, and when she makes her sun just a bit too fiery, then observes that the people below might be getting too hot under its glow, she is perhaps letting me know that in the back of her mind she wonders whether there weren't at least one or two signs that hinted at a coming disaster. Many children born in Southeast Asia have sat back, from the distance of America, and wondered exactly that — whether their parents were *completely* taken by surprise. The children who give most frequent voice to such retrospective, bemusing questions are, I notice, those whose parents are with them — right there, to be asked; *and* whose parents have indicated a willingness to speak about the sort of tragedy that *other* parents are firmly determined to put behind them at all costs. Sarann didn't much want to talk with her father about this matter. She told me why: "He gets very sad when we talk about Cambodia, unless he starts in first. He loves to remember when he and my mother got married, and when we were babies. He will talk, sometimes, about our escape. But he doesn't like me to ask him questions! He likes to say what he remembers, and then he likes us to stop. If we want to keep on, he says we can, but he leaves the room!

"My friends tell me what they hear from their parents, so I learn that way. In school they tell us, too — the history and geography teacher. But I don't go home and recite to my father what I learned. He would say 'thank you' just after I started, and ask to be excused! When he wants us to stop speaking about a subject, he tells us that he is worried about his car. The car is old, and we're always worried about it, but sometimes my father worries more than at other times!"

The girl's wry, ironic, psychologically subtle mind impressed me as especially nourished by the good fortune she had met in the United States — a sponsoring family (group of families, actually) with real warmth and sensitivity, and persisting interest in what unfolded over the years for Sarann, her father, her sister and brother. She herself knew that the various American "contacts" other families from Southeast Asia had been given, in the early days of their arrival, soon vanished, or in truth, turned sour. Moreover, the girl's father is an especially industrious person, a devoted parent. He has become an auto mechanic, an able one at that. Sarann herself has even announced a desire, one day, to drive a convertible. Why? She likes the feel of the wind rushing at her face, her hair. She makes a point, when on a bus, of sitting near the window. She also keeps her eyes on the variations of American cars, and of imports. When she becomes meditative, she reminds herself that this kind of knowledge would hardly be hers, had she stayed in Cambodia. The same inclination to make cross-cultural comparisons holds when she considers the virtues of her already considerable, and always growing education. She goes to a fairly modern school, is bright and dedicated, has had good luck with teachers. One of them, in particular, a woman of Irish Catholic background, has worked hard to help Sarann speak strong, lively, fluent English. Her vocabulary has increased enormously, and she loves to try out words she has recently learned — sometimes falling flat on her face, she realizes. How does she know when that has happened, when the word does not fit the occasion? "The teacher's eyebrows always rise when I make a mistake," Sarann tells me; then she lets me know that the teacher doesn't, however, call her "wrong." The next step is for Sarann to try again, and she does so, willingly — her eyes glued to her teacher's eyes. If the girl is successful, her teacher's eyes *sparkle* — a word Sarann learned a few days before one of my visits. She used it to describe the nodding, affirmative look in that teacher's eyes when a word fitted correctly into a sentence.

Her moods alternate: She is enamored of America's language, automotive technology, hospitals, schools, food, clothing, music (soft rock). She is highly conscious of Cambodia; but America is the country where she now lives: "My country is Cambodia, but I can be an American if I want. I will always be Cambodian, but in America that's all right; there are no Khmer here to force you to their side. People can be different here." With that sort of national appraisal she indicates growing appreciation of a country increasingly familiar to her. No one can predict where and how she will live her life, but her teachers think she'll want to stay here. They notice increasing interest in all things American (movies, travel pictures of other parts of the country) and less inclination to mention Asia, the past. Even so, Sarann tells me that when she does her "pledge of allegiance" to the (American) flag, she thinks of Cambodia as well as America: "I salute America, and I salute Cambodia!" I doubt that double loyalty will ever disappear from her astute mind, quick to notice social nuances at school, in the bus she rides, on the street. People wonder where she comes from, she tells me often — and their act of paying attention to her reinforces her sense of being *from* somewhere, as well as being, probably, here to stay, with growing contentment. Once she showed me that in drawing she was equally adept with an American flag and with the one that represents Kampuchea, formerly Cambodia (Figure 27).[14] She carefully counted the fifty stars she placed on one flag, carefully constructed for the other a yellow silhouette of the ancient Angkor Wat temple, which she placed on the otherwise all-red background. She had made a conscientious effort in school to learn all the particulars of both flags. When she handed them to me "for keeps" they were glued together, her name under each — a veritable document in a study of "the political life of children," and a child's statement of her twin loyalties.

As for Khek Van Trangh, who lives a block away from Sarann, and attends the same school, his future is harder to predict, because he has talked excitedly about a number of occupations he intends to pursue — for example, to become an air-force pilot and help build up an air force for his native Cambodia. For most of the three years I knew him fairly well, I saw no loss of interest in that prospective career — until a soft-spoken and pensive teacher worried aloud to me,[15] several times, why a boy of (then) twelve, should be so determined to leave this country in order to fight jet-plane wars over Southeast Asia. Hadn't Khek seen enough of war, of wanton murder, of sadism and bestiality? The Khmer, who killed many in his extended family, had forced the survivors into exile.

I never asked Khek this sort of question directly, but I did ask him to tell me why he wanted so much to fly planes, and bombers at that. He was direct, blunt, as befitted his occupational aspiration: "You mustn't forget what has happened to your people. I'm here, now, in America, but I may not stay here. My sisters [he has four of them] say they'll never go back; but I would like to go back, and when I get there, I'd like to be as strong as anyone, so strong that no one will come and kick me and hold a machine gun to my head. That's what happened to us in Cambodia. My father says we don't have to be the ones to get even; those soldiers [the Khmer] will suffer one of these days — they'll pay for what they did. But how do we know? I remember when the planes were flying over the camps in Thailand. I thought: No one here can make that plane do anything! The plane is free!"

He has drawn planes, and they are substantial and most certainly free — high up in the sky, near the blazing sun. Below, in one such picture (Figure 28), there is mayhem and murder, houses on fire, a tank's gun blazing. Who wouldn't want to escape from such a scene — or from another, that of the refugee camps, where people sit and wait and sit and wait and try to be grateful that they've been lucky enough to survive. They are there, alive, fed, clothed, given a bed, and so out of the jungle, and no longer walking and walking, endlessly walking, with marauding, blood-thirsty bands of soldiers a constant danger. Khek's description of what he went through *on land* to get out of Cambodia is reason enough for him to concentrate on the sky: "I was sure we'd all fall into a pit, or a swamp, and disappear. We walked and walked, and my feet hurt so bad I wished someone would come and chop them off. *'Don't say that,'* my father kept shouting at me, but I couldn't keep myself quiet! I had sores and cuts, and blood covered my toes and my ankles, and there were bites, and we didn't have much to eat and the water, we knew, would get us sick. 'We'll all die' — when *my father* said that, I knew we were going to die *very soon!* Then, they came, the Khmer: they killed lots of people. We were lying there: *'Believe* you're dead,' my father shouted at us; then he kept reminding us, whispering it: 'Believe you're dead.' I did. I expected to stop breathing. I *tried* to stop, but I couldn't. I've wondered ever since if you can say to yourself: no more breaths — and it'll work. I don't think so. Lying there, I saw the planes. Someone was bombing us, I thought — but it was the Khmer being bombed. We lived. The planes saved us."

Khek envisions himself a Cambodian warrior of a new kind: the pilot of a supersonic jet, able to streak across his country's skies, command its people's attention — in a healing, redemptive fashion: "If we could be there, watching over our country, all the murderers would tremble with fear. *They'd* have to believe they were going to die! They *would* die, if we could figure out where they were. We could have our friends on the ground, and they could send messages to us through the radio, if they saw the Khmer. Then, we'd fly low, and we'd *waste* them!"

I notice his use of "waste." He is an American boy in this respect. I also look, one day, yet again at some of his drawings and paintings, and I realize how much he has learned about America in a few years. He has drawn Superman several times for me. He has drawn sleek jets. He has drawn the Cambodian countryside but has placed in it men with radio transmitters, headphones on their ears: modern communications at work — his fellow fighters for Cambodian freedom. He has drawn helicopters and told me how unforgettable their noise is. He wishes, actually, he *could* be a silent, utterly self-reliant superman: no engine to fail, no fire to endanger life, no shortage of fuel to fear. His supermen, as he draws them, are indeed Promethean — and I realize how deathly afraid he has been in his brief life, how haunted he still is by the irrational power of life and death that his fellow human beings possess.

The boy wants revenge, a listener realizes; he wouldn't mind if his new country, the United States, invaded his old country, Cambodia. Indeed, he would like the United States to invade all three countries of the old, "Indo-China peninsula."[16] I learn of this preference one day when we are taking a walk. He has just finished one of his jet-plane pictures, and I decide to tell him that I'd once been in the Air Force. I tell him that much only — and his eyes widen, he peppers me with questions. When? Where? Doing what? How long? When he finds out that the time was the late 1950s, that I worked as a doctor in a Mississippi Air Force hospital, that the United States in those days had yet to be involved in Southeast Asia, he is both disappointed and pleased. He has learned (while growing up in the United States) to dislike our military role in Vietnam, Laos, Cambodia — learned to blame this country, in part, for the tragedies that befell those nations. He is glad I wasn't "there," involved in "those battles." Yet, because he naturally detests the communists of Vietnam and Cambodia, he is no ordinary critic of America's recent foreign policy. He wishes we'd somehow won, and won quickly. He also wishes I'd been a pilot. He'd respect both my country and me more had each of those two wishes been fulfilled!

I tell him that I doubt America will soon be involved in Asia in the way in which the 1960s and early 1970s saw us involved. I tell him about some of my psychiatric work with Air Force pilots[17] — because he has asked me whether I knew pilots, and what they were like. "They are like you and me, Khek," I say — "sometimes brave and courageous, sometimes quite afraid." He doesn't think the latter applies: "A pilot can't be afraid. He's flying at supersonic speeds. He has to be strong all the time. Otherwise he'll die." When he says those last few words, I think of his father's words to him, as they all trekked west to Thailand, their fate uncertain at best. I hesitate, think of how to frame what I know in my heart, my gut, I want to say. The words come out like this: "Pilots are like you and me, as I said, Khek. They can be scared, and yet get through their missions. Frankly, some of them came to see me to tell me how scared they were at times. And you know what? Once they'd unloaded that on me — bombed me with their fears! — they often began to be less afraid."

Corny sounding, but true, I thought to myself. Then I waited. Khek would have no part of this somewhat contrived conversation into which we'd stumbled. He showed me what a macho pre-adolescent American youth he'd become. He told me of a Clint Eastwood film he'd seen — what a tough guy Eastwood was, how fearless he was all the time. I began to disagree. I said I knew the Eastwood films — as the father of three teenaged American sons would. I remembered some moments when Eastwood had been very much afraid. He hadn't "cut and run," as the saying in our West goes; he never behaved in a cowardly way. But he'd been afraid — and maybe the ability to feel that emotion was part of his strength. (No more of this, I thought: column talk from the "Living" pages of the newspapers!) Khek seemed to agree. He was quiet. We ended our walk fairly soon thereafter.

Next week Khek, to my surprise, resumed exactly where we'd left off. He told me that when he came to the United States he'd made a vow to himself, as he was struggling to learn Boston's streets, the language its people spoke, their customs and routines, that he'd never appear "weak" to others — lest they take advantage of him: "I saw that there were real tough guys in my class, in the second grade, and I copied them. They were big people to me! They called me their 'recruit,' and they protected me. They taught me all the words they used — 'cool' and 'man' and 'awesome' — and when the teacher heard me using those words at recess she said I was becoming American 'real fast.' I was proud. I went home and told my parents about the words — but they didn't use them at work, and I'm glad. They would have lost their jobs, maybe! [They worked in a fast-food restaurant.]"

Later our conversation took a different tack. Amid all the "tough-guy" talk, Khek stopped suddenly. He had heard sounds in the sky. A flock of geese appeared, flying low: they were returning north in a hurry, full of noise and flutter, in a nearly perfect formation save for one straggler, who was hurrying almost desperately to find a place in the broad, elegant, audible letter V, spread across a partly cloudy, early September sky. Khek stood there and watched, as I did. He asked if I knew where the geese were headed. I told him I thought they'd been in Florida (like people, only for the summer, not the winter) and now were going to Canada. He worried about the lonely goose that had fallen away from the others. But the outsider seemed to be catching up as the entire honking flock left our field of vision. Khek continued to stand where he'd been standing, his hands in his pockets, his eyes scanning the horizon for the birds that had turned, progressively, from dots on the sky into a dark blur. Soon the infinity of space swallowed this dramatic spectacle, this reminder of nature's rhythms and forms, its order, its predictability. One word from Khek: "awesome." I was delighted — having struggled with my own sons over their use of that word: exactly the right occasion, this time! Then Khek kicked the dry, late summer, urban dirt — and spotting a stray ice-cream wrapper, went to it, picked it up, crunched it in his hand, looked for a place to deposit it. Nothing in sight! I resisted an impulse and stood there waiting. He stood still, in silence. Now, as anxiety grew in me, I found myself worrying about the wrapper in his hand: where to drop it?

I realized that it wasn't the wrapper that was really on my mind — but Khek's sudden transformation into a quiet, reflective person, one who responded to nature's gifts and worried about man's desecration of them. Finally Khek began moving, but slower than usual. He seemed relaxed, his body slack instead of taut. His stride was steady, not hurried or choppy. He noticed the several varieties of trees along the other side of the street, and asked me to identify them. I did so with enthusiasm, a bit relieved that we were talking again. He listened with evident interest, then caught with his eyes some ordinary street pigeons. He stared and stared at them, as they poked the paltry ground, an unprofitable stretch, I thought. But they were triumphant, and in their success proceeded to gobble, gobble whatever crumbs or gravel they had discovered. Khek watched unwaveringly. But a noisy passing car, too close to the curb, with fumes pouring out of its exhaust pipe, scared the birds off. "They are smart to leave," he observed. I told him they might well be right back; but the pigeons made a more decisive break. They climbed higher, higher — soared out of sight. "Where will they go?" "To another block of Jamaica Plain," I answered.

We continued walking, and soon Khek had come back to talk of school, but the content was different: "When I was young, I never thought I'd end up here! I remember my older brother [killed by the Khmer] when he went to school; his school was a small hut, with one teacher. I remember her face; she smiled a lot. Now I'm here in Boston, in the United States of America. I might stay here for the rest of my life! My country might not even let me back, if I wanted to go there. They might say I'm not welcome! That's what my father says will happen! So, I must study at school, and do well — and prepare to be an American! Our family — we landed here; we traveled far, like those birds, the geese. Now, we'll find a place here for our home, and we'll feel safe, I hope." Like the pigeons, I thought to myself, as I watched him, again watching a flock of them.

Khek resumed his talking (after the pigeons had been prompted to flee again), was full of ideas about courses to take, possible careers available to such as him, a bright, alert, assertive child: "I could still be a pilot, or I could become an engineer. Our teacher has told us what engineers do. Her brother is one. Some engineers work on planes; they design them and build them and test them. I'd love to be an engineer of planes. If I could design planes to fly like those geese — that would be fun! I could fly the planes I'd designed! I could get a good job and live in America, and some day, I could return to Cambodia, but I'd be an American citizen, and that way they'd let me in — as a visitor. I could see Cambodia, then come back home, to here, Boston — or someplace in this country. I don't know where they make planes."

I named a few places, and then it was time to return to his school. The next week, when we did some drawings, Khek took his paper and crayons to a far corner of the classroom, saying he didn't know what to draw. I stayed at the desk where I was. About fifteen minutes later, as I did a drawing myself, and read some notes of conversations I'd had with other children, Khek came close and handed me a drawing (Figure 29). I looked, and was warmed; I smiled; I looked at him. He smiled. Our eyes met knowingly: the sky, the geese, their formation, the straggler, a benevolently grinning sun, and below, the land, grass, a pathway, two small but distinct figures. Khek said this to me: "Do you think they watch us, like we watch them? Do you think *they* wonder where *we're* going?" I could only say "maybe" — and stop and think. How much this boy had taught me about the manner in which children leave a nation, go to another nation, become exiles, learn to feel at home in a new place, dream still of a return, feel increasingly comfortable where they are, hold on to old social and cultural values, gain new ones, and finally, feel less and less part of one country, more and more a part of another one — and in their minds wonder, and like geese, wander, as they try to figure out the why, the where, the whither of this world.

IX

POLITICAL MORALITY:
THE HARD DREAM
OF SURVIVAL

NOVELISTS are blessed with the gift of knowing that a minor aspect of a life, explored long and carefully enough, may tell a whole lot about that life and its larger dimensions. When I started concentrating my thought on the "subject" of "political socialization," I found myself annoyed by some of the distractions that befell the children and me, time and again — their desire to talk about *other* matters, their refusal to let my abstract research interests budge them from *their* day's agenda. I tried to be patient and polite, but I certainly remember many moments when I felt tired, bored, indifferent, and I have to add, sullen, irritable, annoyed, angry. Often teachers got the brunt of my anger; sometimes I got it myself, through depression. I could be traveling in some foreign place, with only a limited amount of time and getting noticeably older each day. Why don't "they" (the children) just answer those questions more precisely? Why don't "they" (the teachers) remember what I said, what I asked? This self-centeredness, this willfulness, is not what one likes to discuss as an aspect of one's "methodology." Still, psychiatric research need not alone assume the self-accusing burden of sinful pride (or as we call it, these days, narcissism).[1]

"We're all sinners," my mother told my brother and me in childhood, speaking a homespun Midwestern religious banality she yet knew we needed to hear when we turned on ourselves with boastful self-recriminations. When I heard my very sensitive and thoughtful psychoanalyst say, on a New Orleans early summer day in 1960, that "we're all struggling with narcissism, including people like me, who study it and write articles about it," I thought I was in the presence of a special moment of wisdom. But then I had one of those "free associations," a remembrance of my mother's voice saying "We're all sinners." I was further surprised when, having told the doctor what she used to say, he immediately observed: "She was right." I'd expected him to wait and see what my mother was doing, once more, in this room; or to ask me why I thought I'd brought *her* up at that moment. Instead he was joining forces with her — a little too abruptly, I thought. (A lapse in "proper analytic technique"? Evidence of "countertransference"? Oh, hell! On with it: ten more minutes, and then a good gin and tonic at the nearby Pontchartrain Hotel.)

Only later did I realize how softly the doctor had spoken those words of agreement — a touching willingness to join his thoughts to mine, to say that yes, the bottles *are* labeled differently, but there *is* a common store of good sense in this life; and so, I won't take your "association" to be a measure of "hostility" or as "resistance" (both expressed in your "defensive" manner: the resort to thinly veiled, brittle sarcasm), but, rather, I'll speak my quiet but firm *yes*. A telling *yes* it was, and I remember it now, as I think of all the stray moments, the diversions, the detours, the blind alleys, the dead-end streets in those years of research with children in various countries and continents — only to find, in so many of the apparently "wrong" experiences (meaning they touched on what seemed, at the time, the irrelevant, the inconsequential), a wonderful glimmer of a child's truth, there and waiting to be understood, if I'd only appreciate my good fortune and get down to work.

It went like this one day in South Africa, a day that seemed taxing, unrewarding, a day further burdened (I have to be as honest as I know how to be here) by the people I was with — yes, including the children. They were a collection of cocky Afrikaner children of the Transvaal, four boys and four girls, sturdily built,

full-faced, their waxen hair mostly brown and blond and displayed
to good effect by a brisk wind from the south. They had just had
a "period" of "physical education," and so they were sweaty —
but still excited: the adrenaline yet to wane. We sat on the grass
and talked. We were no longer strangers. I knew them fairly well,
and I was going to say goodbye. I was scheduled to leave Johannesburg in a couple of days to go back to the States.[2] (How easily
one starts to call one's country, when abroad long enough, by the
familiar names used by others — in South Africa or Ulster, "the
States," in Nicaragua or Brazil, "the North Americans.") The children were hospitable, and I *did* like them, individually and at
moments. Usually, during those *other* moments, when I don't like
a child, or a group of children, in order to protect myself from
devastating self-criticism, I have learned to become sentimental,
hide behind one of the oldest tricks adults use — to trivialize
children (and themselves) by calling the young ones "lovely" or
"innocent" or "nice." That morning, however, the "defense mechanism" failed to work. I remember its collapse physically, in a tight
band of pain across my forehead; a telltale lack of attention to what
was being said; an urge to look at the watch; the yawn rising, a
hard one to stifle; awareness that the stomach was empty, and
craving the addict's balm, ice cream. What the hell — call it quits,
get out of here: a short but sweet goodbye.

But the children had their own plans and strategies, as they
always do. They had decided to ask me *their* questions, and they
did, resolutely and with evidence of sincere reflection. Not the
first time, I thought to myself — but why now? I want *out*, still!
Then Hendrick, one of the toughest of these children, in the literal
sense that he was tall, muscular, agile for his twelve years, and a
born leader, I had noticed, as he smiled with this child, got firm
with another one, pulled back at just the right moment, asserted
himself ever so tactfully but to obvious effect — Hendrick took
the chance every commander has to take. He asked for silence,
and when he didn't fully get it, he insisted: Hey . . . hush! What
he got he immediately used: a message from "them" to me, hope
that I might have a good voyage home, a wish that I come back;
and then, one more matter: "Please tell your people that we are

not bad, our country, that we make mistakes, but we are not bad."

I was suddenly awake, no longer conscious of pain in the head or yearning in the stomach. I was also wary of the ploy that often works on the cleverly gullible liberal bourgeoisie. The persecutor asks us to feel the "agony" of others, and thereby spare ourselves the difficulty of taking a stand, especially one that might turn out to be costly. I waited, and decided not to bite on what I decided was bait — not to ask the question or utter the comment that would allow Hendrick, and maybe some of his pals, to elaborate upon his remark and let me know (for the thousandth time) that South Africa is "unique," and that I mustn't "judge" it by my standards, by anyone else's, for that matter, and that much soul-searching was taking place in the country, and besides, if I were born there (meaning born there as a white man) would I not be like "them," and if I answered in a manner that didn't suit "them," then wouldn't I be a smug moralist, a glib rhetorician, utterly untested by life; but rather, eager to impose judgments on the lives of others in order to bolster my own unearned, or gratuitous, self-respect.

And so I kept quiet. Hendrick was undeterred. Actually, I realized days later, he didn't want me to talk and talk. The boy came closer to me — though not so close that he got out of range of his schoolmates — and said that he had been thinking about his country, South Africa, and my country, the United States, and he wanted to say something before I went home. I sat motionless and silent, save for one small practical gesture, not unfamiliar by now to these children — the routine flick of my tape recorder switch. I was becoming bored, again: This boy has a damn speech to make, and it'll be stuffy, I know! But you take what you can get, and for Christ's sake, that *is* why you're here, in this godforsaken (remote) part of this (morally) godforsaken country. And so — go ahead, Hendrick, and then *I'll* go ahead; that is, go. He did. And I now excerpt: "I know you don't like our country's apartheid. I asked my father and mother last night if they thought you did or you didn't [like it] and they said no, for sure. I knew you didn't last year, by your questions. My older brother said they were loaded!

"We like you, even so! We wanted you to have this."

Hendrick comes up to me, gives me a package, attractively gift wrapped. I ask if I may open it, having exuded both counterfeit thankfulness and genuine surprise. Now I was curious — maybe, half honestly, half out of a mannerly interest, and even that feigned. I started opening the fairly wide but quite thin and light gift, and quickly I realized it as a painting. Boy, these kids are really putting me on! Really tugging at me, too! Really conning me? Will Hendrick be working for Prime Minister Botha's successor one of these days? Will Hendrick *be* that successor? Finally, I have taken off the wrapping paper and the ribbon, managed to put them aside in a reasonably neat, orderly pile, and have time to inspect what is there, waiting to be regarded. I think I'd planned — in the moment available to me — a casual scrutiny, then the requisite, cursory rewrapping, then the plunge to my rented car and, thank God, the freedom of a solitary drive, a tape recorder emptied of its disc, and buried amid the rumpled, sweat-soiled shirts: an ice cream the next goal, and some coffee and a cup of ice. (Why do these South Africans keep telling me they don't serve iced coffee, but smile quite willingly when I ask for a hot cup, then, a glass of ice cubes, please? They always oblige, and watch me go through my motions, and seem grateful for having helped me out.)

I find myself looking closely, though. Looking and looking. I'm not sure what to make of what I see: a sturdy canvas, at the left side of which (I notice at first glance) a war seems to be going on, with people aiming rifles at each other (Figure 30). To the immediate right, however, is a charming South African landscape, with a farmer's cottage or two nestled in the tall grass, with roads winding innocuously through the dramatically jagged "high country" — the land's surfaces merging into one another, the various planes contrasting and defining one another. A young artist's rendering in the manner of Cézanne. (The work was Hendrick's, I knew, from our experiences together.) Then, of course, the sky, that clear, bracing, limitless horizon those beleaguered Boers must have taken as God's widest possible smile when they first came hereabouts, a century or so ago: the trek from the bloody British, those smoothies who know how to wrap craven material greed in their world-renowned politesse. I've seen thousands of drawn or painted suns, but his was some sun, full and central to its targeted land and beaming, but groaning, too, its face showing pain, perhaps at the sight of people fighting with guns next to such a blessedly beautiful country.

Finally, I look carefully at the gray-black structure on the right of this painting. What in the world is it? A building, obviously — but what kind of building? I'm also used to buildings: thousands of buildings — houses, usually, with their balanced windows and brick chimneys, gently emitting smoke (the more relaxed children) or belching it out in fiery assertiveness, if not rage. But this is an irregular and massive presence, not meant to be interesting and attractive, or truculently revealing, but to dominate everything near and far. There is only one break in the thing — and it is, strangely, on the roof! Inside are — well, *What?* I examine the painting more conscientiously. I have, by now, lost a cavalier sentimentality that glosses over an occupational hazard in my kind of work: the tedium and worse, the sinful arrogance, which prompts a perceived sameness — *another* house, *another* sun, and I have to admit, *another* child who thinks he or she is the most gifted prize the Lord has ever awarded this overcrowded planet. (Has no *doctor* ever had such a sense of being special, of having unique worth?)

I begin to falter — do what too often I don't feel the need to do, even though, dammit, I ought to feel such a need every time I'm with a child: I look up, utterly lost, look to the artist for a hint, maybe, please. Hendrick, however, doesn't rush to reassure, to explain, to apologize. He does inhale a deeper than usual breath, though: Oh Lord, I think, what kind of speech am I to hear — yet another Afrikaner apologia! But I can't seem to lunge or hurl or block or whatever the hell the right football word or image is. I stand mute. Hendrick starts talking: "You see, South Africa has bad troubles, we admit. We have our people fighting; the skin colors separate us. [I am struck by the odd way he puts it, so detached, almost clinically so. I'd never heard a South African child use that manner of articulation. I perk up; I *really* perk up.] We'll keep on having fights here, I know. They may get so bad that lots of people will get killed. It's not getting better, everyone says."

He stops, I say nothing. He continues: "Well, it's not only South Africa. We admit, we're 'in the swamp'[3] [a localism I'd heard a lot: in hot water] and even my mother [an optimist, everyone says], isn't sure we'll get out. She told us one Sunday, after Church, that she thought our country, South Africa, might be headed for a big, big 'calamity.' The minister had just given a sermon on a 'calamity'; he meant when the Good people and the Bad people have this last fight, and no one knows, while they're fighting, who will win, except God, and He never tells you what's going to happen while it's happening. My father said oh no, not our country; we'll be all right until the last big fight, when the whole world gets in there, and that means the people who have already died, everyone, not just us. God isn't going to pick on South Africa specially — that's what Daddy said. And my mother said to him: You're too hopeful, one hundred percent too hopeful!"

Another pause, and I feel like a chastened child, who ought to take his medicine, listen to the sermon. I look at the other children: they are attentive, unsmiling. Come on, Hendrick, get on with it. Where else, but in South Africa, among Afrikaner boys and girls of nine, ten, eleven would this kind of drawn-out ceremony, this presentation, this artistic *explication de texte* go on — and on and on, without someone, somehow, breaking the spell, stirring up a laugh, a bout of distracting activity? These *are* "latency age" kids, aren't they — or does adolescence come earlier, hereabouts, than at least one sometime pediatrician ever guessed?

More of Hendrick: "Before you go, we wanted to give you this. I asked everyone what we should give you. Jon said candy and cookies and ice cream, but we decided that, after you'd eaten it, there'd be nothing to bring back to the States. Freddy said a big cake, but the same thing there! Marie said she'd bake *such* a cake, that all of us, even before lunch, couldn't eat it up, and so there would be plenty left, and so you *could* take some back. It might get a little stale, but it would be the gift, the thought, that mattered! But a stale cake — what would your wife and your sons think! Then Annie said we should take some snaps of our country, and put them in a photo album-book, and that would be a real good present, and you could remember us that way, and we could arrange to be in the pictures. We know you like our country a lot — the hills over there and the sunsets. We have the best sunsets in the world — you said that several times. You see, we remember!"

A very short stop, to gas up with the thin Transvaal air (my mind by now, mercifully, is a blank): "But Theo — she was the one: she said we should paint you a big picture, because that's what you like best of all, and you're here to collect as many as you can, and this one should be better than the others, because we'd have lots of time to paint it, not just do it 'on the run,' when you're here, and you ask, but way before. At first we thought we'd all pitch in and do it together, and we tried, but we got into an argument about what we should paint, you see, and it got to be lots of shouting, and so Theo started to cry, and she said she wished she'd never, ever come up with *that* idea! Then, I said, okay, just let's stop this, and I'll try to paint something, and Theo said *please*. I said if it's all right with everyone, and so we agreed I'd try. We did have another idea, to get you a book, but the store is closed for repair [a drugstore, which carries a small supply of books, mostly detective stories, and a few travel yarns, one of which I suspect I might have been given, had this plan been pursued]. I said, give me a day, and I'll work at it 'right along, right along' [another localism]. And here's what we have!"

A smile from me. I thank them. I've already perfunctorily thanked them, but I get more enthusiastically grateful — and am rewarded with their big smiles. Still, I am puzzled by this building, and Hendrick hasn't solved this puzzle for me. He sees me looking, looking. He realizes that I am stumped. He explains: "I didn't know what to paint, so I thought I'd try to paint the hills over there, and I was going to make a sunset, but the painting would have to be so dark, and my sister said no, that's a bad idea. I figured out what to do, and I made a sketch, and I was going to do it the next morning. Then, I had supper, and I went to bed. The next thing, I woke up, and I had a bad dream, and I was afraid. There had been a nuclear war I think; or someone said there might be one in a few days, and South Africa would be in the war — *us!* I think I might have been watching the [South

African State] television with my mother and father. My mother got very worried, and she said we should hide, maybe in our game room; it's below the surface. My father laughed; he said that you can't hide from a nuclear bomb. But he said it's crazy to think that anyone would want to bomb *us*. That's when my mother reminded him about the Russians! He's always saying they're out to destroy us, and if they are, then this could be the time, the minute! I asked whether the blacks could ever get the nuclear bomb. *No,* my father said, *never;* but the Russians could give them a few. We got out our Bible and we sat there praying. And I remember hearing something from Luke, maybe — my father was reading it, but he knew it by heart, and I know the story, of Jesus and His disciples, and they're on a boat, and the lake gets real stormy, and the boat is sinking. It is full of water. Then Jesus makes the storm quiet down, and the disciples are impressed. I guess He told them that they shouldn't be so afraid, because they are with Him, and if they really believe in what He is doing, then they have no right to doubt Him, or doubt that He'll help them get through the trouble, the storm.

"I guess my father was reading that part of the Bible, or he was saying it from memory; I don't remember. All I know is that my father said, not to worry, because we have nuclear bombs in South Africa, so we can fight back — he knows we do, he's positive. But my mother started crying, and she said millions of people will die, and if they do, Jesus will be angry; He'll be *very* angry at us, and He might decide none of us, no one, deserves to be alive, and that will be the end. Then I think we heard a loud noise, and we weren't sure what it was, and it might have been an explosion, we weren't sure, and my mother and father said His name: Jesus! Then I woke up!"

When he'd finished with that narration he had converted a politely quiet audience into an anxiously, utterly silent one — spellbound children and a puzzled doctor. Why this dream? My professional reflexes buzzed away. But I didn't know what to ask or say — and time was running out, in Hendrick's dream and in our time together in that town of South Africa's heartland. I decided to be less passive, though. I asked Hendrick, finally, what the building was — knowing, by then, that he'd bravely attempted to evoke the mysteries of a nuclear reactor! He answered me in a softer than usual voice, not hushed, simply respectful: "I don't know what a nuclear bomb looks like. I think it's a box. I thought I'd make a reactor, or a missile pad, where the bomb is inside, and it's sent out through the roof. I was using my imagination; that's what our art teacher says to do! I don't know why I put the building here. I guess it's because a few weeks ago I heard our minister say that Jesus wanted us to live each day as though it's your last, and then you'll be a better Christian. When I woke up from that dream I thought of what the minister said a few weeks ago, and I said to myself: Hendrick, what if there aren't any more days after this one? What would you do? Well, I didn't have an answer! But when I was painting this, I thought: I guess I'd better put that nuclear stuff in. My mother said in the dream — I forgot to tell you — that it's crazy, what people do: how we kill each other, how we treat each other. And I knew Jesus would say that — I mean, the next morning I was sure Jesus would say what my mother said. So, I decided to paint it in; I figured you'd be going home soon, and we heard on television that your country has lots of missiles and bombs, nuclear bombs."

He stops speaking. I am uneasy; I don't fully follow the logic of his narrative. He seems tired of talking. He looks at his friends, as if to take their measure. How are they doing, feeling — responding to him? But suddenly he resumes — plunges to the finish line: "I thought as I was painting this: What are you doing, Hendrick, painting this? You're crazy! Then I thought — hey, we're all crazy, to have these things on our planet! Then I thought, my God Almighty: if one of these goes off, everyone will die, every single one of us, probably, in South Africa! What difference will it make — where we live, and whether we're old or young. No one would be here. The colored ones would be gone, and the black ones, and the Indians — and us, too, the white people! It makes you wonder! We should stop fighting! That's why I made this picture — so we could all be warned! The picture was originally going to be just the center part. I think I wanted to say what I thought Jesus would say — like our minister tells us: If you're trying to say something and you're having trouble, or if you're trying to decide what to do, and having trouble, then ask yourself: what would Jesus say, what would He do? He'd probably tell us to think of how terrible the nuclear bomb is, and so, try to stay alive, and not die. Try to survive; and stop your fights!"

No more from Hendrick. Not one of us so much as moves. I look at Hendrick and wonder why I hadn't had even more talks with him — but then, a lifetime spent in South Africa still wouldn't be enough, with all the surprises children can offer us at unpredictable moments. I catch myself, as I sit there, also realizing, again, that children everywhere can stop us short with their unnerving moments of innocent good sense — even as they can, also, mouth all our (adult) stupid nonsense — and sometimes, one hopes and prays, give voice to our more honorable and decent thoughts. Just as a rush of these ideas was going through my by now surprised, and I have to say, worried head (Is Hendrick "all right"? Why this dream? Why this picture, really?), young Theo spoke up: "Hendrick, that was a hard dream to follow — that was a hard dream to have, I mean. We're glad you did the painting like you did! It's great! I hope the world will get better, and we never have a nuclear war, *ever!* That's what your picture says — that we should remember!"

Applause. They bring me another present, cookies they'd all made — Afrikaner cookies, an old Dutch recipe. They also give me some picture postcards of their village. They ask me, as we say our final goodbye, whether I'll show the painting to my family, and Hendrick asks whether they'll "understand" it. I tell him I think they will; and I further tell him that he is not as alone as he may think — that others I've known, in other countries, have worried about what nuclear bombs and missiles would do to this planet, and even drawn pictures that convey the fears they quite properly have. His face registers his wonderful thirst for knowledge, his alertness to all that is going on around him. He asks for specifics, and I tell him about some children I've known in Poland and in Northern Ireland, and in fact, in my own country — what they have said about the threat a nuclear war poses to the survival of millions of families. I promise to send him anything I write on the subject — and he seems not only pleased, but proud, as if to say that what seemed like a tough, restless, confusing night (a bizarre dream unsettling a boy whose feet are usually quite solidly planted on the earth) had turned into an occasion to think about important questions, to learn. We had a warm goodbye, all of us, and since that day I have returned to the tape and the memory of that poignant celebration many times — when I hear talk of nuclear war, and too, when I read the latest evidence of what the Afrikaner-led South African government is doing to consolidate its apartheid policies. Here were young Afrikaners; here was, not improbably, a future Afrikaner leader, and yet his moral anguish as a dreamer was all too evident. When do the Hendricks of this world stop having such dreams, lose interest in such urgent ethical matters, forsake willingness to make such a painting?

Since that late-summer day several years ago I've done what I told Hendrick and myself I'd try to do — take stock of what I've heard from other children about this most fearful of all political issues. In the last chapter of *The Moral Life of Children* I provided an account of the work I've attempted with American children in hopes of learning whether or how their general situation in life touches upon their moral thinking about nuclear weapons.[4] I have not had the time to pursue in other countries a similar, relatively systematic research effort, but I most certainly have heard children like Hendrick and the Polish boy quoted in Chapter V make vivid reference to the possibility of destructive nuclear war. What I have heard may be called the expression of a political morality — children who remind themselves and us that a nuclear war might well take place unless national politics everywhere is tethered firmly to a commanding ethics of survival, the gist of Hendrick's dream: Even the cherished apartheid of his Afrikaner people won't with-stand the nuclear Armageddon his night-fevered mind tried to fathom. When I leave Belfast or Johannesburg, Rio de Janeiro or Managua, Quebec, Thailand's refugee camps, Warsaw, *and* when I leave the American homes where I've been lucky to be able to sit and drink coffee and watch television and eat snacks and play games with boys and girls and listen to them trying to make sense of this world, and watch them doing so with crayons and paints and big or small pieces of paper — in all those moments a political morality is never too distant. These children realize that what their countries or other countries do may well affect how, or indeed whether, they will live. Hendrick, well fed, destined for college and a comfortable life, worries that a nuclear warhead can kill everyone, everything. Other children, chronically malnourished and with little hope of even a minimally secure life, worry that a government seemingly indifferent to them will turn actively hostile, send out the police with orders to shoot and shoot and shoot. Anyone who doubts the capacity of children for this kind of political and moral consciousness[5] ought to visit an *elementary* school in Soweto, or simply stand high on a favela and ask children about the city they prowl by day or night — "so that," as one child told me, "there will be another tomorrow." *I* hear that statement and take note of its quality of terse, sad, eloquence. *He* is telling me about death as a fact, a constant, immanent likelihood — and not because he has been reading the nineteenth- and twentieth-century existentialists. Death by nuclear bombs, death by starvation — death either way, these children know, is death by wrongdoing. The nations of the world should beware, should do better, Hendrick said, and so have injunctions to that effect also been uttered by countless black children segregated in Soweto. Occasionally the indignation of those young political moralists will out — hence the dozens and dozens of black children who were killed in 1976 when they spoke their minds and marched together down their dusty unpaved streets.

Nuclear technology — its presence as a threat to our survival — has not gone unnoticed by some children; *but* people like me, doing their research and also worried as ordinary individuals, alive on this dangerous planet, with virtual extinction a possibility, must be very careful to do justice to what is *actually* happening in the minds of children, and not confuse our preoccupations with theirs. The political morality of a Brazilian favelado child, for instance, or one from Soweto, does not include the nuclear threat as an issue of high priority. In Belfast, I heard scant mention of nuclear threats directly — though I regret to say that I did hear children wish that *their* side had possession of a nuclear bomb or two. Would they use such a bomb? They hope not, but: "If the Brits kept pushing us, and we had it [the bomb], we could scare them; we could say that if you don't get out of here and leave us alone, then you'll all *have* to leave, because we'll make you!" An absurd and (one prays) utterly impossible military scenario — a ten-year-old child's extravagant fantasy life. Still, political desperation is at work on those rowdy, agitated streets; and such a political life is accompanied by a sort of moral deterioration, so that boys and girls, even ten-year-olds, justify or recommend what they also know they shouldn't be proposing. The boy just quoted, at another moment (when the IRA and *its* moral and political imperatives were safely filed, psychologically) had this to say about a nuclear bomb, even one: "Lots and lots of people would die right away, and it would be awful. I think one or two of those bombs, and all of Ireland would be gone!" He'd learned that from the nuns — but then, he'd learned many things from the nuns that he managed to forget for long stretches of time: the Sermon on the Mount, for instance, which at an earlier age he had virtually committed to memory. Belfast's Protestant children are not beyond a similar inclination to evoke the wildest military strategies, atomic warfare included, and a correlative realization that such an initiative would mark the end of just about everything for everyone.

It would be quite unfair of me, I believe, to say that these Irish children are in any proper sense of the word obsessed with the nuclear threat. Nor am I prepared to accept the observation that their failure so to be alarmed represents a genre of psychopathology, "denial," or "numbing,"[6] whereas, in contrast, certain upper-middle-class children in the United States are quite worried on this score, or some well-to-do children who live near Queens University in Belfast; or some Brazilian children of very thoughtful Copacabana and Ipanema families. We all use "denial," and I fear we're all able to be "numb" to much of the tragedy that constantly takes place on this earth — and not necessarily because we are "sick" or even callous. Millions fall ill, are malnourished, barely survive, languish near death, or indeed, are dying — whole countries, in fact. Am I the victim of "psychic numbing" should I fail to think about such people, day in and day out? How often do I think about apartheid, in all its horrible urgency as a moral and political matter for the entire world? When I don't (as I don't for days upon days), am I "denying," or am I in a "numbed" state? These are vexing matters, and not illuminated by resort to psychological name-calling, though one's *own* manifestations of psychopathology somehow never become the target for psychiatric labeling.

If psychoanalysis has taught us anything, it is that generalizations apply to individual predilections. Here, of course, the priorities are mine; I incline to use psychiatric nomenclature as a weapon against "them," the ones who aren't following (my) suit. The self-serving aspect of such a temptation is all too obvious. We find it easy to disregard *why* it is that some of our fellow human beings, out of the complexities and ambiguities of their lives, may happen to find themselves dwelling on concerns other than ours. Not only South Africans are capable of falling prey to apartheid; many of us build in our minds our own moral and political apartheid — keeping ourselves and our values and our psychology on one ethical plane, and looking down with condescension, or an inadequate sociology, or a skimpy body of research, upon the "others." Afrikaner children turn on English children, and vice versa. Protestant children of Belfast turn on the Catholic children of Belfast, and vice versa. Scholars quarrel, professional associations become viciously and personally antagonistic, those who argue for "peace" end up being pugnacious. Neither the Ku Klux Klan nor the South African government nor my benighted next-door neighbor have a monopoly on pride or prejudice.

I think I've seen enough children in enough countries, by now, to be able to say that even though I believe that the threat of a nuclear war is the greatest of all dangers to everyone on this earth, and therefore the most important political issue for every nation, the great majority of the children, the parents I have met here and abroad do not feel that way. We need to learn what children *persistently* feel, and to accomplish this goal we need to observe their lives, and what happens in living those lives. I will never forget that stunning moment with Hendrick in South Africa. How tenaciously I have held to it! Here was a boy who, for a moment at least, broke free of the very constraints his nationality, his political socialization, strove to uphold. When I tell Hendrick's story at psychiatric and psychoanalytic seminars or conferences, I'm always asked to consider my own "involvement." A colleague asks me whether "the boy may not have been expressing a transference reaction." He points out that I'd spent rather a long time with those children, years of trips to their community, hence the likelihood of some boys and girls, at least, being won over to my concerns, at least somewhat, and at least for a limited time. He also points out that such a psychological outcome would be likely to surface at the end of a visit, when it might be safely acknowledged, and sad to say, conveniently forgotten thereafter.

Yes, I responded, I agree. Still, few children in any country have abandoned their preoccupations in favor of mine. Hendrick had his own reasons to take the moral pronouncements of Jesus seriously, and to heed (albeit in his own way!) the South African government's sometimes apocalyptic statements. He is not the first South African to fear the worst about the direction his nation is taking, or the first one to try to imagine some perspective in which the hatred and fighting generated by apartheid might somehow be alleviated. Even a prominent government official told me, the second time we met, that he wished "we could find a huge distraction in our country, so no one would pay any more attention to race." He was talking, at the time, about sports as a possible candidate for such a distraction.[7] Hendrick might have an idea for that nationalist leader — but then, how *does* one encourage the rulers of a nation to adopt a view of things that puts the world's survival ahead of saving their own skins? One child's middle-of-the-night analytic effort cannot be expected to answer that question.

I have noticed, in areas such as Poland, Nicaragua, Ulster, South Africa, and the United States as well, where nuclear bombs are made openly or secretly, or where war (internal or external) is a constant threat or a chronic reality, that a few boys and girls do indeed mention, anxious or angry or grimly humorous, the dangers such bombs pose to all of us. Hence the Polish boy quoted in Chapter V, who said what Poles have been thinking and saying for generations: a plague on both their houses — his wry hope that Russian and German-based nuclear missiles would wipe out both countries, leaving a beloved Poland, finally, once and for all, rid of those two overpowering national presences.

Nuclear missiles appear in all too casual a light in the drawings of Nicaraguan children, aroused to heights of nationalism by a government bound to teach them a specific politics. Not that teachers or parents or government officials want to tell those children of a likelihood of a nuclear war in Central America. The children, rather, hear accounts of nuclear missiles in the same way as an earlier generation learned of ordinary weapons. Their natural powers of accentuation, exaggeration, or overstatement, however, draw them to introduce nuclear devices into their artwork, into their stories about what might happen, about what must never happen. As one explores with them what they actually know, how they learned it, how seriously they take their views, or pictures, one is reminded, yet again, that even in Nicaragua the dangerous realities of nuclear weaponry do not go unrecognized. In a rural community near León, I heard children give plenty of evidence of their awareness. A boy of thirteen was afraid the United States would try to "wipe out" his country with one of their "big bombs." Just to check, I asked what kind of bombs they were. He said, "the kind that kills everyone for miles and miles." He didn't know the word "nuclear," but he knew what it was possible in the 1980s for human beings to do: "Let them drop their big bombs! If we're going to be their slaves, it's better that we die!" I thought the statement a bit too rehearsed and rhetorical, but the child had made the words his very own. He was excited. He used his right fist to pound a table. He gritted his teeth. I had to remind myself that people like me also memorize our phrases and make them our own.

In Brazil I heard the children of government technocrats, and of men who run large industries, talk about their strong worries that the United States and the Soviet Union will somehow, some day "blow up all the countries, not only each other." These are children whose social and economic background is very much like that of the upper-middle-class American children whose moral fears about the nuclear bomb I have described in *The Moral Life of Children*. There is, however, this critical difference: The American children worry about their own government's purposes as well as those of the Soviet Union. In Brazil the children who are so apprehensive (I have yet to hear a favela child talk at any length about nuclear bombs) are sure that *their* country will never "scare" the world in the way the United States does. The thirteen-year-old boy in São Paulo who used that word, "scare," intended fully the implications of a deliberate intent. He gave his reasons for such a conclusion, telling as much about his mind's Brazilian nationality as about his sensitive internationalist worries: "Your country, U.S.A., is a big giant, and it loses its temper, and then everyone is afraid. Your country scares all the other countries in North America and South America. We don't know what you'll do. We owe so much money to you. My father is a banker, and he says it's hopeless — every time we try to get free of the United States, they put another piece of rope around our wrists! He likes your country, but he says it's too rich and too strong, and we're too poor and too weak, even though we're making big, big gains. The whole world should control these weapons — and it's not fair that so many countries should be trembling every time the American government coughs. My father says if I went to the United States of America I'd see how rich it is, but even so, he loves coming home to Brazil after he's been in New York. He thinks there won't be a nuclear war, and our Brazil won't go bankrupt. He says it's right for us in school to say we must never have a nuclear war. 'But go tell them that in Washington,' he told my friends. They said they would! My father told them he knows them up there, and they listen to no one except themselves! They don't respect us here. They prefer England. They have never respected us. In a hundred years — maybe then it'll be different. When we open up the Amazon country, Washington will try to take away all our wealth, but we'll stop them! We'll say no. Maybe *we'll* have to build nuclear bombs one of these days! When countries get rich they make bigger bombs, and they can start wars and ruin every-one, even if they live far away!"

In country after country, children's worries about the nuclear bomb have become tangled with the particular nationalist fears, preoccupations, anticipations, or disappointments that those same children have been adapting into their own political life. Perhaps the most bloodthirsty comment I have ever heard from a child about the nuclear bomb was made only half in jest by a Polish girl of thirteen in Krakow: "I wish we could get a Soviet nuclear missile and turn it on our government people, there in Warsaw. That would be what they deserve!" I waited for a sardonic look on her face that I'd come to expect from her. But no, she did not flinch or look as though she were kidding me. Would she *really* want such a device used? Yes, she said — and no more. I was ready to turn to another line of questioning when she added: "No, I guess I wouldn't — but they deserve the worst. Besides, this is all 'have a wish' talk! I have a wish — to be free of our government, but no one knows how to do it."

I was relieved that she relaxed a bit, yet the child's vehemence was unforgettable. As I indicated in writing about Poland, I have never seen children so radically disenchanted with their own government. In Ulster, after all, the Catholic children don't regard the British authorities as part of *any* government — rather, as hateful foreigners. Even in Soweto the black children do feel themselves to be South Africans, though ones receiving terribly unjust treatment; and yet, their rage against the government does not express itself in the strenuous disassociation I have heard Polish children assert. In Soweto the militant young want to fight, yes — but fight *their* government. (A slogan: "We will make our government change, if we have to die trying!") In Poland the young talk about the government as if the two or three million communists in the country are a foreign scum beyond even the comprehension of a South African apartheid apologist. No wonder such children embrace the desperation of a nuclear assault only half in jest.

Meanwhile children like Hendrick, all over the world, continue to learn what their various nations expect of them, and so, what they are to expect for themselves. Hendrick expects a life of reasonable comfort and personal authority. Soweto's children expect a life of exclusion, indignity, powerlessness. A nation's politics becomes a child's everyday psychology. No child I have met, during twenty-five years of work in the United States and many other countries, has failed to remind me, at some time in our acquaintance, of his or her desire to see this century out, to welcome the onset of the third millennium. A not surprising wish — a reasonable expectation for some, and, alas, a distant dream for many children now living in Soweto or in Brazil's favelas. Talk of dates and decades comes naturally to children; at an age when they learn to count, learn their birthdays, they learn months and years that help them identify one another. I am the one who was born on this day of this year, and you are the one born on that day of that year. I am the one born here, in this city of this country at this time, and you were born over there, in that city of that country at that time — nationality as a means of self-definition. The future years as a means of assuring oneself of an existence that began at a particular moment in the past.

In a moment of introspection Hendrick told me late on a rainy August day what he heard in church — that we live until God wants us, and we don't die any earlier: a perhaps garbled theology his minister was urging as Biblical truth in that obscure and tormented South African community. But the boy grabbed the interpretation eagerly — a comfort not unlike that offered by the knowledge of one's birthday, and for some, of one's nationality: a lifeboat in an infinite ocean of a universe. No wonder nuclear bombs alarmed him, prompted his restlessness, his "hard dreams." Hendrick's was a dream of fierce insistence, a child proclaiming in his middle-of-the-night thoughts what Rilke said: "Survival is all." Even the mightiest peoples and nations, these days, can't take such survival for granted, Hendrick knew. He had absorbed surely one of the more important moral and political lessons to be learned by any child anywhere.

NOTES

INTRODUCTION

1. In September 1956. The boy came from the suburban town of Arlington, west of Boston.
2. The supervisor was George Gardner, M.D. — a wise, if sometimes brusque, child psychoanalyst, and at the time, Chief of Child Psychiatry at Children's Hospital. I learned a lot from him about children, and a few things, too, about the common "problems" of doctors such as myself, who work with children!
3. Records such as this were put away by my wife when we dismantled our home to go South, to become involved with the school-desegregation struggle and the sit-in movement. We will eventually send all these old records, along with the tapes of interviews with children, and the thousands of drawings and paintings they have kindly given us over the years, to the University of North Carolina Library.
4. The reader might want to notice the way in which those children's preoccupations and hurdles were described in volume I of *Children of Crisis: A Study of Courage and Fear* (Boston: Atlantic–Little, Brown, 1967).
5. Included, in time, will be the documentation of our work abroad — tapes, edited and unedited transcripts, notes and journals, drawings and paintings, photographs.
6. The interview took place June 17 and 18, 1965, in Greenville, Mississippi.
7. See, especially, his *Nature and Destiny of Man* (New York: Scribner's, 1949), and *Moral Man and Immoral Society* (New York: Scribner's, 1934). I have tried to indicate my debt to Niebuhr's thinking in an essay, "Reinhold Niebuhr's Nature and Destiny of Man" written for *Daedalus* (Winter 1973). When in medical school I audited his lectures, heard him deliver his jeremiad-sermons, and I still think he has yet to be equaled as an American political observer, never mind shrewd Christian moralist.
8. In a long interview, held at the Southern Regional Council, where we then worked: August 1963. We heard, of course, similar analyses rendered in the powerful sermons he offered at the Ebenezer Baptist Church on many a Sunday of that year and others to follow.
9. See Volume IV of *Children of Crisis: Eskimos, Chicanos, Indians* (Boston: Atlantic–Little, Brown, 1977).
10. I well remember Robert Kennedy's serious preparation for the same lectureship in 1966. He reviewed not only South Africa's racial problems but those of the United States. Eight years after he'd been in South Africa, six years after his death, I heard his name constantly evoked there by black, colored, and not a few white children.
11. I went to South Africa with my English-born father, whose uncle had fought

in the Boer War on behalf of Her Majesty, Queen Victoria, and with my young son, who kept on asking me (at age ten) why the black and colored people "put up with the treatment" they received, and who asked his grandfather why England had been so eager to control Cape Town and other South African territory — talking about "political socialization"!

12. The fifth volume, *Privileged Ones: The Well-off and the Rich in America*, was published simultaneously with the fourth volume (Boston: Atlantic–Little, Brown, 1977).

13. See the chapters on "Method" in all five volumes of *Children of Crisis*; also see the Introduction to *The Moral Life of Children* (Atlantic Monthly Press, 1986).

14. See *Up Against the Wall: The Political and Moral Development of Children in East and West Berlin*, a doctoral thesis by Thomas Davey at Harvard Graduate School of Education, 1984.

15. The regions include the urban and suburban areas of New England, New York State, Illinois, and Ohio, the South's cities and rural areas, the Rio Grande Valley of Texas, New Mexico and Arizona, Alaska.

16. Again, I suggest previous essays I've written on "method" in the *Children of Crisis* series and in *Farewell to the South* (Atlantic–Little, Brown, 1972).

I. POLITICAL AUTHORITY AND THE YOUNG

1. See especially the first part of the essay, in *Selected Essays: 1934–1943*, chosen and translated by Richard Rees (New York: Oxford University Press, 1962).

2. First published by Yale University Press in 1965; an important, pioneering empirical effort to learn what American children think about political events.

3. See, especially, their research written up in *The Development of Political Attitudes in Children*, by R. Hess and J. Torney (Chicago: Aldine, 1967), and *Children in the Political System*, by D. Easton and J. Dennis (New York: McGraw–Hill, 1969). Both books give an account of original research completed several years earlier. The term "political socialization" was given prominence, if not coined, by Herbert Hyman, who did not conduct studies of his own, but wrote a series of theoretical essays on the subject: *Political Socialization* (Chicago: Free Press, 1959).

4. "The Adolescence of Political Socialization," in *Sociology of Education*, Vol. 45 (Spring, 1972).

5. In 1971.

6. See Mary Ellen Goodman's *Race Awareness in Young Children* (New York: Macmillan, 1964).

7. I began my work in the South in 1958, but only in 1967 (when the first volume of *Children of Crisis* appeared) was I finally beginning to understand how significantly some children in that region, at that time, apprehended political matters.

8. This matter of questionnaires as against sustained "direct observation" (whether clinical or as a consequence of psychological research) need not be a matter of either-or, nor one of polemics. See the discussion in "Children and the Nuclear Bomb," Chapter 7 in *The Moral Life of Children*.

9. See Piaget, *The Moral Judgment of the Child* (New York: Free Press, 1948). An especially useful book is *The Essential Piaget*, "an interpretive reference and guide," put together by Howard E. Gruber and J. Jacques Vanèche (New

York: Basic Books, 1977). A number of Piaget's most interesting essays are in this collection.

10. See Kohlberg, *The Philosophy of Moral Development* (New York: Harper and Row, 1981). I refer the reader, additionally, to my discussion of the moral conduct of boys and girls, in *The Moral Life of Children*.

11. See Volume IV of *Children of Crisis: Eskimos, Chicanos, Indians* (Boston: Atlantic–Little, Brown, 1977) for a full discussion of the attitudes such children have toward "Anglos," and toward the country "Anglos" control.

12. See Chapter IX of that book: "Children and the Nuclear Bomb" (Boston: Atlantic Monthly Press, 1986).

13. In this regard, my work has been mainly done with American children and South African children. (South Africa has never openly admitted to possession of nuclear bombs. Yet its officials tacitly acknowledge that the country does, indeed, possess nuclear weaponry — and certainly they have advanced research facilities, strictly off limits.)

II. THE HOMELAND: PSYCHOANALYSIS AND THE POLITICAL THOUGHT OF CHILDREN

1. November 12, 1975 in London.

2. Anna Freud used that phrase constantly in her writings (and in every speech). See *Normality and Pathology in Childhood* (New York: International Universities Press, 1965). I have discussed this matter of "direct observation" at some length in "The Achievement of Anna Freud," *Massachusetts Review*, Vol. VII, no. 2 (Spring, 1966); also in *The Mind's Fate* (Boston: Atlantic–Little, Brown, 1975).

3. Psychoanalytic literature is not overly preoccupied with politics or nationalism as influences on mental life, though Freud himself in *Group Psychology and the Analysis of the Ego* (London: Hogarth Press, 1962) was shrewdly knowing about nationalism — and again so in his exchange with Einstein in "Why War?, " a part of Volume 22 of *Collected Works of Sigmund Freud* (London: Hogarth, 1964). An important and helpful text is R. E. Money-Kyrle, *Psychoanalysis and Politics* (New York: Norton, 1951). Erik H. Erikson's early work in this field — the studies of German and Russian "national character" in *Childhood and Society* — was, of course, extremely suggestive (New York: Norton, 1950). A more recent, and quite helpful book in the psychoanalytic tradition is V. Volkan, *Cyprus — War and Adaptation*, with a valuable introduction by John Mack (Charlottesville: University Press of Virginia, 1979).

4. Social psychologists, political scientists, and essayists have offered us a rich literature that documents this symbolic acquisition. Joseph Adelson's work with youths is particularly important: "Growth of Political Ideas in Adolescence: The Sense of Community," *Journal of Personality and Social Psychology*, Vol. 4 (1966), pp. 295–306; and "The Political Imagination of the Young Adolescent," *Daedalus*, Vol. 10 (Fall, 1971), pp. 1013–1050. Joel Agee's fine autobiographical memoir is also highly instructive: *Twelve Years* (New York: Farrar, Straus & Giroux, 1981). Urie Bronfenbrenner's comparison of American and Soviet childhood is a landmark cross-cultural study with much emphasis on the way in which children accommodate themselves to the (symbolic) values of one or

another world: *Two Worlds of Childhood: U.S and U.S.S.R.* (New York: Simon and Schuster, 1970). I have already mentioned the pioneering work of Fred Greenstein; his *Source Book for the Study of Personality and Politics* (Chicago: Markham, 1971) also deserves mention, as does Robert Lane, *Political Thinking and Consciousness* (Chicago: Markham, 1969). Several articles are worthy of careful study: G. Jahoda, "The Development of Children's Ideas About Country and Nationality," *British Journal of Educational Psychology* (February, 1962), pp. 42–60; a paper by D. Jaros and B. Canon, "Transmitting Basic Political Values: The Role of the Educational System," in the *School Review*, Vol. 77 (1969), pp. 94–107; and two articles by M. Jennings and R. Niemi: "Patterns of Political Learning," *Harvard Educational Review*, Vol. 38, no 3 (Summer, 1968); and "The Transmission of Political Values from Parent to Child," in *American Political Science Review*, Vol. 62 (1968), pp. 169–184. Another significant study was that by W. Lambert and O. Klineberg, *Children's Views of Foreign People* (New York: Meredith, 1967).

5. In Wilhelm Reich's *Mass Psychology of Fascism* (New York: Farrar, Straus & Giroux, 1970), he was bold enough to begin making these connections. The psychoanalyst V. Volkan, op. cit., readily noticed such connections as he did his fieldwork research.

6. See Anna Freud, *The Ego and the Mechanism of Defense* (New York: International Universities Press, 1966).

7. An interesting article, on this subject, is "Civic Education, Community Norms and Political Indoctrination" in *The Learning of Political Behavior*, eds. N. Adler and C. Harrington (New York: Scott, Foresman, 1970). This subject of "class" and "political assumptions" needs much more "fieldwork" — explorations in particular neighborhoods. I attempted some preliminary observations in *The Middle Americans* (Boston: Atlantic–Little, Brown, 1971).

8. Of course *thinking* about one's country can, indeed, be an aspect of one's moral thought — as Piaget reminds us in a lovely paper, "The Development in Children of the Idea of the Homeland and of Relations with Other Countries," *International Social Science Bulletin*, Vol. 3 (1951).

9. See a recent effort titled just that, *Freud and Society*, by Jiannis Gabriel (London: Routledge and Kegan Paul, 1983). The bibliography in this book is quite extensive.

10. A more felicitous manner of so doing is to be found in D. W. Winnicott's little gem, "Some Thoughts on the Meaning of the Word Democracy," in *Human Relations*, Vol. III (1950).

11. I refer, concretely, to the virtual absence of a literature of political psychology in the psychiatric and psychoanalytic journal devoted to the problems of children — even though any number of boys and girls, surely, have had occasion to summon up politics in their (exceedingly charged and sometimes volatile) conversations with their doctors.

12. Op. cit.

13. I refer, especially, to a series of discussions with her in 1975, in England.

14. I have recently tried to pay my respects to Kafka's uncannily penetrating psychological knowledge in an Introduction to a new edition of *Metamorphosis* (New York: Limited Editions, 1984).

III. RELIGION AND NATIONALISM: NORTHERN IRELAND

1. The literature that deals with the Catholic and Protestant traditions of Northern Ireland is substantial, to say the least. Conor Cruise O'Brien introduced me to this subject, before I began my research, with his extremely helpful — lively, informative, fair-minded — *States of Ireland* (New York: Random House, 1972). A later book of his, *Herod: Reflections on Political Violence* (London: Hutchinson, 1978), contains remarkably vivid and trenchant essays on the sad and murderous Northern Ireland scene. George Dangerfield's *Damnable Question* (Boston: Atlantic–Little, Brown, 1976) offers a lucid, evenhanded account of a century and more of "Anglo-Irish conflict" — the historical background for today's "Troubles." A similarly historical approach — but with emphasis on documentary compilation — is in Charles Carlton, *Bigotry and Blood* (Chicago: Nelson-Hall, 1977). An even more ambitious "oral documentary" approach is W. H. Van Voris, *Violence in Ulster* (Amherst: University of Massachusetts, 1975). *Ireland: The Challenge of Conflict and Change* (Boulder: Westview, 1983), by Richard Finnegan, is encyclopedic, yet brief — a good beginning. The roots of Catholic nationalism are explored in Robert Kee's ambitious, three-volume *The Green Flag* (London: Quartet, 1976). *Revolution Underground*, by Leon O'Brien (Dublin: Gill and Macmillan, 1976), tells the story of the rise of the Irish Republican Brotherhood in the middle of the nineteenth century and traces its twentieth-century political and social contours.

A number of edifying books offer the reader an education in Northern Ireland's past and present difficulties: *The Narrow Ground*, by A. T. O. Stewart (London: Faber and Faber, 1977); *Governing Without Consensus*, by Richard Rose (Boston: Beacon, 1971); *Queen's Rebels* — an analysis of "Ulster loyalism," by David W. Miller (Dublin: Gill and Macmillan, 1978); *The Northern Ireland Problem*, by Denis P. Barrett and Charles F. Carter (London: Oxford University Press, 1972); *Northern Ireland: Crisis and Conflict* — and how these two nouns abound in the titles of texts of various essays — by John Magee (London: Routledge and Kegan Paul, 1974); *The Protestants of Ulster* by Geoffrey Bell (London: Pluto, 1976); *Belfast: Approach to a Crisis*, by Ian Budge and Cornelius O'Leary (London: Macmillan, 1973); *Peace-Keeping in a Democratic Society: The Lessons of Northern Ireland*, by Robin Evelegh — a British military officer's point of view (London: Hurst, 1978); and finally, a good general history of the Republic of Ireland, *The Making of Modern Ireland*, by J. C. Beckett (London: Faber and Faber, 1966).

Especially helpful for me are Dr. Morris Fraser's *Children in Conflict: Growing Up in Northern Ireland*, a child psychiatrist's account of his work with the children who daily take part in "the Troubles" (New York: Basic Books, 1973), and Roger Rosenblatt's powerfully rendered *Children of War*, which has a detailed account of a talented and seasoned writer's direct observations of Northern Ireland's children (New York: Doubleday, 1983). For those interested in the volatile, charismatic Reverend Ian Paisley, there is *Paisley*, by Patrick Marrinan (Tralee, County Kerry: Anvil, 1973). I have read friendlier accounts of this important figure in Belfast newspapers!

But Northern Ireland has to be understood and appreciated as more than a scene of suspicion, hate, violence. Wonderfully warm, generous, kindhearted, thoroughly interesting, talented, and imaginative people are to be found in those "upper" counties of a particular island, and so I would strongly suggest to the interested reader quite another reading tack: to begin with, the marvelously detailed, eloquent, and knowing *Passing the Time in Ballymenone: Culture and History of an Ulster Community,* by Henry Glassie, a giant work of social and cultural geography (Philadelphia: University of Pennsylvania Press, 1982); *Belfast: Origin and Growth of an Industrial City,* with its wonderful collection of essays in social history, edited by J. C. Beckett and E. Glasscock (London: British Broadcasting Corporation, 1967); *Songs and Sayings of an Ulster Childhood,* by Alice Kane (Toronto: McClelland and Stewart, 1983). *Forces and Themes in Ulster Fiction,* by John Wilson Foster (Dublin: Gill and Macmillan, 1974); and among writers who hail from Ulster, Louis MacNeice's *Collected Poems* (London: Faber and Faber, 1966), and Bernard MacLaverty, whose novel *Cal* negotiates with utter and nonpartisan honesty the truculent ideologies that sustain so many of Northern Ireland's political activists. I would also like to mention two volumes that commemorate and celebrate quite another aspect of a region's creative life — Volumes I and II of *Art in Ulster* (Belfast: Blackstaff Press, 1977). Not all the people one meets in, say, Belfast have war and bigotry on their minds!

2. J. C. Beckett, op. cit.
3. Miller, op. cit.
4. Denis Richards and Anthony Quick, *Britain 1714–1851* (Harlow, Essex, England: Longman, 1972).
5. Foster, op. cit.
6. MacNeice, op. cit.
7. I described this human scene in "Belfast's Children," *New Republic,* October 14, 1981.

IV. IDEOLOGY AND NATIONALISM: NICARAGUA

1. We were able to travel throughout the country, visit nursery schools, libraries, elementary schools, higher schools, and hospitals without interference. We also visited private (Church-run) schools attended by children of well-to-do families.
2. See "Impressions on Nicaragua," *New Oxford Review,* in two parts (April and May, 1984).
3. I strongly recommend for the reader who wants to understand the religious connections to politics made by some of the Sandinista *commandantes* the four-volume work by Ernesto Cardenal, *The Gospel in Solentinaine* (New York: Orbis, 1976). Also, Cardenal's earlier work *In Cuba* (New York: New Directions, 1974). Another valuable book dealing with this issue as it has developed in Nicaragua is Frederick Turner's *Catholicism and Political Development in Latin America* (Chapel Hill: University of North Carolina, 1971). Penny Lernoux's *Cry of the People* (New York: Doubleday, 1980) has been influential — a critical look at the involvement of the United States in "the persecution of the Catholic Church in Latin America." Nicaragua's more recent church-state confrontations are not mentioned, of course. More generally, I recommend Ralph Lee Woodward's *Central America* (New York: Oxford, 1976) for his valuable political and social history of Nicaragua and its neighbors; also, *In-*

evitable Revolutions, by Walter LaFeber (New York: Norton, 1983). An even more general background is offered by Charles Gibson in *Spain in America* (New York: Harper and Row, 1966).

4. The photographer Susan Meiselas gave me vivid accounts of what she'd heard. Her photographic studies of El Salvador and Nicaragua, years in the doing, constitute an invaluable documentary record of what has been taking place in Central America during the late 1970s and the 1980s.

5. A quite modern facility. We spent much time in various parts of the hospital — talked with doctors, nurses, patients, and parents at great length.

6. We also spent much time there, too — as children of the bourgeoisie!

7. See Omar Cabezas, *La Montaña es Algo Más que una Immensa Estepa Verde* (Managua: Editorial Nueva Nicaragua, 1982), which translates as "The Mountain Is Something More Than a Vast Green Steppe." We had a long interview with him in his office — and as he does in his book, he gave us an account of his long ordeal as a Sandinista revolutionary in hiding under Somoza. Of course, Arturo Cruz, also an opponent of Somoza, now sees things differently. See his "Nicaragua's Imperiled Revolution," *Foreign Affairs,* Vol. 61, no. 5 (1983). See also Christopher Dickey's "Central America: From Quagmire to Cauldron," *Foreign Affairs,* Vol. 62, no. 3 (1983). An informative booklet is *Somozas and Sandinistas: The U.S. and Nicaragua in the Twentieth Century,* published by the Council for Inter-American Security, Washington, D.C., in 1982 — an unfriendly look at present-day Sandinista-ruled Nicaragua, with a long bibliography. On the other side, one may call upon *Sandinistas Speak,* which contains the speeches and writings of (and interviews with) Nicaragua's revolutionary leaders (New York: Pathfinder Press, 1982). In the midst of such books, pro and con, I found Robert Stone's powerful novel *A Flag for Sunrise* (New York: Ballantine, 1982) to be more illuminating than all the rhetoric, the accusations, and the counteraccusations. If I were to declare my own "point of view," it would lean heavily on an article by Robert S. Leiken in the *New Republic,* October 8, 1984: "Nicaragua's Untold Stories."

8. See the articles mentioned above in *New Oxford Review.*

V. LANGUAGE, CULTURE, AND NATIONALISM: FRENCH CANADA AND POLAND

1. They were boys and girls attending both public and private schools, ages eight to fourteen. I am grateful to a student of mine, Charles Reynaud, for help in organizing this project and as an occasional translator.

2. *White Niggers of America,* by Pierre Nallières (Toronto: McClelland and Stewart, 1971). A number of books may be consulted by the reader who wishes to explore French Canadian nationalism: for example, Ramsay Cook's anthology, *French Canadian Nationalism* (Toronto: Macmillan, 1969). Also: Peter Desbarats's journalistic study: *The State of Quebec* (Toronto: McClelland and Stewart, 1965). I also recommend *Roots and Values in Canadian Lives,* by J. C. Falardeau (Toronto University Press, 1961); Gerald Gold, *Communities and Culture in French Canada* (Toronto: Holt, Rinehart and Winston, 1973); W. H. Moore, *The Clash: A Study in Nationalities* (London: J. M. Dent, 1918); and *The French Canadians,* by Mason Wade (New York: St. Martin's Press,

1968). Also, Marcel Chaput, *Why I Am a Separatist* (Toronto: Ryerson Press, 1962); and by Ramsay Cook, *Canada and The French Canadian Question* (Toronto: Macmillan, 1966). For those English readers who wish to venture into books written in French, several are of interest: Alfred Lévesque, *La Nation Canadienne-française: son Existence, ses Droits, ses Devoirs . . .* (Montreal, 1934); Pierre Angers, *Problèmes de Culture au Canada français* (Éditions Beauchemin, 1961); and Raoul Blanchard, *Le Canada français* (Paris: Presses Universitaires de France, 1964).

3. I was astonished at how commonly those words are used — a constant means of designating people!

4. Phenomenological research would ignore both the "objective" and "subjective" sides to the question of the significance of language in favor of a detailed study of its continual usage — a reality all its own, whether acknowledged as such by particular psychologists or philosophers; or so certain European phenomenologists would insist.

5. Again and again Edith Stein struggled with the nature of "empathy" (see *On the Problem of Empathy* [The Hague: Nijhoff, 1970]), and so doing, tried to understand how we "understand" one another, with language an aspect of this process, though not by any means the only source of such "understanding." When I hear a French-speaking child in Canada say that "only through French can we really make ourselves known," I think of Husserl and Stein — and I begin to realize that this is no mere matter of intelligibility in the cognitive sense that is at issue!

6. Kierkegaard, in his own dramatically singular fashion, explored the historical linkages between (Christian) Churches and the State, between the authority of God and that of man, as mediated by various secular authorities, whose language (phrases, slogans) become magically endowed, and confused with God's Word (language). See *On Authority* (Princeton: Princeton University Press, 1955), and of course, *The Present Age* (New York: Harper and Row, 1962).

7. The contrast is stunning: the eagerness in the faces of Nicaraguan schoolchildren as they study government-sponsored "political education" courses — and the grim refusal of Polish children to respond to a similar mode of instruction. Bitter humor often prevails in Polish classrooms, one notices — affecting even the more determined (or frightened) teachers, whose weary resignation or ironic detachment is all too obvious.

8. As I heard Polish children and their parents talk, I often thought of a book that appeared a generation ago, *My Language Is Me*, by Beulah Parker (New York: Basic Books, 1962). She told the story of a determined and knowing psychiatrist's effort to understand the statements of an exceedingly troubled boy. The boy says this: "If you understand and appreciate my language, you must understand and appreciate me. My language *is* me." I heard a markedly similar kind of affirmation from many a proud Polish child — an effort to remind me what they are; and, too, what I am not, for I spoke only a smattering of Polish. My interpreter, a sensitive university student who prefers not to be mentioned by name here, told me repeatedly that the children had reminded him that Soviet tanks could take over territory — even bulldoze their way into churches — but a spoken *language* is beyond their power! The reader might want to read Piaget on "language" (its development and cognitive significance

in children) in *Structuralism* (New York: Basic Books, 1970), and in *The Origins of Intelligence in Children* (New York: International Universities Press, 1952). But this political use of language by children has not yet been studied as carefully as it ought to be.

9. It is an irony that the Swiss-born, French-speaking philosopher Jean-Jacques Rousseau long ago advised the Polish government on the manner in which its children might be "politically socialized," as we might put it today. See his eighteenth-century work, *The Government of Poland* (Indianapolis: Bobbs-Merrill, 1972).

Since then any number of writers have tried to evoke Poland's dilemmas — its special circumstances, its history, its continuing struggles. I recommend, especially, Norman Davies's exhaustive two-volume study, *God's Playground: A History of Poland* (New York: Columbia University Press, 1982); also, O. Haleck, *A History of Poland* (New York: David McKay, 1976); Roman Dyboski, *Outlines of Polish History* (Westport, Conn.: Greenwood, 1979); R. F. Leslie, *The History of Poland Since 1863* (Cambridge: Cambridge University Press, 1980); and Antoni Gronowicz, *Polish Profiles* (Westport, Conn.: Hill, 1976). An excellent book about a nation's brave and agonizing effort to achieve social and political democracy — ended all too abruptly, forcibly — is Lawrence Wechsler, *Solidarity* (New York: Simon and Schuster, 1982). Some books that help clarify Poland's political predicament: *Poland in the Twentieth Century*, by M. K. Dziewonowski (New York: Columbia University Press, 1977); *Poland, the Captive Satellite*, by Joseph W. Zurowski (Detroit: Endurance Press, 1977); *The Polish Complex*, a novel, and a powerful evocation of contemporary Polish life, by Tadeusz Konwicki (New York: Farrar, Straus and Giroux, 1982); and Adam Bromke, *Poland's Politics* (Cambridge: Harvard University Press, 1967). For the reader with even more inclination to learn, the historian Norman Davies has assembled an invaluable "select bibliography of works in English," under the title *Poland: Past and Present* (Newtonville, Mass.: Oriental Research Partners, 1977).

VI. RACE AND NATIONALISM: SOUTH AFRICA

1. No book has introduced the world's readers to South Africa more influentially than Paton's *Cry, the Beloved Country* (New York: Charles Scribner's Sons, 1948). I recommend his other books as well: *South Africa and Her People* (London: Lutterworth Press, 1957); *Hope for South Africa* (London: Pall Mall Press, 1958); *Debbie Go Home — Stories* (London: Jonathan Cape, 1961); *Tales from a Troubled Land* (New York: Scribner's, 1961); *Hofmeyr* (London: Oxford University Press, 1964); *The Long View* (London: Pall Mall Press, 1968); *For You Departed* (New York: Scribner's, 1969); *Too Late the Phalarope* (London: Jonathan Cape, 1973).

2. A condition of our meeting was that he go nameless — and that I not mention, in this respect, anyway, the name of the white man who arranged this unforgettable afternoon visit (August 7, 1974 — in Cape Town).

3. Her singular and long Parliamentary opposition to apartheid deserves the gratitude of the world — a person of great courage and strong democratic convictions.

4. In Johannesburg and Pretoria — arranged through the American embassy at the time.

5. He, too, requests anonymity — though will allow me to say that he is a teacher and still very much a dedicated political activist in the struggle against apartheid.

6. See Volume III of *Children of Crisis: The South Goes North* (Boston: Atlantic–Little, Brown, 1972).

7. Not his real name.

8. He may well have wanted to exclude the whites of English ancestry from his personal census!

9. For a splendid discussion of this triptych, by an art historian who is solidly grounded in moral philosophy, see Wayne Andersen, *Gauguin's Paradise Lost* (New York: Viking, 1971).

10. This monument is pictured, and the history it commemorates is chronicled in *The Voortrekker Monument*, a book published by the Board of Control of the Voortrekker Monument, P.O. Box 1595, Pretoria, South Africa. South Africa's history, however, is not, of course, the sole property of its government-inspired and paid writers. If the reader reads nothing else on the subject I strongly urge upon him or her Charles Van Onselen's magisterial *Studies in the Social and Economic History of the Witwatersrand 1886–1914* — the first volume subtitled *New Nineveh*, and the second, *New Babylon* (London: Longman, 1982). These books have the power, lucidity, scope, and brilliance of E. P. Thompson's effort at comprehension of England's "working class in the making" — an exceptionally vivid social history that brings to life the human scene as it developed and changed in the heartland of South Africa. For a general history of South Africa I recommend: *The Oxford History of South Africa*, edited by Monica Wilson and Leonard Thompson (New York: Oxford University Press, 1969); *South Africa: A Modern History*, by T. R. H. Davenport (New York: Macmillan, 1977); *The Afrikaner as Viewed by the English, 1795–1854*, by M. Streak (Cape Town: C. Struik, 1974); *South Africa*, by J. Hoagland (Boston: Houghton Mifflin, 1972); *A History of South Africa*, by C. W. De Kiewiet (London: Oxford University Press, 1957); *Change in Contemporary South Africa*, a particularly informative and wide-ranging collection of essays, with a long and quite important bibliography, edited by Leonard Thompson and Jeffrey Butler (Berkeley: University of California Press, 1975); an excellent analysis of the Afrikaner "civil religion," *The Rise of Afrikanerdom*, by T. Dunbar Moodie (Berkeley: University of California Press, 1975); and not least, Thomas Pakenham's recent *The Boer War* (New York: Random House, 1979).

From a more political angle, these books offered help to an American innocent as he tried to understand a country as complex and volatile as any on this planet: *The Politics of Inequality*, by Gwendolyn M. Carter (New York: Octagon, 1977); and by the same author, *Which Way Is South Africa Going?* (Bloomington: Indiana University Press, 1980); *The Peoples and Policies of South Africa*, by Leo Marquard (London: Oxford University Press, 1969); *South Africa: A Study in Conflict*, by Pierre Van den Berghe (Berkeley: University of California Press, 1967); *Modernizing Racial Discrimination: The Dynamics of South African Politics*, by Herbert Adam (Berkeley: University of California Press, 1971); *Conflict and Progress: Fifty Years of Race Relations in South Africa*, a collection of essays edited by Ellen Hellmann and Henry

Laver (Johannesburg: Macmillan, 1979); *How Long Will South Africa Survive?*
an eminently shrewd analysis of a nation's *realpolitik* — its various centers of
power (New York: Oxford, 1979); *Soweto,* by John Kane-Berman (Johannesburg: Raven, 1978), an important source of information about a community of
more than a million human beings whose social and political struggles have
attracted worldwide notice; *Time Longer Than Rope,* an extraordinarily compelling account by a white South African university professor, a botanist, who
dared challenge apartheid boldly, and who was banned — as was his book
(Madison: University of Wisconsin Press, 1964); *International Pressures and
Political Change in South Africa,* by F. M. A. Clifford-Vaughan (Cape Town:
Oxford University Press, 1978); Anna Starcke's *Survival,* a series of candid
taped interviews with South Africa's power elite (Cape Town: Fafelberg, 1978);
John de St. Jorre, *A House Divided* (New York: Carnegie Endowment, 1977);
and by the same author "South Africa: Is Change Coming?" in *Foreign Affairs,*
Fall, 1981; *Political Imprisonment in South Africa,* an Amnesty International
Report, issued in 1978 (London: Amnesty International Publications); and, a
sad but deeply moving companion volume to the immediately foregoing, *The
Trial of Beyers Naudé* (London: Search Press, 1975), a report by the International Commission of Jurists on the effort of the South African government
to punish a prominent Afrikaner minister who broke with *apartheid;* also on
a personal note, *No Neutral Ground,* by Joel Carlson (New York: Crowell,
1973) — a white lawyer's description of his two-decade-long work on behalf of
black South Africans; and finally, a first-rate journalistic account of South Africa's recent political history, written by a former Harvard student I admired
years ago, and still do, who used the pseudonym James North: *Freedom Rising*
(New York: Macmillan, 1985).

From an economic angle of vision, one immediately mentions a classic of
sorts — *Migrant Labor in South Africa.* The author is Francis Wilson, a professor of economics at the University of Cape Town, a good friend, a brave
and decent man, indeed (Johannesburg: The South African Council of Churches,
1972). Another important book is *Southern African Labor History,* a collection
of essays edited by Eddie Webster (Johannesburg: Raven, 1978). American
readers will, perhaps, want to look at *U.S. Business in South Africa: The
Economic, Political, and Moral Issues,* by Desaix Myers III and a number of
associates (Bloomington: Indiana University Press, 1980). And because Namibia
is really South Africa, still — the International Labor Office's *Labour and
Discrimination in Namibia,* published in 1977, deserves attention.

Needless to say, a more sociological line of inquiry has not been denied
South Africa by its own academic or journalistic observers, and others from
outside who have tried to make sense of that country's customs, laws, social
and racial arrangements. A good start, maybe, for an American reader at least,
might be a reading of *Watts and Woodstock,* whose subtitle is "Identity and
Culture in the United States and South Africa" (New York: Holt, Rinehart and
Winston, 1973). The author, James O'Toole, is a social anthropologist, and he
aims to convey the aspirations, the worries, and the difficulties of people in
our (Los Angeles) Watts community, and of people who live in the Cape Town
Coloured quarter of Woodstock — to compare two worlds. Another book that
takes up in considerable detail the same part of South Africa O'Toole studied,
but from a more historical vantage point, is *The Cape Colour Question,* by W.

M. Macmillan (New York: Humanities Press, 1968). Not that South Africa's "colored" people live only in Cape Town. Western Township, a few miles to the west of downtown Johannesburg, is where my wife and children and I did some of our work; and its life is described with subtlety and accuracy by Marianne Brindley in her *Western Coloured Township: Problems of an Urban Slum* (Johannesburg: Raven, 1976).

With respect to the black people of South Africa, I strongly suggest a start with *The Autobiography of an Unknown South African*, a plainspoken and haunting personal narrative (an "oral history") of a proud and thoughtful man, Naboth Mokgatle, obscure by racial fate rather than as a consequence of his talent, one begins to realize (Berkeley: University of California Press, 1975). More generally, there is *South Africa's Urban Blacks*, a collection of essays by mostly Afrikaner whites of so-called moderate or *verligte* (enlightened) sensibility, edited by Q. Marais and R. Van der Kooy (Pretoria: Centre for Management Studies, 1972). Quite another point of view appears in Joyce Sikakane, *A Window on Soweto* (London: International Defense and Aid Fund, 1977); and in Freda Troup, *Forbidden Pastures: Education Under Apartheid* (London: International Defense and Aid Fund, 1976). Peter Becker, *Tribe to Township* is a more dispassionate (less political) study by an experienced anthropologist (London: Panther, 1974). Similarly with *Townsmen or Tribesmen*, by Philip and Jana Mayer (Cape Town: Oxford University Press, 1984). For another view of black life, especially Soweto's, a work of solid journalistic sociology, there is Denis Herbstein, *White Man, We Want to Talk to You* (New York: Penguin, 1978). Finally, in *South Africa: Sociological Analyses* (Cape Town: Oxford University Press, 1979) edited by A. Paul Hare, Gerd Wiendieck, and Max H. Von Brombsen, the reader will find a wide-ranging and exceptionally forceful collection of social-science essays.

During my research in South Africa I found working with Afrikaner children particularly difficult — the obvious barriers of culture, the moral arguments raised by parents and teachers — no matter my effort to make clear a desire "simply to learn." But that word "simply" is ironically used, one soon enough begins to learn — how complex a task it is for people with different assumptions even to sit in a room and engage in ordinary, casual conversation, never mind the asking and answering of pointed "psychological" or "sociological" questions. In any event, I recommend several interesting and edifying books about the Afrikaner people to the reader who is likely to be as confused and troubled about South Africa's rulers as many have been: W. A. de Klerk's compelling, well-written *The Puritans of Africa: A Story of Afrikanerdom* (New York: Penguin, 1975); J. H. P. Serfontein, *Brotherhood of Power*, a glimpse at the heart of Afrikaner political authority, the so-called *broederbond* (Bloomington: University of Indiana Press, 1978); another book, on the same subject, *The Super-Afrikaners*, by Ivor Wilkins and Hans Strydom (Johannesburg: Jonathan Ball, 1978); *Apartheid*, a collection of essays that shed substantial light on the white as well as black and colored side of South Africa's population. Alex Guma is the editor (New York: International Universities Press, 1978). The subject of Afrikaner "identity" gets a good airing in *Ethnic Power Mobilized*, by Heribert Adam and Hermann Giliomee (New Haven: Yale University Press, 1979); and the quite special and very important matter of the Afrikaner religious world is analyzed trenchantly in *The Church Struggle in South*

Africa, by John W. de Gruchy (Grand Rapids, Mich.: Eerdmans, 1979).

Everyone who is interested in the nation ought to read two books as a matter of necessary and painful education: *Laws Affecting Race Relations in South Africa,* compiled by Muriel Horrell, and published by the South African Institute of Race Relations, Johannesburg, and by the same institution, *Survey of Race Relations in South Africa,* an annual account compiled by various educators at the Institute. These "handbooks," as I've heard them called, tell their own sad, yearly story — and are important monitors for those near to and far from a particular, continuing human tragedy.

I want to mention two visual evocations of that tragedy — first *Soweto Speaks,* which links Peter Magubane's magnificent photographs to Jill Johnson's text (some of it interviews with ordinary men and women). The book was published in 1979 (Johannesburg: Donker). Second, Paul Venter's photographs in *Soweto* (Johannesburg: Perskor, 1977). In contrast, the reader might want to look at a book designed to introduce potential tourists to the undeniably beautiful landscape of the country, as in *South Africa,* by Gerald Cubitt and Arnold Helfet (Cape Town: Struik, 1975).

I also want to mention two intellectual projects with which I became associated, both of them, I think, of enormous value to any reader who wants to take a close look at how South African black and colored people manage their lives under apartheid: John Western's *Outcast Cape Town,* for which I was privileged to write an introduction (Minneapolis: University of Minnesota Press, 1981); and Pamela F. Reynolds, "Children of Crossroads," "an ethnographic study of cognition among seven-year-old Xhosa children" in a Cape Town (urban) environment, a dissertation for the Degree of Doctor of Philosophy at the University of Cape Town (1983). I had the great pleasure of serving on Ms. Reynolds's dissertation committee. Her sensitive work with the children — and their willingness to share with her a view of this world — are immediately apparent to the reader.

Now, to the sheer pleasure of mentioning a nation's extremely impressive literary tradition — one that prompts comparison with a similar achievement by writers of our American South. Is something to be learned from this — the redemptive side of suffering? But oh, the human price paid! It seems in our nature, one surmises, to bear witness — and some find the eloquence to do so in such a manner that grace itself seems at work. True, all the books I've so far mentioned are of interest, or great use — but those which follow are gems of the human spirit, the work of novelists, black and white, who offer us all the complexities and paradoxes (and subtleties and nuances) of our situation as human beings. I start with the best known of South Africa's present-day novelists, Nadine Gordimer, who has been attending to her native land's people, including their racial torment, for many years. A wonderfully eye-opening start for the interested reader would be the collection known as *Some Monday for Sure* (London: Heinemann, 1976), in which (I quote one of my sons, who has taught school in Soweto) "every detail of the whole sad business is described" — and the "business" to which he referred was human, was racial. Her novels are part of our literary and moral landscape and I will mention two recent ones, *The Conservationist* (London: Jonathan Cape, 1974), and *Burger's Daughter* (New York: Viking, 1979). Where would those of us outside of South Africa who have learned to care and worry constantly about that nation, out of concrete human involvement there, be without her sensibility at constant, edifying work? I have already mentioned Alan Paton. Even before I read his writing, I'd come across Dan Jacobson's finely wrought stories, such as those in *The Zulu and the Zeide* (Boston: Atlantic–Little, Brown, 1959), with their touching and exact portrayals of the various incidents and emotional exchanges that make up a nation's "race relations." Those stories are still all too suggestive, and are well worth knowing. I also recommend his recent *Time and Time Again: Autobiographies* (Boston: Atlantic Monthly Press, 1985).

J. M. Coetzee's work continues to gain recognition for what it is — a powerful illumination of all that has become so pervasive, still, on this planet, never mind South Africa: hate, meanness, exploitation, betrayal. *Waiting for the Barbarians* and *Life and Times of Michael K* (New York: Penguin, 1980 and 1984, respectively) are twin moral searchlights, enabling at least some vision for some of us predominantly blind ones. One salutes with similar awe Breyton Breytenbach, yet another Afrikaner who has broken with his own past — and suffered mightily for so doing with such insistence and courage. See his *The True Confessions of an Albino Terrorist* (New York: Farrar, Straus & Giroux, 1985). Another distinguished writer of Afrikaner background who has similarly departed from the fold is André Brink — in the recently published *The Wall of the Plague* (New York: Summit, 1985), or in *Looking on Darkness*, first published in Cape Town (Buren, 1973), as I well remember, having come to the country when that novel was very much on the minds of its many readers.

The black writer-in-exile Peter Abrahams has graced us with an impressive number of books — novels and autobiographical essays. Especially edifying and moving is *Mine Boy* (London: Heinemann, 1946), one of Abrahams's earlier novels, which tells of a black rural man who finds his way into South Africa's urban, industrial world. Abrahams's *Tell Freedom* (New York: Macmillan, 1970) has meant a lot to some of the black youths I've met in Soweto, and deservedly so. Another black writer whose stories are well known in South Africa and abroad is Alex La Guma, originally from Cape Town. He went into exile, having been banned and imprisoned several times. *A Walk in the Night* (Evanston: Northwestern University Press, 1967) offers his powerful short stories. His novel *The Stone Country* (London: Heinemann, 1967) has also meant a lot to "colored" and black intellectuals and young students we've met in South Africa. So too has Modikwe Dikobe, *The Marobi Dance* (London: Heinemann, 1973), a depiction of people caught between tribal life and impoverished urban gang life; and too, Dugmore Boetie's autobiographical *Familiarity Is the Kingdom of the Lost* (London: Cresset, 1969).

I had best begin to bring this bibliographical essay to a conclusion with the reminder that South Africa's literary tradition has not at all been conveyed adequately, even with the foregoing effort! I recommend a look at *A Century of South African Stories*, edited by Jean Marquand (Johannesburg: Donker, 1978) and *A New Book of South African Verse in English*, edited by Guy Butler and Chris Mann (Cape Town: Oxford, 1979) for the reader who wants to become increasingly familiar with that tradition. I also recommend the writing of the storyteller Herman Charles Bosman: his *Mafeking Road* (Cape Town: Human and Rousseau, 1969), and a collection of his stories, *Bosman at His Best*, by the same publisher, in 1965. Olive Schreiner's *The Story of an African Farm* (Johannesburg: Donker, 1979) is a Victorian classic that still has contemporary significance — for the traveler or social observer who spends time in a country whose nineteenth-century rural life has yet to change much in some respects. A frightening update of the prospects of that rural life — and maybe, of South Africa's prospects — has recently been given us by Karel Schoeman in his much-acclaimed *Promised Land* (London: Futura, 1978). As I read my monthly copy of *South African Outlook,* an extraordinary journal published in Cape Town and edited by Francis Wilson, I wonder whether the gloomy Orwellian futurism Graham Greene ascribes to *Promised Land* is not really a present-day realism, a candid acknowledgment of a seemingly endless nightmare, lived by millions: apartheid. In any event, I salute *South African Outlook* and its editor and its many writers — as fine a periodical as one can find anywhere: a brave moral voice, constantly raised on behalf of "all God's children"!

11. Packenham, op. cit.
12. *Voortrekker Monument,* op. cit.
13. Ibid.
14. In fact, just about every South African child I met knew a great deal more about American history than most American children I've known have learned of South African history.
15. Again, the Voortrekker monument reminds visiting Afrikaner children how dangerous the world was — and might again be.
16. In Cape Town, especially, one meets the descendants of English traders, clergymen, intellectuals — and sees the commercial and cultural world they created.
17. New York: Harcourt, Brace and World, 1957.
18. New York: Harcourt, Brace and World, 1959.
19. An American white man has no trouble visiting such neighborhoods. To enter and leave Soweto, however, is quite another matter! One is supposed to obtain permission for each visit to a black "area" — but I never did. The Irish nuns who ran a school in Soweto, and who were so gracious to my sons and me, were quite helpful — encouraged us, as it were, "to come and go and trust in the Lord," as they put it. And we did!
20. I have about a hundred of them; they will go, eventually, to the University of North Carolina Library.
21. I know of no other country where the first and third worlds live so intimately.
22. See Joyce Sikakari's book, op. cit.
23. An extraordinary group of nuns — brave and thoughtful, and yes, ingenious in their various involvements with the Afrikaner bureaucracy.
24. New York: Knopf, 1953.
25. Before a group supporting the Alabama Council on Human Relations.
26. I first met Mrs. Suzman in the 1960s on one of her American visits. She came to the Southern Regional Council, where I worked, and told us of the (then) similarities and differences she had observed between her country's racial situation and that of the South.
27. My friends there, whom I'd best not name, were of inestimable value in helping me work in black and colored neighborhoods.
28. Where my sons and I had been teaching.
29. I ask the reader, in contrast, to look at the drawings of black children I describe in the first three volumes of *Children of Crisis* (Boston: Atlantic–Little, Brown, 1967 and 1972).

30. See the doctoral thesis of Pamela Reynolds, op. cit.
31. Such as those mentioned in note 10, black and colored and white alike.

VII. CLASS AND NATIONALISM: BRAZIL
AND THE UNITED STATES

1. This favela (or urban slum, made up of makeshift houses — lots of scraps of wood, corrugated tin, stretched plastic, dried and caked soil) possessed a dramatic view of Copacabana beach. I would recommend two books on Rio de Janeiro's poor to the reader: *The Lost Ones: Social Forces and Mental Illness in Rio de Janeiro,* by Eugene B. Brody (New York: International Universities Press, 1973), and *The Myth of Marginality: Urban Poverty and Politics in Rio de Janeiro,* by Janice E. Perlman (Berkeley: University of California Press, 1976). The latter offers an excellent bibliography. Needless to say, the reader might also want to read the work of the Brazilian writer Paulo Freire: *Pedagogy of the Oppressed* (New York: Seabury, 1968). There is also Elizabeth Leeds, *Brazil in the 1960s: Favelas and Polity; The Continuity of the Structure of Social Control* (University of Texas Press, 1972); as well as *Reflections on the Brazilian Counter-Revolution,* a collection of essays by F. Fernandes (Armonk, N.Y.: M. E. Sharpe, 1981).
2. The famous statue of Christ, His arms outstretched, which, atop a high hill, dominates the city.
3. He was reminding me what had obtained only a decade or two earlier in our rich country — what he had seen all the time as an old-fashioned "general practitioner" in northern industrial New Jersey. Twice I've tried to do some justice to the genius of someone I was lucky enough to know personally — in *William Carlos Williams: The Knack of Survival in America* (New Brunswick: Rutgers University Press, 1975) and *The Doctor Stories of William Carlos Williams* (New York: New Directions, 1984).
4. Boston: Atlantic Monthly Press, 1986.
5. At Yale Child Study Center, New Haven.
6. Many of these children were taking history courses, and were quite conscious of their nation's various social and political struggles.
7. *The Moral Life of Children* (Boston: Atlantic Monthly Press, 1986).
8. Dr. Sergio Perrot, a pediatrician.
9. In 1985 both Argentina and Brazil had "more freedom," indeed — compared to the relatively recent past.
10. As I have indicated in Chapter I.
11. Though I do in not only *The Middle Americans* (Boston: Atlantic–Little, Brown, 1971) but also *The Old Ones of New Mexico* (Albuquerque: University of New Mexico Press, 1973).
12. Op. cit.
13. See my discussions of this vexing problem in *The Mind's Fate* (Boston: Atlantic–Little, Brown, 1975).
14. Boston: Atlantic–Little, Brown, 1972.
15. Op. cit.
16. I first started working in Harlan County, Kentucky, in 1966.
17. As she transcribed our conversations with the mothers of these children in

preparation for writing chapters of our Volumes I and II of *Women of Crisis* (New York: Delacorte, 1978 and 1980).

18. Especially in the South and the Southwest children are likely to do so — whereas in New England, say, such a separation rarely takes place.

VIII. EXILE AND NATIONALISM: CHILDREN OF SOUTHEAST ASIA

1. See the article in which I described my work there, in the *Washington Post* (November 18, 1984).

2. South Frederick Street, Arlington, Virginia.

3. See the two important books of William Shawcross: *Sideshow* (New York: Simon and Schuster, 1981), and, by the same publisher, in 1984, *The Quality of Mercy*. For a general textbook on Cambodia, see Michael Vickery, *Cambodia* (Boston: South End Press, 1984).

4. On another occasion he pressed his finger so hard on the Cambodian spot of the map that he proclaimed afterward: "My fingerprint will stay there forever!"

5. The following psychological, psychiatric, and pediatric articles about children of Southeast Asia, "unaccompanied" or "accompanied," are of some interest: Neal Boothby, "The Horror, the Hope," *Natural History*, Vol. 1 (1983), 64–71; J. D. Cohen, "Southeast Asian Refugees and School Health Personnel," *Journal of School Health*, Vol. 53 (1983), 151–158; B. Dashowsky and D. W. Teele, "Infectious Disease Problems in Indochinese Refugees," *Pediatrics Annual*, Vol. 12 (1983), 232–244; I. M. Eisenbruch, "Vietnamese Refugees in an English Town," in *Explorations in Cross-Cultural Psychology*, J. B. Deregowski, S. Dziurawiec, and R. C. Annis, eds. (Lisse, Holland: Swets and Zeitlinger, 1983), pp. 229–249; R. K. Harding and J. G. Looney, "Problems of Southeast Asian Children in a Refugee Camp," *American Journal of Psychiatry*, Vol. 134 (1977), pp. 407–411; K-M. Lin, M. Masuda, and L. Tazuma, "Adaptational Problems of Vietnamese Refugees: III. Case Studies in Clinic and Field: Adaptive and Maladaptive," *Psychiatric Journal of the University of Ottawa*, Vol. 7 (1982), pp. 173–183; M. Masuda, K-M. Lin, and L. Tazuma, "Adaptation Problems of Vietnamese Refugees: II. Life Changes and Perception of Life Events," *Archives of General Psychiatry*, Vol. 37 (1980), pp. 447–450; R. Rahe, J. Looney, H. Ward, T. Tung, and W. Liu, "Psychiatric Consultation in a Vietnamese Refugee Camp," *American Journal of Psychiatry*, Vol. 135 (1978), pp. 185–190; L. T. Redick and B. Wood, "Cross-cultural Problems for Southeast Asian Refugee Minors," *Child Welfare*, Vol. 61 (1982), pp. 365–373; D. Scanlan and M. Wyatt, "Tools for Nutrition and Preventive Dental Counselling for Southeast Asian Refugees," *Canadian Dental Hygiene*, Vol. 14 (1980), pp. 60–62; C. L. Williams and J. Westermeyer, "Psychiatric Problems among Adolescent Southeast Asian Refugees: A Descriptive Study," *Journal of Nervous and Mental Disease*, Vol. 171 (1983), pp. 79–85; T. T. Yee and R. H. Lee, "Based on Cultural Strengths, a School Primary Prevention Program for Asian-American Youth," *Community Mental Health Journal*, Vol. 13 (1977), pp. 239–248.

6. He is, actually, doing quite well, as of 1985 — an early adolescent.

7. See R. S. Chavan, *Nationalism in Asia* (New Delhi: Sterling, 1973); also, Maslyn

Williams, *The Land in Between: The Cambodian Dilemma* (New York: Morrow, 1970); and George Hildebrand (with Gareth Porter), *Cambodia: Starvation and Revolution* (New York: Monthly Review Press, 1976); J. McJunkin, *Visions of Vietnam* (Novato, Calif.: Presidio Press, 1983); and Thuy Vu 'o 'ng Gia, *Getting to Know the Vietnamese and Their Culture* (New York: Ungar, 1976).

8. See *The Mind's Fate*, op. cit., and the first three volumes of *Children of Crisis*, op. cit.

9. Chavan's book, op. cit., gives us a good idea of the complexity of Asian nationalism.

10. See Shawcross, both books.

11. See the article by Eisenbruch, op. cit.

12. See, also, Neal Boothby, op. cit., and R. Rosenblatt, op. cit.

13. See Boothby, op. cit.

14. She resolutely referred to Cambodia, never used the word Kampuchea.

15. Marjorie Stein. Her thoughts on the child's progress were helpful, indeed.

16. So I learned to call that territory in high school!

17. Done in Keesler Air Force Base, Biloxi, Mississippi, between 1958 and 1960. I was in charge of a neuropsychiatric unit there. See Volume I of *Children of Crisis*, op. cit.

IX. POLITICAL MORALITY:
THE HARD DREAM OF SURVIVAL

1. Christopher Lasch, *The Culture of Narcissism* (New York: W. W. Norton, 1978), does a good job of distinguishing between a Biblical morality and today's "narcissism." I have discussed this subject at length in "Unreflecting Egoism," the *New Yorker*, August 27, 1979.

2. In late August, 1983.

3. To the point that I find myself using the expression with American children — and they know instantly what I mean!

4. Op. cit.

5. I am constantly stunned by the seeming moral attribution by such children — their inclination to judge a political authority to be heinously cruel and arbitrary — until, alas, I have come to witness the cruelty and arbitrariness myself.

6. See Chapter IX of *The Moral Life of Children;* also an article I wrote on this subject in *Harper's*, March, 1985.

7. No children I've met, anywhere, rival South Africa's in continuing and intense dedication to a wide range of athletics. "They are our national passion — sports of all kinds," a Pretoria youth told me upon my first visit to the country, and upon my most recent time there, a decade later, I began to think the use of the word "passion" to be a weak way, indeed, of describing such a feverish mixture of attention, commitment, devotion!

INDEX